Celestial Craft

Celestial Craft

Matthew Petchinsky

Celestial Craft: The Witch's Almanac for 2025 – A Cosmic Guide to Manifestations, Moons, and Mystical Events
By: Matthew Petchinsky

Introduction: Aligning Your Magic with the Stars in 2025

Welcome to *"Celestial Craft: The Witch's Almanac for 2025"*, a guide designed to synchronize your magical practice with the potent energy of the cosmos. In this almanac, you will find a wealth of astrological, lunar, and celestial information curated for witches, spiritual practitioners, astrologers, and anyone with an interest in using the natural rhythms of the universe to empower their life, rituals, and magic.

The cosmos is a powerful partner in magical practice. Each solar eclipse, planetary alignment, and meteor shower carries a unique vibrational energy, influencing everything from your daily interactions to your deepest magical workings. With each event, the universe offers opportunities to manifest your intentions, heal from past wounds, and delve deeper into your spiritual journey. The purpose of this almanac is to give you the tools, insights, and dates needed to maximize the impact of these cosmic moments, ensuring that your practice aligns with the universal flow.

The Purpose of This Almanac

At its heart, this almanac is about timing—understanding and working with celestial events to enhance your spellwork, manifestations, and spiritual growth. In the same way that farmers consult the Farmer's Almanac to time their planting and harvest cycles, witches can use this celestial guide to harness the energy of the stars and planets for their magical work. The timing of spells, meditations, and rituals can dramatically influence their outcomes, and with this almanac, you will be able to chart your own course through the astrological skies of 2025, ensuring that your intentions align with the most powerful celestial moments.

This almanac provides an in-depth look at:

- **Solar and Lunar Events**: Information on solar and lunar eclipses, full moons, new moons, and the daily movement of the sun and moon across the sky.
- **Planetary Movements and Retrogrades**: Detailed guides to the retrogrades of Mercury, Venus, Mars, and the outer planets, as well as planetary conjunctions, oppositions, and other alignments.
- **Meteor Showers and Comets**: Dates and magical significance of meteor showers, and how to incorporate their energy into your spellwork.
- **Zodiac and Astrology**: Monthly horoscopes for each zodiac sign, planetary placements, and insights into how astrological transits influence different areas of life.
- **Seasonal Energy**: Guidance on how to celebrate and utilize the eight Sabbats of the Wheel of the Year, aligning your magic with the Earth's seasonal shifts.
- **Rituals, Spells, and Planting Guides**: Practical instructions for using celestial energies to plant, harvest, and perform spells for love, protection, prosperity, and healing.

Understanding Celestial Timing

In the world of magic, timing is crucial. The positions of the sun, moon, and planets, as well as the changing seasons and movements of the stars, all affect the subtle energetic currents of our world. These currents are what we, as witches, seek to tap into and channel through our rituals and spellwork. By working with celestial events, you can ride the waves of cosmic energy rather than work against them. For example:

- **A Full Moon in Taurus** brings a grounded, earthy energy perfect for spells related to abundance and security.
- **A Solar Eclipse** offers a moment of profound transformation and clarity, where old patterns can be cleared to make way for new beginnings.
- **Mercury Retrograde**, though often feared, provides the perfect opportunity for reflection, review, and revisiting old projects with a fresh perspective.

This almanac offers precise timings for these celestial events so you can plan your rituals, spellwork, and manifestations with confidence. Whether you're crafting a protection spell, casting a love charm, or simply meditating under a meteor shower, this guide will ensure you are in perfect alignment with the universe's rhythm.

Who Can Use This Almanac?

This almanac is for everyone. Whether you're a seasoned practitioner or someone who is just beginning their magical journey, this guide will help you enhance your practice by understanding and aligning with the cosmos. The chapters within offer both detailed information for those who have already developed a relationship with the celestial world and easy-to-follow guides for beginners who are just learning to attune their rituals to the stars.

For witches, the moon and stars have always held a special place in spellcraft. But even if you do not identify as a witch or practice magic in a traditional sense, you can still benefit from this almanac. Astrologers will find it invaluable for interpreting the movements of the planets and how they influence our lives. Gardeners can use the lunar planting guides to ensure the health of their crops and herbs. Those on a spiritual journey may use the energy of celestial events to meditate, reflect, and realign themselves with their life's path. In essence, this almanac is for anyone who wishes to live a life that is more consciously connected to the natural cycles of the universe.

The Power of Solar and Lunar Cycles

The sun and moon are two of the most powerful celestial bodies in our solar system, and their influence on the Earth and its inhabitants is undeniable. Each year, the sun's movement through the zodiac marks the passage of time, dictating the changing seasons and influencing our collective energy. Similarly, the phases of the moon—from new to full and back again—offer opportunities to set intentions, manifest desires, and release what no longer serves us.

- **The Solar Cycle**: Each season has its own magical properties, and the solstices and equinoxes are powerful turning points that witches can use to their advantage. The summer solstice, when the sun is at its peak, is a time for celebration, manifestation, and gratitude, while the winter solstice, the longest night of the year, is perfect for introspection, renewal, and setting intentions for the coming year.
- **The Lunar Cycle**: The phases of the moon have long been associated with different types of magic. The new moon is a time for new beginnings, the waxing moon for building and growing, the full moon for peak energy and manifestation, and the waning moon for release and banishing. This almanac provides specific dates and times for these lunar phases, allowing you to plan your rituals with precision.

Planetary Movements and Retrogrades

The planets, too, have a profound influence on our lives, both individually and collectively. In astrology, the planets are seen as guiding forces, each ruling different aspects of our lives—love, communication, creativity, ambition, and more. When planets retrograde (move backward in the sky from our perspective on Earth), their energy shifts, often causing delays, confusion, and reflection in the areas they govern.

This almanac provides a full retrograde calendar for 2025, helping you understand when these shifts will occur and how to navigate them. Mercury retrograde, for instance, is famous for disrupting communication and travel, but it also offers an opportunity to pause, reflect, and revisit old projects. Venus retrograde can stir up emotions in relationships, but it also presents a chance to reevaluate your values, desires, and connections.

Using Astrology to Enhance Your Magic

Astrology is an ancient tool that helps us understand the universe and our place within it. Each zodiac sign is associated with certain energies and attributes, and the movements of the planets through the signs can greatly affect your magic. By incorporating astrology into your spellwork, you can amplify the energy you're working with and ensure your intentions are in harmony with the stars.

In this almanac, you will find monthly horoscopes for each zodiac sign, offering insights into career, love, health, and spiritual growth. Additionally, the planetary placement guides will help you understand how the movement of planets through the signs affects your rituals and magic. For example, a full moon in Scorpio is perfect for deep, transformative magic, while a new moon in Virgo is ideal for organization, healing, and grounding.

Your Magical Journey with the Universe

As you journey through 2025, this almanac will be your guide to navigating the celestial landscape. The universe is constantly speaking to us, offering guidance and energy in the form of solar eclipses, lunar phases, planetary movements, and more. By tuning into these cosmic signals, you can align your life and your magic with the universe's natural flow, creating powerful change both within and around you.

Whether you're performing rituals under a full moon, planting herbs by lunar phases, or setting intentions during a solar eclipse, remember that you are part of something much larger than yourself. The stars, the moon, the planets—they are all part of the same universal web, and you have the power to tap into their energy to manifest your dreams and create the life you desire.

This almanac is here to help you do just that.

Chapter 1: Introduction to Celestial Witchcraft
Overview of the Magical Practice of Working with Celestial Bodies

Celestial witchcraft is an ancient and powerful tradition that draws upon the energy of the cosmos—the sun, moon, planets, stars, and other celestial phenomena—to fuel magic, spells, rituals, and personal growth. By aligning your magical practice with these celestial bodies, you tap into the universal forces that influence life on Earth, harnessing their energy to manifest your desires, protect yourself and others, and create harmony in your spiritual journey.

In this chapter, we will explore the foundational concepts of celestial witchcraft, providing an understanding of how working with celestial bodies can enhance your magic. From the radiant power of the sun to the transformative pull of the moon, to the influence of the planets and stars, each celestial entity carries its own unique energy, symbolism, and magical properties. Learning to work with these energies can help you become a more attuned and effective practitioner, amplifying your spellwork and bringing you into deeper alignment with the natural rhythms of the universe.

The practice of celestial witchcraft involves several core components:

- **The Sun**: The life-giving energy of the sun, its cycles, and its influence on seasons and Sabbats.
- **The Moon**: The lunar phases and how they govern different types of magic.
- **The Planets**: The role of planets in astrology and how their movements, retrogrades, and alignments impact magical practice.
- **The Stars and Constellations**: How star formations and their energies can be used for protection, guidance, and spell enhancement.
- **Eclipses, Meteor Showers, and Other Astronomical Events**: Harnessing the unique energy of rare celestial phenomena for transformational magic.

By working with these forces, celestial witches can enhance the effectiveness of their spells, time their rituals to coincide with powerful cosmic shifts, and draw upon the deep, ever-present energy of the universe. This approach to magic not only connects practitioners to the Earth's natural cycles but also to the greater cosmic order, creating a sense of harmony between the practitioner and the universe.

The Sun's Role in Magic

The sun is a symbol of life, vitality, success, and power. As the central figure in our solar system, its energy is constant, reliable, and powerful. It governs the day and the year, influencing the seasonal cycles and, consequently, the Wheel of the Year, which many witches follow in their magical practice.

- **Solar Magic**: The sun's energy is ideal for spells related to strength, leadership, abundance, and health. Solar magic is best performed during the day, particularly at noon when the sun is at its highest and most powerful. The energy of the sun is also connected to joy, success, and creativity, making it perfect for spells aimed at manifesting positive outcomes and amplifying personal power.
- **Solar Sabbats**: The solar cycles are marked by the solstices and equinoxes—significant turning points in the Wheel of the Year. The winter solstice (Yule) represents the rebirth of the sun, while the summer solstice (Litha) celebrates the sun at its peak of power. The equinoxes (Ostara and Mabon) symbolize balance, as day and night are equal. These solar events are potent times for rituals that focus on growth, renewal, and celebrating the cycles of life.
- **Working with the Sun's Zodiac**: The sun moves through the twelve signs of the zodiac over the course of a year, spending approximately one month in each sign. Each sign imbues the sun with different qualities. For example, when the sun is in Leo, it is associated with confidence, leadership, and creativity, making it an ideal time for self-empowerment spells. When the sun is in Cancer, its energy is more nurturing and protective, perfect for home and family-related magic.

Lunar Magic: The Power of the Moon

The moon is one of the most important celestial bodies in witchcraft. Its phases—new moon, waxing, full moon, and waning—offer a cyclical rhythm that witches can follow to maximize the potency of their magic. The moon's energy is intimately tied to emotions, intuition, and the subconscious, making it a powerful tool for witches who work with divination, dream magic, and inner transformation.

- **The Phases of the Moon**:
  - **New Moon**: The new moon is a time for new beginnings, fresh starts, and setting intentions. It is a time to plant the seeds of your desires, whether through spells of manifestation, personal development, or setting goals.
  - **Waxing Moon**: As the moon grows toward fullness, the waxing phase is ideal for spells that focus on growth, increase, and expansion. This is the time to take action on your intentions, build energy, and work towards your goals.
  - **Full Moon**: The full moon is the most potent time for magic, as the moon's energy is at its peak. It is a time for manifestation, bringing things to fruition, and performing

powerful spells of culmination and completion. The full moon is also associated with heightened intuition, making it a powerful time for divination and psychic work.

- ◦ **Waning Moon**: As the moon decreases in size, the waning phase is a time for banishing, releasing, and letting go of anything that no longer serves you. It is ideal for spells of protection, cleansing, and removing negative energy from your life.
- **The Moon's Influence on Emotion and Intuition**: The moon is closely tied to the water element, which governs emotions, intuition, and psychic abilities. This is why many witches feel a stronger connection to their inner selves during certain phases of the moon, particularly the full and new moons. Lunar magic is perfect for working with emotional healing, introspection, and developing your psychic senses.
- **Moon Signs**: In addition to its phases, the moon also moves through the twelve zodiac signs, staying in each sign for about two and a half days. The moon's sign can influence the energy of your rituals. For example, a full moon in Scorpio is excellent for deep emotional healing and transformative magic, while a new moon in Gemini is ideal for communication and intellectual pursuits.

The Planets: Astrology and Magic

The planets are another key component of celestial witchcraft, each representing different aspects of life and the human experience. In astrology, the planets are believed to exert influence over different areas of our lives, and by working with their energy, witches can enhance spells that correspond to those areas.

- **Mercury**: Governs communication, intellect, and travel. Mercury's energy is ideal for spells related to clear communication, learning, and making decisions. However, during Mercury retrograde, it is best to focus on reflection, revisiting old ideas, and resolving past conflicts rather than starting new projects.
- **Venus**: Represents love, beauty, and relationships. Venus's energy is perfect for love spells, beauty rituals, and spells related to self-love and attraction.
- **Mars**: Symbolizes action, courage, and passion. Mars's energy is useful for spells that require strength, assertiveness, and protection.
- **Jupiter**: Associated with expansion, luck, and prosperity. Jupiter's energy is ideal for spells that focus on growth, abundance, and success.
- **Saturn**: Governs discipline, structure, and responsibility. Saturn's energy is useful for long-term goal setting, grounding, and protection rituals.
- **Retrogrades**: When a planet is in retrograde, its energy turns inward, and its usual outward expression can be disrupted. Retrogrades are excellent times for introspection, resolving old issues, and performing spells that focus on reflection and healing. Mercury retrograde, for example, can be used for rituals aimed at resolving miscommunications or reviewing old projects with fresh insight.

The Stars and Constellations

The stars and constellations are a vast and timeless source of magical energy. While the planets govern specific aspects of life, the stars represent a more abstract, guiding energy that witches can draw upon for protection, divination, and guidance.

- **Constellation Magic**: Certain constellations carry powerful symbolism that can be incorporated into spells. For example, the constellation Orion is often associated with strength, protection, and the hunt, while the Pleiades, also known as the Seven Sisters, are linked to feminine energy, mysticism, and the pursuit of knowledge.
- **Working with Fixed Stars**: In astrology, fixed stars are stars that hold a specific point in the sky and can have significant influence when they align with planets in your chart or the sky. Incorporating fixed star magic into your rituals can add a layer of ancient wisdom and guidance.

Celestial Events: Eclipses, Meteor Showers, and Other Phenomena

Beyond the daily movements of the sun, moon, and planets, there are rare celestial events that hold immense magical power. Eclipses, meteor showers, and comet sightings are times when the veil between worlds is thinner, and the energy of the universe is heightened.

- **Solar and Lunar Eclipses**: Eclipses are moments of profound transformation. Solar eclipses are ideal for starting new projects or making major life changes, while lunar eclipses are perfect for shadow work, banishing old habits, and closing difficult chapters in your life.
- **Meteor Showers**: Meteor showers are excellent times for wish magic and setting intentions. As meteors streak across the sky, they carry with them the energy of change and momentum, making them perfect for spells aimed at rapid manifestation.

How Cosmic Energy Enhances Spells and Rituals

Cosmic energy amplifies spellwork by providing a natural flow of power that witches can tap into. Each celestial body resonates with different frequencies, and by timing your rituals to align with these energies, you can increase the potency of your spells and ensure that your intentions are supported by the universe. When you harness the energy of a full moon, retrograde planet, or solar eclipse, you are not just working in isolation—you are drawing upon the vast, dynamic forces of the cosmos to enhance your magic.

Working with celestial bodies also deepens your connection to the natural world and its cycles. As you become more attuned to the rhythms of the sun, moon, planets, and stars, you may find that your intuition strengthens, your understanding of magic deepens, and your ability to manifest your desires becomes more focused and effective. Through celestial witchcraft, you align yourself with the ever-present, ever-moving forces of the universe, creating a powerful, harmonious connection between your practice and the cosmos.

In the following chapters, we will dive deeper into each of these celestial forces—exploring their energies, magical properties, and how you can use them in your rituals, spellwork, and spiritual practice throughout 2025.

Chapter 2: The Sun's Journey: Solar Eclipses and Solstices in 2025

The sun, a radiant source of life and energy, is central to the practice of celestial witchcraft. Its steady journey across the sky defines the changing of the seasons, influences the growth of plants, and governs the cycles of light and dark that shape our lives. In 2025, several key solar events, including two solar eclipses and the solstices, will present powerful opportunities for manifestation, transformation, and release.

This chapter explores the significance of the sun's movements, the dates and times of solar eclipses and solstices in 2025, and provides rituals and spells that you can perform during these pivotal moments. Working with solar energy enables you to harness the life-giving force of the universe and channel it into your magical practice.

The Power of the Sun in Magic

The sun is associated with vitality, success, clarity, and growth. Its energy is both nurturing and transformative, providing the warmth and light needed for all life to flourish. In magic, the sun represents masculine energy, often associated with action, leadership, and outward expression. Solar energy is especially useful in spells and rituals focused on growth, empowerment, and manifestation.

When working with solar energy, timing is essential. The sun's journey is marked by several key points in the year: the equinoxes, solstices, and eclipses. Each of these events offers a unique energetic opportunity to align your magical practice with the rhythms of the universe.

Solar Eclipses in 2025: Dates, Times, and Significance

Solar eclipses are among the most potent and transformative celestial events. They occur when the moon passes between the Earth and the sun, temporarily obscuring the sun's light. This moment of darkness within the day is a powerful symbol of transition, offering an opportunity for personal and spiritual transformation.

In 2025, two solar eclipses will occur:

Solar Eclipse 1: March 29, 2025 — Total Solar Eclipse

- **Date**: March 29, 2025
- **Type**: Total Solar Eclipse
- **Visibility**: Visible in parts of the Pacific Ocean, North America, and the Arctic.
- **Time**: Peak eclipse occurs around 3:00 PM UTC, though the exact timing will vary based on your location.

Significance:

This total solar eclipse marks a profound time for change and new beginnings. Total eclipses are powerful moments of transformation, symbolizing the temporary "death" of the sun's light before it is reborn. This event represents a time to confront deep-seated fears, release what no longer serves you, and make way for new opportunities. The eclipse energy is intense, offering a chance to let go of past burdens and emerge with renewed clarity and purpose.

Ritual for the March 29, 2025, Total Solar Eclipse: Eclipse of Renewal
Materials:

- Black candle (to represent the shadow)
- White candle (to represent the return of light)
- A small mirror or piece of reflective glass
- A bowl of water (to represent emotional cleansing)
- Pen and paper

Instructions:

1. **Preparation**: Find a quiet, comfortable space where you can sit and observe the eclipse (if visible in your location) or focus your energy on the event. Ensure you have your materials nearby.
2. **Shadow Work**: Begin by lighting the black candle, which represents the shadow period of the eclipse. Write down any fears, doubts, or patterns you wish to release. Reflect on what has been holding you back, whether emotionally, mentally, or spiritually.
3. **Release**: Once you have identified the energies you wish to release, burn the paper with the flame of the black candle, symbolically releasing those burdens. Watch the paper burn and imagine those energies dissipating into the universe.
4. **Cleansing**: Take the bowl of water and gaze into it as you hold the small mirror above it. As the paper burns, dip the mirror into the water, symbolizing the cleansing of your inner self. Imagine the water absorbing the remaining negativity and washing away old patterns.
5. **Rebirth**: Light the white candle to symbolize the return of the sun's light and the beginning of a new cycle. Sit with the flame for a few moments and visualize the light of the sun filling you with new strength, purpose, and clarity.
6. **Closing**: When the ritual is complete, extinguish the candles, thanking the sun and moon for their guidance. If safe, dispose of the water outside, pouring it on the ground as an offering of release.

Solar Eclipse 2: September 21, 2025 — Partial Solar Eclipse

- **Date**: September 21, 2025
- **Type**: Partial Solar Eclipse
- **Visibility**: Visible in parts of the Atlantic Ocean, South America, and parts of Europe.
- **Time**: Peak eclipse around 1:15 PM UTC.

Significance:

Partial eclipses carry a gentler energy than total eclipses, but they are still significant moments for introspection and change. This September eclipse comes just days before the autumn equinox, making it an ideal time to reflect on your personal harvest—what you have achieved throughout the year, and what you are ready to release as you move toward the darker half of the year.

Ritual for the September 21, 2025, Partial Solar Eclipse: Harvest of Intentions

Materials:

- A candle (orange or gold to represent the sun's energy)
- A bundle of dried herbs (such as sage or rosemary) for burning
- A journal or notebook
- A small bowl of soil or sand

Instructions:

1. **Preparation**: Find a space where you can sit quietly, preferably outside or near a window where you can connect with the solar energy. Set up your materials before you begin.
2. **Reflection**: Light the candle and hold your journal in your hands. Reflect on the goals or intentions you set earlier in the year. Write down what you have achieved, what you are grateful for, and what you are ready to release as the year moves toward its close.
3. **Cleansing**: Take the bundle of dried herbs and light it. Let the smoke cleanse your space and your mind. As the herbs burn, imagine them clearing away any lingering doubts or frustrations that have built up over the year.
4. **Planting New Seeds**: Place the small bowl of soil or sand in front of you. For each new intention you wish to set for the coming months, draw a symbol in the sand with your finger. As you draw each symbol, imagine planting the seed of that intention, which will grow and flourish in the months ahead.
5. **Closing**: When you are finished, snuff out the candle and allow the herbs to burn out naturally. Take a moment to sit in stillness, absorbing the energy of the eclipse and your new intentions.

Celebrating the Solstices for Manifestation and Release

In addition to solar eclipses, the solstices are key points in the sun's journey that mark the changing of the seasons and offer powerful moments for magical work. The solstices occur when the sun reaches its highest or lowest point in the sky, signaling either the longest or shortest day of the year.

Summer Solstice (Litha) — June 21, 2025

- **Date**: June 21, 2025
- **Significance**: The summer solstice, also known as Litha, is the longest day of the year and marks the height of the sun's power. This is a time for celebrating abundance, growth, and manifestation. The energy of the summer solstice is one of joy, expansion, and creativity, making it an ideal time for spells focused on success, prosperity, and personal empowerment.

Ritual for the Summer Solstice: Manifesting Abundance
Materials:

- Yellow or gold candle (representing the sun)
- A crystal associated with the sun (such as citrine or sunstone)
- A small pouch for holding your intentions
- Fresh flowers (for decoration and offering)

Instructions:

1. **Preparation**: On the morning of the solstice, find a sunny outdoor space or an area where sunlight streams in. Arrange your materials, including the candle, flowers, and crystal.
2. **Manifestation**: Light the candle and hold the crystal in your hand. Close your eyes and visualize the sun's light filling your entire body, energizing you and bringing you into alignment with the universe's abundance. Focus on the goals you want to manifest in the coming months—whether they are related to career, love, or personal growth.
3. **Setting Intentions**: Write your intentions on small pieces of paper and place them in the pouch. As you do so, say aloud, "With the power of the sun, I manifest [your intention]." Feel the sun's energy fueling your intentions with light and warmth.
4. **Offering**: As a token of gratitude, offer the fresh flowers to the earth or place them on your altar. Allow the candle to burn down safely, keeping the crystal with you to carry the sun's energy throughout the day.

Winter Solstice (Yule) — December 21, 2025

- **Date**: December 21, 2025
- **Significance**: The winter solstice, or Yule, marks the longest night of the year and the rebirth of the sun. It is a time for introspection, renewal, and setting intentions for the year ahead. The winter solstice is often associated with rest, reflection, and honoring the cycles of death and rebirth, making it a powerful time for release and new beginnings.

Ritual for the Winter Solstice: Rebirth and Renewal
Materials:

- Evergreen branches (to symbolize eternal life)
- A black candle (for release)
- A white candle (for renewal)
- A small bell or chime

Instructions:

1. **Preparation**: On the evening of the winter solstice, find a quiet space where you can sit and reflect. Decorate your space with evergreen branches, which represent the eternal cycle of life and death.
2. **Releasing the Old**: Light the black candle and sit in darkness for a few moments, contemplating what you are ready to release from the past year. As you reflect, say aloud, "I release all that no longer serves me." Visualize the darkness absorbing your worries, fears, and burdens.
3. **Welcoming the Light**: When you are ready, light the white candle to symbolize the return of the sun's light. Ring the bell or chime to welcome the rebirth of the sun, and say aloud, "I welcome the light of the new year." Focus on what you wish to bring into your life in the coming year—new beginnings, opportunities, and growth.
4. **Closing**: Allow the white candle to burn down safely, keeping the evergreen branches on your altar or in your home as a reminder of the eternal cycles of life.

Conclusion

In 2025, the sun's journey through solar eclipses and solstices offers profound opportunities for both manifestation and release. Whether you are harnessing the transformative power of an eclipse or celebrating the changing seasons through solstice rituals, the sun provides a steady source of life-giving energy to enhance your magic.

By working in harmony with these solar events, you align yourself with the natural cycles of the universe, empowering your spellwork and deepening your connection to the cosmic forces that shape our world.

Chapter 3: Sunrise and Sunset Times by Month

The sun's daily journey across the sky, from sunrise to sunset, provides natural points of power that witches can harness in their magical practice. Sunrise symbolizes new beginnings, hope, and the birth of new ideas or projects, while sunset marks closure, release, and the completion of cycles. Understanding the timing of sunrise and sunset allows you to work in alignment with these natural rhythms, choosing the perfect moment for your spells and rituals to achieve maximum effectiveness.

In this chapter, we will explore how to use sunrise and sunset for spell timing, and you'll find detailed charts of sunrise and sunset times for each month of 2025. These times are presented for general reference, and while actual times may vary depending on your specific location, they offer a framework for planning your magical work.

Using Sunrise and Sunset in Magic

The daily cycle of the sun is one of the most potent and reliable sources of energy available to witches. Sunrise, noon, sunset, and twilight each carry unique energies that can be used for different types of magic. Understanding how to use these windows of time will enhance your spellwork, connecting your rituals to the flow of solar energy.

Sunrise Magic

- **Symbolism**: Sunrise represents birth, new beginnings, hope, and renewal. It is the time when the sun begins its journey across the sky, bringing light to the world after the darkness of night. This moment is ideal for spells of growth, inspiration, clarity, and manifestation.
- **Types of Magic**: Sunrise is perfect for initiating new projects, setting intentions, and working spells related to personal growth, success, and prosperity. It is also an excellent time for rituals involving healing, as the fresh energy of the dawn brings new vitality.
- **Sunrise Ritual Ideas**:
  - A spell for new beginnings, focusing on manifesting goals for the day or the long term.
  - A morning meditation to connect with the sun's energy and set intentions for the day.

Sunset Magic

- **Symbolism**: Sunset marks the end of the day, a time for reflection, closure, and release. The fading light of the sun as it sets on the horizon represents the completion of a cycle, making it the ideal moment to focus on endings, transitions, and letting go.
- **Types of Magic**: Sunset is ideal for banishing spells, protection rituals, and releasing anything that no longer serves you—whether it's a habit, a relationship, or an emotional burden. This is also a good time for spells related to protection and cleansing.
- **Sunset Ritual Ideas**:
  - A banishing spell to release negativity or unwanted influences.

◦ A closing ritual to mark the end of a project, relationship, or phase of life.

Noon and Twilight Magic

- **Noon**: When the sun reaches its zenith, it symbolizes maximum power and energy. Noon is a time for spells that require strength, vitality, and a boost of confidence or courage. This is the peak of solar energy, making it a great time for manifestation, success, and empowerment spells.
- **Twilight**: Twilight, the time just after sunset, holds a mystical energy that balances both light and dark. It is an in-between space, perfect for divination, dream work, and magic related to transitions or transformation. Twilight rituals can also help you connect with your subconscious and the unseen realms.

Sunrise and Sunset Charts for Spell Timing

The following charts provide the approximate times of sunrise and sunset for each month of 2025. These times are based on a mid-latitude location in the Northern Hemisphere. Keep in mind that sunrise and sunset times can vary depending on your geographic location, and seasonal shifts will impact these times. For exact local times, consult an online tool or weather app specific to your area.

January 2025

- **Sunrise**:
    ◦ January 1: 7:21 AM
    ◦ January 15: 7:19 AM
    ◦ January 31: 7:05 AM
- **Sunset**:
    ◦ January 1: 4:42 PM
    ◦ January 15: 4:58 PM
    ◦ January 31: 5:23 PM
- **Magical Focus**: The energy of January, with its slow lengthening of days, is ideal for spells of renewal, protection, and planting the seeds for long-term goals.

February 2025

- **Sunrise**:
    ◦ February 1: 7:04 AM
    ◦ February 15: 6:49 AM
    ◦ February 28: 6:30 AM
- **Sunset**:
    ◦ February 1: 5:25 PM
    ◦ February 15: 5:42 PM

- ◦ February 28: 6:01 PM
- **Magical Focus**: February's growing light encourages spells of love, relationships, and healing. This is a great time to focus on heart-centered magic and self-care.

March 2025

- **Sunrise**:
    - ◦ March 1: 6:29 AM
    - ◦ March 15: 7:11 AM (due to Daylight Saving Time)
    - ◦ March 31: 6:43 AM
- **Sunset**:
    - ◦ March 1: 6:02 PM
    - ◦ March 15: 7:16 PM
    - ◦ March 31: 7:29 PM
- **Magical Focus**: The vernal equinox (March 20, 2025) marks a time of balance between day and night. This is ideal for spells of equilibrium, fertility, and new growth.

April 2025

- **Sunrise**:
    - ◦ April 1: 6:42 AM
    - ◦ April 15: 6:24 AM
    - ◦ April 30: 6:02 AM
- **Sunset**:
    - ◦ April 1: 7:30 PM
    - ◦ April 15: 7:46 PM
    - ◦ April 30: 8:03 PM
- **Magical Focus**: April's increasing daylight hours are perfect for spells of abundance, career advancement, and prosperity.

May 2025

- **Sunrise**:
    - ◦ May 1: 6:00 AM
    - ◦ May 15: 5:43 AM
    - ◦ May 31: 5:28 AM
- **Sunset**:
    - ◦ May 1: 8:04 PM
    - ◦ May 15: 8:19 PM
    - ◦ May 31: 8:36 PM

- **Magical Focus**: With longer days and warmer temperatures, May is a wonderful time for spells of creativity, love, and personal empowerment.

June 2025 (Summer Solstice)

- **Sunrise**:
    - June 1: 5:27 AM
    - June 15: 5:20 AM
    - June 21 (Solstice): 5:22 AM
    - June 30: 5:27 AM
- **Sunset**:
    - June 1: 8:36 PM
    - June 15: 8:45 PM
    - June 21 (Solstice): 8:49 PM
    - June 30: 8:50 PM
- **Magical Focus**: June 21 marks the summer solstice, the longest day of the year. This is an incredibly powerful time for rituals of manifestation, success, and personal strength.

July 2025

- **Sunrise**:
    - July 1: 5:28 AM
    - July 15: 5:37 AM
    - July 31: 5:54 AM
- **Sunset**:
    - July 1: 8:50 PM
    - July 15: 8:44 PM
    - July 31: 8:28 PM
- **Magical Focus**: July's fiery energy is perfect for spells of passion, action, and courage. It's an ideal time to work on achieving personal goals.

August 2025

- **Sunrise**:
    - August 1: 5:56 AM
    - August 15: 6:10 AM
    - August 31: 6:28 AM
- **Sunset**:
    - August 1: 8:26 PM
    - August 15: 8:06 PM
    - August 31: 7:38 PM

- **Magical Focus**: As summer winds down, focus on spells of harvest, gratitude, and bringing your efforts to completion.

September 2025 (Autumn Equinox)

- **Sunrise**:
    - September 1: 6:30 AM
    - September 15: 6:46 AM
    - September 21 (Equinox): 6:53 AM
    - September 30: 7:02 AM
- **Sunset**:
    - September 1: 7:36 PM
    - September 15: 7:12 PM
    - September 21 (Equinox): 6:59 PM
    - September 30: 6:35 PM
- **Magical Focus**: The autumn equinox (September 21) is a time of balance, as day and night are equal. This is perfect for rituals of balance, harmony, and introspection.

October 2025

- **Sunrise**:
    - October 1: 7:03 AM
    - October 15: 7:20 AM
    - October 31: 7:42 AM
- **Sunset**:
    - October 1: 6:33 PM
    - October 15: 6:11 PM
    - October 31: 5:44 PM
- **Magical Focus**: October, with its shortening days, is a great time for protection spells, ancestral work, and preparing for the darker half of the year.

November 2025

- **Sunrise**:
    - November 1: 7:43 AM
    - November 15: 8:00 AM
    - November 30: 8:19 AM
- **Sunset**:
    - November 1: 5:43 PM
    - November 15: 5:24 PM
    - November 30: 5:09 PM

- **Magical Focus**: November's fading light is ideal for introspection, protection, and release work. It is a time to turn inward and prepare for winter.

December 2025 (Winter Solstice)

- **Sunrise**:
    - December 1: 8:20 AM
    - December 15: 8:33 AM
    - December 21 (Solstice): 8:37 AM
    - December 31: 8:41 AM
- **Sunset**:
    - December 1: 5:09 PM
    - December 15: 5:05 PM
    - December 21 (Solstice): 5:06 PM
    - December 31: 5:12 PM
- **Magical Focus**: December 21 marks the winter solstice, the longest night of the year. This is a time for rituals of reflection, rebirth, and renewal.

Conclusion

The daily rise and fall of the sun offers an abundance of opportunities to incorporate solar energy into your magical practice. Whether you are focusing on the dawn's fresh energy for new beginnings or tapping into the setting sun's power for closure and release, sunrise and sunset provide natural windows for spellwork. Use the detailed charts in this chapter to plan your rituals with the sun's energy in mind, ensuring that your magic is always aligned with the flow of the cosmos.

Chapter 4: The Moon's Phases: Full Moons of 2025

The moon is a powerful and mystical force in witchcraft, governing emotions, intuition, cycles of change, and the ebb and flow of life. As witches, we align ourselves with the moon's phases to harness its energy, which amplifies our magic and connects us to the deeper rhythms of the universe. Each phase of the moon has its own unique energy, with the full moon being the most potent time for manifestation, divination, and completing spells that require intense lunar power.

This chapter provides a detailed overview of the full moons of 2025, including their specific dates, times, and astrological meanings. You will also find suggested rituals, divination practices, and spellwork that align with each full moon, allowing you to harness its energy for maximum effect.

Understanding the Phases of the Moon

Before we dive into the full moons of 2025, it's important to understand the moon's phases and their significance in magic:

- **New Moon**: A time for new beginnings, setting intentions, and starting fresh projects. This phase represents potential and growth.
- **Waxing Moon**: As the moon grows from new to full, this phase is ideal for spells related to building, expansion, and attracting positive outcomes.
- **Full Moon**: The full moon is the culmination of the moon's energy and is a time of peak power, ideal for manifestation, completion, and divination. The full moon is perfect for bringing spells to fruition and for magical work that requires intense lunar energy.
- **Waning Moon**: As the moon shrinks from full to new, this phase is associated with banishing, releasing, and letting go of what no longer serves you.

The full moon, in particular, is a time when the moon's energy is at its height. It is a time for clarity, emotional insight, and the completion of goals or projects. Full moon rituals and spells focus on manifestation, release, and connecting deeply with your inner self and the universe.

Full Moons of 2025: Dates, Times, and Meanings

Each full moon of 2025 carries its own unique energy, influenced by the zodiac sign it occurs in. Below, you'll find the full moon dates, times, and astrological meanings, along with specific rituals and spell ideas for each full moon.

1. Full Wolf Moon – January 13, 2025

- **Date**: January 13, 2025
- **Time**: 7:26 AM UTC
- **Zodiac Sign**: Cancer
- **Meaning**: The Full Wolf Moon in Cancer brings emotional insight and the energy of nurturing, protection, and home. It is a time to focus on family, personal comfort, and healing from emotional wounds. Cancer's influence makes this full moon deeply intuitive, making it an ideal time for inner reflection and psychic work.

Ritual: Nurturing the Self

- **Materials**: A blue or silver candle, a bowl of water, and a small mirror.
- **Instructions**: Light the candle and place the bowl of water before you. Sit comfortably and gaze into the mirror, focusing on your own reflection. Reflect on the emotional needs you have been neglecting and how you can better nurture yourself. Use the water to symbolically wash away any emotional blocks or fears, then set new intentions for emotional well-being.

Spellwork Focus: This is a great time for spells of emotional healing, protection, and nurturing relationships. Work on strengthening bonds with loved ones or creating a safe, comforting home environment.

2. Full Snow Moon – February 12, 2025

- **Date**: February 12, 2025
- **Time**: 10:20 PM UTC
- **Zodiac Sign**: Leo
- **Meaning**: The Full Snow Moon in Leo is all about creativity, self-expression, and confidence. Leo's bold and passionate energy makes this full moon a perfect time for personal empowerment, leadership, and artistic pursuits. It's an excellent time to shine and showcase your talents, as well as to embrace self-love.

Ritual: Embracing Your Inner Light

- **Materials**: A gold candle, a piece of citrine or sunstone, and a personal journal.
- **Instructions**: Light the candle and place the citrine or sunstone in front of you. As the flame flickers, meditate on your personal strengths and the ways you can shine brighter in your life. Write down affirmations of self-love and personal empowerment in your journal. Hold the stone in your hands and imagine your inner light growing stronger, infusing you with confidence and joy.

Spellwork Focus: Perform spells related to personal power, creativity, and success. This is a great time for confidence-building rituals and for working on manifesting your creative projects or career goals.

3. Full Worm Moon – March 14, 2025

- **Date**: March 14, 2025
- **Time**: 3:02 PM UTC
- **Zodiac Sign**: Virgo
- **Meaning**: The Full Worm Moon in Virgo encourages grounding, organization, and self-care. Virgo's analytical energy helps you focus on details, health, and routines. This is an ideal time to declutter your life—physically, emotionally, and mentally. It's also a powerful full moon for self-improvement and refining your goals.

Ritual: Clearing the Path

- **Materials**: A white candle, a small broom or besom, and a bowl of salt.
- **Instructions**: Light the white candle and place the bowl of salt at the entrance of your sacred space. Use the broom to symbolically sweep away old, stagnant energy from your space, beginning at the entrance and moving outward. As you sweep, visualize clearing the way for new opportunities and fresh energy to enter your life.

Spellwork Focus: This full moon is perfect for cleansing and purification rituals. It's also an excellent time for spells related to health, wellness, and creating structure in your life. Focus on self-discipline and letting go of unhealthy habits.

4. Full Pink Moon – April 13, 2025

- **Date**: April 13, 2025
- **Time**: 9:17 AM UTC
- **Zodiac Sign**: Libra
- **Meaning**: The Full Pink Moon in Libra brings harmony, balance, and a focus on relationships. Libra's diplomatic and peaceful nature encourages you to seek equilibrium in all areas of your life, particularly in partnerships. This is a time for working on love spells, strengthening relationships, and finding balance between your personal needs and the needs of others.

Ritual: Harmonizing Relationships

- **Materials**: A pink candle, rose petals, and a piece of rose quartz.
- **Instructions**: Light the pink candle and place the rose quartz in front of you. Scatter the rose petals around the candle. As you gaze into the flame, reflect on your relationships—both romantic and platonic. Hold the rose quartz in your hand and visualize harmony and love flowing through your connections. You may also write a letter of forgiveness or gratitude to someone you care about and burn it in the candle flame to release any tension or negativity.

Spellwork Focus: This full moon is ideal for spells focused on love, partnership, and balance. It's a great time to perform rituals that enhance harmony in relationships or to attract new love into your life.

5. Full Flower Moon – May 12, 2025

- **Date**: May 12, 2025
- **Time**: 4:29 AM UTC
- **Zodiac Sign**: Scorpio
- **Meaning**: The Full Flower Moon in Scorpio brings deep transformation and emotional intensity. Scorpio's passionate energy makes this full moon an excellent time for shadow work, releasing what no longer serves you, and embracing personal transformation. It's a powerful moon for digging deep into your subconscious and working through hidden emotions.

Ritual: Transformation Through Shadow Work

- **Materials**: A black candle, a journal, and a bowl of water.
- **Instructions**: Light the black candle and sit in a quiet space with your journal. Reflect on the aspects of your life or self that need transformation. Write down what you are ready to release—whether it's an emotional pattern, a fear, or an old grudge. After writing, dip your fingers into the bowl of water and sprinkle the water over the journal pages as a symbolic cleansing.

Spellwork Focus: This is a perfect time for deep emotional healing, shadow work, and spells related to transformation. Focus on banishing negative patterns and embracing your personal power.

6. Full Strawberry Moon – June 11, 2025

- **Date**: June 11, 2025
- **Time**: 10:17 PM UTC
- **Zodiac Sign**: Sagittarius
- **Meaning**: The Full Strawberry Moon in Sagittarius is all about adventure, expansion, and seeking the truth. Sagittarius' optimistic and fiery energy encourages exploration, both physically and mentally. This is a great time for travel magic, expanding your horizons, and setting your sights on new goals.

Ritual: Expanding Your Horizons

- **Materials**: A purple candle, a map or globe, and a piece of amethyst.
- **Instructions**: Light the purple candle and place the map or globe in front of you. Hold the amethyst in your hands and close your eyes, imagining the possibilities for your future adventures or personal growth. Focus on where you'd like to expand—whether in travel, knowledge, or spiritual exploration. Mark those intentions on the map or write them down on paper.

Spellwork Focus: This full moon is perfect for spells of exploration, travel, and personal growth. It's an excellent time for setting goals related to learning, spiritual growth, or expanding your horizons.

7. Full Buck Moon – July 10, 2025

- **Date**: July 10, 2025
- **Time**: 3:08 PM UTC
- **Zodiac Sign**: Capricorn
- **Meaning**: The Full Buck Moon in Capricorn brings discipline, structure, and long-term planning. Capricorn's practical and grounded energy helps you focus on building strong foundations for your future. This full moon is ideal for career advancement, financial planning, and setting long-term goals.

Ritual: Building Foundations for Success

- **Materials**: A green candle, a piece of onyx or obsidian, and a notebook.
- **Instructions**: Light the green candle and place the onyx or obsidian in front of you. In your notebook, write down your long-term goals, particularly those related to your career, finances, or personal growth. As you write, focus on the steps you need to take to achieve these goals, and visualize yourself steadily building toward success.

Spellwork Focus: Focus on career spells, financial growth, and personal discipline. This is an excellent time for setting practical, long-term goals and performing spells to ensure their success.

8. Full Sturgeon Moon – August 9, 2025

- **Date**: August 9, 2025
- **Time**: 7:51 AM UTC
- **Zodiac Sign**: Aquarius
- **Meaning**: The Full Sturgeon Moon in Aquarius encourages innovation, independence, and community-focused magic. Aquarius' visionary energy makes this full moon ideal for thinking outside the box, breaking free from old limitations, and focusing on humanitarian goals.

Ritual: Visionary Magic

- **Materials**: A blue candle, a piece of labradorite, and a piece of paper.
- **Instructions**: Light the blue candle and hold the labradorite in your hands. Focus on an area of your life where you feel restricted or where you want to break free. On the piece of paper, write down your vision for the future, emphasizing freedom, creativity, and innovation. Burn the paper in the candle's flame, releasing your vision to the universe.

Spellwork Focus: This is the perfect time for spells related to freedom, breaking away from old patterns, and community building. Focus on innovative projects, new ideas, and group-related magic.

9. Full Harvest Moon – September 8, 2025

- **Date**: September 8, 2025
- **Time**: 5:10 AM UTC
- **Zodiac Sign**: Pisces
- **Meaning**: The Full Harvest Moon in Pisces is deeply intuitive, emotional, and spiritual. Pisces' dreamy energy makes this full moon ideal for divination, dream magic, and connecting with your higher self. It's a time to focus on your spiritual path and the subtle energies around you.

Ritual: Dream Magic

- **Materials**: A white candle, lavender oil, and a dream journal.
- **Instructions**: Light the white candle and anoint yourself with lavender oil to calm your mind. Before going to sleep, meditate on your dreams and any messages you wish to receive from the spirit realm. Keep a dream journal next to your bed, and as you wake, record any significant dreams or insights.

Spellwork Focus: This full moon is ideal for dream work, psychic development, and divination. It's also a great time for spiritual cleansing and deep meditation.

10. Full Hunter's Moon – October 7, 2025

- **Date**: October 7, 2025
- **Time**: 11:26 PM UTC
- **Zodiac Sign**: Aries
- **Meaning**: The Full Hunter's Moon in Aries brings boldness, action, and assertiveness. Aries' fiery energy is perfect for taking decisive action, pursuing goals, and focusing on personal empowerment. This is a time for courage, confidence, and going after what you want without hesitation.

Ritual: Fire of Courage

- **Materials**: A red candle, a piece of carnelian, and a small piece of paper.
- **Instructions**: Light the red candle and place the carnelian in front of you. On the piece of paper, write down a goal or challenge you want to overcome. As you gaze into the flame, visualize yourself successfully achieving this goal with courage and strength. Burn the paper in the candle's flame as a symbol of your commitment to taking action.

Spellwork Focus: Focus on spells of courage, strength, and personal empowerment. This is a great time to tackle challenges head-on and pursue your ambitions with confidence.

11. Full Beaver Moon – November 6, 2025

- **Date**: November 6, 2025
- **Time**: 4:20 PM UTC
- **Zodiac Sign**: Taurus
- **Meaning**: The Full Beaver Moon in Taurus is about stability, abundance, and sensuality. Taurus' grounded energy helps you focus on material wealth, comfort, and enjoying life's pleasures. This full moon is ideal for spells related to prosperity, home, and physical well-being.

Ritual: Manifesting Abundance

- **Materials**: A green candle, a coin, and a bowl of earth or soil.
- **Instructions**: Light the green candle and hold the coin in your hands. Focus on manifesting abundance, wealth, and stability in your life. Bury the coin in the bowl of earth, symbolizing the planting of seeds for future prosperity. Leave the candle to burn down safely as you meditate on the energy of abundance flowing into your life.

Spellwork Focus: This full moon is perfect for prosperity spells, grounding, and creating comfort in your home. Focus on spells related to financial growth, physical health, and enjoying the material world.

12. Full Cold Moon – December 6, 2025

- **Date**: December 6, 2025
- **Time**: 9:53 AM UTC
- **Zodiac Sign**: Gemini
- **Meaning**: The Full Cold Moon in Gemini encourages communication, learning, and adaptability. Gemini's intellectual energy makes this full moon an excellent time for spells related to communication, writing, and social connections. It's also a great time to focus on learning new skills and sharing your ideas with others.

Ritual: Words of Power

- **Materials**: A yellow candle, a feather, and a pen.
- **Instructions**: Light the yellow candle and hold the feather in your hand. On a piece of paper, write down your intentions for clearer communication, learning, or intellectual growth. As you write, imagine the words flowing with the energy of the universe, empowered by the full moon. Afterward, read your words aloud to activate their power, and keep the paper on your altar for the next lunar cycle.

Spellwork Focus: This is a great time for communication spells, intellectual pursuits, and learning new skills. Focus on improving communication in your relationships, manifesting new knowledge, or sharing your ideas with the world.

Divination and Lunar Spells for the Full Moon

The full moon is a time when psychic abilities and intuition are heightened, making it the perfect time for divination practices such as tarot reading, scrying, or rune casting. Here are a few practices you can incorporate into your full moon rituals:

- **Tarot Readings**: Perform a tarot reading under the light of the full moon to gain insight into your current situation, challenges, and opportunities. The full moon's energy will amplify your intuition and help you receive clearer messages.
- **Scrying**: Use a bowl of water, a crystal ball, or a mirror to perform scrying during the full moon. The moon's light will illuminate your visions and help you connect with your subconscious mind.
- **Lunar Meditations**: Meditate under the full moon to connect with its energy. Visualize the moon's light filling your body and clearing away any emotional or energetic blockages.
- **Dream Magic**: Sleep with a piece of moonstone or quartz under your pillow on the night of the full moon to enhance your dreams and receive messages from your subconscious or the spirit realm.

Conclusion

The full moons of 2025 present powerful opportunities for growth, transformation, and manifestation. By aligning your rituals, spells, and divination practices with the specific energy of each full moon, you can harness the lunar power to enhance your magic and bring your desires to fruition. Whether you're focusing on personal empowerment, emotional healing, or spiritual growth, the full moon's light will guide you on your magical journey throughout the year.

Chapter 5: The New Moons and Manifestation

The new moon marks the beginning of the lunar cycle and is a potent time for setting intentions, planting the seeds of new projects, and manifesting your desires. Unlike the full moon, which is all about culmination and realization, the new moon symbolizes potential, new beginnings, and the quiet, introspective energy that comes with starting fresh. In this chapter, we'll explore the dates and significance of each new moon in 2025, how to work with the unique energy of the dark moon, and practical guides for setting intentions that align with your deepest desires.

The Power of the New Moon

The new moon is the phase of the moon when it is invisible in the night sky, hidden from view as it lies between the Earth and the sun. This darkened sky represents a blank slate, a time of quiet reflection and renewal. Because the moon is "dark" during this phase, the new moon holds subtle, inward-focused energy that is ideal for manifestation work. It is the moment when we align with the universe's cycles to plant the seeds for what we wish to grow and achieve in the coming weeks and months.

In magical terms, the new moon is associated with:

- **New Beginnings**: Starting new projects, forming new habits, and setting goals for personal and professional growth.
- **Introspection and Reflection**: Reflecting on past cycles, understanding what worked and what didn't, and aligning your future actions with your higher purpose.
- **Manifestation**: Using focused intention-setting rituals to manifest desires and bring new opportunities into your life.
- **Spiritual Cleansing**: Releasing old energy, negative influences, or emotional baggage to make room for fresh energy.

During the new moon, we are encouraged to look within and think about what we truly want to bring into our lives. This is a powerful time for manifestation, but it's also a quiet, inward-focused energy that allows us to be clear and deliberate about our intentions.

How to Work with Dark Moon Energy

The "dark moon" refers to the final phase of the waning moon, just before the new moon. This is the point at which the moon is completely dark, and it carries a different type of energy compared to the new moon itself. While the new moon is a time of beginnings, the dark moon is a moment for deep reflection, shadow work, and release.

Working with the Dark Moon:

- **Shadow Work**: The dark moon is an ideal time to explore your shadow self—the parts of yourself that you may not always acknowledge or want to face. Use this time for introspection, journaling, or meditation to confront hidden fears, emotions, or behaviors that are holding you back. By bringing these aspects of yourself into the light, you can release their hold on you.
- **Releasing Old Patterns**: Before you begin manifesting new desires, the dark moon is a perfect time to let go of old patterns, habits, or relationships that no longer serve your growth. Perform a simple banishing ritual or write down what you want to release and burn the paper to symbolically free yourself from these burdens.
- **Deep Cleansing**: Use the energy of the dark moon for spiritual cleansing. This can involve physically cleaning your space, cleansing your aura with sage or incense, or taking a ritual bath with herbs like rosemary, lavender, or sea salt to wash away stagnant energy.

By embracing the dark moon phase, you clear the way for the new moon's energy to enter your life. This creates a powerful cycle of release and renewal, setting the stage for more effective and focused manifestations during the new moon.

New Moon Manifestation Rituals

When working with the new moon for manifestation, the key is to set clear, focused intentions. This is the time to be specific about what you want to bring into your life, and to put your desires into action through rituals and visualization. The new moon is about sowing the seeds of your intentions, with the understanding that they will grow and come to fruition in the coming lunar cycle.

Here's a basic new moon manifestation ritual that can be adapted for each new moon throughout 2025:

Basic New Moon Manifestation Ritual
Materials:

- A white or silver candle (to symbolize the moon's energy).
- A journal or piece of paper and a pen.
- A small bowl of water (to represent the element of emotion and flow).
- A crystal associated with manifestation (such as clear quartz, citrine, or amethyst).

Instructions:

1. **Set the Scene**: Find a quiet, comfortable space where you won't be disturbed. Light the candle and sit in front of it with your journal or paper. If possible, position yourself near a window where you can feel connected to the night sky, even if the moon isn't visible.
2. **Clear Your Mind**: Take a few deep breaths to center yourself. Hold the crystal in your hands and focus on the energy of new beginnings. Close your eyes and reflect on what you wish to bring into your life. This could be related to love, career, health, personal growth, or any other area of your life that you want to improve or manifest something new.
3. **Set Your Intentions**: Write down your intentions for this lunar cycle. Be specific about what you want to manifest. Instead of general statements like "I want to be successful," phrase your intention as a clear, actionable goal, such as "I am attracting new opportunities in my career that align with my talents and passions."
4. **Focus on the Outcome**: As you write, visualize what it will feel like when your intentions have manifested. Imagine yourself living that reality, feeling the joy, satisfaction, or peace that comes with achieving your goals.
5. **Activate Your Intentions**: After writing your intentions, hold the paper or journal over the bowl of water and say aloud, "As the moon grows, so do my intentions. I am ready to receive what I have asked for. So it is." Visualize the water absorbing your intentions and the energy of the new moon amplifying them.
6. **Closing**: Allow the candle to burn down safely, and keep the crystal with you for the remainder of the lunar cycle as a reminder of your intentions. Over the next few days, revisit your intentions, and take small, tangible steps toward manifesting them.

New Moon Dates and Guides for Setting Intentions in 2025

Each new moon in 2025 carries the energy of the zodiac sign it occurs in, offering specific opportunities for manifestation. Below, we'll explore the new moon dates, times, and the themes associated with each one, along with suggestions for aligning your intentions with the astrological energies of the moment.

1. New Moon in Capricorn – January 28, 2025

- **Date**: January 28, 2025
- **Time**: 2:10 AM UTC
- **Focus**: Ambition, long-term goals, discipline, career.
- **Intentions**: Set intentions related to career advancement, financial stability, or long-term projects. Capricorn's energy supports focus, determination, and perseverance, making this a perfect time to plan for success and lay down solid foundations for the future.

Capricorn New Moon Ritual: Write down your career or financial goals for the year, focusing on tangible outcomes. Perform a grounding meditation to solidify your vision, and place your written goals under a piece of obsidian or garnet to represent the strength and stability of Capricorn energy.

2. New Moon in Aquarius – February 26, 2025

- **Date**: February 26, 2025
- **Time**: 9:29 PM UTC
- **Focus**: Innovation, independence, social connections, humanitarian efforts.
- **Intentions**: Focus on intentions related to innovation, community, or personal freedom. Aquarius energy is perfect for breaking free of old patterns, embracing new ideas, and working on goals that benefit not only yourself but also the collective.

Aquarius New Moon Ritual: Write your intentions on a piece of biodegradable paper and release them into the wind outside, symbolizing your openness to new possibilities and innovative ideas. Meditate on how your personal growth can contribute to the greater good.

3. New Moon in Pisces – March 28, 2025

- **Date**: March 28, 2025
- **Time**: 4:16 PM UTC
- **Focus**: Spiritual growth, creativity, intuition, emotional healing.
- **Intentions**: Set intentions for spiritual development, creative expression, or emotional healing. Pisces brings a deeply intuitive, dreamy energy, making this new moon ideal for tapping into your inner world and exploring your subconscious desires.

Pisces New Moon Ritual: Create an altar with symbols of water (a bowl, shells, or ocean-themed objects) and perform a visualization meditation in which you allow your imagination to flow freely, envisioning your dreams and desires coming to life.

4. New Moon in Aries – April 26, 2025

- **Date**: April 26, 2025
- **Time**: 12:43 AM UTC
- **Focus**: Action, courage, leadership, new beginnings.
- **Intentions**: Aries is the first sign of the zodiac, making this a time for bold new beginnings, leadership, and taking action. Set intentions related to new projects, personal courage, or stepping into a leadership role in your life.

Aries New Moon Ritual: Light a red candle and focus on activating your inner fire. Write your intentions as declarations of action (e.g., "I am taking bold steps toward my goals"), and visualize yourself fearlessly pursuing your desires.

5. New Moon in Taurus – May 25, 2025

- **Date**: May 25, 2025
- **Time**: 8:12 PM UTC
- **Focus**: Stability, abundance, sensuality, self-worth.
- **Intentions**: Set intentions focused on financial security, physical well-being, or enhancing your self-worth. Taurus energy is about grounding, stability, and enjoying the material pleasures of life.

Taurus New Moon Ritual: Create a ritual bath using sea salt, rosemary, and lavender. As you soak, meditate on abundance and prosperity flowing into your life. Visualize yourself surrounded by wealth, comfort, and security, and set intentions to build this in the material world.

6. New Moon in Gemini – June 24, 2025

- **Date**: June 24, 2025
- **Time**: 4:03 AM UTC
- **Focus**: Communication, learning, adaptability, curiosity.
- **Intentions**: Focus on intentions related to learning new skills, improving communication, or exploring new ideas. Gemini's energy supports intellectual growth and social connections, making it a great time for brainstorming and networking.

Gemini New Moon Ritual: Write your intentions on small pieces of paper and place them inside a book or journal. Focus on gaining knowledge and wisdom in areas that will help you achieve your goals. Light a yellow candle to symbolize the clarity of mind and intellectual pursuit.

7. New Moon in Cancer – July 23, 2025

- **Date**: July 23, 2025
- **Time**: 11:38 PM UTC
- **Focus**: Home, family, emotional security, nurturing.
- **Intentions**: Set intentions around building stronger relationships with family, creating emotional security, or nurturing yourself and others. Cancer's energy is deeply nurturing and protective, making this new moon perfect for focusing on matters of the heart and home.

Cancer New Moon Ritual: Create a sacred space in your home where you can reflect on your emotional needs and the relationships that matter most to you. Light a silver or blue candle, and set your intentions for creating emotional harmony and security within yourself and your loved ones.

8. New Moon in Leo – August 22, 2025

- **Date**: August 22, 2025
- **Time**: 9:57 AM UTC
- **Focus**: Creativity, confidence, self-expression, joy.
- **Intentions**: Focus on personal empowerment, creativity, and self-expression. Leo's bold, joyful energy encourages you to shine brightly and pursue your passions without fear. This is a great time to set intentions for creative projects or to boost your self-confidence.

Leo New Moon Ritual: Perform a creative ritual in which you express your desires through art, music, or writing. Light a gold or orange candle and envision yourself stepping into the spotlight, confident and radiant. Set intentions for personal success and joyful self-expression.

9. New Moon in Virgo – September 21, 2025

- **Date**: September 21, 2025
- **Time**: 6:21 AM UTC
- **Focus**: Health, organization, service, self-improvement.
- **Intentions**: Set intentions for improving your health, refining your daily routines, or offering service to others. Virgo's practical energy helps you focus on self-improvement and paying attention to the details that lead to success.

Virgo New Moon Ritual: Organize a space in your home that feels cluttered or chaotic. As you tidy up, focus on creating an environment that supports your goals for self-improvement, health, and well-being. Light a white candle and set intentions for greater clarity and discipline in your life.

10. New Moon in Libra – October 21, 2025

- **Date**: October 21, 2025
- **Time**: 2:18 PM UTC
- **Focus**: Balance, relationships, harmony, beauty.
- **Intentions**: Focus on creating balance in your relationships, personal life, and environment. Libra's energy is about harmony, diplomacy, and beauty, making this a great time for intentions related to love, partnerships, and aesthetics.

Libra New Moon Ritual: Decorate your space with fresh flowers, crystals, or objects that symbolize beauty and balance. Light a pink or green candle, and set your intentions for creating harmonious relationships and a peaceful, beautiful environment.

11. New Moon in Scorpio – November 19, 2025

- **Date**: November 19, 2025
- **Time**: 10:43 AM UTC
- **Focus**: Transformation, power, emotional depth, secrets.
- **Intentions**: Focus on deep emotional transformation, personal empowerment, and uncovering hidden truths. Scorpio's intense energy supports shadow work, deep healing, and manifesting personal power.

Scorpio New Moon Ritual: Perform a ritual of transformation by writing down an aspect of yourself or your life that you wish to change or release. Burn the paper in a black candle's flame, symbolizing the death of the old and the rebirth of the new.

12. New Moon in Sagittarius – December 19, 2025

- **Date**: December 19, 2025
- **Time**: 6:12 AM UTC
- **Focus**: Adventure, higher learning, expansion, optimism.
- **Intentions**: Set intentions related to travel, learning, or expanding your horizons. Sagittarius encourages optimism, growth, and exploring the unknown, making this an ideal time for setting intentions that push you beyond your comfort zone.

Sagittarius New Moon Ritual: Write your intentions on a piece of paper and place it under a map or globe. Light a purple candle, and visualize yourself embarking on new adventures, whether physical, intellectual, or spiritual. Focus on expanding your life in meaningful ways.

Conclusion

The new moons of 2025 offer powerful opportunities to set intentions, begin new projects, and manifest your desires. By aligning your intentions with the unique energy of each new moon, you can harness the power of the lunar cycle to bring about transformation, growth, and success in all areas of your life. Whether you're focusing on love, career, health, or spiritual development, the new moon's energy provides the perfect moment to plant the seeds of your dreams and watch them grow.

Chapter 6: The Retrograde Calendar for 2025

In astrology, planetary retrogrades are often viewed as challenging periods when the energy of a planet appears to reverse, causing delays, confusion, or revisiting past issues. While retrogrades can feel disruptive, they also provide unique opportunities for introspection, reevaluation, and course correction. For witches and spiritual practitioners, retrograde periods can be used to enhance spells of reflection, healing, and transformation, allowing us to work with the planetary energies in new, powerful ways.

This chapter will provide a comprehensive retrograde calendar for 2025, explanations of what each planetary retrograde represents, and how to navigate these periods with aligned spellwork. Each planet governs specific aspects of life, and when retrograde, it invites us to turn inward and revisit these areas. With the right approach, retrogrades can be used to our advantage for growth, release, and spiritual evolution.

Understanding Retrogrades

A planetary retrograde occurs when a planet appears to move backward in the sky from Earth's perspective. While no planet actually reverses its orbit, the optical illusion of retrograde motion happens due to the differing speeds of Earth and other planets as they orbit the sun. Astrologically, retrogrades are seen as times when the planet's energy is turned inward rather than expressed outwardly, often leading to delays, disruptions, or the resurfacing of unresolved issues related to the planet's influence.

Each planet rules specific aspects of life, and its retrograde can influence those areas in unique ways:

- **Mercury**: Governs communication, travel, and technology.
- **Venus**: Rules love, relationships, and beauty.
- **Mars**: Influences action, energy, and conflict.
- **Jupiter**: Governs growth, expansion, and luck.
- **Saturn**: Rules discipline, responsibility, and long-term commitments.
- **Outer Planets (Uranus, Neptune, Pluto)**: Influence deeper, longer-term transformations in societal structures, spirituality, and power dynamics.

While retrogrades are often seen as disruptive, they offer opportunities for reflection, review, and personal growth. Retrograde periods are perfect for revisiting old projects, healing past wounds, and reassessing your goals and strategies. Instead of starting new endeavors, retrogrades are best used for resolving unfinished business, gaining clarity, and adjusting your approach.

Retrograde Calendar for 2025

Below is the detailed calendar of retrograde periods for 2025, including Mercury, Venus, Mars, Jupiter, Saturn, and the outer planets. Each section provides insight into the astrological meaning of the retrograde and specific advice for spellwork during these times.

Mercury Retrograde in 2025

Mercury retrograde is infamous for disrupting communication, travel, and technology, often leading to misunderstandings, delays, or glitches in daily life. However, it is also a powerful time for reflection, revisiting past decisions, and resolving unfinished business. Mercury retrograde invites you to slow down, reassess your thoughts, and work on improving communication in your life.

Mercury Retrograde Dates:

1. **January 1 – January 25, 2025** (in Capricorn)
2. **May 18 – June 11, 2025** (in Gemini)
3. **September 9 – October 1, 2025** (in Libra)

Astrological Influence:

- **Capricorn Retrograde (January)**: This retrograde focuses on career, long-term goals, and structures in your life. Expect to revisit old plans or face delays in work-related projects. It's a good time to reassess your ambitions and align them with your long-term vision.
- **Gemini Retrograde (May-June)**: With Mercury ruling Gemini, this retrograde will heavily influence communication and social interactions. Misunderstandings are common, so be extra cautious with your words. Use this time to reconnect with old friends or review past communications.
- **Libra Retrograde (September-October)**: Relationships, contracts, and legal matters may require reassessment during this retrograde. Focus on finding balance in your personal and professional relationships and avoid making rushed decisions.

Spellwork During Mercury Retrograde:

- **Reconciliation Spells**: Use Mercury retrograde to heal miscommunications or misunderstandings. This is a great time to perform spells that help resolve conflicts or reopen lines of communication with those from your past.
- **Reflective Journaling**: Dedicate time to journaling or meditating on past decisions and communications. Mercury retrograde encourages introspection, making it an excellent time to assess whether you've been expressing yourself truthfully.
- **Divination for Clarity**: Use divination tools like tarot or runes to gain insight into unresolved issues. Mercury retrograde can bring hidden truths to the surface, allowing you to address situations with newfound clarity.

Venus Retrograde in 2025

Venus retrograde occurs roughly every 18 months and is a significant period for reviewing relationships, love, and aesthetics. During Venus retrograde, existing relationships may be tested, and past lovers or unresolved emotional issues may resurface. It's a time to reassess your values around love, beauty, and self-worth.

Venus Retrograde Dates:

• **November 1 – December 14, 2025** (in Sagittarius and Scorpio)

Astrological Influence:

• **Sagittarius (November 1 – November 29)**: In Sagittarius, Venus retrograde may cause you to question your values in relationships, especially concerning freedom, adventure, and personal growth. It's a time to reassess whether your relationships support your individual journey.
• **Scorpio (November 29 – December 14)**: In Scorpio, this retrograde intensifies emotional connections and may bring hidden fears or issues of trust to the surface. It's a time for deep emotional healing and transformation in relationships.

Spellwork During Venus Retrograde:

• **Love Reassessment Rituals**: Venus retrograde is a perfect time to reflect on your relationships. Perform spells focused on clarifying your needs in love and partnership, whether through journaling, tarot, or heart-opening meditations.
• **Beauty Rituals for Self-Love**: Instead of external beauty spells, focus on self-love and self-worth. Use this time to strengthen your inner sense of value and nurture your emotional needs.
• **Cord-Cutting Rituals**: If past relationships or unresolved emotional connections are resurfacing, consider performing a cord-cutting ritual to release energetic ties that no longer serve your highest good.

Mars Retrograde in 2025

Mars retrograde occurs approximately every two years and can bring issues related to energy, motivation, and conflict to the surface. When Mars is retrograde, it's common to feel a lack of drive, or conversely, to experience frustration as repressed anger or unresolved conflicts emerge. Instead of charging forward, Mars retrograde encourages you to pause and reconsider your actions.

Mars Retrograde Dates:

- **December 6, 2025 – February 23, 2026** (in Gemini)

Astrological Influence:

- **Mars in Gemini**: Mars retrograde in Gemini will particularly affect communication, decision-making, and how you express your desires or frustrations. Arguments may arise from miscommunication or misunderstandings, and it's crucial to be mindful of your words during this period.

Spellwork During Mars Retrograde:

- **Conflict Resolution Spells**: Perform spells aimed at resolving conflict or diffusing anger. Use calming herbs like lavender or chamomile in your rituals to promote peace and harmony.
- **Rest and Rejuvenation**: Since Mars governs energy and drive, this retrograde is an ideal time for self-care rituals and spells to recharge your physical and emotional energy. Focus on healing and renewal rather than pushing forward aggressively.
- **Protection Spells**: Mars retrograde can stir up aggression or frustration. Cast protective spells or create talismans to shield yourself from negative energies and conflict during this time.

Jupiter Retrograde in 2025

Jupiter, the planet of expansion, luck, and growth, goes retrograde once a year for about four months. During this period, outward expansion may slow down, but it is an ideal time to turn inward and reflect on your personal growth, beliefs, and long-term vision. Jupiter retrograde encourages philosophical exploration and spiritual introspection.

Jupiter Retrograde Dates:

- **March 6 – July 30, 2025** (in Taurus)

Astrological Influence:

- **Jupiter in Taurus**: Jupiter retrograde in Taurus focuses on issues of stability, material wealth, and personal values. You may be encouraged to reassess your financial goals, material possessions, and how you create abundance in your life. This is also a time to reflect on the relationship between growth and sustainability.

Spellwork During Jupiter Retrograde:

- **Abundance Reassessment Rituals**: Use Jupiter retrograde to reevaluate your financial goals and how you manifest abundance. Perform grounding rituals to strengthen your connection to the Earth and ensure that your goals align with sustainable growth.
- **Spiritual Growth Meditations**: This is a powerful time for introspection and expanding your spiritual practice. Meditate on your beliefs and values, and perform spells for wisdom, personal growth, and spiritual insight.
- **Goal Reassessment**: If you've been pursuing big dreams or expansion, Jupiter retrograde is a time to pause and reassess your direction. Perform rituals that focus on refining your long-term vision and adjusting your approach if necessary.

Saturn Retrograde in 2025

Saturn is the planet of discipline, structure, and responsibility. When Saturn goes retrograde, it's a time to review commitments, assess long-term goals, and confront challenges around authority, discipline, and personal boundaries. Saturn retrograde often brings lessons or karmic patterns that require resolution.

Saturn Retrograde Dates:

- **June 1 – November 15, 2025** (in Pisces)

Astrological Influence:

- **Saturn in Pisces**: Saturn retrograde in Pisces highlights spiritual discipline, boundaries in emotional and creative expression, and the need for structure in your dreams and ideals. You may feel the need to reevaluate how you manage responsibilities related to spirituality, compassion, or emotional boundaries.

Spellwork During Saturn Retrograde:

- **Karmic Cleansing**: Saturn retrograde is a great time to perform spells focused on clearing past karma or unresolved lessons. This could involve journaling about past challenges or performing a cord-cutting ritual to release negative patterns.
- **Long-Term Goal Reassessment**: Revisit your long-term goals, especially those related to your spiritual practice, creativity, or emotional well-being. Perform a ritual to solidify your commitment to these goals while making any necessary adjustments.

- **Setting Boundaries**: If you've been struggling with setting or maintaining boundaries, this is the ideal time to perform spells that help reinforce your personal limits and protect your emotional and spiritual space.

Outer Planet Retrogrades in 2025

The outer planets (Uranus, Neptune, and Pluto) spend nearly half of each year in retrograde, and their influence is less personal, focusing on collective or generational shifts. However, their retrogrades can still impact your spiritual practice, particularly if they are strongly positioned in your natal chart.

Uranus Retrograde (Taurus): August 28, 2025 – January 27, 2026

- **Focus**: Uranus retrograde encourages reflection on personal freedom, innovation, and the need for change. In Taurus, it's about rethinking your approach to stability, finances, and personal values.

Neptune Retrograde (Pisces): June 30 – December 6, 2025

- **Focus**: Neptune retrograde is a time to reflect on your spiritual beliefs, dreams, and intuition. In Pisces, it encourages you to reconnect with your spiritual path and seek clarity in areas where illusions or fantasies may have clouded your vision.

Pluto Retrograde (Aquarius): April 3 – September 8, 2025

- **Focus**: Pluto retrograde is a period of deep transformation, urging you to confront power dynamics, personal shadows, and issues of control. In Aquarius, it highlights societal changes, collective transformation, and the need to innovate old systems.

Spellwork During Outer Planet Retrogrades:

- **Deep Transformation Rituals**: Use Pluto retrograde to perform shadow work, releasing deep-seated fears or power struggles. Focus on personal transformation and spiritual rebirth.
- **Clarity and Vision Spells**: Neptune retrograde is an ideal time for divination, dream work, and seeking spiritual clarity. Perform spells that enhance your intuition and connection to the divine.
- **Freedom and Innovation Rituals**: Uranus retrograde encourages you to break free from old limitations. Perform spells that promote personal liberation, innovation, and forward-thinking change.

Conclusion

Retrograde periods may feel challenging, but they offer valuable opportunities for reflection, healing, and personal growth. By understanding the astrological influence of each planet and tailoring your spellwork to align with these energies, you can turn the disruption of retrogrades into powerful moments of transformation and introspection. Instead of resisting the changes these periods bring, embrace them as opportunities to pause, reassess, and make more informed, intentional choices in your magical and everyday life.

Chapter 7: Meteor Showers and Their Magical Significance

Meteor showers are some of the most awe-inspiring celestial events visible from Earth. These showers occur when Earth passes through the debris left behind by comets or asteroids, resulting in streams of meteors (also called "shooting stars") streaking across the night sky. Throughout history, meteor showers have been associated with divine messages, prophecies, and magical energy. In witchcraft, meteor showers are seen as powerful moments to harness the energy of the cosmos for wishes, spells, and manifestations.

This chapter delves into the magical significance of meteor showers, offering practical advice on how to incorporate their energy into your spellwork. You'll find detailed information on the peak dates of major meteor showers in 2025, as well as rituals and spells designed to align with these celestial events.

The Magical Significance of Meteor Showers

In magical traditions, meteor showers are considered times when the veil between the physical and spiritual realms thins, making it easier to connect with the cosmos, divine forces, or the spirit world. The sudden burst of energy from meteors crashing into Earth's atmosphere creates a unique opportunity to channel powerful forces for spellwork and manifestation.

Meteor showers are commonly associated with:

- **Wish Fulfillment**: The falling stars are thought to carry the energy of manifestation. Making a wish during a meteor shower is believed to heighten the likelihood of your wish coming true.
- **Change and Transformation**: Just as meteors burn brightly and disappear, meteor showers symbolize sudden changes, transitions, and new beginnings. They are ideal for spells focused on transformation, clearing away the old to make way for the new.
- **Divine Communication**: Meteors have long been viewed as messengers from the gods or the universe. A meteor shower can be used to receive guidance from higher powers, enhance intuition, and deepen your connection with the spiritual realm.
- **Release and Renewal**: Like comets shedding their debris, meteor showers offer the perfect time to release what no longer serves you and clear stagnant energy from your life.

The energy of a meteor shower is both swift and intense, making it perfect for rituals that require a burst of power to get things moving quickly. Whether you're making a wish, seeking guidance, or initiating a major transformation, meteor showers can amplify your magic and bring your intentions to fruition with greater speed and potency.

Harnessing Meteor Shower Energy for Wishes and Spells

To harness the energy of a meteor shower, it's important to be intentional about the timing and preparation of your rituals. Meteor showers provide concentrated bursts of cosmic energy that can be directed toward specific intentions, such as wishes, transformation, or divination.

Here are some general guidelines for working with meteor showers:

1. **Timing**: The peak of the meteor shower is the most powerful time to perform magic. However, the night before and after the peak can also be potent if the weather or viewing conditions aren't ideal on the peak night.
2. **Outdoor Rituals**: If possible, perform your ritual outdoors, directly under the night sky, where you can watch the meteors and connect to their energy. If you're unable to be outside, set up your ritual space indoors but near a window to maintain a visual connection with the sky.
3. **Intention Setting**: Before the meteor shower, spend some time reflecting on what you want to manifest or change in your life. Use this time to get clear about your intentions so you can direct your energy during the shower.
4. **Wish Magic**: When you see a meteor, immediately make your wish, either aloud or silently. For stronger manifestation, visualize the wish coming true as you speak it. You can also use talismans or crystals to amplify the energy of your wish.
5. **Offerings and Gratitude**: After making your wish or casting your spell, leave a small offering to honor the cosmos and the forces you are working with. This could be flowers, herbs, a few drops of water, or a simple prayer of gratitude.

Meteor Showers in 2025: Peak Viewing Dates and Magical Suggestions

Below is a detailed guide to the major meteor showers of 2025, including their peak viewing dates and the specific magical energies associated with each. For each meteor shower, you'll find a brief overview of the astrological or symbolic meaning, along with suggested rituals and spellwork ideas to help you tap into their power.

1. Quadrantids Meteor Shower (January 3–4, 2025)

- **Peak Dates**: January 3–4, 2025
- **Estimated Peak Rate**: Up to 120 meteors per hour
- **Best Viewing**: After midnight, in the Northern Hemisphere
- **Origin**: Debris from asteroid 2003 EH1

Magical Significance:

The Quadrantids meteor shower occurs in the deep winter, a time for quiet introspection and renewal. As the first major meteor shower of the year, the Quadrantids carry energy associated with new beginnings and personal transformation. The cold, crisp air of January creates a perfect environment for introspective work and setting long-term goals for the year ahead.

Suggested Spellwork:

- **New Year's Manifestation Ritual**: Use the energy of the Quadrantids to set powerful intentions for the new year. Write your wishes for the coming year on small pieces of paper, and burn them in a fire-safe container as you watch the meteors. Visualize your intentions being carried into the universe with each shooting star.
- **Divination for the Year Ahead**: Perform a tarot or rune reading under the meteor shower to gain insight into the upcoming year. Ask for guidance on what you should focus on in the year ahead and how to align your actions with your higher purpose.

2. Lyrids Meteor Shower (April 22–23, 2025)

- **Peak Dates**: April 22–23, 2025
- **Estimated Peak Rate**: 15–20 meteors per hour
- **Best Viewing**: Late night to pre-dawn, globally visible
- **Origin**: Debris from Comet Thatcher (C/1861 G1)

Magical Significance:

The Lyrids meteor shower occurs during spring, a time of growth, fertility, and renewal. The energy of the Lyrids is closely associated with creativity, inspiration, and personal breakthroughs. This is an ideal time to plant the seeds of new projects, especially those related to creativity or personal expression.

Suggested Spellwork:

- **Creative Inspiration Ritual**: Under the Lyrids, perform a ritual to spark creativity and fresh ideas. Light a blue or violet candle and sit under the night sky with a journal. As you watch the meteors, write down any new ideas or insights that come to you. Visualize your creative energy expanding with each shooting star.
- **Personal Breakthrough Spells**: If you've been feeling stuck or blocked, use the energy of the Lyrids to break through obstacles. Write down a personal barrier you want to overcome and burn the paper as you make a wish for freedom and clarity.

3. Eta Aquarids Meteor Shower (May 5–6, 2025)

- **Peak Dates**: May 5–6, 2025
- **Estimated Peak Rate**: 40–60 meteors per hour
- **Best Viewing**: Predawn, best seen in the Southern Hemisphere
- **Origin**: Debris from Halley's Comet

Magical Significance:

The Eta Aquarids meteor shower is linked to the famous Halley's Comet and carries the energy of deep transformation and cosmic insight. Occurring during spring, the Eta Aquarids are ideal for spells focused on personal evolution, shedding old patterns, and embracing new growth.

Suggested Spellwork:

- **Transformation Ritual**: Use this time to release old habits, beliefs, or situations that are holding you back. Write down what you wish to release and bury the paper in the earth, symbolizing your readiness to shed the old and embrace transformation.
- **Cosmic Connection Meditation**: Sit under the night sky during the Eta Aquarids and meditate on your connection to the universe. Focus on receiving messages from the cosmos, and allow your intuition to guide you toward new insights and spiritual growth.

4. Delta Aquarids Meteor Shower (July 28–29, 2025)

- **Peak Dates**: July 28–29, 2025
- **Estimated Peak Rate**: 15–20 meteors per hour
- **Best Viewing**: Predawn, best seen in the Southern Hemisphere
- **Origin**: Debris from Comet 96P/Machholz

Magical Significance:

The Delta Aquarids occur in the heat of summer, during a time of abundance and fulfillment. The energy of this meteor shower is associated with community, collective growth, and humanitarian efforts. It's a time to focus on how you contribute to the greater good and to align your actions with your values.

Suggested Spellwork:

- **Community Building Ritual**: Use the Delta Aquarids to focus on building and strengthening connections within your community. Light a green candle and meditate on how you can serve others. Set intentions for creating harmony and unity in your family, social circle, or spiritual group.
- **Manifesting Collective Goals**: If you're working toward a shared goal with others, perform a manifestation ritual under the Delta Aquarids. Visualize the success of your collective efforts and ask the universe to bless your group's endeavors.

5. Perseids Meteor Shower (August 12–13, 2025)

- **Peak Dates**: August 12–13, 2025
- **Estimated Peak Rate**: 60–100 meteors per hour
- **Best Viewing**: Midnight to pre-dawn, Northern Hemisphere
- **Origin**: Debris from Comet Swift-Tuttle

Magical Significance:

The Perseids are one of the most well-known and active meteor showers of the year, occurring in late summer when the energy is vibrant and strong. The Perseids are ideal for wish-making, personal empowerment, and manifesting bold new visions. This meteor shower's bright, fiery energy supports action, creativity, and fast results.

Suggested Spellwork:

- **Wish Fulfillment Ritual**: During the Perseids, make a wish for something you truly desire. Hold a clear quartz crystal in your hand as you watch the meteors and speak your wish aloud as each shooting star passes. Place the crystal on your altar afterward to keep the energy of your wish alive.

- **Empowerment Spells**: Perform spells that focus on self-confidence, personal power, and courage. Light a red or orange candle and visualize yourself stepping into your power and achieving your goals with determination and passion.

6. Orionids Meteor Shower (October 21–22, 2025)

- **Peak Dates**: October 21–22, 2025
- **Estimated Peak Rate**: 20–30 meteors per hour
- **Best Viewing**: Midnight to pre-dawn, globally visible
- **Origin**: Debris from Halley's Comet

Magical Significance:

The Orionids meteor shower occurs in the autumn, a season of change and reflection. The energy of the Orionids is associated with letting go, transformation, and preparing for the darker half of the year. It's a time to release what no longer serves you and embrace personal growth.

Suggested Spellwork:

- **Release Ritual**: Write down anything you wish to let go of—whether it's a fear, a toxic relationship, or an old belief. Burn the paper in a fire-safe container as you watch the meteors, and imagine the smoke carrying your burdens away. Use the energy of the Orionids to create space for new growth in your life.
- **Preparing for Change**: As you prepare for the darker half of the year, use the Orionids to set intentions for personal transformation. Focus on what you need to release to move forward with clarity and purpose in the months ahead.

7. Geminids Meteor Shower (December 13–14, 2025)

- **Peak Dates**: December 13–14, 2025
- **Estimated Peak Rate**: 100–120 meteors per hour
- **Best Viewing**: All night, Northern Hemisphere
- **Origin**: Debris from asteroid 3200 Phaethon

Magical Significance:

The Geminids meteor shower occurs near the winter solstice, a time of reflection, closure, and preparation for the new year. The energy of the Geminids supports grounding, introspection, and finalizing long-term goals. This is a great time to look back on the year and bring any unfinished business to a close.

Suggested Spellwork:

- **Year-End Reflection Ritual**: Sit under the night sky and reflect on the past year. Write down your accomplishments, lessons learned, and any areas where you've grown. As you watch the Geminids, thank the universe for the blessings and challenges you've experienced, and set your intentions for the coming year.

- **Grounding and Protection Spells**: The Geminids' earthy energy is perfect for grounding and protection work. Perform a grounding meditation under the meteors, visualizing yourself rooted firmly in the earth. Use black tourmaline or smoky quartz to create a protective shield around yourself as you prepare for the new year.

Conclusion

Meteor showers offer powerful bursts of cosmic energy that can enhance your spells, wishes, and manifestations. By aligning your magic with the peak viewing times of meteor showers in 2025, you can harness the universe's energy for personal transformation, wish fulfillment, and spiritual growth. Whether you're making a wish, releasing old patterns, or preparing for new beginnings, these celestial events provide an unparalleled opportunity to connect with the cosmos and deepen your magical practice.

Chapter 8: Comets: Rare Celestial Visitors

Comets have captivated humanity for millennia, regarded as rare celestial visitors with mystical significance and powerful energy. Unlike meteor showers, which occur regularly as Earth passes through the debris of comets or asteroids, comets themselves are far rarer and often unpredictable in their appearances. These "cosmic wanderers" are composed of ice, dust, and gases, originating from the outer regions of our solar system. When they approach the sun, they ignite and form a glowing coma and tail, creating a stunning visual display in the night sky.

In mythology and folklore, comets have been seen as omens—both of change and transformation, and at times of foreboding or significant events. In witchcraft and spiritual practice, comets are viewed as carriers of profound energy, signaling moments of cosmic alignment that invite deep reflection, magical manifestation, and personal transformation.

This chapter explores the forecasts for comet appearances in 2025 and provides insight into their spiritual significance. We will also explore how to incorporate the unique energy of comets into your magical practice, offering rituals, spells, and meditations designed to harness their power for transformation and spiritual awakening.

The Spiritual Significance of Comets

Comets have been interpreted differently across cultures and spiritual traditions, but they share a universal association with the unknown, the mystical, and the transformative. They are often seen as harbingers of great change, with their rare and sudden appearance breaking the routine of the sky. In ancient times, comets were believed to be messages from the gods, omens of events such as the rise or fall of empires, the birth or death of kings, or significant natural events.

In witchcraft and modern spirituality, comets represent:

- **Change and Transformation**: Comets are powerful symbols of sudden and profound transformation. Their appearance in the sky signals a time to embrace change, let go of the old, and prepare for new beginnings.
- **Messages from the Cosmos**: Comets are seen as messengers from the outer realms of the universe, bringing divine or spiritual guidance. Their appearance can serve as a reminder to pay attention to spiritual signs, dreams, or synchronicities in your life.
- **Cycles of Renewal**: Comets remind us of the cyclical nature of the universe. Like the comet's journey from the far reaches of the solar system to the inner realms near the sun, they symbolize renewal and the eternal cycles of birth, death, and rebirth.
- **Awakening and Enlightenment**: Because comets are so rare and visually striking, they are often associated with moments of spiritual awakening or sudden insights. When a comet appears, it may be a sign that you are being called to awaken to a higher level of consciousness or awareness.

In magical practice, the energy of a comet can be harnessed for rituals that focus on transformation, divination, and the release of stagnant energy. These celestial visitors offer a unique window of opportunity to align with cosmic forces and embrace the changes they herald.

Forecasts for Comet Appearances in 2025

While the appearance of comets can be unpredictable, astronomers are able to forecast certain comets that will be visible from Earth in 2025. The following is a detailed list of the comets expected to make appearances this year, along with their astrological and spiritual meanings.

1. Comet 12P/Pons-Brooks

- **Expected Visibility**: July – August 2025
- **Peak Viewing**: Early August 2025
- **Best Viewing Locations**: Northern Hemisphere (visible with binoculars or telescopes)
- **Orbital Period**: Approximately 71 years

Astronomical Overview:

Comet 12P/Pons-Brooks is a periodic comet with a roughly 71-year orbit around the sun. Its return to visibility in 2025 will mark a significant event, as the comet last passed through the inner solar system in 1954. This comet is known for its bright coma and prominent tail, which can be observed with binoculars or telescopes under clear skies.

Spiritual Significance:

Comet Pons-Brooks carries the energy of long cycles, renewal, and deep transformation. Its extended period reminds us of the importance of patience, reflection, and the gradual unfolding of destiny. The comet's return after seven decades symbolizes the cyclical nature of life and the opportunity to revisit long-term goals, karmic lessons, or unfinished business from previous generations.

Magical Focus:

- **Ritual of Renewal**: The appearance of Comet Pons-Brooks is an ideal time for rituals of renewal and transformation. If there are long-standing goals or personal patterns you wish to change, now is the time to focus on bringing closure to old cycles and beginning new ones. Perform a ritual to release the past and set new intentions for the future.
- **Karmic Reflection**: Use this time to reflect on the karmic lessons you've encountered over the past years or even decades. Meditate on how far you've come and what unresolved energies still linger. Perform a divination ritual using tarot or runes to gain insight into your karmic path and the lessons you need to integrate.

2. Comet 109P/Swift-Tuttle

- **Expected Visibility**: October – November 2025
- **Peak Viewing**: Late October 2025
- **Best Viewing Locations**: Northern Hemisphere (visible with binoculars)
- **Orbital Period**: 133 years

Astronomical Overview:

Comet 109P/Swift-Tuttle is the parent comet of the famous Perseids meteor shower, and it last approached Earth in 1992. With its long orbital period, this comet won't return for another century after 2025. However, during its current pass, it will be visible in the night sky, primarily in the Northern Hemisphere, offering a rare chance to connect with this ancient celestial traveler.

Spiritual Significance:

Swift-Tuttle's energy is strongly connected to cycles of release and transformation, as it is the source of the Perseids meteor shower, known for its fiery energy. The comet itself embodies the themes of patience, long-term spiritual growth, and cosmic renewal. Its presence offers a reminder of the power of perseverance and the slow but steady evolution of the soul.

Magical Focus:

- **Manifestation of Long-Term Goals**: This comet's long orbital period mirrors the slow but powerful progress of long-term manifestations. Focus on setting intentions that require patience and sustained effort. Perform a candle spell where you light a new candle each night for several days leading up to the comet's peak visibility, symbolizing the steady growth of your manifestation.

- **Cosmic Communication Ritual**: Swift-Tuttle's connection to the Perseids offers a unique opportunity for receiving messages from the cosmos. Use this time for deep meditation, scrying, or dream work to connect with higher realms or receive guidance from the universe. You may find that spiritual messages or insights come through clearly during this period.

3. Comet 7P/Pons-Winnecke

- **Expected Visibility**: June 2025
- **Peak Viewing**: Mid-June 2025
- **Best Viewing Locations**: Northern Hemisphere (visible with binoculars or small telescopes)
- **Orbital Period**: 6.37 years

Astronomical Overview:

Comet 7P/Pons-Winnecke is a short-period comet that orbits the sun approximately every six and a half years. In 2025, it will be visible in June, making it a relatively frequent visitor compared to other comets. While not as visually dramatic as some of the longer-period comets, its frequent appearances make it a symbol of recurring cycles and renewal.

Spiritual Significance:

Pons-Winnecke brings the energy of recurring cycles and the importance of regular reflection and realignment with your spiritual path. Its relatively short orbital period encourages a focus on shorter-term goals and milestones in life. The comet's energy reminds you to periodically check in with yourself, reassess your progress, and make necessary adjustments.

Magical Focus:

- **Cycle of Intentions Ritual**: As Comet Pons-Winnecke passes through the sky, use this time to revisit and refine your current goals. Reflect on the intentions you set during previous lunar cycles or seasonal transitions. Perform a ritual in which you assess your progress and adjust your intentions for the coming months.
- **Self-Reflection Meditation**: The frequent return of this comet encourages regular self-assessment. During its visibility, meditate on the cycles in your life—both physical and spiritual. What patterns have emerged repeatedly, and how can you work with these cycles to create positive change? Incorporate journaling or divination to explore these themes further.

4. Potential New Comet Discovery (Comet C/2025 A1)

- **Expected Visibility**: November – December 2025
- **Peak Viewing**: Late November to early December 2025
- **Best Viewing Locations**: To be determined (expected to be visible with the naked eye)
- **Orbital Period**: Unpredictable, potential long-period comet

Astronomical Overview:

As of early 2024, astronomers are tracking a newly discovered comet, currently designated C/2025 A1. While its exact visibility and appearance are still being calculated, it is expected to be visible from Earth in late 2025, potentially becoming a bright naked-eye comet. This comet may offer a once-in-a-lifetime viewing opportunity, depending on its trajectory and interaction with the sun.

Spiritual Significance:

New comets, particularly those with unpredictable or long orbital periods, carry a potent energy of the unknown. They are symbols of cosmic mystery, unexpected change, and divine intervention. The sudden appearance of a new comet can be seen as a sign of a major turning point, both personally and collectively, offering the chance for new beginnings or transformative spiritual growth.

Magical Focus:

- **Embracing the Unknown**: Use this new comet's appearance to embrace the energy of the unknown. Perform a ritual of surrender, where you release your need for control and open yourself to the possibilities that the universe may present. Light a silver candle and meditate on trusting the cosmic flow.
- **Initiating New Spiritual Journeys**: The discovery of a new comet is a powerful symbol of fresh starts and unexplored potential. Use this time to initiate a new spiritual practice or embark on a new magical journey. Perform a ritual to dedicate yourself to a new path, allowing the comet's energy to guide and inspire you.

Working with Comet Energy in Magic

The rare appearance of comets makes them potent symbols of cosmic power and transformation. When a comet is visible, its energy is at its peak, offering a limited window of time to tap into its influence. Here are some ways to work with comet energy in your magical practice:

1. Transformation Rituals

Comets are associated with sudden and profound transformation. If you're seeking to make a significant change in your life—whether in your career, relationships, or spiritual path—a comet's appearance can provide the momentum needed to catalyze that change. Perform a transformation ritual during the comet's visibility, focusing on releasing old patterns and embracing a new chapter in your life.

2. Divination and Cosmic Messages

Comets are often seen as messengers from the cosmos. Use their energy to enhance your divination practice, whether through tarot, runes, or scrying. During a comet's appearance, ask for guidance or clarity on a particular issue, and trust that the universe will deliver the answers through dreams, signs, or intuitive insights.

3. Cosmic Cleansing and Renewal

The fiery nature of a comet's tail, created as it burns through the atmosphere, makes it a powerful symbol of purification. Use this energy for cleansing rituals. Whether you're cleansing your home, your aura, or your emotional energy, focus on releasing the old and allowing the comet's light to renew and refresh your spirit.

4. Wish Fulfillment

Like meteor showers, comets are associated with wish-making. However, the rarity of comets gives their wish-fulfillment energy an extra boost. Write down your most important wishes or desires, and perform a wish spell under the comet's light, visualizing your intentions being carried to the cosmos by the comet's tail.

Conclusion

Comets are rare, powerful celestial visitors that offer unique moments for spiritual growth, transformation, and divine connection. Their appearances in 2025 bring opportunities to work with cosmic energy in profound ways, whether you're seeking to initiate new beginnings, gain spiritual insights, or embrace significant change in your life. By attuning yourself to the energy of these comets and incorporating them into your magical practice, you can deepen your connection to the cosmos and harness the rare power of these celestial travelers.

Chapter 9: Planetary Alignments and Their Influence

Planetary alignments and conjunctions have fascinated astrologers and spiritual practitioners for centuries. These cosmic events occur when two or more planets appear to meet or align in the sky from our vantage point on Earth. These powerful celestial moments create windows of heightened energy, offering opportunities to perform spells and rituals with amplified potency. Whether it's a conjunction between Venus and Mars that heightens romantic energy or a Jupiter-Saturn alignment that invites long-term success and growth, planetary alignments allow us to harness the unique synergy between the planets for magic and manifestation.

This chapter explores the major planetary alignments and conjunctions in 2025, their astrological meanings, and how to tap into their energy through spellwork. You'll find specific dates for key alignments as well as practical rituals for love, career, personal power, balance, and spiritual growth that are aligned with these celestial events.

Understanding Planetary Alignments and Conjunctions

In astrology, a **planetary alignment** occurs when planets align closely along the same celestial longitude, while a **conjunction** refers to the moment when two or more planets appear very close to each other in the sky, typically within a few degrees. Conjunctions are considered especially powerful because they combine the energies of the involved planets, often leading to a blending or intensification of their respective influences.

The energy of planetary alignments and conjunctions depends on the characteristics of the planets involved:

- **Venus** influences love, beauty, relationships, and self-worth.
- **Mars** rules action, courage, conflict, and passion.
- **Jupiter** governs expansion, abundance, wisdom, and luck.
- **Saturn** brings discipline, structure, responsibility, and long-term planning.
- **Mercury** rules communication, intellect, and travel.
- **Neptune** represents dreams, intuition, spirituality, and illusion.
- **Uranus** governs change, innovation, and rebellion.
- **Pluto** influences transformation, power, and deep psychological healing.

When these planets align or form a conjunction, their combined energy creates a powerful backdrop for magical work. By aligning your spells and rituals with these cosmic events, you can draw on their intensified energy to manifest your desires more effectively.

Major Planetary Alignments and Conjunctions in 2025
Below is a detailed guide to the most significant planetary alignments and conjunctions of 2025, including their dates, astrological meanings, and how to work with their energy for spellwork.
1. Venus and Mars Conjunction — February 22, 2025

- **Date**: February 22, 2025
- **Significance**: Venus and Mars are the cosmic lovers, and when they meet in a conjunction, their energy combines to amplify passion, romance, and the balance between love and desire. Venus represents the feminine principle of attraction, beauty, and harmony, while Mars represents the masculine principle of action, courage, and raw energy. Together, they create a powerful synergy for love magic, relationships, and personal empowerment.
- **Astrological Influence**: This conjunction takes place in the sign of Aquarius, encouraging unconventional love, intellectual connections, and freedom within relationships.

Love Spell for Passion and Harmony
Materials:

- A pink candle (for love and harmony)
- A red candle (for passion and desire)
- Rose petals
- A piece of rose quartz and a piece of carnelian

Instructions:

1. Set up your altar with the two candles, placing the pink candle to represent Venus and the red candle to represent Mars. Scatter the rose petals around the candles, and place the rose quartz and carnelian in front of them.
2. Light the pink candle first, focusing on the energy of love, beauty, and harmony. Then light the red candle, invoking the energy of passion, courage, and desire.
3. Visualize the energy of Venus and Mars coming together, blending into a harmonious balance of love and passion. Speak aloud your intention, whether it's to attract a new partner, reignite passion in an existing relationship, or bring harmony to a current connection.
4. Hold the rose quartz (for love) and carnelian (for passion) in your hands as you meditate on your desire. Let the candles burn down safely, and keep the stones on your altar or carry them with you to maintain the energy of the spell.

2. Jupiter and Neptune Conjunction — April 10, 2025

- **Date**: April 10, 2025
- **Significance**: Jupiter, the planet of expansion, wisdom, and abundance, aligns with Neptune, the planet of dreams, intuition, and spirituality. This conjunction creates an energy of heightened spiritual awareness, creativity, and manifestation of dreams. It's an ideal time for spells related to spiritual growth, psychic development, and manifesting long-held dreams or visions.
- **Astrological Influence**: This conjunction takes place in Pisces, a water sign associated with intuition, compassion, and spiritual insight. The alignment of Jupiter and Neptune in Pisces offers an opportunity for profound emotional healing and connection with the higher self.

Manifestation Spell for Dreams and Abundance
Materials:

- A blue candle (for intuition and dreams)
- A gold candle (for abundance and success)
- A bowl of water
- Lavender or jasmine essential oil
- A piece of amethyst and citrine

Instructions:

1. Anoint the blue and gold candles with lavender or jasmine oil to infuse them with the energy of dreams and abundance. Set the blue candle to represent Neptune and the gold candle for Jupiter.
2. Light both candles, and place the bowl of water in front of you to symbolize the flow of abundance and spiritual insight.
3. Hold the amethyst and citrine stones in your hands and close your eyes. Visualize the energy of Jupiter expanding your ability to manifest abundance, while Neptune opens your intuitive channels to receive guidance and inspiration.
4. Speak your intentions aloud, focusing on manifesting your dreams with clarity and confidence. Visualize your dreams becoming reality, flowing to you effortlessly through the power of Jupiter and Neptune's alignment.
5. After the candles have burned down, keep the stones on your altar or carry them with you to stay aligned with the energy of abundance and intuition.

3. Saturn and Uranus Alignment — July 1, 2025

- **Date**: July 1, 2025
- **Significance**: The alignment of Saturn, the planet of discipline and structure, with Uranus, the planet of innovation and change, creates a powerful dynamic for breaking free of old limitations and creating lasting, revolutionary change. This is an ideal time for spells focused on career transformation, breaking free from restrictive situations, and embracing new opportunities.
- **Astrological Influence**: This alignment occurs in Taurus, a sign associated with stability, material wealth, and values. The energy of Saturn and Uranus in Taurus encourages rethinking long-standing structures in your life, especially related to finances, career, and personal values.

Spell for Career Transformation and Breaking Free
Materials:

- A green candle (for career and prosperity)
- A black candle (for banishing limitations)
- A piece of pyrite (for success and wealth)
- A piece of hematite (for grounding and protection)

Instructions:

1. Place the green candle to represent new opportunities in your career and the black candle to represent the banishing of limitations or restrictions.
2. Light the black candle first, focusing on what you need to release to move forward in your career. This could be self-doubt, fear of failure, or a job that no longer serves your highest good.
3. Afterward, light the green candle and visualize new opportunities and career success flowing into your life. Imagine yourself in a position of strength, confidence, and abundance.
4. Hold the pyrite in your hand to amplify the energy of success and the hematite to keep you grounded during this transformation. Speak your intentions aloud, asking for Saturn's discipline to guide you and Uranus's energy to bring about positive change.
5. Let the candles burn down safely, and keep the pyrite and hematite on your desk or workspace to continue attracting career success and protection.

4. Mercury and Venus Conjunction — August 25, 2025

- **Date**: August 25, 2025
- **Significance**: Mercury, the planet of communication, and Venus, the planet of love, align in this conjunction to enhance harmonious communication in relationships. This is a perfect time for spells focused on love, diplomacy, and improving relationships, whether romantic, familial, or professional.
- **Astrological Influence**: This conjunction occurs in Libra, a sign ruled by Venus and associated with balance, beauty, and partnerships. The alignment of Mercury and Venus in Libra promotes peaceful communication, fairness, and the resolution of conflicts through understanding and compassion.

Spell for Harmonious Communication in Relationships
Materials:

- A light blue candle (for communication)
- A pink candle (for love and harmony)
- Rose petals
- A piece of blue lace agate (for clear communication)
- A piece of rose quartz (for love and harmony)

Instructions:

1. Set up your altar with the blue candle for Mercury and the pink candle for Venus. Scatter the rose petals around the candles, and place the blue lace agate and rose quartz in front of them.
2. Light both candles, focusing on the energy of clear, loving communication. Visualize any conflicts or misunderstandings in your relationships being resolved with ease and compassion.
3. Hold the blue lace agate in your hand as you speak aloud your intentions for harmonious communication, whether in a specific relationship or more broadly in your life. Then, hold the rose quartz and focus on cultivating love and understanding in your relationships.
4. Let the candles burn down safely, and keep the stones near your phone, computer, or any space where you engage in communication to continue promoting clear and loving interactions.

5. Pluto and Mars Alignment — November 5, 2025

- **Date**: November 5, 2025
- **Significance**: Mars, the planet of action and conflict, aligns with Pluto, the planet of transformation and power, creating a deeply intense energy that is perfect for spells focused on personal power, transformation, and releasing deeply held fears or limiting beliefs. This alignment invites you to step into your personal power with courage and purpose.
- **Astrological Influence**: This alignment takes place in Capricorn, a sign associated with ambition, discipline, and long-term success. The energy of Mars and Pluto in Capricorn encourages you to take control of your destiny and embrace your inner strength to achieve your goals.

Spell for Personal Power and Transformation
Materials:

- A red candle (for action and strength)
- A black candle (for transformation and release)
- A piece of obsidian (for protection and grounding)
- A piece of garnet (for strength and personal power)

Instructions:

1. Place the red candle for Mars and the black candle for Pluto on your altar. Hold the obsidian in your hand to ground yourself as you prepare for this powerful ritual.
2. Light the black candle first, focusing on what you need to release—whether it's fear, limiting beliefs, or a situation that is holding you back from stepping into your power. Imagine these obstacles burning away in the candle's flame.
3. Light the red candle next, focusing on your inner strength and the courage needed to embrace your power. Hold the garnet in your hand and visualize yourself standing in your full power, ready to take decisive action in your life.
4. Speak aloud your intention for transformation, asking Pluto to help you release what no longer serves you and Mars to give you the strength to move forward boldly.
5. Let the candles burn down safely, and keep the garnet with you to remind you of your personal power and the changes you are embracing.

Conclusion

Planetary alignments and conjunctions are moments of heightened cosmic energy that can significantly enhance your spellwork. Whether you are focusing on love, career, balance, or personal transformation, aligning your magic with these celestial events allows you to harness the combined power of the planets for more effective and powerful results. By understanding the astrological meanings behind these alignments and using the suggested spells in this chapter, you can tap into the energy of the cosmos and bring your desires to fruition with the full support of the universe.

Chapter 10: The Zodiac and Planetary Placements

The interplay between the planets and the zodiac signs they occupy shapes the astrological and energetic landscape each month. Planetary placements in specific zodiac signs create unique energies that influence various aspects of our lives, from communication and relationships to career, spirituality, and personal power. By understanding how each planet's movement through the zodiac affects its energy, you can tailor your magical practice to align with these cosmic influences and enhance the potency of your spells and rituals.

In this chapter, we will provide a detailed monthly breakdown of planetary placements for 2025, along with guidance on how to work with the planetary and zodiac energy each month. You'll find insights into how each planet's influence shifts when it moves through different signs and how you can use this knowledge to craft specific spells for love, career, health, spiritual growth, and more.

Overview of Planetary Influences in Astrology

Before diving into the monthly breakdown, it's essential to understand the core influences of the major planets in astrology. Each planet governs certain areas of life, and the zodiac sign a planet occupies colors how its energy manifests. Here is a brief overview of the planets and their astrological domains:

- **Sun**: Represents the self, identity, and vitality. It governs how we express ourselves and find purpose.
- **Moon**: Governs emotions, intuition, and inner life. It reflects how we feel and process emotional experiences.
- **Mercury**: Rules communication, intellect, learning, and travel. It influences how we think and express ideas.
- **Venus**: Governs love, beauty, relationships, and pleasure. It reflects how we attract love, balance relationships, and enjoy life's pleasures.
- **Mars**: Represents action, passion, energy, and conflict. It governs how we assert ourselves, take action, and pursue desires.
- **Jupiter**: Governs expansion, abundance, wisdom, and growth. It reflects where we find luck, opportunity, and personal growth.
- **Saturn**: Rules discipline, structure, responsibility, and long-term goals. It governs where we must work hard to build stability and achieve success.
- **Uranus**: Represents change, innovation, and rebellion. It influences where we seek freedom, originality, and transformation.
- **Neptune**: Governs dreams, spirituality, illusion, and intuition. It reflects where we seek transcendence, inspiration, and divine connection.
- **Pluto**: Represents power, transformation, and deep psychological growth. It governs areas of life where we undergo profound changes and face issues of control.

When planets travel through the zodiac, they take on the qualities of the sign they occupy, influencing the way their core energies manifest in the world and in our personal lives. The following sections provide a monthly guide to planetary placements in 2025 and how to align your magical work with the unique energy of each month.

January 2025: Capricorn's Stability and Aquarius's Innovation

- **Sun in Capricorn (until January 19), then Aquarius**: Capricorn energy in the early part of the month supports hard work, goal setting, and discipline. As the Sun moves into Aquarius, focus shifts to innovation, independence, and thinking outside the box.
- **Mercury in Capricorn (until January 9), then Aquarius**: Mercury in Capricorn promotes practical, grounded communication, ideal for organizing projects or clarifying long-term goals. Once Mercury moves into Aquarius, communication becomes more inventive and forward-thinking.
- **Venus in Sagittarius (until January 23), then Capricorn**: Venus in Sagittarius encourages adventure and freedom in relationships. After Venus moves into Capricorn, relationships become more focused on commitment, stability, and long-term planning.
- **Mars in Scorpio (until January 4), then Sagittarius**: Mars in Scorpio fosters deep, transformative action. Once Mars moves into Sagittarius, energy becomes more adventurous, bold, and expansive.
- **Jupiter in Taurus**: Jupiter continues its journey through Taurus, emphasizing growth in finances, material abundance, and stability.
- **Saturn in Pisces**: Saturn's placement in Pisces supports long-term spiritual growth, emotional discipline, and dissolving old boundaries.
- **Uranus in Taurus**: Uranus in Taurus continues to encourage innovation in financial matters, values, and material security.
- **Neptune in Pisces**: Neptune remains in its home sign of Pisces, amplifying intuition, dreams, and spiritual growth.
- **Pluto in Capricorn**: Pluto in Capricorn encourages transformation in areas of authority, career, and structures in society and personal life.

Magical Focus for January:

- **Capricorn Energy (until January 19)**: Focus on setting long-term goals, building structures, and creating discipline in your life. Perform grounding and protection spells, and work on career-related magic, particularly for financial stability and success.
- **Aquarius Energy (after January 19)**: Shift to spells that promote freedom, originality, and intellectual pursuits. Embrace creativity and innovation in your magical practice, particularly for spells related to technology, community, and humanitarian goals.

- **Venus in Sagittarius**: Perform love spells that focus on expanding relationships or attracting adventure and excitement. After Venus moves into Capricorn, focus on spells for long-term relationship commitment and stability.

February 2025: Aquarius's Vision and Pisces's Intuition

- **Sun in Aquarius (until February 18), then Pisces**: Aquarius season continues to promote individuality, innovation, and community engagement. When the Sun moves into Pisces, focus shifts to emotional healing, intuition, and spiritual practices.
- **Mercury in Aquarius (until February 20), then Pisces**: Mercury in Aquarius encourages inventive communication and intellectual insights. In Pisces, communication becomes more intuitive and emotionally driven.
- **Venus in Capricorn**: Venus continues its journey through Capricorn, emphasizing loyalty, commitment, and long-term relationship goals.
- **Mars in Sagittarius**: Mars in Sagittarius encourages bold action, adventure, and exploration. This energy is ideal for taking risks and pursuing personal growth.
- **Jupiter in Taurus**: Jupiter's steady presence in Taurus continues to support financial growth and stability.
- **Saturn in Pisces**: Saturn in Pisces encourages emotional and spiritual discipline, focusing on bringing structure to creative and spiritual practices.
- **Uranus in Taurus**: Uranus in Taurus continues to revolutionize areas related to personal values, financial innovation, and material security.
- **Neptune in Pisces**: Neptune amplifies dreams, intuition, and spiritual growth in Pisces, making February a deeply reflective and spiritual time.
- **Pluto in Capricorn**: Pluto continues to bring transformative energy to structures of power and authority, both personal and societal.

Magical Focus for February:

- **Aquarius Energy (until February 18)**: Focus on spells for innovation, community, and intellectual breakthroughs. Magic for social causes, technology, and new ideas will thrive during this time.
- **Pisces Energy (after February 18)**: Shift to more introspective, spiritual, and emotionally driven magic. Work on dream magic, divination, and healing rituals.
- **Mars in Sagittarius**: Perform spells for adventure, growth, and exploration, particularly for expanding your personal boundaries or taking on new challenges.
- **Venus in Capricorn**: Continue focusing on love spells for commitment, long-term relationships, and stability. Incorporate earth elements to ground your intentions.

March 2025: Pisces' Dreams and Aries' Fire

- **Sun in Pisces (until March 20), then Aries**: Pisces season fosters deep intuition, spirituality, and emotional healing. As the Sun enters Aries, there is a surge of energy, action, and bold new beginnings.
- **Mercury in Pisces (until March 10), then Aries**: Mercury in Pisces supports dream work, intuitive communication, and emotional insight. Once Mercury moves into Aries, communication becomes direct, assertive, and action-oriented.
- **Venus in Aquarius (until March 18), then Pisces**: Venus in Aquarius promotes unconventional relationships and intellectual connections. As Venus moves into Pisces, love becomes more compassionate, spiritual, and emotionally deep.
- **Mars in Capricorn**: Mars in Capricorn is focused, disciplined, and goal-oriented, making it a great time for spells related to career success, long-term projects, and material stability.
- **Jupiter in Taurus**: Jupiter in Taurus continues to emphasize growth, abundance, and stability, especially in financial matters.
- **Saturn in Pisces**: Saturn continues its long-term influence in Pisces, promoting emotional discipline and spiritual maturity.
- **Uranus in Taurus**: Uranus's influence in Taurus continues to bring changes and innovation in the realms of finance, personal security, and values.
- **Neptune in Pisces**: Neptune's influence in Pisces remains strong, encouraging introspection, spiritual exploration, and dream work.
- **Pluto in Capricorn**: Pluto in Capricorn continues to challenge structures of authority and power, both on a personal and societal level.

Magical Focus for March:

- **Pisces Energy (until March 20)**: Focus on spiritual growth, emotional healing, and connecting with higher realms through dream magic, meditation, and divination.
- **Aries Energy (after March 20)**: Shift to spells for action, courage, and new beginnings. Use this fiery energy for initiating projects, boosting confidence, and pursuing personal goals with vigor.
- **Venus in Pisces**: Perform love spells focused on emotional connection, compassion, and spiritual alignment. Incorporate water elements for a fluid, heart-centered approach to love magic.
- **Mars in Capricorn**: Continue working with Capricorn's disciplined energy to achieve career and financial goals through structured, goal-oriented spellwork.

April 2025: Aries' Boldness and Taurus' Stability

- **Sun in Aries (until April 19), then Taurus**: Aries season is a time for taking action, starting new ventures, and embracing personal power. As the Sun enters Taurus, the focus shifts to building stability, grounding your efforts, and enjoying the material world.
- **Mercury in Aries (until April 28), then Taurus**: Mercury in Aries promotes fast, assertive communication and decision-making. When Mercury enters Taurus, communication becomes more thoughtful, grounded, and focused on practical matters.
- **Venus in Pisces (until April 11), then Aries**: Venus in Pisces brings compassionate, spiritual love, while Venus in Aries encourages bold expressions of desire, attraction, and passion.
- **Mars in Capricorn (until April 15), then Aquarius**: Mars in Capricorn remains focused on discipline and achieving long-term goals. When Mars enters Aquarius, action becomes more innovative, rebellious, and future-focused.
- **Jupiter in Taurus**: Jupiter's influence in Taurus continues to support financial stability, abundance, and long-term growth.
- **Saturn in Pisces**: Saturn continues to encourage emotional resilience and spiritual discipline.
- **Uranus in Taurus**: Uranus's influence continues to revolutionize areas related to personal values, material security, and finances.
- **Neptune in Pisces**: Neptune's ongoing influence in Pisces encourages deep spiritual connection, intuition, and creative expression.
- **Pluto in Capricorn**: Pluto's transformative energy in Capricorn continues to influence structures of power and authority.

Magical Focus for April:

- **Aries Energy (until April 19)**: Focus on spells for self-confidence, taking bold action, and starting new projects. Use this fiery energy to clear obstacles and initiate change.
- **Taurus Energy (after April 19)**: Shift to spells for stability, abundance, and grounding. Perform rituals that focus on creating long-term success, financial security, and enjoying the pleasures of life.
- **Venus in Aries**: Work on love spells that promote passion, attraction, and bold expressions of desire. Focus on cultivating new romantic connections or reigniting passion in existing relationships.
- **Mars in Aquarius**: Use this innovative energy for spells related to breaking free from old patterns, embracing originality, and pursuing social or technological advancements.

May 2025: Taurus' Grounding and Gemini's Curiosity

- **Sun in Taurus (until May 20), then Gemini**: Taurus season continues to emphasize grounding, material success, and enjoying the pleasures of life. As the Sun enters Gemini, the energy becomes more curious, social, and mentally stimulating.
- **Mercury in Taurus (until May 15), then Gemini**: Mercury in Taurus supports practical communication and decision-making. Once Mercury moves into Gemini, communication becomes fast-paced, intellectual, and focused on learning and social interaction.
- **Venus in Aries (until May 7), then Taurus**: Venus in Aries continues to encourage passionate, bold expressions of love. As Venus moves into Taurus, love becomes more sensual, stable, and focused on physical pleasure and security.
- **Mars in Aquarius**: Mars in Aquarius continues to promote innovative, rebellious action and forward-thinking approaches to personal goals.
- **Jupiter in Taurus**: Jupiter's ongoing presence in Taurus continues to support financial growth and long-term stability.
- **Saturn in Pisces**: Saturn's influence in Pisces encourages emotional discipline and spiritual resilience.
- **Uranus in Taurus**: Uranus continues to bring change and innovation to areas related to values, finances, and material security.
- **Neptune in Pisces**: Neptune's influence remains strong in Pisces, supporting spiritual growth, intuition, and creative inspiration.
- **Pluto in Capricorn**: Pluto continues its transformative work in Capricorn, reshaping structures of power and authority.

Magical Focus for May:

- **Taurus Energy (until May 20)**: Continue working with Taurus energy for spells focused on financial stability, abundance, and grounding. Perform rituals that emphasize enjoying the pleasures of life, such as food, beauty, and comfort.
- **Gemini Energy (after May 20)**: Shift to spells for communication, learning, and social connection. This is a great time for spells related to education, intellectual pursuits, and networking.
- **Venus in Taurus**: Focus on love spells that emphasize sensuality, pleasure, and stability in relationships. Incorporate earth elements to enhance your connection to the physical and material aspects of love.
- **Mars in Aquarius**: Use this energy to embrace innovation, break free from old habits, and pursue unique goals with courage and originality.

June 2025: Gemini's Curiosity and Cancer's Nurturing

- **Sun in Gemini (until June 21), then Cancer**: Gemini season continues to promote curiosity, learning, and social engagement. As the Sun enters Cancer, the focus shifts to home, family, emotional security, and nurturing.
- **Mercury in Gemini (until June 22), then Cancer**: Mercury in Gemini supports intellectual curiosity, quick thinking, and communication. Once Mercury enters Cancer, communication becomes more emotionally driven and focused on family and personal matters.
- **Venus in Taurus (until June 5), then Gemini**: Venus in Taurus continues to emphasize stable, sensual love. As Venus moves into Gemini, relationships become more social, communicative, and intellectually stimulating.
- **Mars in Aquarius (until June 2), then Pisces**: Mars in Aquarius encourages bold, innovative action. When Mars enters Pisces, action becomes more intuitive, emotional, and spiritually motivated.
- **Jupiter in Taurus**: Jupiter's influence in Taurus continues to promote growth and stability in material and financial matters.
- **Saturn in Pisces**: Saturn in Pisces encourages emotional discipline, spiritual growth, and boundary setting in emotional and spiritual matters.
- **Uranus in Taurus**: Uranus continues to bring innovation to areas related to material security and personal values.
- **Neptune in Pisces**: Neptune remains in Pisces, supporting creativity, dreams, and spiritual exploration.
- **Pluto in Capricorn**: Pluto continues its transformative work in Capricorn, focusing on power dynamics and long-term structural changes.

Magical Focus for June:

- **Gemini Energy (until June 21)**: Focus on spells for communication, learning, and intellectual pursuits. This is a great time to improve communication skills, work on writing projects, or enhance your social networks.
- **Cancer Energy (after June 21)**: Shift to spells for home, family, emotional security, and protection. Focus on creating a nurturing, supportive environment for yourself and your loved ones.
- **Venus in Gemini**: Perform love spells that emphasize communication, intellectual connection, and social engagement in relationships. This is an ideal time to strengthen the mental and verbal aspects of love.

- **Mars in Pisces**: Use this time for spells related to emotional healing, spiritual growth, and creativity. Mars in Pisces encourages introspection and gentle action, making it ideal for dream work, meditation, and healing rituals.

July 2025: Cancer's Nurturing and Leo's Confidence

- **Sun in Cancer (until July 23), then Leo**: Cancer season continues to focus on home, family, emotional security, and nurturing. When the Sun moves into Leo, the energy shifts to self-confidence, creativity, and personal expression.
- **Mercury in Cancer (until July 9), then Leo**: Mercury in Cancer supports emotionally intuitive communication and conversations centered on home and family. In Leo, Mercury encourages bold, confident, and creative communication.
- **Venus in Gemini (until July 7), then Cancer**: Venus in Gemini promotes intellectual connections and social relationships. Once Venus moves into Cancer, love becomes more nurturing, protective, and emotionally focused.
- **Mars in Pisces (until July 20), then Aries**: Mars in Pisces supports intuitive, spiritual action. When Mars moves into Aries, it brings boldness, courage, and action-oriented energy, perfect for initiating new projects.
- **Jupiter in Taurus**: Jupiter's steady influence in Taurus continues to promote material growth and financial stability.
- **Saturn in Pisces**: Saturn continues to support emotional maturity, spiritual discipline, and boundary setting in creative and spiritual matters.
- **Uranus in Taurus**: Uranus continues its work of bringing innovation to areas related to security, finances, and personal values.
- **Neptune in Pisces**: Neptune's influence in Pisces remains strong, supporting spiritual exploration, intuition, and creativity.
- **Pluto in Capricorn**: Pluto continues to bring transformative energy to power structures and long-term goals.

Magical Focus for July:

- **Cancer Energy (until July 23)**: Focus on spells for emotional healing, home protection, and nurturing relationships. This is a great time for spells that bring comfort, security, and emotional stability to yourself and your loved ones.
- **Leo Energy (after July 23)**: Shift to spells for self-expression, creativity, and confidence. Perform rituals that boost your charisma, courage, and leadership abilities.
- **Venus in Cancer**: Work on love spells that emphasize emotional connection, family harmony, and nurturing love. Incorporate water elements to enhance emotional bonding in your spells.

- **Mars in Aries**: Use this fiery energy for spells of action, courage, and personal empowerment. Focus on initiating new ventures, boosting your confidence, and taking bold steps toward your goals.

August 2025: Leo's Confidence and Virgo's Precision

- **Sun in Leo (until August 23), then Virgo**: Leo season continues to promote confidence, creativity, and self-expression. As the Sun moves into Virgo, the focus shifts to precision, organization, and personal improvement.
- **Mercury in Leo (until August 25), then Virgo**: Mercury in Leo supports bold, confident communication. When Mercury moves into Virgo, communication becomes more analytical, detail-oriented, and focused on practical matters.
- **Venus in Cancer (until August 12), then Leo**: Venus in Cancer promotes nurturing, protective love. As Venus moves into Leo, love becomes more passionate, expressive, and romantic.
- **Mars in Aries (until August 6), then Taurus**: Mars in Aries brings bold, action-oriented energy. Once Mars moves into Taurus, action becomes more deliberate, steady, and focused on building long-term success.
- **Jupiter in Taurus**: Jupiter's ongoing influence in Taurus continues to promote abundance, stability, and material growth.
- **Saturn in Pisces**: Saturn continues its work in Pisces, promoting spiritual growth, emotional discipline, and resilience.
- **Uranus in Taurus**: Uranus's presence in Taurus encourages innovation and change in areas related to finances, values, and material security.
- **Neptune in Pisces**: Neptune's energy remains strong in Pisces, supporting dream work, spiritual growth, and creativity.
- **Pluto in Capricorn**: Pluto's transformative influence continues to reshape power dynamics and long-term goals.

Magical Focus for August:

- **Leo Energy (until August 23)**: Focus on spells for personal power, confidence, and creative expression. This is a great time to perform rituals that boost your charisma, leadership abilities, and self-confidence.
- **Virgo Energy (after August 23)**: Shift to spells for organization, precision, and personal improvement. Focus on refining your goals, improving your skills, and bringing more structure to your life.
- **Venus in Leo**: Perform love spells that emphasize romance, passion, and bold expressions of affection. Use fire elements to amplify the intensity of your love magic.
- **Mars in Taurus**: Focus on spells for long-term success, financial stability, and perseverance. Use earthy elements to ground your energy and build solid foundations for your goals.

September 2025: Virgo's Precision and Libra's Balance

- **Sun in Virgo (until September 23), then Libra**: Virgo season continues to emphasize organization, precision, and personal improvement. As the Sun moves into Libra, the focus shifts to balance, harmony, and relationships.
- **Mercury in Virgo (until September 9), then Libra**: Mercury in Virgo supports detailed, practical communication. Once Mercury enters Libra, communication becomes more diplomatic, balanced, and focused on partnerships.
- **Venus in Leo (until September 16), then Virgo**: Venus in Leo continues to promote passionate, expressive love. As Venus moves into Virgo, love becomes more grounded, practical, and focused on service and support.
- **Mars in Taurus**: Mars in Taurus continues to promote steady, deliberate action toward building long-term success and material security.
- **Jupiter in Taurus**: Jupiter's influence in Taurus continues to promote financial abundance, stability, and growth.
- **Saturn in Pisces**: Saturn's influence in Pisces supports emotional discipline, spiritual growth, and the dissolution of old boundaries.
- **Uranus in Taurus**: Uranus's presence in Taurus continues to bring innovation to areas related to personal values, finances, and material security.
- **Neptune in Pisces**: Neptune's influence in Pisces remains strong, supporting spiritual exploration, creativity, and intuition.
- **Pluto in Capricorn**: Pluto continues its transformative influence in Capricorn, reshaping power structures and long-term goals.

Magical Focus for September:

- **Virgo Energy (until September 23)**: Focus on spells for self-improvement, organization, and health. This is a great time to perform rituals that enhance your efficiency, productivity, and attention to detail.
- **Libra Energy (after September 23)**: Shift to spells for balance, harmony, and relationships. Perform rituals that bring equilibrium to your life, whether in love, work, or personal well-being.
- **Venus in Virgo**: Work on love spells that focus on practical support, service, and grounded affection. Focus on building relationships that are based on mutual respect and long-term stability.
- **Mars in Taurus**: Continue working with Taurus's steady energy to manifest long-term success, financial growth, and perseverance. Perform spells that build strong foundations for your goals and desires.

October 2025: Libra's Balance and Scorpio's Depth

- **Sun in Libra (until October 23), then Scorpio**: Libra season continues to focus on balance, harmony, and relationships. As the Sun moves into Scorpio, the energy becomes more intense, transformative, and focused on deep emotional connections and personal power.
- **Mercury in Libra (until October 24), then Scorpio**: Mercury in Libra promotes diplomatic, harmonious communication. Once Mercury enters Scorpio, communication becomes more intense, emotionally driven, and focused on uncovering hidden truths.
- **Venus in Virgo (until October 12), then Libra**: Venus in Virgo continues to promote practical, supportive love. As Venus moves into Libra, relationships become more focused on balance, beauty, and partnership.
- **Mars in Taurus (until October 29), then Gemini**: Mars in Taurus promotes steady, grounded action. When Mars enters Gemini, action becomes more mentally driven, flexible, and focused on communication and learning.
- **Jupiter in Taurus**: Jupiter's ongoing influence in Taurus continues to promote financial growth, stability, and abundance.
- **Saturn in Pisces**: Saturn continues its work in Pisces, promoting emotional discipline, spiritual growth, and boundary setting.
- **Uranus in Taurus**: Uranus continues to bring change and innovation to areas related to personal values, finances, and material security.
- **Neptune in Pisces**: Neptune's influence in Pisces remains strong, encouraging creativity, intuition, and spiritual growth.
- **Pluto in Capricorn**: Pluto continues to transform structures of power and authority, both personally and collectively.

Magical Focus for October:

- **Libra Energy (until October 23)**: Focus on spells for balance, harmony, and relationships. Perform rituals that restore equilibrium in your life and strengthen partnerships.
- **Scorpio Energy (after October 23)**: Shift to spells for transformation, power, and deep emotional healing. Scorpio's intense energy is ideal for shadow work, banishing negative influences, and diving into the depths of your psyche.
- **Venus in Libra**: Perform love spells that focus on creating harmony, beauty, and mutual respect in relationships. Focus on enhancing the balance between giving and receiving in love.
- **Mars in Gemini**: Use this energy for spells that require mental agility, communication, and flexibility. Focus on improving your communication skills, learning new things, or adapting to changing circumstances.

November 2025: Scorpio's Depth and Sagittarius's Expansion

- **Sun in Scorpio (until November 22), then Sagittarius**: Scorpio season continues to promote transformation, emotional depth, and personal power. As the Sun moves into Sagittarius, the energy becomes more expansive, adventurous, and focused on personal growth and exploration.
- **Mercury in Scorpio (until November 13), then Sagittarius**: Mercury in Scorpio supports intense, transformative communication. When Mercury enters Sagittarius, communication becomes more optimistic, philosophical, and focused on exploring new ideas.
- **Venus in Libra (until November 8), then Scorpio**: Venus in Libra continues to promote balanced, harmonious relationships. As Venus moves into Scorpio, love becomes more passionate, intense, and transformative.
- **Mars in Gemini**: Mars in Gemini promotes mental agility, communication, and flexibility in action. This is an ideal time for spells that require adaptability, learning, or social engagement.
- **Jupiter in Taurus**: Jupiter's influence in Taurus continues to support financial stability, abundance, and material growth.
- **Saturn in Pisces**: Saturn's influence in Pisces continues to promote emotional discipline, spiritual growth, and the dissolution of old boundaries.
- **Uranus in Taurus**: Uranus continues its work of bringing innovation and change to areas related to finances, values, and material security.
- **Neptune in Pisces**: Neptune's influence in Pisces remains strong, supporting intuition, creativity, and spiritual exploration.
- **Pluto in Capricorn**: Pluto continues to bring transformation to areas related to power, authority, and long-term structures.

Magical Focus for November:

- **Scorpio Energy (until November 22)**: Focus on spells for personal transformation, emotional healing, and power. Perform rituals that help you release negative influences, dive into shadow work, and reclaim your personal strength.
- **Sagittarius Energy (after November 22)**: Shift to spells for personal growth, adventure, and expanding your horizons. Use this time for spells that help you explore new opportunities, travel, or expand your spiritual knowledge.
- **Venus in Scorpio**: Perform love spells that focus on deep emotional connections, passion, and transformation in relationships. This is a great time for healing past wounds or intensifying romantic bonds.
- **Mars in Gemini**: Use this energy for spells that require communication, learning, and adaptability. Focus on improving your intellectual skills or navigating complex social situations with ease.

December 2025: Sagittarius's Expansion and Capricorn's Discipline

- **Sun in Sagittarius (until December 22), then Capricorn**: Sagittarius season promotes growth, adventure, and personal exploration. As the Sun moves into Capricorn, the focus shifts to discipline, long-term planning, and achieving success through hard work.
- **Mercury in Sagittarius (until December 15), then Capricorn**: Mercury in Sagittarius promotes optimistic, philosophical communication. Once Mercury enters Capricorn, communication becomes more focused on practical matters, discipline, and long-term goals.
- **Venus in Scorpio (until December 4), then Sagittarius**: Venus in Scorpio promotes passionate, transformative love. As Venus moves into Sagittarius, relationships become more adventurous, optimistic, and focused on personal growth.
- **Mars in Gemini (until December 16), then Cancer**: Mars in Gemini supports mental flexibility and communication. When Mars enters Cancer, action becomes more emotionally driven, focused on home, family, and personal security.
- **Jupiter in Taurus**: Jupiter's influence in Taurus continues to promote financial growth, stability, and abundance.
- **Saturn in Pisces**: Saturn's influence in Pisces continues to support emotional discipline, spiritual growth, and boundary setting.
- **Uranus in Taurus**: Uranus's presence in Taurus continues to bring innovation and change to areas related to finances, values, and material security.
- **Neptune in Pisces**: Neptune's influence in Pisces remains strong, supporting creativity, intuition, and spiritual exploration.
- **Pluto in Capricorn**: Pluto continues to transform structures of power, authority, and long-term goals, both personally and collectively.

Magical Focus for December:

- **Sagittarius Energy (until December 22)**: Focus on spells for personal growth, adventure, and expanding your horizons. Use this time for spells that help you explore new opportunities, learn new things, and embrace new experiences.
- **Capricorn Energy (after December 22)**: Shift to spells for discipline, long-term success, and achieving your goals. Perform rituals that focus on creating stability, building structures, and working toward long-term ambitions.
- **Venus in Sagittarius**: Perform love spells that emphasize adventure, growth, and freedom in relationships. This is a great time to explore new romantic possibilities or expand your understanding of love.
- **Mars in Cancer**: Use this energy for spells related to home, family, and emotional security. Focus on creating a safe, nurturing environment for yourself and your loved ones.

Conclusion

The planetary movements through the zodiac in 2025 offer powerful opportunities to tailor your magical practice to the unique energies each month brings. By aligning your spells and rituals with the planetary and zodiac influences, you can enhance the effectiveness of your magic and flow in harmony with the cosmos. Whether you are focusing on love, career, personal growth, or spiritual development, this guide will help you make the most of each month's astrological landscape, empowering you to manifest your desires with greater ease and clarity.Bottom of Form

Chapter 11: Aries to Pisces: Horoscope Guidance for 2025

Astrology offers powerful insights into the energies that will shape each zodiac sign's journey throughout the year. In this chapter, we provide detailed yearly horoscopes for each zodiac sign, offering a month-by-month guide for 2025. These horoscopes delve into key themes such as career, love, health, and spiritual growth, helping you align your goals and decisions with the cosmic influences at play.

This chapter offers comprehensive guidance for every sign of the zodiac, beginning with Aries and concluding with Pisces, ensuring you have the knowledge needed to make the most of each month.

Aries (March 21 – April 19)

Overview of 2025

For Aries, 2025 will be a year of growth, courage, and newfound clarity. With your ruling planet Mars providing ample energy throughout the year, you'll feel the urge to take bold actions in both your personal and professional life. The first half of the year will challenge you to let go of what no longer serves you, while the second half will focus on building new foundations for your future.

Monthly Insights

- **January**: The year begins with a focus on career and long-term goals, as Mars moves into Sagittarius, encouraging you to take risks in your professional life. Reflect on your ambitions and make plans for the year ahead.
- **February**: Venus and Mars in your social house bring harmony to relationships. Whether you're single or attached, this is a great time for forming new connections or strengthening existing ones.
- **March**: With the Sun entering Aries, your energy levels peak. This is the perfect time to start new projects, assert your independence, and prioritize self-care. Health is excellent, but don't burn out.
- **April**: Mercury and Venus in Taurus invite you to focus on financial stability. Consider revising your budget or looking for new ways to boost your income. Practical, grounded decisions will lead to success.
- **May**: Jupiter in Taurus continues to boost your financial sector, bringing growth and abundance. This is a powerful time for career advancement or expanding a business.
- **June**: Romance flourishes as Venus enters your home sector, bringing harmony to family life. If you've been considering making home improvements, now is the time to do so.
- **July**: Mars in Cancer may create emotional turbulence. Focus on nurturing your inner self, and don't let minor frustrations turn into conflicts. Meditation or yoga can help restore balance.
- **August**: Creative energy surges this month, thanks to the Sun's movement into Leo. Channel this energy into artistic endeavors, and don't be afraid to express your ideas boldly.
- **September**: With Mars entering Libra, relationships take center stage. Whether it's romantic or professional partnerships, cooperation and compromise will be key.

- **October**: Career momentum builds as the Sun in Libra shines a spotlight on professional partnerships. It's a great time for networking and expanding your social circle.
- **November**: Personal transformation is highlighted as Scorpio season encourages deep emotional healing. Consider engaging in therapy or shadow work to clear lingering emotional blocks.
- **December**: The year ends with a focus on travel and expansion, as the Sun moves into Sagittarius. This is a great time for spiritual growth, adventure, and expanding your worldview.

Taurus (April 20 – May 20)
Overview of 2025

Taurus, 2025 will be a year of solidifying your foundations, particularly in your finances, career, and personal life. Jupiter's presence in your sign for most of the year will bring growth and expansion, but also the need for careful planning and perseverance. Focus on practical steps toward your goals while embracing opportunities for abundance and stability.

Monthly Insights

- **January**: The year begins with financial focus as Jupiter in your sign amplifies your potential for growth. Review your long-term goals, and take action on career or financial investments.
- **February**: Venus in your career sector highlights opportunities for professional advancement. Relationships with colleagues will be harmonious, making this a great time for teamwork and collaboration.
- **March**: As the Sun enters Aries, you may feel the need to retreat and reflect. Take time for self-care and address any emotional wounds that need healing before the Sun moves into your sign next month.
- **April**: With the Sun in Taurus, you feel more grounded and confident. This is your time to shine, especially in career and personal development. Financial decisions made now will bring long-term rewards.
- **May**: Jupiter continues its journey through your sign, bringing abundance in all areas of life. Focus on personal growth, and don't be afraid to take risks in pursuit of your goals.
- **June**: Love takes center stage as Venus moves into your romance sector. If you're in a relationship, deepen your emotional bond. Singles may meet someone special during this time.
- **July**: Mars in Cancer brings family and home matters to the forefront. Take care of domestic responsibilities and nurture close family relationships.
- **August**: With the Sun in Leo, creative energy flows, especially in your personal projects or home environment. Use this time to add beauty to your surroundings and express your inner artist.
- **September**: Mercury in Virgo sharpens your communication skills. It's an ideal time for work-related presentations, contract negotiations, and detail-oriented tasks.
- **October**: Venus in your relationship sector brings harmony to your love life. Focus on deepening connections with loved ones, and consider engaging in shared activities to strengthen bonds.

- **November**: Scorpio season invites you to transform any areas of stagnation in your relationships or personal growth. Be willing to let go of old habits or dynamics that no longer serve you.
- **December**: As the Sun enters Sagittarius, focus on long-term financial planning. It's a good time to revisit investments, budgets, and long-term career goals.

Gemini (May 21 – June 20)
Overview of 2025
For Gemini, 2025 is a year of communication, learning, and social expansion. With key planetary movements influencing your personal growth, this is a time to deepen your intellectual pursuits, build strong connections, and focus on personal and professional development. Your natural curiosity will lead you to exciting new opportunities, but be mindful of staying focused and grounded.

Monthly Insights

- **January**: The year begins with a focus on personal transformation. Mars in Sagittarius encourages you to confront any hidden fears or unresolved issues in relationships.
- **February**: Communication is key this month, as Mercury in Aquarius sharpens your ability to express yourself clearly. Focus on networking and expanding your social circle.
- **March**: The Sun in Pisces brings attention to your career. Creative solutions to challenges will pay off, and this is an ideal time for professional growth and recognition.
- **April**: Relationships are highlighted as Mercury in Taurus brings practical communication in love and partnerships. Focus on building stable, lasting connections.
- **May**: Jupiter in Taurus enhances your financial potential, encouraging you to take a grounded approach to wealth-building. Long-term planning will bring lasting rewards.
- **June**: Venus in Cancer brings emotional harmony to your home and family life. Focus on creating a nurturing environment and resolving any family tensions.
- **July**: Mars in Cancer may heighten emotions, leading to potential conflicts. Be mindful of how you express your feelings, and seek balance in family and domestic matters.
- **August**: Creativity surges as the Sun in Leo amplifies your artistic talents. Channel this energy into passion projects, especially those related to writing, art, or public speaking.
- **September**: Mercury in Virgo sharpens your mind for analytical work. This is a great time for revisiting past projects, organizing your thoughts, and clearing up miscommunications.
- **October**: Venus in Libra brings harmony to your social life. Romantic connections may deepen, and singles may find themselves drawn to new, meaningful relationships.
- **November**: The Sun in Scorpio encourages introspection and personal transformation. Focus on emotional healing and self-improvement through spiritual practices.
- **December**: As the year ends, the Sun in Sagittarius highlights personal growth through travel, education, and new experiences. This is a great time to expand your horizons and pursue new adventures.

Cancer (June 21 – July 22)
Overview of 2025

For Cancer, 2025 is a year of emotional growth, home improvements, and personal transformation. Saturn in Pisces throughout the year will encourage you to build emotional resilience, while Jupiter's influence brings financial opportunities and stability. This year will push you to find a balance between nurturing others and taking care of your own needs.

Monthly Insights

- **January**: The year begins with a focus on relationships, as Venus in your romance sector brings harmony and love. Focus on deepening emotional connections with loved ones.
- **February**: Career takes center stage as Mars in Sagittarius energizes your work life. Push yourself to achieve professional goals and take on leadership roles.
- **March**: The Sun in Pisces highlights your spiritual growth. This is a great time for reflection, meditation, and focusing on your emotional well-being.
- **April**: Financial stability is enhanced by Mercury and Venus in Taurus, bringing growth opportunities in your career. Focus on long-term planning and investments.
- **May**: Jupiter continues to bring abundance in financial matters, while Venus in Cancer enhances your personal life. Love and family relationships flourish.
- **June**: Mars in Cancer energizes your personal goals, pushing you to take action in your home life. It's a great time for home improvements and family-related decisions.
- **July**: With the Sun in Leo, focus on building self-confidence and expressing your personal talents. It's a great time for creative endeavors and boosting your self-esteem.
- **August**: Venus in Leo brings romance and passion into your life. If you're single, this could be a time to attract new love, while couples can reignite their connection.
- **September**: Health and well-being come into focus as Mercury in Virgo encourages you to take better care of yourself. Reassess your routines and focus on self-care.
- **October**: Venus in Scorpio enhances intimacy in relationships. This is a time for emotional healing, particularly in close partnerships.
- **November**: With the Sun in Scorpio, personal transformation is highlighted. Dive deep into shadow work and explore what needs healing in your emotional life.
- **December**: The year ends with a focus on your career and public image. As the Sun enters Sagittarius, focus on long-term professional growth and future goals.

Leo (July 23 – August 22)
Overview of 2025

Leo, 2025 will be a year of personal empowerment, creative expression, and relationship growth. With key planetary transits activating your sector of self-expression and romance, this is a time to shine in both your personal and professional life. Expect exciting opportunities for personal growth and leadership, but be mindful of maintaining balance and self-care amidst your ambitions.

Monthly Insights

- **January**: Career matters take precedence as Mars in Sagittarius encourages you to take bold actions in your professional life. Take initiative and pursue leadership opportunities.
- **February**: Relationships flourish as Venus moves through your social sector. Whether in love or friendship, focus on building strong, supportive connections.
- **March**: The Sun in Aries brings a burst of energy to your personal goals. This is a great time to pursue your passions and take bold steps toward your dreams.
- **April**: Financial matters stabilize as Jupiter in Taurus enhances your earning potential. Focus on building long-term financial security through smart investments.
- **May**: Venus in Cancer brings harmony to your home life. It's a great time for strengthening family bonds and creating a peaceful domestic environment.
- **June**: Mars in Cancer encourages you to focus on emotional healing and personal well-being. Don't hesitate to prioritize your mental and emotional health this month.
- **July**: With the Sun in Leo, this is your time to shine. Focus on creative projects, personal expression, and building your self-confidence. The world is your stage!
- **August**: Venus in Leo amplifies romance, beauty, and self-love. Take this time to indulge in self-care, beautify your surroundings, and deepen romantic relationships.
- **September**: Health and wellness come into focus as Mercury in Virgo encourages you to fine-tune your daily habits. Focus on creating a balanced routine that supports your overall well-being.
- **October**: Venus in Libra enhances communication and social connections. This is a great time for networking, making new friends, and improving relationships through thoughtful dialogue.
- **November**: With the Sun in Scorpio, home and family matters come into focus. Consider making improvements to your living space or resolving lingering family issues.
- **December**: The year ends with an adventurous spirit as the Sun moves into Sagittarius. Embrace opportunities for travel, learning, and expanding your horizons.

Virgo (August 23 – September 22)
Overview of 2025

Virgo, 2025 will be a year of growth, introspection, and practical progress. With Jupiter in Taurus influencing your house of long-term goals and personal beliefs, you'll be motivated to focus on financial stability and professional development. Saturn in Pisces will challenge you to reassess your relationships and emotional boundaries, pushing you toward more authentic connections.

Monthly Insights

- **January**: The year begins with a focus on personal relationships. Venus in Sagittarius highlights your love life, encouraging you to find harmony and balance in your partnerships.
- **February**: Career opportunities flourish as Mars in Sagittarius boosts your professional drive. Focus on taking calculated risks and pushing your career goals forward.
- **March**: With the Sun in Pisces, focus on nurturing your relationships and emotional well-being. This is a good time for reflection and healing any lingering emotional wounds.
- **April**: Financial growth is highlighted as Jupiter in Taurus brings abundance in career and money matters. Focus on long-term investments and practical planning.
- **May**: Venus in Gemini brings harmony to your social life. Networking and connecting with others will bring new opportunities, particularly in your career.
- **June**: Health and wellness come into focus as Mars moves into your sector of well-being. This is an ideal time to focus on improving your daily habits and health routines.
- **July**: The Sun in Leo encourages introspection and self-care. Take time for yourself and focus on emotional healing and personal growth.
- **August**: Venus in Leo encourages self-love and creative expression. This is a great time to indulge in hobbies that bring you joy and enhance your sense of fulfillment.
- **September**: With the Sun in Virgo, this is your time to shine. Focus on personal growth, refining your goals, and improving your daily routines. Organize and plan for the year ahead.
- **October**: Financial matters stabilize as Mercury in Libra brings clarity to money-related decisions. It's a good time for budgeting, financial planning, and securing future investments.
- **November**: Venus in Scorpio enhances intimacy and emotional depth in relationships. Focus on healing emotional wounds and deepening your connection with loved ones.
- **December**: The year ends with a focus on long-term goals and financial planning. The Sun in Sagittarius encourages you to think about your future and make decisions that support your growth.

Libra (September 23 – October 22)
Overview of 2025

Libra, 2025 will be a year of balance, transformation, and relationship growth. With Saturn in Pisces influencing your emotional life, you'll be encouraged to set boundaries and focus on building healthier relationships. Jupiter in Taurus brings financial stability and growth opportunities, while key planetary transits highlight your personal development and career progression.

Monthly Insights

- **January**: The year begins with a focus on career advancement as Mars in Sagittarius energizes your professional life. Take initiative and be bold in pursuing new opportunities.
- **February**: Venus in Capricorn highlights your home and family life. Focus on creating a harmonious environment and resolving any lingering family tensions.
- **March**: With the Sun in Pisces, focus on your emotional well-being and spiritual growth. This is a great time for meditation, reflection, and healing emotional wounds.
- **April**: Financial growth is highlighted as Jupiter in Taurus brings abundance in career and wealth. Focus on long-term investments and practical financial decisions.
- **May**: Relationships flourish as Venus in Gemini enhances communication and social connections. This is a great time for networking, meeting new people, and strengthening existing relationships.
- **June**: Mars in Cancer brings emotional intensity to your relationships. Focus on nurturing your connections and resolving any emotional conflicts.
- **July**: With the Sun in Leo, your social life thrives. This is a great time for networking, meeting new people, and enjoying social activities.
- **August**: Venus in Leo enhances romance and creative expression. Focus on deepening your romantic relationships and pursuing hobbies that bring you joy.
- **September**: Mercury in Virgo encourages introspection and self-care. Take time to reflect on your personal growth and make adjustments to your routines as needed.
- **October**: With the Sun in Libra, this is your time to shine. Focus on personal growth, improving relationships, and finding balance in your life.
- **November**: Venus in Scorpio enhances emotional depth in relationships. Focus on healing emotional wounds and strengthening your connection with loved ones.
- **December**: The year ends with a focus on career growth and long-term goals. The Sun in Sagittarius encourages you to pursue new opportunities and think about your future success.

Scorpio (October 23 – November 21)
Overview of 2025

Scorpio, 2025 will be a year of transformation, emotional growth, and financial stability. With key planetary influences affecting your relationships and career, this is a time for deep personal growth and introspection. Jupiter in Taurus brings abundance and stability, while Saturn in Pisces encourages you to focus on emotional healing and building healthier relationships.

Monthly Insights

- **January**: The year begins with a focus on your home and family life. Venus in Capricorn encourages you to create a harmonious domestic environment and strengthen family bonds.
- **February**: Mars in Sagittarius brings energy to your financial sector. Focus on budgeting, saving, and making smart financial decisions that will benefit you in the long run.
- **March**: The Sun in Pisces highlights your creative talents and emotional well-being. This is a great time for artistic expression and personal reflection.
- **April**: With Jupiter in Taurus, financial growth and career advancement are highlighted. Focus on long-term planning and practical decisions that will secure your future.
- **May**: Relationships take center stage as Venus in Gemini enhances communication and connection. Focus on building meaningful relationships with loved ones and colleagues.
- **June**: Mars in Cancer brings emotional intensity to your personal life. Focus on resolving any emotional conflicts and nurturing your relationships.
- **July**: The Sun in Leo encourages you to take bold actions in your career. This is a great time for professional advancement and leadership roles.
- **August**: Venus in Leo brings passion and romance into your life. Whether single or in a relationship, focus on deepening your emotional connection with others.
- **September**: Mercury in Virgo enhances your communication skills. This is a great time for networking, learning, and sharing your ideas with others.
- **October**: With the Sun in Scorpio, this is your time for personal transformation. Focus on deep emotional healing, releasing old patterns, and stepping into your power.
- **November**: Financial growth continues as Jupiter in Taurus brings stability and abundance. Focus on long-term investments and financial planning.
- **December**: The year ends with a focus on personal growth and self-improvement. The Sun in Sagittarius encourages you to explore new opportunities and embrace personal growth.

Sagittarius (November 22 – December 21)
Overview of 2025

Sagittarius, 2025 will be a year of exploration, growth, and financial stability. With Jupiter in Taurus influencing your career and financial sectors, this is a time for practical decision-making and long-term planning. Saturn in Pisces encourages you to focus on emotional well-being and building stronger connections with loved ones. Your natural curiosity will lead you to new adventures, but be mindful of staying grounded in your pursuits.

Monthly Insights

- **January**: The year begins with a focus on personal growth and emotional healing. Venus in Capricorn encourages you to create a harmonious domestic environment and strengthen family bonds.
- **February**: Mars in Sagittarius energizes your personal goals and ambitions. Focus on pursuing your passions and taking bold steps toward your dreams.
- **March**: The Sun in Pisces highlights your emotional well-being and family life. This is a great time for introspection and healing emotional wounds.
- **April**: Financial growth is highlighted as Jupiter in Taurus brings abundance in your career and money matters. Focus on long-term financial planning and practical decisions.
- **May**: Relationships take center stage as Venus in Gemini enhances communication and social connections. Focus on building meaningful relationships with loved ones and colleagues.
- **June**: Mars in Cancer brings emotional intensity to your personal life. Focus on resolving any emotional conflicts and nurturing your relationships.
- **July**: The Sun in Leo encourages you to take bold actions in your career. This is a great time for professional advancement and leadership roles.
- **August**: Venus in Leo brings passion and romance into your life. Whether single or in a relationship, focus on deepening your emotional connection with others.
- **September**: Mercury in Virgo enhances your communication skills. This is a great time for networking, learning, and sharing your ideas with others.
- **October**: With the Sun in Scorpio, focus on personal transformation. Engage in deep emotional healing and let go of old habits or beliefs that no longer serve you.
- **November**: Financial stability continues as Jupiter in Taurus brings opportunities for career growth and financial abundance. Focus on making practical, long-term decisions.
- **December**: The year ends with a focus on personal growth and exploration. The Sun in Sagittarius encourages you to pursue new opportunities and embrace your natural curiosity.

Capricorn (December 22 – January 19)
Overview of 2025

Capricorn, 2025 will be a year of professional growth, personal transformation, and relationship stability. With Saturn, your ruling planet, influencing your emotional life, you'll be encouraged to set boundaries and focus on building healthier relationships. Jupiter in Taurus brings financial abundance and career opportunities, while key planetary transits highlight your personal development and relationship dynamics.

Monthly Insights

- **January**: The year begins with a focus on career advancement as Mars in Sagittarius energizes your professional life. Take bold actions in pursuit of new opportunities and leadership roles.
- **February**: Venus in Aquarius highlights your social connections. Focus on building strong relationships and expanding your social network.
- **March**: The Sun in Pisces encourages introspection and emotional healing. This is a great time for reflection, self-care, and healing any lingering emotional wounds.
- **April**: Financial growth is highlighted as Jupiter in Taurus brings abundance in your career and money matters. Focus on long-term financial planning and practical decisions.
- **May**: Relationships flourish as Venus in Gemini enhances communication and connection. Focus on building meaningful relationships with loved ones and colleagues.
- **June**: Mars in Cancer brings emotional intensity to your relationships. Focus on nurturing your connections and resolving any emotional conflicts.
- **July**: The Sun in Leo encourages bold actions in your personal life. This is a great time for self-expression and personal growth.
- **August**: Venus in Leo brings passion and romance into your life. Focus on deepening your emotional connection with loved ones.
- **September**: Mercury in Virgo enhances your communication skills. This is a great time for networking, learning, and sharing your ideas with others.
- **October**: With the Sun in Libra, focus on creating balance in your life. This is a great time for improving relationships and finding harmony in your personal and professional life.
- **November**: Financial growth continues as Jupiter in Taurus brings stability and abundance. Focus on long-term investments and practical decisions.
- **December**: The year ends with a focus on personal growth and self-improvement. The Sun in Sagittarius encourages you to embrace new opportunities and think about your long-term goals.

Aquarius (January 20 – February 18)
Overview of 2025

Aquarius, 2025 will be a year of innovation, personal growth, and relationship development. With Saturn in Pisces influencing your financial and emotional sectors, you'll be encouraged to focus on building stability and emotional resilience. Jupiter in Taurus brings abundance and financial growth, while key planetary transits highlight your personal development and relationship dynamics.

Monthly Insights

- **January**: The year begins with a focus on personal growth and emotional healing. Venus in Capricorn encourages you to create a harmonious domestic environment and strengthen family bonds.
- **February**: Mars in Sagittarius energizes your personal goals and ambitions. Focus on pursuing your passions and taking bold steps toward your dreams.
- **March**: The Sun in Pisces highlights your emotional well-being and family life. This is a great time for introspection and healing emotional wounds.
- **April**: Financial growth is highlighted as Jupiter in Taurus brings abundance in your career and money matters. Focus on long-term financial planning and practical decisions.
- **May**: Relationships take center stage as Venus in Gemini enhances communication and social connections. Focus on building meaningful relationships with loved ones and colleagues.
- **June**: Mars in Cancer brings emotional intensity to your personal life. Focus on resolving any emotional conflicts and nurturing your relationships.
- **July**: The Sun in Leo encourages bold actions in your personal life. This is a great time for self-expression and personal growth.
- **August**: Venus in Leo brings passion and romance into your life. Whether single or in a relationship, focus on deepening your emotional connection with others.
- **September**: Mercury in Virgo enhances your communication skills. This is a great time for networking, learning, and sharing your ideas with others.
- **October**: With the Sun in Libra, focus on creating balance in your life. This is a great time for improving relationships and finding harmony in your personal and professional life.
- **November**: Financial stability continues as Jupiter in Taurus brings opportunities for career growth and financial abundance. Focus on making practical, long-term decisions.
- **December**: The year ends with a focus on personal growth and exploration. The Sun in Sagittarius encourages you to pursue new opportunities and embrace your natural curiosity.

Pisces (February 19 – March 20)
Overview of 2025

Pisces, 2025 will be a year of emotional growth, spiritual development, and personal transformation. With Saturn in your sign throughout the year, you'll be encouraged to set boundaries, build emotional resilience, and focus on your personal growth. Jupiter in Taurus brings financial stability and opportunities for career advancement, while key planetary transits highlight your spiritual journey and relationships.

Monthly Insights

- **January**: The year begins with a focus on emotional healing and personal growth. Venus in Capricorn encourages you to create a harmonious domestic environment and strengthen family bonds.
- **February**: Mars in Sagittarius energizes your career goals. Focus on professional growth and take bold steps toward achieving your long-term ambitions.
- **March**: The Sun in Pisces highlights your personal growth and spiritual development. This is a great time for introspection, meditation, and healing emotional wounds.
- **April**: Financial growth is highlighted as Jupiter in Taurus brings abundance in your career and money matters. Focus on long-term financial planning and practical decisions.
- **May**: Relationships flourish as Venus in Gemini enhances communication and connection. Focus on building meaningful relationships with loved ones and colleagues.
- **June**: Mars in Cancer brings emotional intensity to your personal life. Focus on nurturing your relationships and resolving any emotional conflicts.
- **July**: The Sun in Leo encourages self-expression and personal growth. This is a great time for creative projects and boosting your self-confidence.
- **August**: Venus in Leo brings passion and romance into your life. Whether single or in a relationship, focus on deepening your emotional connection with others.
- **September**: Mercury in Virgo enhances your communication skills. This is a great time for networking, learning, and sharing your ideas with others.
- **October**: With the Sun in Libra, focus on creating balance in your life. This is a great time for improving relationships and finding harmony in your personal and professional life.
- **November**: Financial stability continues as Jupiter in Taurus brings opportunities for career growth and financial abundance. Focus on making practical, long-term decisions.
- **December**: The year ends with a focus on personal growth and spiritual development. The Sun in Sagittarius encourages you to embrace new opportunities and think about your long-term goals.

Conclusion

2025 offers each zodiac sign unique opportunities for personal growth, career advancement, love, and spiritual transformation. By aligning your actions with the planetary influences detailed in this chapter, you can make the most of the year's cosmic energies and work toward your goals with clarity and purpose. Whether you're focusing on career success, deepening relationships, or enhancing your well-being, the stars are here to guide you on your journey throughout the year.

Chapter 12: The Wheel of the Year and Seasonal Sabbats

The Wheel of the Year is a cycle of seasonal festivals, or Sabbats, that celebrate the cycles of nature and the changing of the seasons. These eight festivals, rooted in ancient pagan traditions, mark the turning points in the Earth's journey around the Sun. For witches and practitioners of earth-based spirituality, the Sabbats are times of celebration, reflection, and ritual, providing an opportunity to align with the natural rhythms of the Earth.

This chapter explores each of the eight Sabbats—Imbolc, Ostara, Beltane, Litha, Lughnasadh, Mabon, Samhain, and Yule—detailing their history, meanings, and correspondences. You'll find suggestions for seasonal rituals, altar ideas, and ways to honor these sacred days. Whether you're celebrating alone or with a group, these festivals offer powerful moments to connect with the cycles of nature and deepen your spiritual practice.

Overview of the Sabbats

The Wheel of the Year is divided into two halves: the light half (spring and summer) and the dark half (autumn and winter). The eight Sabbats are evenly spaced throughout the year, each corresponding to a key point in the Earth's seasonal journey.

- **Imbolc (February 1st–2nd)**: A festival of light and purification, marking the midway point between winter and spring.
- **Ostara (March 20th–23rd)**: The spring equinox, celebrating balance, renewal, and the rebirth of life.
- **Beltane (April 30th–May 1st)**: A fire festival celebrating fertility, passion, and the blossoming of life.
- **Litha (June 20th–23rd)**: The summer solstice, honoring the peak of the Sun's power and the abundance of nature.
- **Lughnasadh (August 1st)**: A festival of the first harvest, celebrating abundance, gratitude, and community.
- **Mabon (September 20th–23rd)**: The autumn equinox, a time of balance, reflection, and giving thanks for the harvest.
- **Samhain (October 31st–November 1st)**: The final harvest festival, honoring the ancestors and marking the beginning of the dark half of the year.
- **Yule (December 20th–23rd)**: The winter solstice, celebrating the return of the Sun and the rebirth of light.

Each of these Sabbats carries unique energies and offers opportunities for specific types of magical work, from manifesting abundance at Beltane to releasing the old at Samhain. By celebrating the Sabbats, witches and spiritual practitioners attune themselves to the rhythms of the Earth and the cycles of life, death, and rebirth.

Imbolc (February 1st–2nd)
Overview
Imbolc, also known as Brigid's Day, marks the midpoint between winter and spring. It is a time of purification, renewal, and hope as the first signs of life begin to stir in the frozen Earth. Traditionally, Imbolc was a fire festival dedicated to the goddess Brigid, a deity of healing, fertility, and inspiration.

Imbolc is a time to clear away the old and prepare for the new. It's a season of light, as candles and fires are lit to symbolize the returning strength of the Sun.

Correspondences

- **Colors**: White, silver, red, pale yellow
- **Symbols**: Candles, snowdrops, Brigid's cross, fire, seeds
- **Herbs**: Rosemary, bay, basil, angelica, snowdrops
- **Crystals**: Amethyst, garnet, onyx, citrine
- **Deities**: Brigid, Persephone, Demeter

Rituals for Imbolc

- **Candle Lighting Ceremony**: Light candles or a fire in your hearth to honor the growing light and the return of the Sun. Focus on clearing out old, stagnant energy and inviting fresh inspiration.
- **Cleansing and Purification**: Perform a cleansing ritual for your home by sweeping out old energy, using incense like sage or rosemary, or sprinkling blessed water. Imbolc is a perfect time to cleanse yourself, your space, and your tools.
- **Planting Seeds of Intention**: Imbolc is an ideal time for setting intentions for the coming year. Plant literal seeds or symbolically plant your goals and desires, knowing that they will grow and flourish as the year progresses.

Ostara (March 20th–23rd)
Overview

Ostara is the spring equinox, a time when day and night are of equal length, symbolizing balance and the renewal of life. Named after the Germanic goddess Eostre, this Sabbat celebrates fertility, rebirth, and the awakening of nature after the long winter. It is a time of planting and new beginnings.

The themes of Ostara center around balance, growth, and transformation. As the Earth reawakens, so do we, making this a perfect time for personal and spiritual renewal.

Correspondences

- **Colors**: Green, yellow, pastel shades, pink, lavender
- **Symbols**: Eggs, rabbits, flowers, seeds, butterflies
- **Herbs**: Daffodils, tulips, jasmine, lavender, chamomile
- **Crystals**: Rose quartz, moonstone, aquamarine, amethyst
- **Deities**: Eostre, Persephone, Demeter, Gaia

Rituals for Ostara

- **Egg Ritual for New Beginnings**: Paint or decorate eggs, which symbolize fertility and new beginnings. Bury them in your garden or keep them on your altar as a reminder of the potential for growth and transformation.
- **Planting Ritual**: Physically or symbolically plant seeds to represent the goals or intentions you wish to grow in the coming year. As you plant, visualize your dreams taking root and growing strong.
- **Balance Meditation**: On the equinox, meditate on balance in your life. Consider the areas where you feel imbalanced and how you can restore harmony, just as the Earth finds balance between light and dark.

Beltane (April 30th–May 1st)
Overview
Beltane is one of the most joyous and energetic Sabbats on the Wheel of the Year, celebrating fertility, passion, and the blossoming of life. Traditionally, Beltane was marked by the lighting of bonfires and the dancing of the maypole, symbolizing the union of the masculine and feminine energies of nature.

This fire festival honors the life force that fuels all living things. It's a time to celebrate love, creativity, sensuality, and abundance.

Correspondences

- **Colors**: Green, red, pink, yellow
- **Symbols**: Flowers, maypole, bonfires, ribbons, blossoms
- **Herbs**: Hawthorn, marigold, rose, lavender, thyme
- **Crystals**: Emerald, rose quartz, garnet, malachite
- **Deities**: Flora, Pan, Freyja, Cernunnos, Aphrodite

Rituals for Beltane

- **Fire Ritual**: Build a bonfire or light candles to celebrate the power of the Sun and the vitality of life. As you light the fire, visualize your desires growing stronger, fueled by the energy of the flames.
- **Maypole Dance**: If possible, participate in a maypole dance or create a small maypole on your altar. The weaving of the ribbons symbolizes the intertwining of energies and the creation of new life.
- **Love Magic**: Beltane is a time for love and romance. Perform love spells, rituals to attract a partner, or rituals to deepen an existing relationship. Use rose petals, jasmine, and love-inspiring crystals to enhance the magic.

Litha (June 20th–23rd)
Overview

Litha, also known as Midsummer or the Summer Solstice, celebrates the height of the Sun's power. The longest day and shortest night of the year, Litha is a celebration of abundance, fertility, and the joy of life. It marks the peak of summer and the abundance of nature's gifts.

Litha is a time of power and light, perfect for working magic related to abundance, prosperity, and personal empowerment.

Correspondences

- **Colors**: Gold, yellow, orange, green, blue
- **Symbols**: Sun wheels, bonfires, herbs, solar symbols, oak leaves
- **Herbs**: St. John's wort, chamomile, mugwort, elderflower, lavender
- **Crystals**: Citrine, tiger's eye, carnelian, sunstone
- **Deities**: Sun gods (Apollo, Ra, Lugh), Oak King, Freyja

Rituals for Litha

- **Sun Magic**: Perform rituals outside during the day, connecting with the Sun's energy. Use solar symbols like sunflowers or gold candles to focus on drawing in abundance, personal power, and vitality.
- **Prosperity Spells**: Litha is an ideal time for spells related to wealth and success. Light a gold or green candle and visualize prosperity flowing into your life. You can also create a charm or talisman to attract abundance.
- **Herb Gathering**: Traditionally, herbs gathered at midsummer were believed to be at the height of their power. Collect herbs like lavender, rosemary, or mugwort to use in magical workings throughout the year.

Lughnasadh (August 1st)
Overview

Lughnasadh, also known as Lammas, is the first of the three harvest festivals and celebrates the beginning of the grain harvest. Named after the Celtic god Lugh, this Sabbat is a time of gratitude, abundance, and preparation for the darker half of the year. It marks the gathering of the first fruits and grains and is a celebration of the Earth's generosity.

Lughnasadh is a time to give thanks for the abundance in our lives and to prepare for the coming of autumn.

Correspondences

- **Colors**: Gold, yellow, orange, brown
- **Symbols**: Wheat, corn, bread, sickles, fruits
- **Herbs**: Wheat, corn, heather, blackberry, sunflower
- **Crystals**: Amber, citrine, peridot, aventurine
- **Deities**: Lugh, Demeter, Ceres, Persephone

Rituals for Lughnasadh

- **Gratitude Ritual**: Create an altar with grains, bread, and fresh fruits. Give thanks for the abundance in your life and offer part of your harvest (whether literal or symbolic) back to the Earth in gratitude.
- **Bread Making**: Bake bread as an offering to the Earth and as a symbol of the harvest. While kneading the dough, focus on your gratitude for the nourishment and abundance in your life.
- **Harvest Ritual**: Perform a ritual to celebrate the "harvests" in your life—whether they are related to career, relationships, or personal growth. Reflect on what you have achieved and prepare for the work that lies ahead as the year begins to wane.

Mabon (September 20th–23rd)

Overview

Mabon, the autumn equinox, is a time of balance, reflection, and thanksgiving. Just like Ostara in the spring, Mabon represents a point of balance between light and dark, day and night. It is the second harvest festival, and a time to reflect on the fruits of the Earth and our personal harvests.

Mabon invites us to give thanks for the abundance in our lives, to share our blessings with others, and to prepare for the darker, introspective half of the year.

Correspondences

- **Colors**: Red, orange, brown, gold
- **Symbols**: Cornucopia, apples, grapes, acorns, leaves
- **Herbs**: Sage, ivy, apple, blackberry, cinnamon
- **Crystals**: Jasper, carnelian, tiger's eye, smoky quartz
- **Deities**: Mabon, Demeter, Persephone, Thor

Rituals for Mabon

- **Balance Ritual**: Meditate on balance in your life, focusing on areas that feel imbalanced. Use the equinox as an opportunity to restore harmony between work and rest, giving and receiving, and light and shadow.
- **Thanksgiving Feast**: Host a meal with friends or family, sharing the bounty of the season. Prepare dishes using seasonal fruits, vegetables, and grains, and give thanks for the abundance in your life.
- **Apple Ritual**: The apple, a symbol of knowledge and wisdom, is associated with Mabon. Perform a ritual using apples, either by sharing them with loved ones, making apple cider, or using them in divination.

Samhain (October 31st–November 1st)

Overview

Samhain is one of the most important Sabbats on the Wheel of the Year, marking the end of the harvest season and the beginning of winter. It is a time to honor the ancestors, reflect on the cycle of life and death, and embrace the mysteries of the unseen world. As the veil between the worlds is thinnest on Samhain, it is an ideal time for divination and connecting with the spirit realm.

Samhain is a time of death and rebirth, a liminal moment when we honor what has passed and prepare for the new beginnings to come.

Correspondences

- **Colors**: Black, orange, dark purple, silver
- **Symbols**: Skulls, pumpkins, candles, cauldrons, skeletons
- **Herbs**: Mugwort, rosemary, sage, apples, wormwood
- **Crystals**: Obsidian, black tourmaline, onyx, amethyst
- **Deities**: Hecate, Morrigan, Anubis, Persephone

Rituals for Samhain

- **Ancestor Altar**: Create an altar to honor your ancestors, placing photos, mementos, and offerings of food or drink. Light candles to guide the spirits of your loved ones and spend time reflecting on their wisdom and influence in your life.
- **Divination**: Samhain is the perfect time for scrying, tarot, or rune readings. Use this night to gain insight into the future and connect with spiritual guides or ancestors for wisdom.
- **Release Ritual**: Perform a ritual to release old patterns, habits, or grief. Write down what you wish to release and burn the paper in a cauldron or fire, symbolically letting go of what no longer serves you.

Yule (December 20th–23rd)
Overview

Yule, the winter solstice, is a celebration of the rebirth of the Sun. It marks the longest night and the shortest day of the year, after which the days begin to lengthen again. Yule is a time of hope, renewal, and the promise of returning light.

Traditionally, Yule was celebrated with bonfires, feasting, and the burning of the Yule log, symbolizing the return of the Sun's warmth and life-giving energy.

Correspondences

- **Colors**: Red, green, gold, silver, white
- **Symbols**: Evergreen boughs, Yule log, holly, mistletoe, candles
- **Herbs**: Pine, cedar, cinnamon, cloves, holly, ivy
- **Crystals**: Garnet, ruby, clear quartz, citrine
- **Deities**: Sun gods (Apollo, Ra, Sol), Holly King, Odin, Freyja

Rituals for Yule

- **Yule Log Ceremony**: Burn a Yule log in your hearth or light a symbolic log candle on your altar. As the log burns, release the old year and welcome the rebirth of light and new possibilities.
- **Evergreen Magic**: Decorate your home with evergreens like pine, cedar, and holly, which symbolize eternal life and the endurance of nature through the winter. You can also create wreaths or garlands as a way to honor the season.
- **Winter Solstice Meditation**: On the longest night, meditate on the themes of renewal, rebirth, and hope. Reflect on the lessons of the past year and set intentions for the year to come as the Sun's strength begins to grow.

Conclusion

The Wheel of the Year offers a powerful framework for aligning your spiritual practice with the natural rhythms of the Earth. By celebrating the Sabbats, you honor the cycles of birth, growth, death, and rebirth that govern both the natural world and our own lives. Each festival brings its own unique energies and magical opportunities, allowing you to attune to the shifting seasons and embrace the wisdom they offer. Whether through rituals of gratitude at Lughnasadh or deep transformation at Samhain, the Wheel of the Year provides moments of sacred connection and spiritual growth throughout the year.

Chapter 13: Moon Sign Magic

The Moon plays a powerful role in magical practice, representing intuition, emotions, the subconscious, and the cycles of nature. In astrology, the Moon's zodiac sign deeply influences how we feel, respond to situations, and interact with others on an emotional level. When the Moon transits through each zodiac sign, it offers unique energies that can enhance your spellwork and rituals.

This chapter explores the connection between the Moon's zodiac sign and magic, providing insights into how the Moon's position in the zodiac influences different types of spellwork. Additionally, it includes a detailed moon sign chart for 2025, outlining the best times to perform specific spells based on the Moon's zodiacal position each month.

Understanding Moon Sign Magic

The Moon travels through the entire zodiac, spending approximately two to three days in each sign. This constant motion creates a fluctuating emotional landscape, which can be harnessed for various magical purposes. While the **lunar phase** (new moon, waxing, full, waning) is traditionally the primary focus in moon magic, the Moon's position in the zodiac provides additional layers of energy that can fine-tune your rituals and enhance their effectiveness.

How the Moon's Zodiac Sign Affects Magic

Each zodiac sign brings its unique qualities and influences the type of magic that will be most potent during the Moon's transit. Here is an overview of the Moon in each sign and how to align your spellwork with the Moon's zodiac placement:

Moon in Aries

- **Keywords**: Action, courage, assertiveness, initiation
- **Magic Focus**: The Moon in Aries is a time of high energy, ideal for spells that require boldness, decisiveness, and action. Use this time for initiating new projects, boosting confidence, and taking risks.
- **Best for**: Courage spells, success rituals, physical strength, overcoming fear, starting new ventures.

Moon in Taurus

- **Keywords**: Stability, material security, sensuality, patience
- **Magic Focus**: The Moon in Taurus is perfect for grounding and stabilizing your energy. This is a good time for spells focused on long-term goals, financial security, and building lasting foundations.
- **Best for**: Prosperity magic, home and family security, love spells with a focus on commitment, health and wellness, spells for abundance.

Moon in Gemini

- **Keywords**: Communication, adaptability, intellect, curiosity
- **Magic Focus**: The Moon in Gemini brings mental agility and curiosity, making it ideal for spells related to communication, learning, and quick thinking. This is a great time for networking, expanding your knowledge, or working on writing projects.
- **Best for**: Communication spells, learning and memory enhancement, social magic, divination, intellectual pursuits.

Moon in Cancer

- **Keywords**: Emotion, intuition, home, protection
- **Magic Focus**: Cancer is the Moon's natural home, amplifying emotional sensitivity and intuition. This is a time for deep emotional work, protection magic, and spells that nurture the home and family.
- **Best for**: Healing and nurturing spells, home protection, fertility, family matters, emotional healing, psychic development.

Moon in Leo

- **Keywords**: Confidence, creativity, leadership, passion
- **Magic Focus**: The Moon in Leo is all about personal empowerment, self-expression, and creativity. This is a great time for spells that boost confidence, enhance your public image, or spark creative endeavors.
- **Best for**: Glamour spells, self-confidence, leadership, creativity and artistic expression, love and attraction.

Moon in Virgo

- **Keywords**: Organization, health, service, practicality
- **Magic Focus**: Virgo energy is perfect for organizing, planning, and attending to the details. Use this time for spells focused on health, well-being, and refining your plans for the future.
- **Best for**: Health and wellness magic, organizational spells, rituals for purification, self-improvement, job and work-related magic.

Moon in Libra

- **Keywords**: Balance, harmony, beauty, relationships
- **Magic Focus**: The Moon in Libra is ideal for spells related to love, partnerships, and bringing balance to various areas of your life. This is a great time for relationship healing, creating harmony, and working on legal matters.
- **Best for**: Love spells, relationship harmony, beauty magic, peace-making, legal and contractual matters.

Moon in Scorpio

- **Keywords**: Transformation, intensity, power, secrets
- **Magic Focus**: Scorpio's energy is intense and transformative, making it ideal for deep emotional work, banishing negative influences, and uncovering hidden truths. This is a powerful time for shadow work and transformation spells.
- **Best for**: Banishing spells, protection, transformation and rebirth, psychic development, deep emotional healing, uncovering secrets.

Moon in Sagittarius

- **Keywords**: Exploration, freedom, adventure, growth
- **Magic Focus**: The Moon in Sagittarius brings expansive, optimistic energy, ideal for spells related to growth, adventure, and personal expansion. Use this time to focus on travel, learning, and broadening your horizons.
- **Best for**: Travel magic, higher learning, exploration, luck and optimism, manifesting new opportunities, long-distance communication.

Moon in Capricorn

- **Keywords**: Discipline, ambition, authority, structure
- **Magic Focus**: Capricorn energy is practical and disciplined, making it ideal for spells focused on career, long-term goals, and building solid foundations. This is a good time for business and financial magic.
- **Best for**: Career and business success, financial growth, goal-setting, discipline and self-control, leadership and authority.

Moon in Aquarius

- **Keywords**: Innovation, independence, community, intuition
- **Magic Focus**: The Moon in Aquarius brings a focus on innovation, individuality, and community. This is a good time for spells that break away from tradition, encourage independence, or help you connect with like-minded people.
- **Best for**: Social justice, community building, innovation, breaking free from constraints, intuitive and futuristic magic, technology-related spells.

Moon in Pisces

- **Keywords**: Spirituality, intuition, dreams, compassion
- **Magic Focus**: Pisces energy is deeply spiritual and intuitive, making it a great time for dream work, divination, and spells related to compassion and emotional healing. This is also a perfect time for exploring your subconscious and psychic abilities.
- **Best for**: Dream magic, psychic development, emotional healing, compassion, spiritual growth, water element magic.

Working with Moon Sign Magic in Your Practice

When planning your magical work, aligning your spells with the Moon's zodiac sign can significantly enhance the energy you're working with. For example, if you want to cast a spell for financial prosperity, the Moon in Taurus or Capricorn would provide the most supportive energy for such work. If you're focusing on self-love and creativity, the Moon in Leo might be more appropriate.

Here are some tips for incorporating Moon sign magic into your practice:

1. **Plan Ahead**: Use the moon sign chart (provided below) to plan your rituals and spellwork according to the Moon's zodiac placement.
2. **Combine Lunar Phases with Moon Signs**: Enhance your magic by combining the Moon phase with its zodiac sign. For example, during a Full Moon in Scorpio, you might focus on releasing emotional baggage or uncovering hidden truths.
3. **Meditate with the Moon Sign Energy**: On the day of a powerful Moon transit, take time to meditate and connect with the specific energy of the sign. Visualize how you can integrate its qualities into your spellwork.
4. **Journal Your Results**: Keep a moon magic journal where you document your spellwork and rituals based on the Moon's zodiac sign. Over time, you'll notice patterns in how each Moon sign affects your practice.

Monthly Moon Sign Charts for 2025

Below is a monthly breakdown of the Moon's journey through the zodiac in 2025. Each day, the Moon shifts between signs, and understanding this movement helps you plan your magical work for the most supportive energies. The chart includes the date ranges for each Moon sign each month, allowing you to tailor your spells to the lunar energies available.

January 2025 Moon Sign Chart

- **Jan 1-2**: Moon in Capricorn
- **Jan 3-4**: Moon in Aquarius
- **Jan 5-7**: Moon in Pisces
- **Jan 8-9**: Moon in Aries
- **Jan 10-12**: Moon in Taurus
- **Jan 13-14**: Moon in Gemini
- **Jan 15-17**: Moon in Cancer
- **Jan 18-19**: Moon in Leo
- **Jan 20-21**: Moon in Virgo
- **Jan 22-23**: Moon in Libra
- **Jan 24-26**: Moon in Scorpio
- **Jan 27-28**: Moon in Sagittarius
- **Jan 29-30**: Moon in Capricorn
- **Jan 31**: Moon in Aquarius

February 2025 Moon Sign Chart

- **Feb 1-2**: Moon in Aquarius
- **Feb 3-5**: Moon in Pisces
- **Feb 6-7**: Moon in Aries
- **Feb 8-9**: Moon in Taurus
- **Feb 10-12**: Moon in Gemini
- **Feb 13-14**: Moon in Cancer
- **Feb 15-17**: Moon in Leo
- **Feb 18-19**: Moon in Virgo
- **Feb 20-21**: Moon in Libra
- **Feb 22-23**: Moon in Scorpio
- **Feb 24-26**: Moon in Sagittarius
- **Feb 27-28**: Moon in Capricorn

March 2025 Moon Sign Chart

- **Mar 1-2**: Moon in Aquarius
- **Mar 3-4**: Moon in Pisces
- **Mar 5-7**: Moon in Aries
- **Mar 8-9**: Moon in Taurus
- **Mar 10-11**: Moon in Gemini
- **Mar 12-14**: Moon in Cancer
- **Mar 15-16**: Moon in Leo
- **Mar 17-18**: Moon in Virgo
- **Mar 19-20**: Moon in Libra
- **Mar 21-22**: Moon in Scorpio
- **Mar 23-24**: Moon in Sagittarius
- **Mar 25-26**: Moon in Capricorn
- **Mar 27-28**: Moon in Aquarius
- **Mar 29-30**: Moon in Pisces
- **Mar 31**: Moon in Aries

April 2025 Moon Sign Chart

- **Apr 1**: Moon in Aries
- **Apr 2-3**: Moon in Taurus
- **Apr 4-6**: Moon in Gemini
- **Apr 7-8**: Moon in Cancer
- **Apr 9-10**: Moon in Leo
- **Apr 11-12**: Moon in Virgo
- **Apr 13-14**: Moon in Libra
- **Apr 15-17**: Moon in Scorpio
- **Apr 18-19**: Moon in Sagittarius
- **Apr 20-21**: Moon in Capricorn
- **Apr 22-23**: Moon in Aquarius
- **Apr 24-25**: Moon in Pisces
- **Apr 26-27**: Moon in Aries
- **Apr 28-29**: Moon in Taurus
- **Apr 30**: Moon in Gemini

May 2025 Moon Sign Chart

- **May 1-2**: Moon in Gemini
- **May 3-4**: Moon in Cancer
- **May 5-6**: Moon in Leo
- **May 7-8**: Moon in Virgo
- **May 9-10**: Moon in Libra
- **May 11-13**: Moon in Scorpio
- **May 14-15**: Moon in Sagittarius
- **May 16-17**: Moon in Capricorn
- **May 18-20**: Moon in Aquarius
- **May 21-22**: Moon in Pisces
- **May 23-25**: Moon in Aries
- **May 26-27**: Moon in Taurus
- **May 28-29**: Moon in Gemini
- **May 30-31**: Moon in Cancer

June 2025 Moon Sign Chart

- **Jun 1**: Moon in Cancer
- **Jun 2-3**: Moon in Leo
- **Jun 4-5**: Moon in Virgo
- **Jun 6-7**: Moon in Libra
- **Jun 8-9**: Moon in Scorpio
- **Jun 10-12**: Moon in Sagittarius
- **Jun 13-14**: Moon in Capricorn
- **Jun 15-16**: Moon in Aquarius
- **Jun 17-18**: Moon in Pisces
- **Jun 19-20**: Moon in Aries
- **Jun 21-22**: Moon in Taurus
- **Jun 23-24**: Moon in Gemini
- **Jun 25-26**: Moon in Cancer
- **Jun 27-28**: Moon in Leo
- **Jun 29-30**: Moon in Virgo

July 2025 Moon Sign Chart

- **Jul 1**: Moon in Virgo
- **Jul 2-3**: Moon in Libra
- **Jul 4-5**: Moon in Scorpio
- **Jul 6-7**: Moon in Sagittarius
- **Jul 8-10**: Moon in Capricorn
- **Jul 11-12**: Moon in Aquarius
- **Jul 13-14**: Moon in Pisces
- **Jul 15-16**: Moon in Aries
- **Jul 17-18**: Moon in Taurus
- **Jul 19-20**: Moon in Gemini
- **Jul 21-23**: Moon in Cancer
- **Jul 24-25**: Moon in Leo
- **Jul 26-27**: Moon in Virgo
- **Jul 28-29**: Moon in Libra
- **Jul 30-31**: Moon in Scorpio

August 2025 Moon Sign Chart

- **Aug 1**: Moon in Scorpio
- **Aug 2-3**: Moon in Sagittarius
- **Aug 4-5**: Moon in Capricorn
- **Aug 6-7**: Moon in Aquarius
- **Aug 8-9**: Moon in Pisces
- **Aug 10-12**: Moon in Aries
- **Aug 13-14**: Moon in Taurus
- **Aug 15-16**: Moon in Gemini
- **Aug 17-18**: Moon in Cancer
- **Aug 19-20**: Moon in Leo
- **Aug 21-22**: Moon in Virgo
- **Aug 23-24**: Moon in Libra
- **Aug 25-27**: Moon in Scorpio
- **Aug 28-29**: Moon in Sagittarius
- **Aug 30-31**: Moon in Capricorn

September 2025 Moon Sign Chart

- **Sep 1**: Moon in Capricorn
- **Sep 2-3**: Moon in Aquarius
- **Sep 4-5**: Moon in Pisces
- **Sep 6-7**: Moon in Aries
- **Sep 8-9**: Moon in Taurus
- **Sep 10-11**: Moon in Gemini
- **Sep 12-13**: Moon in Cancer
- **Sep 14-15**: Moon in Leo
- **Sep 16-17**: Moon in Virgo
- **Sep 18-19**: Moon in Libra
- **Sep 20-21**: Moon in Scorpio
- **Sep 22-23**: Moon in Sagittarius
- **Sep 24-25**: Moon in Capricorn
- **Sep 26-27**: Moon in Aquarius
- **Sep 28-29**: Moon in Pisces
- **Sep 30**: Moon in Aries

October 2025 Moon Sign Chart

- **Oct 1-2**: Moon in Aries
- **Oct 3-4**: Moon in Taurus
- **Oct 5-6**: Moon in Gemini
- **Oct 7-8**: Moon in Cancer
- **Oct 9-11**: Moon in Leo
- **Oct 12-13**: Moon in Virgo
- **Oct 14-15**: Moon in Libra
- **Oct 16-17**: Moon in Scorpio
- **Oct 18-19**: Moon in Sagittarius
- **Oct 20-22**: Moon in Capricorn
- **Oct 23-24**: Moon in Aquarius
- **Oct 25-26**: Moon in Pisces
- **Oct 27-28**: Moon in Aries
- **Oct 29-30**: Moon in Taurus
- **Oct 31**: Moon in Gemini

November 2025 Moon Sign Chart

- **Nov 1**: Moon in Gemini
- **Nov 2-3**: Moon in Cancer
- **Nov 4-6**: Moon in Leo
- **Nov 7-8**: Moon in Virgo
- **Nov 9-10**: Moon in Libra
- **Nov 11-12**: Moon in Scorpio
- **Nov 13-14**: Moon in Sagittarius
- **Nov 15-17**: Moon in Capricorn
- **Nov 18-19**: Moon in Aquarius
- **Nov 20-22**: Moon in Pisces
- **Nov 23-24**: Moon in Aries
- **Nov 25-27**: Moon in Taurus
- **Nov 28-29**: Moon in Gemini
- **Nov 30**: Moon in Cancer

December 2025 Moon Sign Chart

- **Dec 1-2**: Moon in Cancer
- **Dec 3-4**: Moon in Leo
- **Dec 5-6**: Moon in Virgo
- **Dec 7-9**: Moon in Libra
- **Dec 10-11**: Moon in Scorpio
- **Dec 12-13**: Moon in Sagittarius
- **Dec 14-15**: Moon in Capricorn
- **Dec 16-17**: Moon in Aquarius
- **Dec 18-19**: Moon in Pisces
- **Dec 20-22**: Moon in Aries
- **Dec 23-24**: Moon in Taurus
- **Dec 25-26**: Moon in Gemini
- **Dec 27-29**: Moon in Cancer
- **Dec 30-31**: Moon in Leo

Conclusion

Understanding how the Moon's transit through the zodiac influences your emotions, intuition, and spellwork can add depth and precision to your magical practice. By using the moon sign charts provided, you can plan your rituals, spells, and intentions according to the most supportive lunar energies. Whether you're focusing on love, career, emotional healing, or personal growth, aligning your work with the Moon's zodiac sign enhances your connection to the cosmos and amplifies the power of your magic.

Chapter 14: Spellwork for the Elements: Earth, Air, Fire, Water

In witchcraft and magical practice, the four classical elements—Earth, Air, Fire, and Water—are essential forces that shape the natural world and the universe. Each element carries distinct qualities, energies, and correspondences that can be harnessed in spellwork for different purposes. Working with the elements allows practitioners to align with the foundational forces of nature, invoking their powers to enhance spells, rituals, and magical intentions.

This chapter provides an in-depth exploration of elemental magic, detailing how to time spells according to elemental days, celestial events, and the Moon's phases. Additionally, you'll find correspondences for each element and guidance on how to incorporate these forces into your magical practice.

The Four Elements in Magic

The elements are central to many magical traditions. In astrology, each zodiac sign is governed by one of the four elements, while in magic, they correspond to different forms of energy, intentions, and manifestations. Each element also governs specific magical practices, making them ideal for certain types of spells and rituals. Here's an overview of the characteristics of each element:

Earth Element

- **Qualities**: Grounded, stable, practical, nurturing, patient
- **Magic Focus**: Earth governs all things related to stability, growth, abundance, and material security. It is the element of manifestation and fertility, making it perfect for spells involving prosperity, health, grounding, and protection.
- **Tools and Symbols**: Stones, crystals, soil, pentacle, herbs
- **Zodiac Signs**: Taurus, Virgo, Capricorn
- **Direction**: North
- **Season**: Winter
- **Colors**: Green, brown, black
- **Deities**: Gaia, Demeter, Cernunnos, Rhea

Air Element

- **Qualities**: Intellectual, communicative, free-flowing, adaptable, curious
- **Magic Focus**: Air governs communication, ideas, creativity, and mental clarity. It is associated with inspiration, wisdom, and the mind. Air spells are often related to intellect, learning, divination, and the power of words.
- **Tools and Symbols**: Feathers, incense, athame, smoke
- **Zodiac Signs**: Gemini, Libra, Aquarius
- **Direction**: East
- **Season**: Spring
- **Colors**: Yellow, white, light blue
- **Deities**: Hermes, Athena, Thoth, Mercury

Fire Element

- **Qualities**: Passionate, transformative, energetic, bold, destructive, creative
- **Magic Focus**: Fire is the element of energy, action, transformation, and willpower. It governs spells related to passion, creativity, strength, and courage. Fire can be used in both constructive (creation) and destructive (banishing) magic.
- **Tools and Symbols**: Candles, flames, sun symbols, cauldrons
- **Zodiac Signs**: Aries, Leo, Sagittarius
- **Direction**: South
- **Season**: Summer
- **Colors**: Red, orange, gold
- **Deities**: Brigid, Hestia, Pele, Sekhmet

Water Element

- **Qualities**: Emotional, intuitive, fluid, receptive, nurturing
- **Magic Focus**: Water governs emotions, intuition, dreams, and healing. It is linked to the subconscious, psychic abilities, and purification. Water spells are commonly used for emotional healing, fertility, love, and dream work.
- **Tools and Symbols**: Chalices, seashells, water, mirrors
- **Zodiac Signs**: Cancer, Scorpio, Pisces
- **Direction**: West
- **Season**: Autumn
- **Colors**: Blue, silver, teal
- **Deities**: Aphrodite, Yemaya, Poseidon, Isis

Timing Spells According to Elemental Days

Each day of the week is associated with a particular planet, which corresponds to certain elements. By timing your spells according to the day and the element associated with it, you can amplify the energy of your magical workings.

Elemental Days of the Week

- **Monday (Moon)**: Water – A day for intuition, emotions, dreams, and psychic work. Use for spells related to emotional healing, fertility, and divination.
- **Tuesday (Mars)**: Fire – A day for courage, strength, and action. Best for spells requiring boldness, such as protection, banishing, and motivation.
- **Wednesday (Mercury)**: Air – A day for communication, learning, and intellect. Ideal for spells related to knowledge, wisdom, creativity, and mental clarity.
- **Thursday (Jupiter)**: Fire/Earth – A day of abundance, prosperity, and growth. Thursday's energy supports financial success, career spells, and long-term planning.
- **Friday (Venus)**: Water – A day of love, beauty, and relationships. Use for love spells, friendship, emotional healing, and creativity.
- **Saturday (Saturn)**: Earth – A day for discipline, protection, and long-term goals. Perfect for grounding spells, protection rituals, and banishing negativity.
- **Sunday (Sun)**: Fire – A day for success, personal power, and creativity. Use for rituals focused on self-confidence, leadership, and life direction.

Correspondences of Elements with Moon Phases

The Moon's phases are integral to many forms of magic, and each phase corresponds to a particular type of spellwork. Combining the Moon's phase with the elemental energy you need can amplify the potency of your rituals.

New Moon (Initiation and Beginnings)

- **Elemental Focus**: Air
- **Best for**: New beginnings, setting intentions, intellectual pursuits, creativity, and planning. The New Moon is a time to tap into the Air element for spells related to inspiration, new ideas, and communication.
- **Spell Example**: A spell to gain clarity on a new project or venture, using the Air element to stimulate mental focus and fresh perspectives.

Waxing Moon (Growth and Expansion)

- **Elemental Focus**: Earth
- **Best for**: Prosperity, abundance, growth, and material gains. The Waxing Moon phase is ideal for spells related to increasing wealth, health, and physical resources.
- **Spell Example**: A prosperity spell using Earth-based materials like soil or crystals to attract financial abundance or career growth.

Full Moon (Power and Manifestation)

- **Elemental Focus**: Fire
- **Best for**: Manifestation, empowerment, and transformation. The Full Moon is a powerful time to harness Fire energy for spells that require courage, passion, and creativity.
- **Spell Example**: A ritual for manifesting a personal goal or desire, using the Fire element through candle magic to intensify the spell's outcome.

Waning Moon (Release and Banishment)

- **Elemental Focus**: Water
- **Best for**: Letting go, emotional healing, banishing negativity, and purification. The Waning Moon is aligned with Water, making it perfect for cleansing rituals and spells to release emotional burdens.
- **Spell Example**: A cleansing bath ritual using the Water element to release stress, negative emotions, or unhealthy attachments during the Waning Moon.

Timing Spells with Celestial Events

In addition to the Moon phases, other celestial events such as eclipses, meteor showers, and planetary alignments provide opportunities for powerful spellwork. Here's how you can align the elements with these celestial events.

Solar Eclipses (Transformation and Rebirth)

- **Elemental Focus**: Fire and Air
- **Magic Focus**: Solar eclipses are potent moments for transformation, especially when breaking free from old patterns or starting anew. Use the combined energies of Fire for action and Air for clarity in your spells.
- **Best for**: Transformation, manifesting change, new beginnings, courage spells, personal empowerment.

Lunar Eclipses (Emotional Healing and Closure)

- **Elemental Focus**: Water and Earth
- **Magic Focus**: Lunar eclipses are tied to deep emotional shifts and closures. Use Water for emotional healing and Earth for grounding during this potent time for releasing old patterns.
- **Best for**: Emotional healing, closure, letting go of toxic relationships, and ancestral work.

Meteor Showers (Wishes and Manifestation)

- **Elemental Focus**: Air and Fire
- **Magic Focus**: Meteor showers carry the energy of the cosmos and are often seen as moments of wishing or manifesting. Air provides inspiration and mental clarity, while Fire adds the passion and energy needed to drive your desires forward.
- **Best for**: Wish magic, manifestation, dream work, and long-term goal setting.

Planetary Alignments (Amplified Magic)

- **Elemental Focus**: Depends on the planets involved
- **Magic Focus**: When planets align, the elemental energies associated with each planet are heightened. For example, a Venus and Mars conjunction would amplify Water (love) and Fire (passion), making it ideal for spells focusing on relationships, creativity, or desire.
- **Best for**: Love, balance, career advancement, creativity, and passion.

How to Incorporate the Elements into Your Spellwork

Incorporating the elements into your magical practice doesn't require elaborate tools or rituals—often, it's about simply attuning yourself to the elemental energy that best matches your intentions. Here are a few ways to integrate elemental correspondences into your spells:

1. Altar Elements

Incorporate symbols of each element on your altar to represent the balance of Earth, Air, Fire, and Water. For example:

- Earth: Crystals, soil, plants, stones
- Air: Feathers, incense, bells
- Fire: Candles, a cauldron, sun symbols
- Water: A chalice, seashells, mirrors, or bowls of water

2. Elemental Incantations

Use elemental invocations in your spells to call upon the energy of a specific element. For example, before casting a protection spell, invoke Earth energy by chanting:

"I call upon the Earth, steady and strong,
To ground me, protect me, where I belong."

3. Elemental Talismans

Create talismans or charms infused with the energy of a particular element to carry with you. For prosperity, use Earth-based items like green stones or herbs. For communication spells, choose a feather or other Air symbol to enhance mental clarity.

4. Elemental Offerings

As part of your spell or ritual, offer something back to the element you're working with. For example, when working with Earth, bury a crystal or seeds as an offering. When working with Fire, burn a piece of parchment with your intention written on it.

Conclusion

Understanding the elemental forces of Earth, Air, Fire, and Water allows you to work in harmony with the natural world and enhance the potency of your spells. By timing your spells according to elemental days, Moon phases, and celestial events, you can attune your magical practice to the most supportive energies. Whether you're grounding with Earth, manifesting with Fire, seeking wisdom with Air, or healing with Water, the elements provide a powerful foundation for every aspect of your magical journey.

Chapter 15: Best Times for Planting and Harvesting

For centuries, witches and practitioners of earth-based spirituality have turned to the cycles of the Moon to guide their planting and harvesting practices. The Moon's influence on the tides extends to all forms of growth, including plants. By aligning your gardening efforts with lunar phases and astrological signs, you can enhance the health and vitality of your plants, as well as the potency of the herbs you grow for magical purposes.

This chapter provides a detailed lunar gardening guide for witches, offering insights into the optimal times for planting, harvesting, and incorporating herbs into your magical practice. You will learn how the phases of the Moon and its transit through the zodiac affect the growth cycles of plants, and how to use this knowledge to plan your garden and create more potent herbal remedies, charms, and spells.

The Principles of Lunar Gardening

Lunar gardening is based on the belief that the Moon's gravitational pull affects water in the soil in much the same way it affects the tides. The waxing and waning cycles of the Moon influence the movement of moisture in the earth and the vitality of seeds and plants.

The primary components of lunar gardening include:

- **Moon Phases**: The Moon's waxing (increasing in light) and waning (decreasing in light) phases influence different aspects of plant growth.
- **Zodiac Signs**: Each zodiac sign has its own elemental and energetic influence on plants, and the Moon's transit through these signs affects the optimal times for planting and harvesting.
- **Planetary Influences**: Understanding how planetary movements, especially Mercury retrogrades and other planetary retrogrades, impact growth cycles can enhance your gardening success.

By timing your planting, pruning, and harvesting according to the Moon and astrological signs, you can enhance the growth and potency of your plants and herbs.

The Moon Phases and Gardening

Each phase of the Moon exerts a different influence on plant growth, and knowing how to align your gardening tasks with the lunar cycle is key to success in the garden. Here's a breakdown of how each phase of the Moon affects plants:

New Moon (Initiation and Beginnings)

- **Best for**: Planting seeds, transplanting, starting new projects.
- **Magic Focus**: The New Moon is a time for setting intentions, making it ideal for planting seeds—both literal and metaphorical—that you wish to grow into abundance.
- **Gardening Tasks**: Plant crops that produce above-ground fruits or vegetables, such as leafy greens, tomatoes, and beans. This is also a great time to plant fast-growing crops that you want to harvest quickly.

Waxing Crescent Moon (Growth and Building)

- **Best for**: Fertilizing, planting, grafting, nurturing new growth.
- **Magic Focus**: The Waxing Moon phase supports growth and expansion. This is an ideal time for cultivating abundance and nurturing things you wish to grow strong, whether they are plants or goals.
- **Gardening Tasks**: Continue planting above-ground crops, particularly those that have long growing seasons. Water your plants deeply and add compost or fertilizer to encourage robust growth.

First Quarter Moon (Strength and Expansion)

- **Best for**: Planting crops that require strong roots, supporting structural growth.
- **Magic Focus**: This phase is about building strength and resilience. Focus on cultivating strong foundations in your garden and in your life.
- **Gardening Tasks**: This is a good time to plant crops that benefit from sturdy stems or deep roots, such as corn, sunflowers, and cucumbers. It's also a good time for grafting and pruning.

Waxing Gibbous Moon (Anticipation and Maturation)

- **Best for**: Pruning, feeding, building soil health.
- **Magic Focus**: The Waxing Gibbous phase builds momentum toward the Full Moon. Use this time to nurture the strength and health of your plants and focus on personal or magical endeavors nearing fruition.
- **Gardening Tasks**: Prune back any dead or unhealthy growth, add nutrient-rich compost or fertilizers, and ensure that plants have the support they need to thrive. This is a time for checking the health of your garden and making necessary adjustments.

Full Moon (Abundance and Manifestation)

- **Best for**: Harvesting, pruning, magical work with herbs, and spells of abundance.
- **Magic Focus**: The Full Moon brings everything to its peak. This is the best time to harvest herbs for magic, as the plants will be at their most potent during this phase.
- **Gardening Tasks**: Harvest crops, especially those grown for fruit, leaves, or flowers, like tomatoes, lettuce, and herbs. It's also a good time for pruning to encourage future growth. If you're making herbal tinctures, salves, or teas, the Full Moon is when your harvested plants will be most magical and medicinally potent.

Waning Gibbous Moon (Reflection and Preparation)

- **Best for**: Harvesting root vegetables, weed control, and composting.
- **Magic Focus**: The Waning Moon is a time of release and preparation for the next cycle. Focus on clearing away what no longer serves you, both in your garden and in your life.
- **Gardening Tasks**: Harvest root crops such as carrots, potatoes, and beets. This is also a good time to focus on clearing away dead plants and weeds, as they are easier to manage when the Moon is waning.

Last Quarter Moon (Releasing and Decline)

- **Best for**: Clearing, pruning, weeding, pest control.
- **Magic Focus**: This phase is associated with banishing and letting go, making it an ideal time for weeding your garden and releasing any unwanted energies from your life.
- **Gardening Tasks**: Focus on removing dead or diseased plants, cutting back vines or trees, and eliminating pests. You can also prepare your soil for the next cycle by adding compost and allowing it to rest.

Waning Crescent Moon (Rest and Renewal)

- **Best for**: Clearing space, resting, spiritual renewal, magical reflection.
- **Magic Focus**: The Waning Crescent is a time for rest and reflection. Allow your garden to rest as well, and focus on spiritual renewal and planning for the next cycle.
- **Gardening Tasks**: Avoid planting or pruning during this phase. Focus on preparing your tools and planning for future planting cycles. Use this time to clear out old garden beds and clean your gardening tools.

Planting by the Zodiac Signs

In addition to the Moon phases, the Moon's position in the zodiac also influences plant growth. Each zodiac sign brings its elemental influence to the garden, and certain signs are considered more fertile than others. Here is how each zodiac sign affects gardening, along with the types of plants best suited to each sign:

Fertile Signs (Best for Planting)

- **Cancer**: The most fertile sign. Best for planting crops that need moisture, such as leafy greens, melons, and herbs. Ideal for any type of nurturing or growth.
- **Scorpio**: Fertile and productive. Good for planting root crops, herbs, and medicinal plants. Scorpio's depth makes it excellent for long-lasting crops.
- **Pisces**: Fertile and abundant. Excellent for planting flowers, herbs, and plants used in magic or medicine. Pisces energy enhances intuitive plant work and spiritual connections with the garden.
- **Taurus**: Productive and stable. Best for root crops, leafy vegetables, and anything requiring solid growth and stability, such as trees or shrubs.

Semi-Fertile Signs (Good for Planting with Focus)

- **Libra**: Airy and balanced. Good for flowers, vines, and decorative plants. Libra's energy supports beauty and harmony in the garden.
- **Capricorn**: Grounded and determined. Best for planting root vegetables and plants that require long-term growth. Capricorn is ideal for slow-growing crops and establishing long-term garden projects.

Barren Signs (Not Ideal for Planting)

- **Aries**: A barren, fiery sign. Best for pruning, weeding, or clearing space. Avoid planting during Aries, as its energy can scorch new growth.
- **Leo**: Another barren, fiery sign. Ideal for harvesting or removing old plants, but not for planting. Use Leo's energy for pruning or harvesting fruits that need strong sun energy.
- **Sagittarius**: A semi-barren sign. While Sagittarius has a restless and expansive energy, it's not ideal for planting. Instead, focus on weeding, pruning, or general garden maintenance.
- **Aquarius**: A barren, airy sign. Avoid planting during this time. Instead, focus on tasks such as aerating the soil, organizing your garden, or making future planting plans.
- **Gemini**: A barren, airy sign. Best for pruning, weeding, or harvesting. While not suitable for planting, Gemini's quick energy is good for taking care of busy tasks like weeding or pruning vines.

Optimal Times for Planting, Harvesting, and Herbal Magic
Combining lunar phases, zodiac signs, and specific celestial events can create optimal windows for planting, harvesting, and using herbs in your magical practice. Here's a guide to planning your gardening year, including the best times for different tasks:

1. Planting for Growth

- **Best Moon Phases**: New Moon to First Quarter, Waxing Gibbous Moon
- **Best Signs**: Cancer, Taurus, Pisces, Scorpio
- **Ideal for**: Starting new garden projects, planting seeds, transplanting seedlings, and beginning crops that require a long growing season. Plant leafy greens, herbs, vegetables, and any crops that bear fruit above ground during these phases and signs.

2. Harvesting Herbs for Magic

- **Best Moon Phases**: Full Moon for peak potency, Waxing Gibbous for herbal magic focused on growth and abundance, Waning Gibbous for release and transformation.
- **Best Signs**: Pisces for spiritual herbs, Scorpio for deep emotional healing herbs, Cancer for nurturing herbs, Taurus for strong and stable plants.
- **Ideal for**: Harvesting herbs intended for use in magic, including tinctures, oils, teas, and charms. Herbs harvested during the Full Moon will be at their most potent, especially when used for healing, protection, or prosperity magic.

3. Pruning and Weeding

- **Best Moon Phases**: Last Quarter Moon, Waning Crescent Moon
- **Best Signs**: Aries, Leo, Gemini, Sagittarius
- **Ideal for**: Clearing out dead or overgrown plants, weeding the garden, and pruning trees or shrubs. This is a time for removing anything that no longer serves your garden and making space for new growth in the next cycle.

4. Root Crop Planting and Harvesting

- **Best Moon Phases**: Waning Moon (especially Last Quarter)
- **Best Signs**: Capricorn, Scorpio, Taurus, Virgo
- **Ideal for**: Planting and harvesting root crops such as carrots, potatoes, onions, and beets. The waning Moon pulls energy down into the Earth, making it an ideal time for nurturing strong root systems or harvesting underground crops.

5. Preparing Soil and Fertilizing

- **Best Moon Phases**: Waxing Crescent, First Quarter Moon
- **Best Signs**: Taurus, Virgo, Capricorn, Cancer
- **Ideal for**: Adding compost, enriching soil, or preparing garden beds for future planting. Use this time to focus on building the health and vitality of the earth itself, ensuring strong plant growth in the future.

Incorporating Magical Practices into Gardening

For witches and magical practitioners, gardening is not only about growing food and herbs but also about connecting with the Earth and using plant allies in spellwork. Here are some ways to combine magic with your gardening:

1. Moon Gardening Rituals

Create simple rituals to honor the Moon's influence on your garden. For example, perform a New Moon planting ritual where you bless your seeds with intentions for growth, prosperity, or healing. During the Full Moon, hold a ritual of gratitude and harvest your herbs for magic, knowing they are at their peak potency.

2. Herbal Talismans

As you plant your herbs, imbue them with your intentions. For example, plant rosemary for protection, lavender for peace, and basil for prosperity. As the plants grow, they will absorb the magical energy of the Earth and Moon, becoming powerful allies in your spells.

3. Elemental Gardening

Align your gardening tasks with the four elements. When working with Earth, focus on planting and rooting your garden. Call upon Fire's energy when pruning or harvesting sun-loving crops. Use Water's energy for nourishing and healing your plants, and invoke Air for inspiration when planning new garden designs.

Conclusion

Lunar gardening is a practice that allows witches and magical practitioners to align their gardening efforts with the cycles of the Moon, the zodiac, and the elements. By timing your planting, pruning, and harvesting according to these natural rhythms, you can enhance the vitality of your garden and the potency of the herbs you grow for magical purposes. Whether you're tending to a large garden or growing a small collection of herbs in your home, working with the Moon and the elements can deepen your connection to the Earth and empower your magical practice.

Chapter 16: Manifestation Spells by Celestial Event

Celestial events have long been revered as powerful moments for magical practice, especially when it comes to manifestation spells. The movements of the Sun, Moon, planets, and other cosmic bodies create energetic windows of opportunity that can amplify your intentions and bring them into reality. By aligning your manifestation spells with specific celestial events, you can harness the natural energies of the universe to bring about your desires with greater potency.

This chapter explores a variety of powerful rituals for manifesting during key cosmic alignments, including eclipses, planetary conjunctions, retrogrades, meteor showers, and other astronomical phenomena. Each ritual is designed to align your personal intentions with the celestial energy at play, offering step-by-step instructions and guidance on how to use these events for maximum manifestation power.

Understanding Celestial Energy and Manifestation

Celestial events create shifts in the energetic landscape, often opening portals for transformation, growth, and change. Different types of cosmic phenomena carry unique frequencies that can be channeled into specific kinds of manifestation spells. Understanding these influences allows you to work in harmony with the cosmos to co-create the reality you desire.

Types of Celestial Events and Their Magical Influence

1. **Eclipses**: Powerful moments of shadow and light, perfect for transformation and resetting your life path.
2. **Planetary Conjunctions**: Alignments that create strong synergies between planetary energies, amplifying certain types of magic (e.g., love, career, spiritual growth).
3. **Retrogrades**: Times of reflection and recalibration, ideal for manifesting change through introspection, release, and revision.
4. **Meteor Showers**: Magical moments associated with making wishes and manifesting dreams, often tied to fast results.
5. **Solstices and Equinoxes**: Seasonal markers that bring balance, renewal, and shifts in energy, perfect for manifesting growth, clarity, or new beginnings.

Manifestation Spells for Eclipses

Eclipses are among the most potent celestial events for magical work. They represent moments of powerful transformation, where the Sun and Moon align in a way that can significantly influence both the mundane and magical worlds. Eclipses are particularly effective for resetting your intentions, letting go of old patterns, and manifesting major life changes.

Solar Eclipse Manifestation Ritual

A **solar eclipse** occurs when the Moon passes between the Earth and the Sun, casting a shadow and blocking the Sun's light. This event symbolizes the union of conscious (Sun) and subconscious (Moon) energies, creating a perfect moment for manifesting life-changing goals and personal empowerment.

Best for: New beginnings, career advancement, self-confidence, personal transformation, and manifesting long-term goals.

Materials:

- A gold or yellow candle (representing the Sun)
- A silver or white candle (representing the Moon)
- A piece of gold or yellow paper
- A pen
- Sunstone or citrine crystal (for empowerment)
- Sage or incense for cleansing

Instructions:

1. **Prepare Your Space**: Cleanse your sacred space with sage or incense. Place the gold and silver candles on your altar, representing the Sun and the Moon.
2. **Set Your Intention**: Write your manifestation goal on the gold or yellow paper. Be specific about what you want to manifest, focusing on long-term desires like career success, personal empowerment, or transformation.
3. **Light the Candles**: As you light the gold (Sun) candle, say aloud:
   "I call upon the power of the Sun to bring light, clarity, and strength into my life."
   Light the silver (Moon) candle and say:
   "I call upon the wisdom of the Moon to guide my intuition and align my heart with my desires."
4. **Visualize**: Hold the Sunstone or citrine in your hands and visualize your intention coming to life. Imagine the union of the Sun and Moon creating a pathway for your desires to manifest.
5. **Speak Your Intention**: Recite your written intention aloud, then fold the paper and place it under the Sunstone or citrine.
6. **Close the Ritual**: Allow the candles to burn down completely, then bury the paper in the Earth or keep it in a sacred space until your manifestation comes to fruition.

Lunar Eclipse Manifestation Ritual

A **lunar eclipse** occurs when the Earth passes between the Sun and the Moon, blocking the Moon's light. Lunar eclipses are powerful times for releasing old patterns, emotional healing, and manifesting deep inner transformation.

Best for: Emotional healing, releasing limiting beliefs, banishing negativity, manifesting personal growth, and spiritual transformation.

Materials:

- A black candle (for release)
- A white candle (for renewal)
- A piece of paper and pen
- A clear quartz crystal (for clarity and healing)
- Sage or palo santo for cleansing

Instructions:

1. **Cleanse Your Space**: Burn sage or palo santo to cleanse the area where you will perform the ritual. Place the black and white candles on your altar.
2. **Write Your Release**: On the piece of paper, write down what you want to release—whether it's a limiting belief, a toxic relationship, or an old pattern that no longer serves you.
3. **Light the Black Candle**: As you light the black candle, say aloud:
   "I release all that no longer serves me. I let go of the past and make space for new beginnings."
4. **Burn the Paper**: Carefully burn the paper in the flame of the black candle (in a fireproof bowl), symbolizing the release of what you no longer need.
5. **Light the White Candle**: As you light the white candle, say aloud:
   "I welcome new light, healing, and growth into my life. I manifest clarity and positive transformation."
6. **Hold the Crystal**: Hold the clear quartz crystal in your hands and visualize yourself surrounded by light. Imagine the old energy being replaced with new, vibrant energy.
7. **Close the Ritual**: Allow both candles to burn down completely. Keep the crystal on your altar or near you as a reminder of the transformation you've initiated.

Manifestation Spells for Planetary Conjunctions

When planets align, their energies combine to create powerful influences that can be harnessed in your magical practice. Different planetary conjunctions offer unique opportunities for manifesting love, abundance, personal power, and spiritual growth.

Venus and Jupiter Conjunction Manifestation Ritual

A **Venus and Jupiter conjunction** is one of the most fortunate and expansive planetary alignments. Venus, the planet of love and beauty, combines with Jupiter, the planet of luck and abundance, to create a powerful window for manifesting love, prosperity, and joy.

Best for: Manifesting love, financial abundance, beauty, happiness, and success.

Materials:

- A pink or green candle (for Venus)
- A gold candle (for Jupiter)
- Rose petals or a favorite flower (symbolizing beauty and love)
- A small bowl of water (symbolizing flow and abundance)
- A piece of rose quartz or jade (for love and prosperity)

Instructions:

1. **Set Up Your Space**: Create a sacred space with the pink (or green) and gold candles. Place the bowl of water in front of the candles and scatter rose petals around the area.

2. **Set Your Intention**: Hold the rose quartz or jade and focus on what you want to manifest. Whether it's financial abundance, a new love, or increased happiness, be specific in your desires.

3. **Light the Candles**: Light the Venus (pink/green) candle and say:

   "I call upon Venus, the goddess of love and beauty, to bring harmony, joy, and love into my life."

   Light the Jupiter (gold) candle and say:

   "I call upon Jupiter, the planet of abundance, to bring prosperity, success, and happiness into my life."

4. **Visualize Your Desire**: Hold the crystal over the bowl of water and visualize your desire flowing into the water, filling it with the energy of love and abundance.

5. **Speak Your Intention**: Say aloud:

   "With the power of Venus and Jupiter, I manifest [state your desire]. I open myself to receive the blessings of love, prosperity, and joy."

6. **Close the Ritual**: Allow the candles to burn down. Keep the water in the bowl for 24 hours on your altar, then pour it into the Earth as an offering. Keep the crystal as a talisman to remind you of your intention.

Mars and Pluto Conjunction Manifestation Ritual

A **Mars and Pluto conjunction** brings intense, transformative energy, combining Mars' action and courage with Pluto's power of deep transformation. This alignment is perfect for manifesting personal power, breaking through obstacles, and initiating profound change in your life.

Best for: Manifesting personal power, overcoming obstacles, transformation, breaking through fears, and embracing your strength.

Materials:

- A red candle (for Mars)
- A black candle (for Pluto)
- A piece of obsidian or garnet (for protection and power)
- A small mirror (for reflection and transformation)

Instructions:

1. **Cleanse Your Space**: Use sage or palo santo to cleanse your sacred space. Place the red and black candles on either side of the mirror.
2. **Set Your Intention**: Hold the obsidian or garnet in your hands and think about what you want to manifest—whether it's personal empowerment, overcoming fears, or breaking through a difficult situation.
3. **Light the Red Candle**: As you light the red candle, say:
   "I call upon the power of Mars to ignite my strength, courage, and determination. I am ready to act."
4. **Light the Black Candle**: As you light the black candle, say:
   "I call upon the power of Pluto to guide me through transformation and help me shed what no longer serves me."
5. **Focus on the Mirror**: Look into the mirror and see yourself as the empowered, transformed version of who you want to become. Visualize the obstacles in your path dissolving as you step into your personal power.
6. **Speak Your Intention**: Recite:
   "With the combined power of Mars and Pluto, I manifest my strength and transformation. I break free from all that holds me back, and I rise as my most powerful self."
7. **Close the Ritual**: Allow the candles to burn down. Keep the mirror on your altar as a reminder of your transformation, and carry the obsidian or garnet as a protective talisman.

Manifestation Spells for Retrogrades

Retrogrades, especially **Mercury retrograde**, are often seen as challenging times, but they also offer opportunities for introspection, reflection, and recalibration. Retrogrades are perfect for manifestation spells that focus on revision, breaking bad habits, and releasing old energy to make space for new growth.

Mercury Retrograde Manifestation Ritual

Mercury retrograde is known for disrupting communication, travel, and technology, but it's also an ideal time for clearing away old energy and reworking past plans. Use this retrograde energy to revise, reflect, and manifest clarity in areas that have been stuck.

Best for: Revising plans, improving communication, breaking bad habits, and manifesting clarity and understanding.

Materials:

- A blue candle (for communication)
- A piece of paper and pen
- A clear quartz crystal (for clarity)
- Lavender oil or incense (for peace and calm)

Instructions:

1. **Cleanse Your Space**: Light lavender incense or diffuse lavender oil to create a calming atmosphere.
2. **Write Your Revision**: On a piece of paper, write down something you want to revise or improve in your life. It could be a relationship, a project, or a habit you want to break.
3. **Light the Blue Candle**: As you light the blue candle, say:
   "I call upon Mercury to bring clarity, reflection, and understanding. I welcome this time of revision and renewal."
4. **Visualize Your Revision**: Hold the clear quartz crystal and visualize the situation or habit improving. Imagine yourself communicating clearly, making wise decisions, and releasing old patterns.
5. **Speak Your Intention**: Recite:
   "During this retrograde, I manifest clarity, healing, and renewal. I release what no longer serves me and welcome new understanding and growth."
6. **Close the Ritual**: Allow the candle to burn down. Keep the paper in a safe place, and reflect on your progress throughout the retrograde period. Revisit your intention once Mercury turns direct.

Manifestation Spells for Meteor Showers

Meteor showers are magical cosmic events often associated with making wishes and manifesting dreams. The sudden burst of energy from a meteor shower can be used to accelerate manifestation spells, particularly those focused on dreams, success, and rapid changes.

Meteor Shower Manifestation Ritual

Best for: Making wishes, manifesting dreams, bringing swift change, and aligning with cosmic energies.

Materials:

- A wish stone (such as a piece of clear quartz or a stone you find special)
- A piece of paper and pen
- A white candle
- A blanket (if performing the ritual outdoors)

Instructions:

1. **Prepare Your Space**: If possible, perform this ritual outdoors under the meteor shower. Lay out a blanket and set up your candle. If indoors, simply place your candle in a window where you can see the night sky.
2. **Set Your Intention**: Write your wish or dream on a piece of paper. Be clear and specific about what you want to manifest.
3. **Light the White Candle**: As you light the candle, say:
   "I call upon the magic of the stars, the cosmic forces that connect us all. I make my wish with an open heart, trusting the universe to bring it to life."
4. **Make Your Wish**: Hold your wish stone in your hands and focus on your desire. Visualize the meteor shower's energy flowing into your wish, accelerating its manifestation.
5. **Release Your Wish**: Hold the piece of paper to your chest and then release it to the wind or burn it (safely) in the candle's flame as a symbol of releasing your wish to the universe.
6. **Close the Ritual**: Allow the candle to burn down completely. Keep the wish stone with you as a reminder of the power of your wish.

Manifestation Spells for Solstices and Equinoxes

Solstices and equinoxes are key points in the Wheel of the Year that mark significant shifts in energy. These celestial events offer powerful opportunities for manifestation, depending on the season and the balance of light and dark.

Winter Solstice Manifestation Ritual

The **Winter Solstice** is the longest night of the year, marking the rebirth of the Sun and the return of light. It's a powerful time for manifesting renewal, new beginnings, and hope.

Best for: New beginnings, spiritual rebirth, manifesting hope, and planting seeds for the future.

Materials:

- A white or gold candle (symbolizing the returning Sun)
- A small bowl of water (symbolizing renewal)
- A green sprig (such as pine or holly, symbolizing life)

Instructions:

1. **Prepare Your Space**: Cleanse your space with sage or palo santo and place the candle, bowl of water, and green sprig on your altar.
2. **Set Your Intention**: Focus on what new beginning you wish to manifest in the coming year. This could be a new project, relationship, or personal transformation.
3. **Light the Candle**: As you light the candle, say:
   "On this longest night, I welcome the return of the Sun, the light of hope and renewal. I manifest new beginnings and open myself to the possibilities of the year to come."
4. **Make Your Offering**: Place the green sprig in the bowl of water, symbolizing the rebirth of life and your intentions for growth. Visualize your wish growing and flourishing as the light of the Sun returns.
5. **Close the Ritual**: Allow the candle to burn down completely. Keep the green sprig on your altar as a reminder of the life and light you've invited into your life.

Conclusion

By aligning your manifestation spells with celestial events such as eclipses, planetary conjunctions, retrogrades, meteor showers, and solstices, you can tap into the powerful forces of the universe to bring your desires into reality. Each cosmic event carries unique energies that amplify different types of magic, offering you opportunities to create, transform, and manifest with greater potency. Whether you are seeking love, abundance, personal growth, or spiritual transformation, the stars and planets are your allies in the art of manifestation.

Chapter 17: Prosperity Magic

Prosperity magic focuses on attracting abundance, wealth, financial security, and overall success in your personal and professional life. Whether you're seeking to improve your financial situation, cultivate a mindset of abundance, or manifest opportunities for growth, prosperity magic can help align your energy with the flow of wealth and abundance in the universe.

This chapter explores the principles behind prosperity magic, the best times to perform abundance spells, and step-by-step rituals for drawing financial blessings into your life. We'll cover lunar and solar phases, planetary alignments, and other cosmic events that can enhance your prosperity magic. You'll also learn how to incorporate specific symbols, herbs, crystals, and deities associated with wealth and abundance.

Understanding Prosperity Magic

Prosperity magic is based on the belief that abundance is a flow of energy that you can tap into. It's not just about material wealth but also about opening yourself to opportunities, resources, and relationships that bring value to your life. Prosperity magic helps you align your thoughts, actions, and spiritual energy with this flow of abundance, creating a positive feedback loop where wealth and success naturally gravitate toward you.

In this form of magic, intention and mindset are crucial. Prosperity magic requires a clear focus on what abundance means to you. It could be financial wealth, career success, spiritual growth, or even emotional richness in relationships. The key is to approach prosperity with gratitude, generosity, and openness, which enhances the magnetic energy you project into the universe.

Timing Prosperity Magic for Maximum Effect

Just like planting seeds for a bountiful harvest, prosperity spells are more effective when aligned with specific lunar phases, planetary transits, and celestial events. Timing your rituals according to the flow of cosmic energies can significantly boost the potency of your manifestation efforts.

Lunar Phases and Prosperity Spells

The phases of the Moon play a major role in prosperity magic, as the Moon governs cycles of growth, abundance, and reflection. Here's how to work with each lunar phase for prosperity spells:

- **New Moon**: The New Moon is a time for setting intentions and planting the seeds of what you want to manifest. This is an excellent time for initiating spells related to new financial ventures, setting wealth goals, or starting a new career path.

  Best for: Starting new projects, attracting new income streams, setting financial goals.

- **Waxing Moon**: As the Moon grows in light, it symbolizes growth and expansion. This is the perfect time for building upon the foundations you set during the New Moon. Prosperity spells performed during the Waxing Moon focus on attracting more abundance and nurturing the growth of wealth and resources.

Best for: Increasing wealth, attracting business opportunities, expanding income.

- **Full Moon**: The Full Moon represents the peak of power and abundance. It is the most potent time for manifesting prosperity and achieving your financial goals. This phase is ideal for rituals that solidify wealth, attract major financial breakthroughs, or secure long-term financial security.

Best for: Manifesting financial windfalls, sealing abundance spells, achieving financial goals.

- **Waning Moon**: The Waning Moon is a time for releasing blockages and letting go of financial patterns that no longer serve you. This phase is ideal for clearing debt, removing financial obstacles, or breaking through limiting beliefs about wealth.

Best for: Clearing debt, removing financial blockages, banishing poverty mindset.

Planetary Correspondences for Prosperity Magic

Each planet governs different aspects of life, including wealth and abundance. By aligning your prosperity spells with the planetary influences, you can harness their energy for greater success.

- **Jupiter (Planet of Wealth and Expansion)**: Jupiter is the planet of abundance, prosperity, and growth. It's the ideal planetary influence for any prosperity spell. Thursdays, ruled by Jupiter, are the best days to work on abundance and success spells.

Best for: Expanding wealth, attracting success, financial growth, business opportunities.

- **Venus (Planet of Money and Luxury)**: Venus governs money, luxury, and beauty. While often associated with love, Venus is also connected to material wealth and the flow of money. Fridays, ruled by Venus, are ideal for spells related to personal finances, luxury, and material abundance.

Best for: Attracting luxury, increasing personal finances, enhancing financial attractiveness.

- **Saturn (Planet of Discipline and Long-Term Success)**: Saturn may seem like a challenging planet for prosperity magic, but its energy of discipline and structure is perfect for manifesting long-term financial security. Saturday, ruled by Saturn, is a good day for spells aimed at building a stable financial future, clearing debt, and setting realistic financial goals.

Best for: Financial planning, long-term stability, clearing debt, building wealth.

- **Sun (Planet of Success and Vitality)**: The Sun represents success, power, and vitality. Prosperity spells performed on Sundays (ruled by the Sun) focus on achieving recognition, career advancement, and personal empowerment, which naturally leads to increased wealth.

Best for: Career success, personal power, recognition, leadership roles.

Astrological Timing

In addition to working with lunar phases and planetary days, it's beneficial to consider the zodiac signs that the Moon or planets are transiting through. Certain signs are more fertile and prosperous for financial growth:

- **Taurus**: Ruled by Venus, Taurus is one of the most fertile signs for prosperity magic. It's perfect for spells focused on building wealth, luxury, and material security.

Best for: Wealth accumulation, luxury, financial stability.

- **Capricorn**: As an Earth sign ruled by Saturn, Capricorn's energy is ideal for spells focused on long-term financial planning, career success, and achieving financial goals through discipline and hard work.

Best for: Career advancement, long-term financial planning, disciplined wealth-building.

- **Libra**: Ruled by Venus, Libra is excellent for manifesting balanced financial opportunities and creating harmony in your financial life.

Best for: Financial balance, partnerships, business negotiations.

- **Scorpio**: While intense, Scorpio's transformative energy can be harnessed for deep financial changes, such as overcoming debt or financial crises and creating new sources of income.

Best for: Financial transformation, debt clearing, finding new income streams.

Powerful Prosperity Rituals and Spells

Below are a few detailed prosperity spells and rituals that you can perform to attract wealth, success, and abundance into your life. Each ritual is aligned with specific cosmic energies for maximum effectiveness.

1. New Moon Prosperity Jar Spell

This spell is perfect for setting new financial intentions during the New Moon. It involves creating a prosperity jar filled with symbols of abundance, which acts as a magnet for wealth and success as the Moon waxes.

Materials:

- A small jar with a lid
- A green candle (for prosperity)
- Coins (as symbols of wealth)
- Dried basil (for abundance)
- Cinnamon sticks (for financial success)

- A small piece of citrine or pyrite (for wealth)
- A piece of paper and pen

Instructions:

1. **Set Up Your Space**: Cleanse your space with sage or incense. Place the green candle in front of you, along with the jar and all ingredients.
2. **Write Your Intention**: On the piece of paper, write down a clear and specific financial goal or intention. It could be something like "I attract new sources of income" or "I welcome financial abundance and security."
3. **Fill the Jar**: As you add each item to the jar, focus on your intention. Start with the coins (symbolizing wealth), then add the basil (for abundance), cinnamon sticks (for success), and the citrine or pyrite (for attracting wealth).
4. **Place the Paper Inside**: Fold your intention paper and place it inside the jar. Seal the jar with the lid.
5. **Light the Green Candle**: As you light the candle, say aloud:
   "With the power of the New Moon, I plant the seed of abundance. I attract wealth, success, and financial growth into my life."
6. **Visualize Your Goal**: Hold the jar in your hands and visualize your financial goal as if it has already manifested. Feel the energy of abundance surrounding you.
7. **Close the Ritual**: Let the candle burn down completely. Keep the jar on your altar or in a safe place where you can see it daily as a reminder of your growing prosperity.

2. Full Moon Wealth Manifestation Ritual

The Full Moon is the most powerful time for manifesting financial abundance and achieving your prosperity goals. This ritual uses the peak energy of the Full Moon to attract wealth and success.

Materials:

- A gold or green candle (for abundance)
- A bowl of water (symbolizing flow and abundance)
- A small piece of paper and pen
- A citrine crystal (for wealth and success)
- A small dish of salt (for purification)

Instructions:

1. **Prepare Your Space**: Cleanse your sacred space with salt or sage. Place the bowl of water in front of you, with the candle next to it and the citrine on your altar.

2. **Write Your Intention**: Write your financial intention or goal on the piece of paper. Be clear and specific about what you want to manifest (e.g., "I manifest $10,000 for a new business venture" or "I attract financial success and stability").

3. **Light the Candle**: As you light the candle, say aloud:
   "Under the light of the Full Moon, I call forth abundance and prosperity. I align with the flow of wealth and success in all aspects of my life."

4. **Place the Paper in the Water**: Gently place the paper with your intention into the bowl of water, allowing it to float. As you do this, visualize your intention growing and expanding like the energy of the Full Moon.

5. **Hold the Citrine**: Hold the citrine crystal in your hands and focus on your intention. Imagine golden light surrounding you and your financial goal, filling you with confidence, success, and abundance.

6. **Visualize Your Manifestation**: Spend a few minutes visualizing yourself enjoying the financial abundance you seek. Imagine the money, opportunities, and success flowing effortlessly into your life.

7. **Close the Ritual**: Allow the candle to burn down completely. Afterward, pour the water outside in a garden or near a tree as an offering to the Earth. Keep the citrine crystal on your altar or carry it with you to continue attracting wealth.

3. Thursday Prosperity Invocation (Jupiter Day)

This simple prosperity invocation ritual is best performed on a Thursday, the day ruled by Jupiter, the planet of abundance and expansion. It uses the energy of Jupiter to call in wealth and success.

Materials:

- A gold candle (for Jupiter)
- A piece of paper and pen
- A coin or token of money (to represent wealth)
- A small bowl of salt or earth (for grounding prosperity)

Instructions:

1. **Cleanse Your Space**: Use sage or incense to cleanse your sacred space. Place the gold candle in front of you, along with the coin and the bowl of salt or earth.

2. **Write Your Intention**: Write your intention for financial success or abundance on the piece of paper. Be clear and specific about what you wish to manifest.

3. **Light the Gold Candle**: As you light the candle, say:
   "I call upon Jupiter, the great planet of abundance, to open the doors of prosperity and wealth in my life. With your expansive energy, I attract financial success and blessings."

4. **Focus on the Coin**: Hold the coin in your hands and visualize it multiplying. See yourself surrounded by wealth and opportunities, with money flowing effortlessly into your life.

5. **Place the Coin in the Salt**: Place the coin in the bowl of salt or earth, symbolizing that your wealth is grounded and secure. Say:
   "As this coin is placed in the Earth, my wealth is grounded, stable, and growing."
6. **Close the Ritual**: Let the candle burn down completely. Keep the coin on your altar or carry it in your wallet as a charm to attract money.

4. Mercury Retrograde Debt Clearing Ritual

Although Mercury retrograde is often associated with communication breakdowns, it's also a powerful time for clearing old debts and releasing financial burdens. This ritual focuses on breaking free from financial limitations and clearing away debt.

Materials:

- A black or white candle (for release and clarity)
- A piece of paper and pen
- A small fireproof bowl
- A hematite stone (for grounding and protection)

Instructions:

1. **Cleanse Your Space**: Use sage or incense to clear your space. Place the black or white candle in front of you, along with the hematite stone.
2. **Write Your Debt**: On the piece of paper, write down the debt or financial burden you want to clear. Be specific, but keep it simple (e.g., "I release $5,000 of debt").
3. **Light the Candle**: As you light the candle, say:
   "I call upon the energy of Mercury retrograde to release and clear all financial burdens from my life. I am free from debt and limitations."
4. **Burn the Paper**: Safely burn the piece of paper in the fireproof bowl, visualizing the debt disappearing into the flame. As the paper burns, imagine the debt dissolving and disappearing from your life.
5. **Hold the Hematite**: Hold the hematite stone in your hands and visualize yourself free from all financial constraints, grounded and empowered. Feel the weight of the debt lifted from your shoulders.
6. **Close the Ritual**: Allow the candle to burn down. Keep the hematite stone on your altar or carry it with you as a protective talisman against financial difficulties.

Symbols, Herbs, and Crystals for Prosperity Magic

In addition to timing your spells with cosmic energies, you can enhance your prosperity magic with specific symbols, herbs, and crystals that carry the vibration of wealth and abundance.

Prosperity Symbols:

- **Pentacle**: Represents protection and wealth, often used to attract financial security.
- **Coins**: Symbolize money and wealth, often used in rituals for manifesting financial abundance.
- **Acorns**: Represent potential and growth, used to attract long-term wealth and success.
- **Keys**: Symbolize unlocking opportunities and pathways to wealth.

Herbs for Prosperity:

- **Basil**: Known for attracting wealth and prosperity.
- **Cinnamon**: Used to bring financial success and speed up the flow of money.
- **Mint**: Associated with money and abundance, perfect for prosperity spells.
- **Bay Leaves**: Used for manifesting wishes, including financial desires.

Crystals for Prosperity:

- **Citrine**: Known as the "merchant's stone," citrine attracts wealth, success, and abundance.
- **Green Aventurine**: A crystal of opportunity, often used in prosperity and success spells.
- **Pyrite**: A powerful stone for attracting wealth, especially in business ventures.
- **Jade**: Symbolizes prosperity, harmony, and success.

Conclusion

Prosperity magic is a powerful tool for aligning your energy with the flow of abundance and wealth in the universe. By carefully timing your spells with lunar phases, planetary influences, and astrological signs, you can maximize the effectiveness of your manifestation efforts. Whether you're focusing on financial growth, clearing debt, or attracting success in your career, prosperity magic empowers you to co-create your reality with intention and focus. Through spells, rituals, and an abundance mindset, you can invite wealth, success, and financial security into your life.

Chapter 18: Love and Relationship Spells

Love and relationship spells have been a central part of magical practice for centuries, from ancient charms to modern-day rituals designed to attract new love, deepen existing relationships, or foster emotional healing. In 2025, the cosmos offers unique astrological alignments and celestial events that can enhance the effectiveness of love magic. This chapter provides astrological insights, best dates for casting love spells, and detailed rituals for attracting love, strengthening relationships, and nurturing emotional intimacy.

By aligning your love magic with the cosmic influences of the planets, particularly Venus (the planet of love) and the Moon (governing emotions), you can synchronize your intentions with the natural rhythms of the universe, amplifying your ability to manifest love, harmony, and connection.

Astrological Insights for Love Magic in 2025

In 2025, several astrological transits provide powerful opportunities to work with love magic. Venus, Mars, and the Moon are the primary celestial bodies to focus on when casting love spells, as they govern relationships, passion, attraction, and emotional intimacy. The retrograde periods of these planets, as well as key alignments, will influence the best times for performing love spells, depending on your goals.

Key Planetary Influences for Love Magic in 2025

- **Venus (Planet of Love and Relationships):** Venus governs all aspects of love, romance, beauty, and harmony. Its position in the zodiac each month influences how we experience love and attraction. The dates when Venus moves into romantic and passionate signs like Taurus, Libra, and Pisces are especially powerful for love spells. In 2025, Venus retrogrades in Gemini (May 18th to June 30th), offering a time for reflection, re-evaluating relationships, and revisiting past love issues.
- **Mars (Planet of Passion and Desire):** Mars governs passion, sexuality, and desire in relationships. Its transits through fire and water signs (Aries, Leo, Scorpio) in 2025 enhance the energy of sexual attraction, chemistry, and physical intimacy. Mars in Cancer (March 16th to May 1st) brings focus to emotional intimacy and nurturing love in home and family settings.
- **The Moon (Emotional Intimacy and Love Magic):** The Moon's phases and transits through the zodiac affect our emotional needs and how we connect on a deeper level. Working with the Moon's energy in love magic allows you to harness the power of the lunar cycle to strengthen emotional bonds, attract love, or heal old wounds. Full Moons in romantic signs such as Libra and Taurus are particularly powerful for love spells.

Astrological Transits and Best Dates for Love Magic in 2025

By paying attention to key astrological dates and aligning your love spells with these energies, you can enhance the potency of your magical workings. Below are some of the best astrological events and dates for love and relationship spells in 2025:

Venus in Pisces: February 25th to March 22nd

Why It's Powerful: Venus in Pisces is a deeply romantic, dreamy, and spiritual influence. It opens the heart to unconditional love, compassion, and emotional connection. This is an excellent time to cast spells for attracting soulmate connections or strengthening spiritual bonds in existing relationships.

Best for: Soulmate connections, spiritual and emotional intimacy, attracting compassionate and harmonious love.

Full Moon in Libra: April 13th

Why It's Powerful: Libra is the sign of partnership, balance, and harmony, making this Full Moon ideal for love spells that focus on deepening romantic connections or fostering equality in relationships. It's a perfect time for spells to enhance communication, mutual respect, and emotional intimacy in partnerships.

Best for: Strengthening existing relationships, fostering harmony and balance, enhancing communication in love.

Venus Retrograde in Gemini: May 18th to June 30th

Why It's Powerful: During Venus retrograde, we are invited to reflect on past relationships, re-evaluate our romantic values, and heal unresolved emotional issues. This is not the best time to begin a new relationship or cast attraction spells, but it is powerful for healing, reconciliation, and reviewing old patterns in love.

Best for: Reconciliation, healing past wounds, breaking old relationship patterns, reflecting on love values.

Mars in Leo: July 26th to September 7th

Why It's Powerful: Mars in Leo amplifies passion, sexual attraction, and bold romantic gestures. It's a time for dramatic displays of love, confidence in romantic pursuits, and rekindling physical intimacy in relationships. This transit also empowers self-love and confidence, making it a great time for spells that boost personal magnetism.

Best for: Sexual attraction, confidence in love, rekindling passion, romantic adventures.

Full Moon in Taurus: October 17th

Why It's Powerful: Taurus, ruled by Venus, is a sign deeply connected to sensuality, stability, and love. This Full Moon offers a potent time for spells that focus on attracting a stable, committed relationship, enhancing sensual intimacy, and building long-term love connections. It's also an ideal time for self-love rituals that focus on body positivity and self-worth.

Best for: Attracting long-term love, sensual intimacy, commitment, self-love.

Mars in Scorpio: November 25th to January 6th, 2026

Why It's Powerful: Mars in Scorpio brings intensity, passion, and deep emotional connection. This is a time for exploring the depths of emotional intimacy, sexual desire, and transformation in relationships. It's ideal for love spells focused on rekindling desire, deepening trust, and working through emotional barriers in romantic relationships.

Best for: Deep emotional connection, sexual transformation, rekindling passion, emotional healing in relationships.

Powerful Love and Relationship Spells for 2025

Here are detailed love spells that align with the best astrological dates of 2025. Whether you're seeking to attract new love, strengthen an existing relationship, or heal from past emotional wounds, these rituals offer step-by-step guidance to help you manifest your heart's desires.

1. Venus in Pisces Soulmate Attraction Spell

This spell is designed to attract a soulmate or deepen the spiritual connection with an existing partner. It takes advantage of Venus in Pisces' dreamy, compassionate energy to call in a love that transcends the material and connects on a soul level.

Materials:

- A pink or white candle (for love and spiritual connection)
- Rose petals or lavender (for love and harmony)
- A piece of rose quartz (for unconditional love)
- A small mirror (to reflect your intention)
- A pen and paper

Instructions:

1. **Prepare Your Space**: Cleanse your space with sage or incense. Set up your altar with the candle, rose petals, rose quartz, and mirror.
2. **Write Your Intention**: On the piece of paper, write a clear intention for the type of soulmate connection you want to attract. Be specific about the qualities you desire in a partner, but also leave room for the universe to guide the right person to you.
3. **Light the Candle**: As you light the pink or white candle, say aloud:
   "I call upon the energy of Venus in Pisces to bring me a love that is deep, spiritual, and pure. I am ready to attract my soulmate, a partner who resonates with my heart and soul."
4. **Place the Rose Quartz on the Mirror**: Place the rose quartz in the center of the mirror, symbolizing the reflection of your soulmate energy into the universe. As you do this, visualize your heart opening to receive love and your soulmate being drawn to you.

5. **Speak Your Intention**: Recite your written intention aloud, then fold the paper and place it under the mirror. Focus on the reflection in the mirror as a symbol of the love you are attracting.

6. **Close the Ritual**: Allow the candle to burn down completely. Keep the rose quartz with you as a talisman of love, and trust that your soulmate will be drawn to you.

2. Full Moon in Libra Relationship Harmony Spell

This spell is ideal for couples who want to strengthen their relationship, resolve conflicts, or foster a deeper sense of harmony and balance. The Full Moon in Libra provides the perfect energy for enhancing communication, understanding, and mutual respect.

Materials:

- A blue or pink candle (for communication and harmony)
- A piece of paper and pen
- A small bowl of rose water (for love and peace)
- A piece of lapis lazuli or blue lace agate (for clear communication)

Instructions:

1. **Prepare Your Space**: Cleanse your space with sage or palo santo. Place the blue or pink candle, the bowl of rose water, and the crystal on your altar.

2. **Write Your Intention**: Write down your intention for the relationship. Be clear about the areas where you want to improve harmony and communication. For example, "I ask for open communication and mutual understanding in my relationship."

3. **Light the Candle**: As you light the candle, say:
   "Under the light of the Full Moon in Libra, I invite balance, harmony, and peace into my relationship. May we communicate with love, listen with compassion, and strengthen our bond."

4. **Dip Your Fingers in the Rose Water**: Gently dip your fingers into the bowl of rose water, then touch your forehead and heart. Visualize love and understanding flowing between you and your partner, healing any conflicts or misunderstandings.

5. **Speak Your Intention**: Recite your written intention aloud, then place the paper under the bowl of rose water. Let the candle burn down completely.

6. **Close the Ritual**: After the ritual, keep the lapis lazuli or blue lace agate with you as a reminder of your intention for clear communication and harmony in your relationship.

3. Venus Retrograde Reconciliation and Healing Spell

During Venus retrograde, the cosmos invites us to reflect on our past relationships, heal emotional wounds, and reconsider our romantic values. This spell is designed to facilitate reconciliation with a loved one or to heal emotional scars from a past relationship.

Materials:

- A white or pink candle (for healing and love)
- A photograph or token of the person (optional, for reconciliation)
- A piece of amethyst or rhodonite (for emotional healing)
- A small bowl of water (for emotional flow)
- A pen and paper

Instructions:

1. **Prepare Your Space**: Cleanse your space with sage or incense. Place the candle, bowl of water, and amethyst or rhodonite on your altar.
2. **Write Your Intention**: On the piece of paper, write down your intention for reconciliation or healing. If you are seeking to reconcile, focus on mutual understanding and forgiveness. If you are healing, focus on releasing pain and opening your heart to future love.
3. **Light the Candle**: As you light the candle, say:
   "During this Venus retrograde, I call upon the power of love and healing. I release the past and open my heart to reconciliation and emotional healing."
4. **Place the Photograph or Token in the Water**: If you are seeking reconciliation, place the photograph or token of the person in the bowl of water. Visualize emotional healing and forgiveness flowing between you. If you are healing, place a symbolic item (such as a small flower or stone) in the water and visualize the pain flowing away.
5. **Hold the Crystal**: Hold the amethyst or rhodonite and focus on emotional healing. Imagine yourself letting go of pain, resentment, or misunderstandings, and feel your heart becoming lighter.
6. **Close the Ritual**: Allow the candle to burn down. Pour the water outside as an offering to the Earth, symbolizing the release of old emotional energy.

4. Mars in Leo Passion and Attraction Spell

Mars in Leo enhances passion, desire, and romantic attraction, making it an ideal time to cast spells for rekindling sexual chemistry, boosting confidence in love, or attracting new romantic opportunities. This spell focuses on increasing passion and magnetism, whether in a new relationship or to reignite an existing one.

Materials:

- A red candle (for passion)
- Cinnamon or patchouli oil (for attraction)
- A red or pink ribbon (for love and passion)
- A piece of carnelian or garnet (for desire and confidence)
- A small mirror (to reflect your inner confidence)

Instructions:

1. **Prepare Your Space**: Cleanse your space with incense or palo santo. Place the red candle, ribbon, carnelian or garnet, and mirror on your altar.
2. **Write Your Intention**: Write down your intention for passion or attraction. Be clear whether you want to rekindle desire in an existing relationship or attract new romantic energy.
3. **Anoint the Candle**: Anoint the red candle with cinnamon or patchouli oil, focusing on your intention to increase passion and attraction.
4. **Light the Candle**: As you light the candle, say:
   "With the fire of Mars in Leo, I ignite passion, desire, and attraction. I am confident, magnetic, and open to the love and passion I deserve."
5. **Tie the Ribbon Around the Candle**: Tie the red or pink ribbon around the base of the candle, symbolizing the binding of passion and love to your life. Visualize the flame of the candle representing the flame of desire growing stronger in your relationship or within yourself.
6. **Use the Mirror**: Look into the mirror and see yourself as confident, desirable, and magnetic. Feel the energy of Mars in Leo empowering you to attract love and passion effortlessly.
7. **Close the Ritual**: Allow the candle to burn down. Keep the carnelian or garnet with you as a talisman of passion and confidence.

Love Deities, Herbs, and Crystals for Love Magic

In addition to timing your spells with cosmic energies, you can enhance your love magic by calling on deities, using specific herbs, and incorporating crystals that resonate with the vibration of love and attraction.

Love Deities:

- **Aphrodite**: Greek goddess of love, beauty, and desire. Call upon Aphrodite to attract romantic love, enhance your beauty, or deepen intimacy.
- **Freyja**: Norse goddess of love, fertility, and passion. Freyja's energy is powerful for manifesting passion, sensuality, and attracting lovers.
- **Oshun**: West African goddess of love, beauty, and rivers. Oshun is invoked for attracting love, joy, and harmony in relationships.
- **Eros**: Greek god of romantic and physical love. Eros' energy is perfect for igniting sexual desire and deepening emotional connections.

Herbs for Love Magic:

- **Rose Petals**: Used in spells for love, attraction, and emotional healing. Rose petals are a symbol of unconditional love and beauty.
- **Lavender**: Associated with harmony and peace, lavender is used in spells to promote calmness and balance in relationships.
- **Cinnamon**: Known for its ability to attract love and passion, cinnamon adds a spark of energy to love spells.
- **Basil**: Used in love spells to attract a partner and foster commitment and fidelity.

Crystals for Love Magic:

- **Rose Quartz**: The ultimate stone of love, rose quartz attracts unconditional love and promotes emotional healing and harmony in relationships.
- **Garnet**: A stone of passion and desire, garnet is perfect for rekindling romance or igniting new love.
- **Rhodonite**: Known for its healing properties, rhodonite helps heal past emotional wounds and opens the heart to new love.
- **Moonstone**: Connected to the Moon's energy, moonstone is a stone of emotional balance, intuition, and deepening romantic bonds.

Conclusion

Love and relationship spells offer a powerful way to align with the universal energies of attraction, intimacy, and emotional connection. By timing your rituals with astrological transits in 2025—particularly Venus, Mars, and the Moon—you can enhance the effectiveness of your spells and invite love, passion, and harmony into your life. Whether you're seeking to attract a soulmate, strengthen an existing relationship, or heal from past emotional wounds, love magic can help manifest your desires with intention and focus. Through careful timing, the use of specific herbs, crystals, and deities, you can create a magical pathway toward deeper, more fulfilling relationships.

Chapter 19: Protection Spells

Protection magic is a fundamental aspect of witchcraft, safeguarding practitioners from negative energies, harmful influences, and unwanted entities. Whether you are looking to protect your home, your energy, or a loved one, protection spells create powerful shields that keep you safe and secure. In 2025, specific celestial events such as eclipses, retrogrades, and lunar phases offer unique windows of opportunity to enhance protection magic. By aligning your protective rituals with these cosmic energies, you can strengthen your wards, banish negativity, and clear harmful influences more effectively.

This chapter covers the celestial events that are particularly potent for protection magic, the best times for banishing and warding off negative energy, and a collection of protection spells to incorporate into your practice. You'll learn how to use the cycles of the Moon, the influence of the planets, and natural elemental forces to create powerful protective barriers.

Celestial Events That Enhance Protection Magic

The cosmos is filled with moments of transformation, intensity, and reflection that can amplify protection magic. When casting protective spells, it is crucial to work with the natural energy flows of the universe, using planetary alignments, eclipses, retrogrades, and specific lunar phases to boost your intention. Each celestial event carries unique energetic qualities that are ideal for different types of protection spells.

Solar and Lunar Eclipses

Eclipses are moments of shadow and light that can enhance protection rituals, especially those aimed at banishing, releasing negativity, and clearing away unwanted influences. The temporary "blotting out" of the Sun or Moon during an eclipse symbolizes a disruption of energy that can be harnessed to reset boundaries and fortify protective shields.

- **Solar Eclipses**: Solar eclipses are ideal for casting protective spells that require empowerment, clarity, and a strong defense against negative forces. These powerful celestial events symbolize a rebirth of energy, making them perfect for setting new protective barriers that are both resilient and far-reaching.

Best for: Setting strong protective shields, empowerment rituals, clearing away harmful external influences.

- **Lunar Eclipses**: Lunar eclipses are especially effective for banishing negativity, cutting ties with harmful energies or people, and clearing away emotional or psychic debris. Since the Moon governs emotions and intuition, lunar eclipses offer a powerful time to remove internal blocks or negative patterns that affect your energy field.

Best for: Banishing negative energy, releasing emotional baggage, clearing psychic or emotional attacks.

Planetary Retrogrades

Retrogrades, particularly those of Mercury, Mars, and Saturn, provide potent opportunities for protection magic. Retrogrades are times of introspection, review, and recalibration, making them ideal for spells focused on banishing, warding, and shielding from past issues that resurface or hidden negative influences.

- **Mercury Retrograde**: Mercury retrograde (happening several times in 2025) is known for its disruption in communication, technology, and travel. However, it is also a powerful time for reflection and clearing away miscommunication or misunderstandings that could be draining your energy. Use this retrograde to shield yourself from confusion, deception, or gossip.

Best for: Protecting against miscommunication, mental clarity, clearing out deceptive energies.

- **Mars Retrograde**: Mars, the planet of action and aggression, can create heightened conflict during its retrograde. This period (November 25, 2025, to January 6, 2026) is ideal for casting protection spells that deflect anger, aggression, or hostile energy directed at you.

Best for: Warding off anger, hostility, physical and emotional protection, calming conflict.

- **Saturn Retrograde**: Saturn governs boundaries, discipline, and long-term structures. During Saturn retrograde, which occurs from June 29, 2025, to November 1, 2025, it's the perfect time for reviewing and strengthening existing protective boundaries, both physical and energetic. This retrograde encourages a re-evaluation of your spiritual defenses and the fortification of protection wards.

Best for: Strengthening personal boundaries, long-term protection, revising protective barriers, karmic protection.

The Moon and Protection Magic

The Moon's phases are essential to protection magic. Different phases of the lunar cycle provide distinct energies that can enhance your protective workings, especially when combined with the Moon's transit through specific zodiac signs. Here's how to use the Moon's energy for protection spells:

- **New Moon**: The New Moon is a time for new beginnings and setting fresh protective boundaries. It's the perfect time to cast spells for setting new wards, creating protection talismans, and initiating defensive magic.

Best for: Creating new protective shields, setting wards, protection talismans.

- **Waxing Moon**: As the Moon grows in light, it brings increased energy to protective spells. Use the Waxing Moon to strengthen existing wards, reinforce boundaries, and enhance the effectiveness of your protective barriers.

Best for: Strengthening existing protective barriers, enhancing defensive magic, building resilience.

- **Full Moon**: The Full Moon is a time of culmination and high energy. It's the most powerful time for casting protection spells that require intense focus, such as those that involve shielding against psychic attacks, spiritual protection, and banishing strong negative influences.

Best for: Powerful shielding, psychic protection, spiritual defenses, banishing negative entities.

- **Waning Moon**: The Waning Moon is the perfect time for banishing spells and clearing away negative energies. This phase is excellent for removing unwanted influences, cleansing your home or energy field, and severing toxic energetic cords.

Best for: Banishing negative energy, severing cords, clearing space for protection, removing spiritual attachments.

Best Times for Banishing and Warding Off Negative Energy

There are specific celestial events, moon phases, and planetary transits in 2025 that are especially conducive to banishing and warding off negative energy. Aligning your protection rituals with these dates can enhance the power and effectiveness of your spells.

New Moon in Capricorn: January 1, 2025

Why It's Powerful: Capricorn's disciplined, grounded energy is ideal for setting long-term protection and boundaries. The New Moon in Capricorn is perfect for creating protection wards that offer both spiritual and physical safety for the year ahead.

Best for: Creating new protective boundaries, shielding your home and space, establishing long-term protection.

Full Moon in Scorpio: May 7, 2025

Why It's Powerful: Scorpio is the sign of transformation, death, and rebirth. A Full Moon in Scorpio brings powerful energy for banishing and releasing deep-seated negative influences or psychic attacks. This is the ideal time for cutting ties with toxic people or energies and for casting spells that transform harmful energies into protection.

Best for: Banishing toxic influences, protection against psychic attacks, cutting energetic cords.

Mercury Retrograde in Gemini: May 18 to June 30, 2025

Why It's Powerful: Mercury retrograde in Gemini can stir up confusion, misunderstandings, and mental chaos. It's an ideal time to cast protection spells to shield against gossip, slander, miscommunication, and mental overwhelm. Use this retrograde to guard against deceptive energies and protect your mental clarity.

Best for: Shielding from gossip, protecting mental clarity, guarding against deception.

Lunar Eclipse in Taurus: November 8, 2025

Why It's Powerful: A lunar eclipse in Taurus creates a powerful opportunity for clearing emotional blockages and setting strong boundaries. Taurus, ruled by Venus, also governs physical and material protection, making this a perfect time for banishing negative influences that affect your emotional well-being and financial security.

Best for: Banishing emotional or financial blockages, clearing negative energy from your home, establishing material protection.

Mars Retrograde in Scorpio: November 25, 2025, to January 6, 2026

Why It's Powerful: Mars retrograde in Scorpio brings intense energy that can reveal hidden sources of conflict, aggression, or manipulation. This period is ideal for casting protection spells that deflect hostility, prevent power struggles, and shield against deep emotional or physical attacks.

Best for: Deflecting anger and hostility, shielding from manipulative forces, emotional and physical protection.

Protection Rituals and Spells for 2025

Below are detailed protection spells and rituals designed to align with the celestial events and lunar phases of 2025. These rituals can be used to safeguard your home, ward off negative influences, and protect your energy field from harm.

1. New Moon in Capricorn Protective Shield Ritual

This ritual harnesses the grounded, disciplined energy of Capricorn to create a long-lasting protective shield around yourself or your home. It's perfect for initiating a new layer of protection for the year ahead.

Materials:

- A black candle (for protection)
- Salt or earth (for grounding)
- A piece of obsidian or black tourmaline (for shielding)
- A small mirror (to reflect negative energy)
- A piece of paper and pen

Instructions:

1. **Cleanse Your Space**: Burn sage or incense to cleanse the area where you will perform the ritual. Place the black candle, salt, and crystal on your altar.
2. **Write Your Intention**: On the piece of paper, write down your protective intention (e.g., "I create a powerful shield of protection around myself and my home, deflecting all negative energy").
3. **Light the Black Candle**: As you light the candle, say aloud:
   "Under the New Moon in Capricorn, I call upon the Earth's strength and stability to create a protective shield. No harm may enter; no negativity may cross."
4. **Circle the Salt Around the Candle**: Sprinkle a circle of salt or earth around the candle, symbolizing the boundary of protection. Place the obsidian or black tourmaline in the center of the circle.
5. **Reflect Negative Energy**: Hold the mirror and visualize any negative energy being reflected away from you or your home. Say aloud:
   "I reflect all harm away from me. This shield protects me from all that seeks to harm or drain my energy."
6. **Close the Ritual**: Let the candle burn down completely. Keep the obsidian or black tourmaline in your home or carry it with you as a protective talisman.

2. Full Moon in Scorpio Banishing Spell

This spell is designed to banish deeply rooted negative energies or influences, using the transformative power of the Full Moon in Scorpio. It's perfect for cutting toxic energetic cords or removing harmful attachments.

Materials:

- A black candle (for banishing)
- A piece of string or cord (to represent the energy being banished)
- A fireproof bowl
- A piece of black tourmaline or obsidian (for protection)
- Sage or palo santo for cleansing

Instructions:

1. **Cleanse Your Space**: Use sage or palo santo to cleanse your space. Set up your altar with the black candle, string, and fireproof bowl.
2. **Write Your Banishing Intention**: On the piece of paper, write down the energy or person you wish to banish from your life. Be clear and specific.
3. **Tie the String**: As you tie knots in the string, focus on the negative energy you wish to remove. Each knot symbolizes an aspect of the energy or attachment being banished.
4. **Light the Black Candle**: As you light the candle, say:
   "Under the Full Moon in Scorpio, I release and banish all harmful influences from my life. I sever the cords of negativity that drain my spirit."
5. **Burn the String**: Carefully burn the string in the flame of the black candle, placing it in the fireproof bowl. Visualize the negative energy dissolving and being released.
6. **Hold the Crystal**: Hold the black tourmaline or obsidian and visualize a protective shield forming around you, blocking any further harm. Say:
   "I am protected. No harm may enter this space."
7. **Close the Ritual**: Allow the candle to burn down completely. Keep the crystal with you as a protective talisman.

3. Mercury Retrograde Communication Protection Spell

Mercury retrograde often brings confusion, miscommunication, and misunderstandings. This spell is designed to shield you from deceptive or harmful communication and to ensure clarity and protection in all interactions.

Materials:

- A blue candle (for clear communication)
- A piece of paper and pen
- A feather or symbol of Air (for Mercury's influence)
- A piece of clear quartz or sodalite (for mental clarity)
- Lavender oil or incense (for calming and clarity)

Instructions:

1. **Cleanse Your Space**: Burn lavender oil or incense to cleanse your space and invite calmness. Place the blue candle, feather, and crystal on your altar.
2. **Write Your Intention**: Write down your intention for protection during Mercury retrograde (e.g., "I am shielded from all miscommunication and deception during this retrograde").
3. **Light the Blue Candle**: As you light the candle, say:
   "During Mercury retrograde, I call upon the power of Air to protect my mind and my words. I speak clearly, and I am protected from all confusion."
4. **Hold the Feather**: Hold the feather (or Air symbol) and visualize a bubble of clarity surrounding you. This bubble prevents any negative or deceptive communication from reaching you.
5. **Focus on the Crystal**: Hold the clear quartz or sodalite and feel your mind becoming clear and focused. Say aloud:
   "My mind is clear, and my words are protected. No harm may come from confusion or deception."
6. **Close the Ritual**: Allow the candle to burn down completely. Keep the crystal with you during Mercury retrograde as a protective charm for clear communication.

4. Mars Retrograde Anger Deflection Spell

Mars retrograde can increase aggression, anger, and conflict. This spell is designed to deflect hostile energy and protect you from emotional or physical harm during this intense retrograde.

Materials:

- A red candle (for Mars)
- A small mirror (for deflecting energy)
- A piece of hematite or black tourmaline (for grounding and protection)
- A bowl of water (for calming energy)
- Sage or palo santo for cleansing

Instructions:

1. **Cleanse Your Space**: Burn sage or palo santo to clear away any lingering negative energy. Place the red candle, mirror, and bowl of water on your altar.
2. **Write Your Intention**: Write down your intention for protection from anger or hostility (e.g., "I deflect all anger and aggression away from me. I am calm and protected").
3. **Light the Red Candle**: As you light the candle, say:
   "During Mars retrograde, I call upon the power of calm and protection. No harm may come to me through anger or conflict."
4. **Use the Mirror**: Hold the mirror and visualize it deflecting all hostile energy away from you. Imagine anger or conflict bouncing off the mirror and being dissolved into the universe.
5. **Place the Mirror in the Water**: Place the mirror face-up in the bowl of water, symbolizing the calming of aggressive energy. Say aloud:
   "All aggression is calmed. Anger dissolves and is reflected away from me."
6. **Hold the Crystal**: Hold the hematite or black tourmaline and feel yourself grounded and protected. Imagine a shield of calmness surrounding you.
7. **Close the Ritual**: Let the candle burn down. Keep the crystal with you for protection during Mars retrograde.

Crystals, Herbs, and Symbols for Protection Magic

Incorporating specific crystals, herbs, and symbols into your protection magic can amplify the power of your spells. Here are some key correspondences for protection spells:

Crystals for Protection:

- **Obsidian**: A powerful protective stone that shields against negativity and psychic attacks.
- **Black Tourmaline**: A grounding stone that deflects harmful energy and creates a strong protective barrier.
- **Hematite**: Known for its grounding and reflective properties, hematite repels negative energy and strengthens personal boundaries.
- **Clear Quartz**: Amplifies protective spells and shields against unwanted influences.

Herbs for Protection:

- **Sage**: Used for cleansing and purifying spaces, sage removes negative energy and creates a shield of protection.
- **Rosemary**: A powerful herb for protection and purification, rosemary is often used in protection rituals and spells.
- **Lavender**: Provides calming protection and helps guard against harmful energies while promoting peace and clarity.
- **Basil**: Used in protection spells to ward off negative influences and bring safety and security to the home.

Symbols for Protection:

- **Pentacle**: A symbol of protection and balance, often used to shield against harm and negative forces.
- **Mirrors**: Used in reflective magic to deflect harmful energy and prevent it from reaching you.
- **Salt**: Known for its purifying and protective properties, salt is often used in protective circles or sprinkled around doorways to keep negative energy out.
- **Keys**: Symbolize unlocking protection and safeguarding boundaries.

Conclusion

Protection magic is a vital part of any witch's practice, creating barriers and wards that shield against negative energy, psychic attacks, and harmful influences. By aligning your protection spells with the celestial events of 2025—such as eclipses, retrogrades, and lunar phases—you can amplify their effectiveness and ensure that you are protected on every level. Whether you are seeking to banish negativity, create new protective boundaries, or ward off specific threats, protection magic offers powerful tools to keep you safe and secure. With the right timing, materials, and intention, you can build a strong energetic fortress that shields you from harm.

Chapter 20: Full Moon Rituals for Each Zodiac Sign

The Full Moon is one of the most potent times for magical work, representing a peak of energy and a time of culmination, manifestation, and heightened spiritual power. Each month, as the Moon reaches its full phase, it transits through a specific zodiac sign, bringing unique energies that influence the focus and intent of our rituals. By aligning your Full Moon rituals with the zodiac sign the Moon is in, you can amplify the power of your spellwork, attuning your magic to the celestial energies of the cosmos.

This chapter offers detailed rituals for each month's Full Moon in 2025, tailored to the astrological sign that governs the Moon at that time. Whether you're looking to manifest abundance, heal emotional wounds, deepen relationships, or release negative energy, these Full Moon rituals are designed to help you align with the lunar and zodiacal energies for maximum magical impact.

January 13, 2025 – Full Moon in Cancer

Cancer, ruled by the Moon, is the sign of home, family, emotions, and intuition. This Full Moon invites deep emotional healing, nurturing, and a focus on personal security. It's a perfect time for spells related to emotional balance, family matters, and protection of your home.

Full Moon in Cancer Ritual: Emotional Healing and Protection
Materials:

- A white candle (for purity and protection)
- A bowl of water (for Cancer's watery influence)
- Seashells or moonstone (for emotional healing)
- Lavender or rose oil (for calming)
- A small piece of paper and pen

Instructions:

1. **Set the Mood**: Cleanse your space with lavender or rose incense. Place the candle, bowl of water, and seashells or moonstone on your altar.
2. **Write Your Intention**: On the piece of paper, write down an emotional wound or something that is causing you emotional imbalance, such as a conflict with a loved one or a fear you wish to release.
3. **Light the Candle**: As you light the candle, say:
   "Under this Full Moon in Cancer, I call upon the healing waters of the Moon to cleanse my heart and mind. I release emotional burdens and open myself to peace."
4. **Focus on the Water**: Hold the bowl of water in your hands and visualize your emotional pain or concern dissolving into the water. Feel the calming, nurturing energy of Cancer soothing your soul.
5. **Place the Paper in the Water**: Fold the paper and place it in the water, symbolizing the release of your emotional burdens. Let the water cleanse and purify your energy.

6. **Close the Ritual**: Allow the candle to burn down. Dispose of the water outside, giving it back to the Earth. Keep the seashell or moonstone near you as a talisman for emotional healing.

February 12, 2025 – Full Moon in Leo

Leo, ruled by the Sun, is the sign of self-expression, creativity, and confidence. This Full Moon is ideal for manifesting personal power, enhancing your charisma, and igniting your creative fire. It's a perfect time for rituals focused on self-love, leadership, and standing in your personal truth.

Full Moon in Leo Ritual: Confidence and Creativity
Materials:

- A gold or yellow candle (for confidence and power)
- Sunflowers or marigold flowers (for Leo's energy)
- Citrine or sunstone (for abundance and self-esteem)
- Cinnamon or clove incense (for passion)
- A mirror (to reflect your inner power)

Instructions:

1. **Prepare Your Space**: Cleanse your space with cinnamon or clove incense. Place the candle, flowers, and citrine or sunstone on your altar.
2. **Write Your Intention**: On a piece of paper, write down an area of your life where you want to increase confidence or creative expression.
3. **Light the Candle**: As you light the gold or yellow candle, say:
   "Under this Full Moon in Leo, I ignite the fire of my personal power. I radiate confidence, creativity, and strength in all I do."
4. **Use the Mirror**: Hold the mirror and look into your reflection, visualizing yourself as powerful, confident, and radiant. Say aloud:
   "I am confident. I am creative. I am a powerful force of light and inspiration."
5. **Visualize Your Manifestation**: Hold the citrine or sunstone in your hands and imagine yourself achieving the success or creative goal you have in mind. See yourself standing in your power.
6. **Close the Ritual**: Allow the candle to burn down. Keep the citrine or sunstone on your altar or carry it with you to maintain the energy of confidence and creativity.

March 14, 2025 – Full Moon in Virgo

Virgo is the sign of organization, health, and service, ruled by Mercury. This Full Moon brings energy for grounding, purification, and setting things in order. It's an ideal time for rituals that focus on health, self-care, and creating structure in your life.

Full Moon in Virgo Ritual: Cleansing and Organization

Materials:

- A green or brown candle (for grounding and healing)
- Rosemary or eucalyptus oil (for cleansing)
- A clear quartz crystal (for clarity)
- A broom or besom (for purification)
- A small notebook or journal

Instructions:

1. **Cleanse Your Space**: Anoint your space with rosemary or eucalyptus oil, focusing on areas that feel cluttered or stagnant.
2. **Set Your Intention**: In your notebook, write down areas of your life where you need more organization or clarity. Be specific about what you want to cleanse or improve (e.g., health routines, work habits, or personal projects).
3. **Light the Candle**: As you light the green or brown candle, say:
   "Under this Full Moon in Virgo, I purify and organize my life. I cleanse away disorder and create harmony and balance."
4. **Use the Broom**: Sweep your space with a broom or besom, symbolically clearing away stagnant energy and any blocks to your goals. Visualize the broom removing physical, mental, or spiritual clutter from your life.
5. **Focus on the Quartz**: Hold the clear quartz crystal and visualize your mind and space becoming clear and organized. Imagine your goals falling into place with ease and clarity.
6. **Close the Ritual**: Let the candle burn down completely. Keep the clear quartz on your desk or workspace to maintain clarity and focus.

April 13, 2025 – Full Moon in Libra

Libra, ruled by Venus, is the sign of balance, harmony, and relationships. This Full Moon is a time to focus on partnership, beauty, and creating equilibrium in your life. It's ideal for spells that foster harmony in relationships, attract love, and bring balance to chaotic situations.

Full Moon in Libra Ritual: Relationship Harmony

Materials:

- A pink or blue candle (for love and harmony)
- Rose petals or jasmine flowers (for love)
- Rose quartz or lapis lazuli (for balanced communication)
- A piece of paper and pen

Instructions:

1. **Cleanse Your Space**: Use rose incense or jasmine oil to cleanse your space and invite loving energy.
2. **Set Your Intention**: Write down an intention related to improving a relationship, whether romantic, familial, or professional. Focus on areas where you want to restore harmony and balance.
3. **Light the Candle**: As you light the pink or blue candle, say:
   "Under this Full Moon in Libra, I invite balance, harmony, and love into my relationships. May peace and understanding flow freely between us."
4. **Use Rose Petals**: Sprinkle rose petals around the candle, symbolizing the love and harmony you wish to cultivate. Visualize the relationship healing and growing in mutual respect and understanding.
5. **Hold the Rose Quartz**: Hold the rose quartz or lapis lazuli in your hands and imagine yourself communicating clearly and with love. Picture any conflicts dissolving into peaceful resolution.
6. **Close the Ritual**: Allow the candle to burn down. Keep the rose quartz or lapis lazuli near you to maintain harmonious communication and love in your relationships.

May 12, 2025 – Full Moon in Scorpio

Scorpio, ruled by Pluto, is the sign of transformation, power, and deep emotional intensity. This Full Moon brings the energy of rebirth and is ideal for rituals focused on releasing emotional baggage, banishing negativity, and transforming difficult situations.

Full Moon in Scorpio Ritual: Emotional Release and Transformation
Materials:

- A black or dark red candle (for transformation)
- A bowl of water (for emotional release)
- A piece of obsidian or black tourmaline (for protection)
- A piece of paper and pen
- Sage or palo santo for cleansing

Instructions:

1. **Cleanse Your Space**: Burn sage or palo santo to clear your space, inviting in the transformative energy of Scorpio.
2. **Set Your Intention**: Write down what you wish to release from your life, whether it's emotional baggage, a toxic relationship, or an unhealthy pattern. Be specific and clear about what you want to let go of.
3. **Light the Candle**: As you light the black or dark red candle, say:
   "Under this Full Moon in Scorpio, I release all that no longer serves me. I transform my pain into power and my wounds into wisdom."
4. **Use the Water**: Hold the bowl of water and visualize your emotional burdens dissolving into it. Imagine the water absorbing all negative energy and emotional pain.
5. **Burn the Paper**: Safely burn the piece of paper with your written intention in the flame of the candle, symbolizing the release of the old. As the paper burns, imagine yourself being freed from the weight of your past.
6. **Close the Ritual**: Pour the water outside, symbolizing the return of your emotional burdens to the Earth. Keep the obsidian or black tourmaline with you as a talisman of protection during your transformation.

June 10, 2025 – Full Moon in Sagittarius

Sagittarius, ruled by Jupiter, is the sign of adventure, expansion, and higher learning. This Full Moon brings energy for exploring new horizons, seeking wisdom, and manifesting personal growth. It's ideal for rituals that focus on travel, learning, and expanding your spiritual path.

Full Moon in Sagittarius Ritual: Expansion and Wisdom

Materials:

- A purple or blue candle (for wisdom and expansion)
- A map or travel-related object (for manifestation)
- Amethyst or turquoise (for spiritual growth)
- A piece of paper and pen

Instructions:

1. **Cleanse Your Space**: Use sage or sandalwood incense to cleanse your space and invite in the expansive energy of Sagittarius.
2. **Set Your Intention**: Write down an intention for growth, whether personal, spiritual, or related to travel or learning. Be clear about the new horizons you wish to explore.
3. **Light the Candle**: As you light the purple or blue candle, say:
   "Under this Full Moon in Sagittarius, I call forth the energy of expansion and adventure. I open myself to new experiences, wisdom, and growth."
4. **Use the Map**: Place a map or travel-related object on your altar to symbolize the new journeys you wish to embark on. Visualize yourself exploring these new horizons with excitement and curiosity.
5. **Hold the Amethyst**: Hold the amethyst or turquoise in your hands and imagine yourself gaining wisdom and insight from your journey. Picture yourself growing spiritually and mentally as you explore new opportunities.
6. **Close the Ritual**: Allow the candle to burn down. Keep the amethyst or turquoise with you as you embark on new adventures and personal growth.

July 9, 2025 – Full Moon in Capricorn

Capricorn, ruled by Saturn, is the sign of discipline, ambition, and structure. This Full Moon brings energy for manifesting long-term goals, building stability, and achieving success through hard work and determination. It's ideal for spells focused on career advancement, financial stability, and personal responsibility.

Full Moon in Capricorn Ritual: Career and Financial Success
Materials:

- A green or brown candle (for stability and growth)
- A small box or jar (for storing your goals)
- A piece of pyrite or garnet (for financial success)
- A piece of paper and pen

Instructions:

1. **Cleanse Your Space**: Burn incense or cedarwood oil to cleanse your space and ground your energy.
2. **Set Your Intention**: Write down a long-term goal related to your career or finances. Be specific about what you want to manifest and what steps you are willing to take to achieve it.
3. **Light the Candle**: As you light the green or brown candle, say:
   "Under this Full Moon in Capricorn, I set my intentions for long-term success. I call upon the energy of stability, discipline, and ambition to help me manifest my goals."
4. **Use the Box or Jar**: Place your written goal in the box or jar, symbolizing the seeds of your ambition being planted. Visualize your goal taking root and growing into a stable, successful outcome.
5. **Hold the Pyrite**: Hold the pyrite or garnet in your hands and feel the energy of success and prosperity flowing into your life. Picture yourself achieving your financial or career goals with ease and determination.
6. **Close the Ritual**: Allow the candle to burn down. Keep the box or jar in a safe place and revisit it whenever you need a boost of motivation. Carry the pyrite or garnet with you to attract financial success and stability.

August 7, 2025 – Full Moon in Aquarius

Aquarius, ruled by Uranus, is the sign of innovation, individuality, and community. This Full Moon is ideal for spells focused on breaking free from old patterns, embracing change, and contributing to collective well-being. It's perfect for rituals that enhance creativity, social change, and personal freedom.

Full Moon in Aquarius Ritual: Embracing Change and Freedom
Materials:

- A blue or silver candle (for change and innovation)
- A piece of paper and pen
- A small piece of clear quartz or labradorite (for new ideas)
- A symbol of freedom (such as a feather or bird figurine)

Instructions:

1. **Cleanse Your Space**: Burn sage or frankincense incense to cleanse your space and invite in the energy of freedom and innovation.
2. **Set Your Intention**: Write down a change you want to make in your life or an old pattern you want to break free from.
3. **Light the Candle**: As you light the blue or silver candle, say:
   "Under this Full Moon in Aquarius, I embrace change and freedom. I break free from old patterns and open myself to new possibilities."
4. **Visualize Your Change**: Hold the clear quartz or labradorite and visualize the change you wish to manifest. Picture yourself breaking free from any limitations and stepping into your personal power.
5. **Use the Symbol of Freedom**: Place the feather or bird symbol on your altar and imagine yourself soaring toward your goals with freedom and confidence.
6. **Close the Ritual**: Allow the candle to burn down. Keep the clear quartz or labradorite with you to maintain clarity and inspiration as you embrace change and new opportunities.

September 5, 2025 – Full Moon in Pisces

Pisces, ruled by Neptune, is the sign of dreams, intuition, and spiritual connection. This Full Moon brings energy for deep emotional healing, psychic awareness, and spiritual growth. It's an ideal time for rituals focused on dream work, divination, and connecting with your higher self.

Full Moon in Pisces Ritual: Intuition and Spiritual Connection
Materials:

- A purple or white candle (for spiritual awareness)
- A piece of amethyst or moonstone (for intuition)
- A bowl of water (for Pisces' watery influence)
- Lavender or sandalwood incense (for calming)
- A journal or dream diary

Instructions:

1. **Cleanse Your Space**: Burn lavender or sandalwood incense to create a calming, spiritual atmosphere.
2. **Set Your Intention**: Write down a spiritual goal or area of your intuition you want to strengthen, such as developing your psychic abilities or gaining clarity in dream work.
3. **Light the Candle**: As you light the purple or white candle, say:
   "Under this Full Moon in Pisces, I open myself to divine guidance and spiritual awareness. I trust my intuition and embrace my spiritual path."
4. **Use the Water**: Hold the bowl of water in your hands and visualize your intuition flowing freely, connecting you to the spiritual realm. Imagine the water enhancing your psychic abilities and deepening your spiritual understanding.
5. **Hold the Amethyst**: Hold the amethyst or moonstone and focus on your third eye, imagining it opening to receive divine messages and insights. Let the energy of the Full Moon in Pisces amplify your intuition.
6. **Close the Ritual**: Allow the candle to burn down. Keep the amethyst or moonstone under your pillow or near your bed to enhance your dream work and intuition. Write down any insights or dreams in your journal.

October 17, 2025 – Full Moon in Taurus

Taurus, ruled by Venus, is the sign of sensuality, stability, and material abundance. This Full Moon is ideal for spells that focus on financial security, manifesting abundance, and enhancing pleasure and comfort in your life. It's also a great time for self-love rituals.

Full Moon in Taurus Ritual: Abundance and Self-Love

Materials:

- A green or pink candle (for abundance and love)
- Rose petals or a favorite flower (for beauty)
- A piece of jade or green aventurine (for prosperity)
- A small jar or bowl of honey (for sweetness and abundance)
- A piece of paper and pen

Instructions:

1. **Cleanse Your Space**: Use rose incense or essential oil to cleanse your space and invite in the energy of beauty, abundance, and love.
2. **Set Your Intention**: Write down your intention for abundance, whether it's financial security, self-love, or material comfort. Be specific about what you want to attract into your life.
3. **Light the Candle**: As you light the green or pink candle, say:
   "Under this Full Moon in Taurus, I manifest abundance, prosperity, and love. I welcome all forms of beauty and comfort into my life."
4. **Use the Honey**: Dip your finger into the honey and place a small amount on your tongue, symbolizing the sweetness and abundance you are inviting into your life. Visualize your intention manifesting with ease and pleasure.
5. **Hold the Jade**: Hold the jade or green aventurine and imagine yourself surrounded by wealth, comfort, and love. Feel the energy of abundance flowing into your life.
6. **Close the Ritual**: Allow the candle to burn down. Keep the jade or green aventurine with you to continue attracting prosperity and abundance into your life.

November 16, 2025 – Full Moon in Gemini

Gemini, ruled by Mercury, is the sign of communication, learning, and adaptability. This Full Moon is ideal for spells focused on enhancing communication, networking, and gaining clarity in mental pursuits. It's perfect for rituals that involve learning new skills, improving relationships through communication, or manifesting new ideas.

Full Moon in Gemini Ritual: Clarity and Communication
Materials:

- A blue or yellow candle (for communication and mental clarity)
- A feather or quill pen (for Mercury's Air influence)
- A piece of lapis lazuli or sodalite (for clear thinking)
- A piece of paper and pen

Instructions:

1. **Cleanse Your Space**: Burn sage or sandalwood incense to cleanse your space and invite clarity.
2. **Set Your Intention**: Write down a communication goal, such as improving a relationship through better dialogue, gaining mental clarity, or expressing yourself more freely.
3. **Light the Candle**: As you light the blue or yellow candle, say:
   "Under this Full Moon in Gemini, I open my mind to clarity and my heart to honest communication. I express myself clearly and effectively in all situations."
4. **Use the Feather**: Hold the feather or quill pen and visualize your words and thoughts flowing freely and with ease. Picture yourself speaking and being heard clearly in all your interactions.
5. **Hold the Lapis Lazuli**: Hold the lapis lazuli or sodalite and imagine your mind becoming clear and focused. See yourself communicating your ideas with confidence and clarity.
6. **Close the Ritual**: Allow the candle to burn down. Keep the lapis lazuli or sodalite with you to maintain clear thinking and effective communication.

December 16, 2025 – Full Moon in Sagittarius

The second Full Moon in Sagittarius for the year brings an even stronger energy of expansion, adventure, and spiritual growth. This Full Moon is ideal for rituals focused on personal freedom, expanding your horizons, and manifesting new spiritual insights. It's also a great time to focus on travel and higher learning.

Full Moon in Sagittarius Ritual: Manifesting Adventure and Growth
Materials:

- A blue or purple candle (for expansion and spiritual insight)
- A small piece of turquoise or lapis lazuli (for wisdom)
- A map or globe (for travel and adventure)
- A piece of paper and pen

Instructions:

1. **Cleanse Your Space**: Burn sage or sandalwood incense to cleanse your space and invite in the expansive energy of Sagittarius.
2. **Set Your Intention**: Write down an intention for personal or spiritual growth, travel, or expanding your knowledge. Be clear about the new adventures you wish to manifest.
3. **Light the Candle**: As you light the blue or purple candle, say:
   "Under this Full Moon in Sagittarius, I open myself to new adventures and spiritual growth. I embrace the wisdom that comes with experience and seek new horizons."
4. **Use the Map**: Hold the map or globe and visualize yourself traveling to new places, learning new things, or embarking on a new spiritual path. Imagine yourself expanding your knowledge and growing in wisdom.
5. **Hold the Turquoise**: Hold the turquoise or lapis lazuli and focus on gaining spiritual insight and personal growth. Visualize yourself achieving your goals with confidence and joy.
6. **Close the Ritual**: Allow the candle to burn down. Keep the turquoise or lapis lazuli with you to inspire wisdom and spiritual growth.

Conclusion

Each Full Moon brings unique astrological energies based on the zodiac sign it inhabits, and by aligning your rituals with these influences, you can tap into the powerful energy of the cosmos. Whether you are working to heal, grow, manifest abundance, or release negativity, the Full Moon offers an opportunity to amplify your magical intentions and align with the natural rhythms of the universe. Use these rituals as a guide throughout 2025 to harness the energy of each Full Moon and create meaningful, transformative changes in your life.

Chapter 21: New Moon Manifestation Guides

The New Moon is a time of beginnings, offering a powerful opportunity to set new intentions, plant seeds for future growth, and initiate fresh projects. Each New Moon occurs in a specific zodiac sign, which influences the type of energy available for your intentions and goals. By aligning your manifestations with the energy of the zodiac sign the New Moon is in, you can maximize your chances of success and ensure that your goals resonate with the natural cosmic forces at play.

In this chapter, we will explore detailed manifestation guides for each New Moon in 2025, providing step-by-step rituals for setting intentions and aligning with the energy of the zodiac. Whether you're looking to start a new project, deepen your spiritual practice, attract abundance, or improve relationships, these New Moon guides will help you focus your energy in harmony with the lunar cycle.

The Power of the New Moon

The New Moon is the phase when the Moon is hidden from view, symbolizing a time of inward focus, reflection, and renewal. It is the perfect time to plant the seeds of new intentions, as the energy of the Moon will grow and develop over the next two weeks, culminating in the Full Moon. Whatever you initiate during the New Moon will gain momentum as the Moon waxes, making this phase ideal for setting goals, creating plans, and beginning new ventures.

Key principles of New Moon manifestation:

- **Introspection**: The dark of the New Moon encourages looking inward to assess what you truly desire.
- **Planting Seeds**: The New Moon is the time to plant the seeds of your intentions that will grow and manifest over the coming lunar cycle.
- **Setting Goals**: Align your goals with the energy of the zodiac sign the New Moon is in for better results.

January 1, 2025 – New Moon in Capricorn

Capricorn is a grounded Earth sign ruled by Saturn, representing ambition, discipline, and long-term planning. This New Moon is ideal for setting intentions related to career, financial stability, and personal responsibility. It's a powerful time for laying the foundation for long-term goals that require patience and hard work.

New Moon in Capricorn Manifestation Ritual: Career and Ambition
Materials:

- A green or brown candle (for stability and growth)
- A piece of paper and pen
- A small jar or box (to store your goals)
- A piece of pyrite or garnet (for success and financial growth)
- Sage or cedarwood oil (for grounding)

Instructions:

1. **Cleanse Your Space**: Burn sage or cedarwood oil to cleanse your space and invite grounded, stable energy.
2. **Set Your Intention**: Write down your long-term goals related to career, finances, or personal growth. Be specific about what you want to achieve and the steps you are willing to take.
3. **Light the Candle**: As you light the green or brown candle, say:
   "Under this New Moon in Capricorn, I set my intentions for success, stability, and growth. I am patient, disciplined, and ready to manifest my goals."
4. **Store Your Goals**: Place the written goals in a small jar or box, symbolizing the seeds of your intentions being planted. Visualize these seeds growing into a strong, stable reality over time.
5. **Hold the Pyrite**: Hold the pyrite or garnet in your hands and imagine yourself achieving your long-term goals with ease and success.
6. **Close the Ritual**: Allow the candle to burn down. Keep the jar or box in a safe place where you can revisit it throughout the year.

January 30, 2025 – New Moon in Aquarius

Aquarius, ruled by Uranus, is the sign of innovation, individuality, and social progress. This New Moon is perfect for setting intentions related to personal freedom, community involvement, or technological advancements. It's a time to focus on breaking free from limitations and embracing new ideas and progressive change.

New Moon in Aquarius Manifestation Ritual: Innovation and Personal Freedom

Materials:

- A blue or silver candle (for change and innovation)
- A feather (for freedom and the Air element)
- A piece of clear quartz or labradorite (for new ideas and insight)
- A piece of paper and pen

Instructions:

1. **Cleanse Your Space**: Use sage or frankincense incense to cleanse your space and invite the energy of innovation and freedom.
2. **Set Your Intention**: Write down a goal or desire related to personal freedom, a new idea, or a progressive change you want to make in your life or community.
3. **Light the Candle**: As you light the blue or silver candle, say:
   "Under this New Moon in Aquarius, I embrace change, innovation, and freedom. I break free from all limitations and welcome new possibilities."
4. **Use the Feather**: Hold the feather and visualize yourself soaring above any obstacles, free to pursue your unique path. Imagine your new idea or intention taking flight and manifesting effortlessly.

5. **Hold the Quartz**: Hold the clear quartz or labradorite and focus on receiving insight and inspiration for your new goals. See yourself thinking clearly and creatively as you move toward your desired future.

6. **Close the Ritual**: Allow the candle to burn down. Keep the quartz or labradorite near your workspace to continue receiving inspiration and clarity.

March 1, 2025 – New Moon in Pisces

Pisces, ruled by Neptune, is the sign of dreams, intuition, and spirituality. This New Moon is a time to focus on spiritual growth, emotional healing, and deepening your connection to your inner self. It's perfect for setting intentions related to dream work, psychic development, and creative endeavors.

New Moon in Pisces Manifestation Ritual: Intuition and Spiritual Growth
Materials:

- A purple or white candle (for spiritual awareness)
- A piece of amethyst or moonstone (for intuition and spiritual growth)
- A bowl of water (for Pisces' watery influence)
- A small journal or dream diary

Instructions:

1. **Cleanse Your Space**: Use lavender or sandalwood incense to create a calming, spiritual atmosphere.
2. **Set Your Intention**: Write down a spiritual or emotional goal, such as strengthening your intuition, deepening your spiritual practice, or healing from emotional wounds.
3. **Light the Candle**: As you light the purple or white candle, say:
   "Under this New Moon in Pisces, I open myself to spiritual growth and divine guidance. I trust my intuition and allow my dreams to guide me."
4. **Use the Water**: Hold the bowl of water in your hands and visualize your spiritual path flowing smoothly, connecting you to your higher self. Imagine your intuition becoming stronger with each passing day.
5. **Hold the Amethyst**: Hold the amethyst or moonstone in your hands and focus on receiving spiritual insights and healing. Feel your connection to the divine deepening as you open yourself to spiritual guidance.
6. **Close the Ritual**: Allow the candle to burn down. Keep the amethyst or moonstone near your bed or meditation space to enhance your spiritual practice and dream work.

March 30, 2025 – New Moon in Aries

Aries, ruled by Mars, is the sign of action, courage, and new beginnings. This New Moon brings energy for initiating projects, taking bold steps toward your goals, and manifesting personal power. It's the perfect time for setting intentions related to leadership, physical vitality, and courage in pursuing new ventures.

New Moon in Aries Manifestation Ritual: Courage and New Beginnings

Materials:

- A red candle (for action and courage)
- A piece of carnelian or garnet (for energy and confidence)
- A small piece of paper and pen
- Cinnamon or ginger incense (for motivation)

Instructions:

1. **Cleanse Your Space**: Burn cinnamon or ginger incense to energize your space and invite bold, courageous energy.
2. **Set Your Intention**: Write down a goal related to taking action, starting a new project, or overcoming a personal challenge. Focus on a specific area where you need courage and motivation.
3. **Light the Candle**: As you light the red candle, say:
   "Under this New Moon in Aries, I ignite the fire of courage within me. I take bold action toward my goals and embrace new beginnings."
4. **Visualize Your Goal**: Hold the carnelian or garnet in your hands and visualize yourself confidently achieving your goal. See yourself taking action with courage and determination.
5. **Close the Ritual**: Allow the candle to burn down. Keep the carnelian or garnet with you as a reminder to stay focused and motivated in pursuing your goals.

April 28, 2025 – New Moon in Taurus

Taurus, ruled by Venus, is the sign of stability, abundance, and sensuality. This New Moon is ideal for manifesting financial security, attracting abundance, and enhancing your relationship with the material world. It's a perfect time to set intentions related to wealth, self-worth, and creating a comfortable, beautiful environment.

New Moon in Taurus Manifestation Ritual: Abundance and Financial Stability

Materials:

- A green candle (for prosperity)
- A small bowl of coins (for abundance)
- A piece of jade or green aventurine (for financial success)
- A piece of paper and pen

Instructions:

1. **Cleanse Your Space:** Burn sandalwood or patchouli incense to ground your space and invite the energy of abundance.
2. **Set Your Intention:** Write down a financial goal or an intention to attract abundance into your life. Be specific about the amount or type of wealth you wish to manifest.
3. **Light the Candle:** As you light the green candle, say:
   "Under this New Moon in Taurus, I call forth abundance, prosperity, and financial stability. I attract wealth with ease and grace."
4. **Use the Coins:** Hold the bowl of coins in your hands and visualize your financial intentions coming to fruition. Imagine the coins multiplying and filling your life with abundance and security.
5. **Hold the Jade:** Hold the jade or green aventurine and feel the energy of prosperity flowing into your life. Picture yourself achieving financial success and stability.
6. **Close the Ritual:** Allow the candle to burn down. Keep the jade or green aventurine in your wallet or on your desk to attract continuous financial success.

May 29, 2025 – New Moon in Gemini

Gemini, ruled by Mercury, is the sign of communication, learning, and adaptability. This New Moon is ideal for setting intentions related to improving communication, learning new skills, and manifesting mental clarity. It's a great time for starting new educational pursuits or enhancing your ability to express yourself clearly.

New Moon in Gemini Manifestation Ritual: Communication and Learning Materials:

- A yellow or blue candle (for clarity and communication)
- A feather or quill pen (for Mercury's influence)
- A piece of lapis lazuli or sodalite (for mental clarity)
- A notebook or journal

Instructions:

1. **Cleanse Your Space:** Burn sandalwood or sage incense to cleanse your space and invite clear thinking and communication.
2. **Set Your Intention:** Write down an intention related to improving communication, learning a new skill, or enhancing mental clarity.
3. **Light the Candle:** As you light the yellow or blue candle, say:
   "Under this New Moon in Gemini, I open my mind to clarity and my voice to truth. I communicate clearly and learn with ease."
4. **Use the Feather:** Hold the feather or quill pen and visualize your thoughts flowing freely and clearly. Imagine yourself learning new things easily and expressing your ideas with confidence.

5. **Hold the Lapis Lazuli**: Hold the lapis lazuli or sodalite and focus on your mind becoming clear and focused. Visualize yourself achieving mental clarity and mastering new skills with ease.
6. **Close the Ritual**: Allow the candle to burn down. Keep the lapis lazuli or sodalite with you when studying or communicating to enhance clarity and focus.

June 27, 2025 – New Moon in Cancer

Cancer, ruled by the Moon, is the sign of home, family, and emotional security. This New Moon is ideal for setting intentions related to home life, nurturing relationships, and creating emotional balance. It's a perfect time to focus on emotional healing, strengthening family bonds, and protecting your personal space.

New Moon in Cancer Manifestation Ritual: Emotional Healing and Home Protection
Materials:

- A white or blue candle (for emotional balance and protection)
- A bowl of water (for Cancer's watery influence)
- A piece of moonstone or rose quartz (for emotional healing)
- A small piece of paper and pen

Instructions:

1. **Cleanse Your Space**: Burn lavender or rose incense to create a calming, nurturing atmosphere.
2. **Set Your Intention**: Write down an intention related to emotional healing, strengthening family bonds, or protecting your home.
3. **Light the Candle**: As you light the white or blue candle, say:
   "Under this New Moon in Cancer, I call forth emotional healing, peace, and protection. I create a safe and nurturing space for myself and my loved ones."
4. **Use the Water**: Hold the bowl of water in your hands and visualize emotional balance and peace flowing into your life. Imagine the water soothing any emotional wounds or conflicts.
5. **Hold the Moonstone**: Hold the moonstone or rose quartz and focus on healing any emotional pain or restoring harmony in your home. Picture yourself and your loved ones surrounded by a protective, nurturing energy.
6. **Close the Ritual**: Allow the candle to burn down. Keep the moonstone or rose quartz in your home to promote emotional balance and protection.

July 27, 2025 – New Moon in Leo

Leo, ruled by the Sun, is the sign of creativity, self-expression, and confidence. This New Moon is perfect for setting intentions related to personal empowerment, creative projects, and manifesting success. It's a great time to focus on boosting your confidence and stepping into the spotlight.

New Moon in Leo Manifestation Ritual: Creativity and Confidence

Materials:

- A gold or orange candle (for confidence and creativity)
- A piece of citrine or sunstone (for self-esteem and success)
- A mirror (to reflect your inner power)
- A small piece of paper and pen

Instructions:

1. **Cleanse Your Space**: Burn cinnamon or clove incense to energize your space and invite creative, confident energy.
2. **Set Your Intention**: Write down a goal related to personal empowerment, creative expression, or achieving success in a project.
3. **Light the Candle**: As you light the gold or orange candle, say:
   "Under this New Moon in Leo, I ignite the fire of creativity and confidence within me. I express myself with power and grace."
4. **Use the Mirror**: Hold the mirror and look into your reflection, visualizing yourself as powerful, confident, and successful. See yourself achieving your goals with ease and radiating creative energy.
5. **Hold the Citrine**: Hold the citrine or sunstone and focus on boosting your confidence and self-esteem. Visualize yourself stepping into the spotlight and manifesting success in all your endeavors.
6. **Close the Ritual**: Allow the candle to burn down. Keep the citrine or sunstone with you to continue attracting confidence and success.

August 26, 2025 – New Moon in Virgo

Virgo, ruled by Mercury, is the sign of organization, health, and service. This New Moon is ideal for setting intentions related to self-care, health routines, and bringing order to your life. It's a great time for focusing on improving your physical well-being, organizing your space, and setting productive routines.

New Moon in Virgo Manifestation Ritual: Health and Organization

Materials:

- A green or brown candle (for health and grounding)
- A piece of clear quartz or jade (for healing and clarity)
- Rosemary or eucalyptus oil (for cleansing)
- A small notebook or planner

Instructions:

1. **Cleanse Your Space**: Use rosemary or eucalyptus oil to cleanse your space and invite healing, organized energy.
2. **Set Your Intention**: Write down an intention related to improving your health, organizing your space, or creating new productive routines.
3. **Light the Candle**: As you light the green or brown candle, say:
   "Under this New Moon in Virgo, I call forth health, clarity, and organization. I create space for healing and balance in my life."
4. **Use the Notebook**: Write down a detailed plan for how you will implement your health or organizational goals. Be specific about the steps you will take to bring more order and well-being into your life.
5. **Hold the Clear Quartz**: Hold the clear quartz or jade and visualize yourself feeling healthy, organized, and in control of your routines. Imagine your life flowing smoothly and efficiently.
6. **Close the Ritual**: Allow the candle to burn down. Keep the clear quartz or jade near your workspace or in your home to promote clarity and organization.

September 24, 2025 – New Moon in Libra

Libra, ruled by Venus, is the sign of balance, beauty, and relationships. This New Moon is ideal for setting intentions related to improving relationships, creating harmony in your life, and manifesting beauty and peace. It's a perfect time to focus on love, partnerships, and bringing balance to any chaotic situations.

New Moon in Libra Manifestation Ritual: Love and Harmony

Materials:

- A pink or blue candle (for love and harmony)
- Rose petals or jasmine flowers (for beauty)
- Rose quartz or lapis lazuli (for balanced communication)
- A piece of paper and pen

Instructions:

1. **Cleanse Your Space**: Use rose incense or jasmine oil to cleanse your space and invite loving, harmonious energy.
2. **Set Your Intention**: Write down an intention related to improving a relationship, attracting love, or creating balance in your life.
3. **Light the Candle**: As you light the pink or blue candle, say:
   "Under this New Moon in Libra, I call forth love, balance, and harmony. I create peace and beauty in all areas of my life."
4. **Use Rose Petals**: Sprinkle rose petals around the candle, symbolizing the love and harmony you wish to cultivate. Visualize your relationships growing in mutual respect and understanding.
5. **Hold the Rose Quartz**: Hold the rose quartz or lapis lazuli in your hands and focus on communicating clearly and with love. Picture yourself bringing balance and peace to all areas of your life.
6. **Close the Ritual**: Allow the candle to burn down. Keep the rose quartz or lapis lazuli near you to maintain harmonious energy in your relationships.

October 25, 2025 – New Moon in Scorpio

Scorpio, ruled by Pluto, is the sign of transformation, power, and deep emotional intensity. This New Moon is ideal for setting intentions related to personal transformation, emotional healing, and releasing old patterns. It's a powerful time for focusing on manifesting change, rebirth, and empowerment.

New Moon in Scorpio Manifestation Ritual: Transformation and Emotional Healing
Materials:

- A black or dark red candle (for transformation)
- A piece of obsidian or black tourmaline (for protection)
- A bowl of water (for emotional release)
- A piece of paper and pen

Instructions:

1. **Cleanse Your Space**: Burn sage or palo santo to clear your space, inviting in the transformative energy of Scorpio.
2. **Set Your Intention**: Write down an intention related to personal transformation, emotional healing, or releasing an old pattern or behavior.
3. **Light the Candle**: As you light the black or dark red candle, say:
   "Under this New Moon in Scorpio, I release all that no longer serves me. I transform my life and heal my heart."
4. **Use the Water**: Hold the bowl of water in your hands and visualize your old patterns or emotional wounds dissolving into the water. Imagine yourself being freed from the weight of your past.
5. **Hold the Obsidian**: Hold the obsidian or black tourmaline and focus on your personal transformation and empowerment. Visualize yourself rising from the ashes of your past, strong and renewed.
6. **Close the Ritual**: Allow the candle to burn down. Pour the water outside as an offering to symbolize the release of old emotional energy. Keep the obsidian or black tourmaline with you as a talisman for protection and strength.

November 23, 2025 – New Moon in Sagittarius

Sagittarius, ruled by Jupiter, is the sign of expansion, adventure, and higher learning. This New Moon is ideal for setting intentions related to personal growth, travel, and spiritual exploration. It's a perfect time to focus on manifesting new opportunities, expanding your knowledge, and embracing new adventures.

New Moon in Sagittarius Manifestation Ritual: Adventure and Growth
Materials:

- A blue or purple candle (for expansion and spiritual insight)
- A map or travel-related object (for manifestation)
- A piece of turquoise or lapis lazuli (for wisdom)
- A piece of paper and pen

Instructions:

1. **Cleanse Your Space**: Burn sage or sandalwood incense to cleanse your space and invite the energy of adventure and expansion.
2. **Set Your Intention**: Write down a goal related to personal growth, travel, or expanding your knowledge. Be specific about the new experiences or opportunities you wish to attract.
3. **Light the Candle**: As you light the blue or purple candle, say:
   "Under this New Moon in Sagittarius, I open myself to new adventures and personal growth. I embrace the wisdom that comes from experience and seek new horizons."
4. **Use the Map**: Place a map or travel-related object on your altar to symbolize the new journeys you wish to embark on. Visualize yourself exploring these new horizons with excitement and curiosity.
5. **Hold the Turquoise**: Hold the turquoise or lapis lazuli and focus on gaining wisdom and insight from your experiences. Picture yourself growing spiritually and mentally as you explore new opportunities.
6. **Close the Ritual**: Allow the candle to burn down. Keep the turquoise or lapis lazuli with you to inspire wisdom and spiritual growth.

December 22, 2025 – New Moon in Capricorn

The second New Moon in Capricorn this year brings an opportunity to review your progress on long-term goals and set new intentions for the coming year. It's a powerful time to focus on manifesting success, building stability, and achieving personal or financial goals.

New Moon in Capricorn Manifestation Ritual: Review and Renew

Materials:

- A green or brown candle (for stability and growth)
- A small jar or box (to store your goals)
- A piece of pyrite or garnet (for success and financial growth)
- A piece of paper and pen

Instructions:

1. **Cleanse Your Space**: Burn sage or cedarwood oil to ground your space and invite stability.
2. **Review Your Progress**: Write down the goals you set earlier in the year and review your progress. Reflect on what has worked and what needs more focus.
3. **Set New Intentions**: Write down new intentions for the coming year, focusing on what you want to manifest in terms of success, career, or finances.
4. **Light the Candle**: As you light the green or brown candle, say:
   "Under this New Moon in Capricorn, I set my intentions for long-term success and stability. I am patient, disciplined, and ready to manifest my goals."
5. **Store Your Goals**: Place the written goals in a small jar or box, symbolizing the seeds of your intentions being planted for the coming year.
6. **Hold the Pyrite**: Hold the pyrite or garnet in your hands and imagine yourself achieving your long-term goals with ease and success.
7. **Close the Ritual**: Allow the candle to burn down. Keep the jar or box in a safe place where you can revisit it throughout the next year.

Conclusion

The New Moon is a powerful time for setting intentions and planting the seeds of future manifestations. By aligning your intentions with the zodiac sign that governs each New Moon, you can harness the unique energy of the cosmos to amplify your goals and bring your desires to fruition. Whether you're focused on personal growth, career success, emotional healing, or spiritual expansion, these New Moon manifestation guides offer step-by-step rituals to help you align with the lunar cycle and manifest your dreams in harmony with the universe.

Chapter 22: Solar Energy and Daylight Spells

The Sun, a powerful and ever-present force, has been revered across cultures for its life-giving energy and association with success, joy, healing, and vitality. In magical practice, the Sun represents strength, clarity, personal power, and the ability to manifest success and positive energy. While the Moon governs emotions, intuition, and the subconscious, the Sun shines on the conscious mind, illuminating our path, fueling our confidence, and empowering our ambitions.

Harnessing the Sun's energy through spells and rituals aligns you with the forces of growth, abundance, health, and happiness. This chapter provides a comprehensive guide to solar magic, teaching you how to channel the Sun's power for success, joy, and healing. We will explore the best times to perform daylight spells, specific solar deities you can call upon, and detailed rituals that use the Sun's radiant energy for manifestation, personal empowerment, and physical well-being.

The Power of the Sun in Magical Practice

The Sun governs the element of Fire, symbolizing life force, action, vitality, and creativity. Its energy is active, masculine, and direct, making it ideal for spells related to success, personal empowerment, and bringing clarity to situations. When you work with solar energy, you are tapping into a source of light, warmth, and nourishment that fuels all living things. In magical terms, the Sun can be called upon to illuminate paths that are unclear, burn away negativity, and provide strength for challenging times.

Key Qualities of Solar Energy

- **Vitality and Health**: The Sun provides the energy necessary for life, making it a powerful force for healing spells and rituals focused on physical vitality and well-being.
- **Success and Achievement**: Solar energy fuels ambition and confidence, helping you manifest success in your endeavors and overcome obstacles.
- **Joy and Happiness**: The Sun is a symbol of light, joy, and positivity. It can be used in spells to banish depression, increase happiness, and invite more light into your life.
- **Clarity and Focus**: Just as the Sun lights up the day, its energy can bring mental clarity, helping you make decisions and see situations more clearly.
- **Personal Empowerment**: Solar energy strengthens self-confidence, willpower, and personal power, making it ideal for spells focused on self-development and leadership.

Harnessing Solar Energy in Spellwork

To effectively harness the power of the Sun in your magical practice, it's important to time your spells and rituals to correspond with the daily and seasonal cycles of solar energy. The Sun's movement from sunrise to sunset, as well as its annual journey through the zodiac, offers many opportunities to channel its energy for success, joy, and healing.

Daily Solar Cycle

- **Sunrise**: The rising Sun brings new beginnings, renewal, and the promise of potential. It is a powerful time for setting intentions, starting new projects, and invoking the energy of hope and success.
- **Noon**: At noon, the Sun is at its zenith, representing the height of power, clarity, and energy. This is an ideal time for spells requiring maximum strength, success in business, leadership, and confidence.
- **Sunset**: As the Sun sets, it ushers in a time of reflection, release, and closure. Sunset is perfect for spells focused on letting go of the past, ending toxic cycles, and preparing for a fresh start.

Seasonal Solar Cycle

- **Summer Solstice (Litha)**: The longest day of the year, the Summer Solstice celebrates the peak of the Sun's power and is a time for abundance, growth, and prosperity. Spells for success, fertility, and manifesting abundance are especially potent on this day.
- **Winter Solstice (Yule)**: The Winter Solstice marks the rebirth of the Sun after the longest night, symbolizing hope, renewal, and the return of light. It's a powerful time for spells that focus on rebirth, new beginnings, and manifesting positive change after a dark period.
- **Spring Equinox (Ostara)**: The Spring Equinox represents balance between light and dark, making it an excellent time for spells that focus on balance, growth, and new opportunities.
- **Autumn Equinox (Mabon)**: This day of equal light and darkness is a time for harvest and gratitude. It is a good time for spells that focus on reaping rewards, bringing projects to fruition, and celebrating success.

Solar Deities to Call Upon

Throughout history, many cultures have honored solar deities as powerful forces of life, success, and healing. Calling upon these deities in your solar spells can help you harness their specific attributes and amplify the energy of your rituals.

Ra (Egyptian Sun God)

- **Attributes**: Ra is the god of the Sun, creation, and life. He represents power, vitality, and success.
- **Use in Spells**: Call upon Ra for spells related to leadership, personal power, and overcoming obstacles.

Apollo (Greek God of the Sun and Healing)

- **Attributes**: Apollo governs music, healing, prophecy, and the Sun. He is associated with light, clarity, and health.
- **Use in Spells**: Invoke Apollo for healing rituals, spells for mental clarity, and success in creative endeavors.

Helios (Greek God of the Sun)

- **Attributes**: Helios is the personification of the Sun, driving his chariot across the sky each day. He represents unwavering strength and light.
- **Use in Spells**: Call upon Helios for strength, endurance, and illuminating the truth in situations.

Amaterasu (Japanese Sun Goddess)

- **Attributes**: Amaterasu is the goddess of the Sun and the universe. She brings light, warmth, and life to all beings.
- **Use in Spells**: Invoke Amaterasu for rituals that focus on personal growth, spiritual enlightenment, and bringing light into dark situations.

Sol (Norse Sun Goddess)

- **Attributes**: Sol drives the Sun's chariot through the sky. She represents life force, success, and perseverance.
- **Use in Spells**: Call upon Sol for spells focused on perseverance through challenges, manifesting success, and personal empowerment.

Solar Spells for Success, Joy, and Healing

Solar energy is dynamic and empowering, making it ideal for a variety of spells. Below are specific rituals for success, joy, and healing, all designed to harness the radiant energy of the Sun to bring light and positivity into your life.

1. Success and Abundance Spell

This spell is perfect for manifesting success in your career, business, or personal endeavors. It draws upon the power of the Sun to amplify your efforts and bring about favorable outcomes.

Materials:

- A gold or yellow candle (for success and abundance)
- A piece of pyrite or citrine (for prosperity)
- Sunflowers or marigold flowers (for solar energy)
- Cinnamon or basil (for prosperity)
- A piece of paper and pen

Instructions:

1. **Prepare Your Space**: Cleanse your space with cinnamon or basil incense to invite prosperous energy.
2. **Set Your Intention**: Write down a specific goal or area of your life where you seek success. Be clear and detailed about what you wish to achieve.
3. **Light the Candle**: As you light the gold or yellow candle, say:
   "I call upon the power of the Sun to bring success and abundance into my life. I ignite the flame of prosperity and watch it grow."
4. **Use the Sunflowers**: Place the sunflowers or marigolds around the candle, symbolizing the energy of the Sun nourishing your goals.
5. **Hold the Pyrite**: Hold the pyrite or citrine in your hands and visualize your goal manifesting with ease and success. Imagine the Sun's light shining on your path, illuminating opportunities.
6. **Close the Ritual**: Allow the candle to burn down completely. Keep the pyrite or citrine on your desk or workspace to continue attracting success.

2. Solar Healing Ritual

The Sun's energy is not only powerful but also deeply healing. This spell draws on the Sun's warmth and vitality to heal physical ailments, restore energy, and promote overall well-being.

Materials:

- A white or yellow candle (for healing and vitality)
- A bowl of water (for cleansing)
- A piece of sunstone or amber (for healing energy)
- A few drops of rosemary or eucalyptus oil (for healing)

Instructions:

1. **Prepare Your Space**: Cleanse your space with rosemary or eucalyptus oil to promote healing.
2. **Set Your Intention**: Focus on the area of your body or life that requires healing. Be clear about what you wish to heal, whether it's physical, emotional, or spiritual.
3. **Light the Candle**: As you light the white or yellow candle, say:
   "I call upon the healing energy of the Sun to restore my vitality and bring health and wellness into my life."
4. **Use the Water**: Hold the bowl of water and visualize it being charged with the healing energy of the Sun. Imagine the water glowing with golden light, filled with the power to cleanse and heal.
5. **Hold the Sunstone**: Hold the sunstone or amber in your hands and focus on the healing energy flowing into your body. Visualize the Sun's warmth removing illness or pain, leaving you feeling restored and energized.
6. **Close the Ritual**: Allow the candle to burn down. Use the charged water to anoint your body or pour it over your hands and feet as a final act of healing. Keep the sunstone or amber with you as a talisman of healing.

3. Joy and Positivity Spell

This spell is designed to banish negativity and invite more joy and happiness into your life. It uses the Sun's energy to brighten your outlook and fill your life with light and positivity.

Materials:

- A yellow or orange candle (for joy and happiness)
- Sunflowers or daisies (for solar energy)
- A piece of citrine or clear quartz (for positive energy)
- A small mirror (to reflect light)

Instructions:

1. **Prepare Your Space**: Cleanse your space with citrus or peppermint incense to invite light and joy.
2. **Set Your Intention**: Focus on an area of your life where you need more positivity or want to banish negative thoughts or energy. Be clear about the joy you wish to attract.
3. **Light the Candle**: As you light the yellow or orange candle, say:
   "I call upon the power of the Sun to fill my life with light, joy, and happiness. I banish all darkness and invite positivity to reign."
4. **Use the Sunflowers**: Place the sunflowers or daisies around the candle, symbolizing the light and happiness you wish to invite into your life.
5. **Use the Mirror**: Hold the mirror and reflect the light of the candle onto yourself, visualizing the Sun's energy brightening your life and filling you with joy. Imagine any negativity being burned away by the light.
6. **Hold the Citrine**: Hold the citrine or clear quartz and focus on the feeling of happiness and positivity filling your heart. Visualize yourself smiling, laughing, and feeling light and carefree.
7. **Close the Ritual**: Allow the candle to burn down. Keep the citrine or clear quartz with you to maintain positive energy throughout your day.

4. Solar Confidence and Personal Power Spell

This spell is perfect for boosting self-confidence, enhancing personal power, and stepping into leadership roles. It harnesses the strength of the Sun to empower you and give you the courage to pursue your goals with confidence.

Materials:

- A gold or orange candle (for power and confidence)
- A piece of carnelian or tiger's eye (for courage and strength)
- Cinnamon or clove incense (for motivation)
- A small mirror (to reflect your inner power)

Instructions:

1. **Prepare Your Space**: Burn cinnamon or clove incense to energize your space and invite strength and confidence.
2. **Set Your Intention**: Write down a goal or area of your life where you want to feel more confident and empowered. Be specific about the kind of personal power you wish to cultivate.
3. **Light the Candle**: As you light the gold or orange candle, say:
   "I call upon the power of the Sun to strengthen my confidence and empower my spirit. I step boldly into my personal power and shine my light on the world."

4. **Use the Mirror**: Hold the mirror and look into your reflection, visualizing yourself as confident, powerful, and capable. See yourself succeeding in your goals and standing in your full power.

5. **Hold the Carnelian**: Hold the carnelian or tiger's eye in your hands and focus on the energy of courage and confidence flowing through you. Imagine yourself taking bold steps toward your goals with unwavering self-assurance.

6. **Close the Ritual**: Allow the candle to burn down. Keep the carnelian or tiger's eye with you as a reminder of your strength and confidence.

Solar Symbols, Herbs, and Crystals for Solar Magic

To enhance your solar spells, you can incorporate specific symbols, herbs, and crystals that resonate with the Sun's energy.

Solar Symbols:

- **Sun Disk**: Represents the power of the Sun, life force, and success.
- **Lion**: Symbol of strength, courage, and leadership.
- **Phoenix**: Represents rebirth, transformation, and rising from the ashes.
- **Gold Coins**: Symbol of wealth, success, and abundance.

Herbs for Solar Magic:

- **Sunflowers**: Associated with the Sun, success, and happiness.
- **Marigolds**: Used in spells for protection, success, and positivity.
- **Cinnamon**: Adds energy, power, and motivation to solar spells.
- **Basil**: Attracts prosperity, abundance, and protection.

Crystals for Solar Magic:

- **Citrine**: A powerful crystal for success, abundance, and joy.
- **Sunstone**: Represents vitality, personal power, and healing.
- **Tiger's Eye**: Used for courage, protection, and personal empowerment.
- **Amber**: Carries the energy of the Sun and is used for healing, vitality, and positivity.

Conclusion

The Sun's energy is a potent force for success, joy, healing, and personal empowerment. By harnessing its power in your spells and rituals, you can tap into a source of vitality and strength that illuminates your path and fuels your ambitions. Whether you are seeking success in your career, healing for your body, or more joy in your life, solar magic offers powerful tools for manifesting your desires and stepping into the light of your full potential. Through careful timing, the use of solar symbols, herbs, and crystals, and alignment with the Sun's cycles, you can create radiant spells that bring success, happiness, and well-being into your life.

Chapter 23: Lunar Eclipses and Their Impact

Lunar eclipses are potent and transformative celestial events that occur when the Earth passes between the Sun and the Moon, casting a shadow on the Moon's surface. During these powerful moments, the Moon's usual brilliance is dimmed, symbolizing a temporary disruption of energy, a pause in the lunar cycle, and a time of intense transformation. In magical practice, lunar eclipses are associated with endings, release, and deep spiritual shifts, providing a potent opportunity to engage in shadow work, banishing rituals, and letting go of patterns, emotions, or situations that no longer serve you.

This chapter explores the astrological and magical significance of lunar eclipses, offering detailed information on the lunar eclipses occurring in 2025 and how to harness their transformative energy for your magical practice. You'll find specific dates for each eclipse, an understanding of the astrological influences at play, and rituals tailored to each lunar eclipse to help you align with the energies of release, transformation, and spiritual growth.

Understanding Lunar Eclipses in Magic

Lunar eclipses are powerful celestial events that intensify the normal energy of a Full Moon. While Full Moons are typically a time for manifestation, celebration, and culmination, lunar eclipses add a layer of intensity and complexity, making them more about endings, revelations, and profound change. During a lunar eclipse, hidden truths often come to light, emotions are heightened, and deep-seated issues may rise to the surface for resolution.

Key Themes of Lunar Eclipses:

- **Release and Letting Go**: Lunar eclipses are ideal for releasing old patterns, habits, or emotional baggage that you've been holding onto. It's a time for cutting ties with situations, relationships, or mindsets that no longer serve your highest good.
- **Transformation and Change**: Eclipses signify major turning points, often forcing transformation. They provide the energetic push needed to evolve, offering a powerful opportunity for spiritual growth and self-awareness.
- **Revelations and Truth**: Eclipses often reveal what has been hidden, both externally and within yourself. Long-buried truths may come to light, and it's important to face these revelations with honesty and openness.
- **Shadow Work**: Lunar eclipses are an ideal time for shadow work—confronting the aspects of yourself that you may have ignored or suppressed. This deep inner work can lead to healing and empowerment as you release old fears and traumas.

Lunar eclipses act as cosmic resets, allowing you to clear away the past and create space for new beginnings. The energy of a lunar eclipse can feel overwhelming at times, but when channeled correctly, it can lead to profound personal growth and transformation.

Lunar Eclipses in 2025: Dates and Astrological Significance

In 2025, there will be two significant lunar eclipses, each with its own unique energy and astrological influence. These eclipses will provide opportunities for magical workings focused on release, transformation, and the revelation of truth.

1. March 14, 2025 – Total Lunar Eclipse in Virgo

Astrological Significance: Virgo is an Earth sign ruled by Mercury, associated with organization, health, work, and service. This lunar eclipse in Virgo highlights the need to release perfectionism, control, and rigidity. It calls for letting go of habits that no longer support your well-being, especially those related to health, daily routines, and work-life balance.

Magical Focus: This eclipse is an ideal time to focus on releasing unhealthy patterns in your life, particularly around your self-care, productivity, or critical thinking. It's also a good time for clearing emotional and mental clutter, detoxifying your mind and body, and releasing the need for perfection.

Themes:

- Releasing control and perfectionism
- Cleansing and detoxifying (physically, mentally, and emotionally)
- Letting go of rigid routines or limiting beliefs around work and health
- Focusing on self-compassion and balance

2. September 7, 2025 – Partial Lunar Eclipse in Pisces

Astrological Significance: Pisces, ruled by Neptune, is a Water sign associated with intuition, dreams, spirituality, and emotional depth. This lunar eclipse in Pisces encourages deep emotional release, the healing of spiritual wounds, and the surrender of illusions. It calls for letting go of anything that hinders your spiritual growth, such as addictive behaviors, emotional dependencies, or self-deception.

Magical Focus: This eclipse is perfect for shadow work and spiritual healing. It's a powerful time to release emotional baggage, unresolved trauma, and toxic attachments. With Pisces' energy, you can tap into your intuition and dreams to gain insights into what needs to be healed and released. This eclipse also offers an opportunity to dissolve emotional barriers and open yourself to spiritual growth and divine connection.

Themes:

- Emotional healing and release
- Letting go of illusions, addictions, and toxic emotional patterns
- Heightening intuition and spiritual awareness
- Releasing fear and embracing spiritual surrender

Rituals and Spells for Each Lunar Eclipse in 2025

Below are detailed rituals designed to align with the specific energies of each lunar eclipse in 2025. These rituals focus on release, transformation, and spiritual growth, helping you harness the power of these potent celestial events.

Total Lunar Eclipse in Virgo – March 14, 2025

Ritual: Releasing Perfectionism and Cultivating Balance

This ritual is designed to help you release rigid patterns of control, perfectionism, or unhealthy routines. The Virgo eclipse encourages letting go of the need to be perfect in all aspects of life and embracing self-compassion, balance, and well-being.

Materials:

- A white or green candle (for healing and release)
- A small piece of paper and pen
- A bowl of water (for cleansing)
- A piece of clear quartz or amethyst (for clarity and healing)
- Lavender or rosemary incense (for calming and clarity)

Instructions:

1. **Prepare Your Space**: Cleanse your space with lavender or rosemary incense to create a calming, clear atmosphere.
2. **Set Your Intention**: Reflect on areas of your life where you've been overly critical, rigid, or perfectionistic. Write down the habits or patterns you wish to release, particularly those that affect your health, work, or sense of self-worth.
3. **Light the Candle**: As you light the white or green candle, say:
   "Under this eclipse in Virgo, I release the need for perfection. I let go of control, rigidity, and unhealthy habits that no longer serve me."
4. **Use the Water**: Hold the bowl of water and visualize it as a cleansing force, washing away your worries, perfectionism, and any harmful routines. Imagine yourself being cleansed of all that holds you back from balance and well-being.
5. **Burn the Paper**: Safely burn the piece of paper with your written habits or behaviors in the candle flame, symbolizing their release. As the paper burns, feel yourself letting go of the need for control and embracing a more balanced, compassionate approach to life.
6. **Hold the Crystal**: Hold the clear quartz or amethyst in your hands and visualize yourself feeling calm, balanced, and free from self-criticism. Imagine the crystal amplifying your intention to release and heal.
7. **Close the Ritual**: Allow the candle to burn down completely. Pour the water outside as a final act of release and renewal. Keep the clear quartz or amethyst near you to maintain clarity and balance.

Partial Lunar Eclipse in Pisces – September 7, 2025
Ritual: Emotional Release and Spiritual Healing

This ritual is designed to help you release emotional and spiritual blockages that prevent you from fully embracing your intuition and spiritual path. The Pisces eclipse offers a powerful opportunity for emotional healing and spiritual renewal, allowing you to let go of toxic attachments and embrace spiritual surrender.

Materials:

- A blue or white candle (for healing and intuition)
- A small mirror (for reflection and truth)
- A piece of paper and pen
- A bowl of saltwater (for cleansing and emotional release)
- A piece of moonstone or rose quartz (for emotional healing)
- Lavender or sandalwood incense (for spiritual clarity)

Instructions:

1. **Prepare Your Space**: Burn lavender or sandalwood incense to create a sacred, calming atmosphere.
2. **Set Your Intention**: Reflect on the emotional patterns, toxic attachments, or illusions you wish to release. Write down what you are ready to let go of, particularly in relation to your emotional well-being or spiritual growth.
3. **Light the Candle**: As you light the blue or white candle, say:
   "Under this eclipse in Pisces, I release all emotional pain, toxic attachments, and illusions. I open my heart to healing and spiritual growth."
4. **Use the Mirror**: Hold the mirror and gaze into your reflection. As you look at yourself, reflect on the emotional or spiritual patterns that have held you back. See them clearly and with compassion, acknowledging what you are ready to release.
5. **Use the Saltwater**: Dip your fingers into the bowl of saltwater and anoint your forehead, heart, and hands, symbolizing the cleansing and release of emotional burdens. As you do this, visualize the saltwater dissolving your pain, fear, or toxic emotions.
6. **Burn the Paper**: Safely burn the piece of paper with your written emotional patterns or attachments in the candle flame. As the paper burns, imagine these patterns being released from your life, leaving space for healing and spiritual renewal.
7. **Hold the Moonstone**: Hold the moonstone or rose quartz in your hands and focus on emotional healing and spiritual connection. Visualize yourself surrounded by the energy of peace, love, and divine support.

8. **Close the Ritual**: Allow the candle to burn down completely. Pour the saltwater outside, releasing your emotional burdens to the Earth. Keep the moonstone or rose quartz near your bed or on your altar to support continued emotional healing.

Magical Timing for Lunar Eclipses

While lunar eclipses offer potent energy for release and transformation, it's important to be mindful of the energy they bring. Unlike a traditional Full Moon, which is a time for manifestation, lunar eclipses are better suited for rituals of letting go, closure, and clearing away obstacles. Here are some tips for working with lunar eclipse energy:

- **Focus on Release**: Use lunar eclipses to let go of what no longer serves you, whether it's old habits, toxic relationships, limiting beliefs, or emotional pain.
- **Avoid New Beginnings**: The chaotic and intense energy of a lunar eclipse is not ideal for starting new projects or setting new intentions. Instead, focus on clearing the way for future manifestations.
- **Embrace Shadow Work**: Lunar eclipses are a perfect time for shadow work—exploring the darker aspects of your psyche, confronting fears, and releasing deep-seated emotional or psychological blocks.
- **Ritual Timing**: Perform your rituals during the actual eclipse for maximum potency, or within 24 hours before or after the eclipse to align with the transformative energy.

Lunar Eclipse Symbols, Herbs, and Crystals

To enhance your lunar eclipse rituals, you can incorporate specific symbols, herbs, and crystals that resonate with the energy of release, transformation, and emotional healing.

Symbols for Lunar Eclipses:

- **The Snake**: A symbol of transformation, shedding old skins, and renewal.
- **The Phoenix**: Represents death and rebirth, rising from the ashes of the past.
- **The Moon**: Represents emotions, intuition, and the subconscious mind.
- **Scissors or a Knife**: Symbolizes cutting ties and releasing old attachments.

Herbs for Lunar Eclipses:

- **Sage**: Used for clearing negative energy and purifying the space.
- **Mugwort**: Heightens intuition and supports shadow work during the eclipse.
- **Lavender**: Calms the emotions and promotes spiritual clarity during times of transformation.
- **Rosemary**: Used for protection and mental clarity when confronting deep emotional issues.

Crystals for Lunar Eclipses:

- **Amethyst**: A powerful crystal for spiritual clarity, emotional healing, and release.
- **Black Tourmaline**: Offers protection and grounding during intense emotional work.
- **Moonstone**: Enhances intuition and emotional healing, supporting the release of emotional patterns.
- **Obsidian**: A stone of protection and deep emotional cleansing, ideal for shadow work.

Conclusion

Lunar eclipses are transformative moments that offer powerful opportunities for release, healing, and spiritual growth. By aligning your magical practice with the energy of lunar eclipses, you can clear away old patterns, embrace personal transformation, and make space for new beginnings in the future. Each eclipse carries its own astrological significance, offering unique energies to support your journey of healing and self-discovery. Whether you are focused on emotional release, letting go of limiting beliefs, or deepening your spiritual practice, lunar eclipses provide a potent backdrop for profound change and personal evolution.

Chapter 24: Mercury Retrograde Spells and Solutions

Mercury retrograde is one of the most well-known and widely discussed astrological events, often associated with communication breakdowns, travel delays, technological malfunctions, and general confusion. While many view Mercury retrograde as a time of frustration and miscommunication, in magical practice, this period offers valuable opportunities for reflection, reassessment, and protection. By working with the energy of Mercury retrograde rather than resisting it, you can perform powerful spells for clarity, introspection, and protection, turning a potentially chaotic time into one of personal growth and spiritual realignment.

This chapter explores the magical significance of Mercury retrograde, offering insight into how to use its energy constructively. You'll learn how to craft spells for reflection, protection, and clearing confusion, as well as how to protect yourself from the potential negative effects of Mercury retrograde. Whether you're a seasoned practitioner or new to magic, these spells and solutions will help you navigate Mercury retrograde with grace and purpose.

Understanding Mercury Retrograde in Magic

Mercury, the planet of communication, intellect, travel, and technology, rules over how we express ourselves, how we think, and how we connect with others. When Mercury is in retrograde (appearing to move backward in the sky), these areas of life often feel disrupted. Communication may break down, plans may go awry, and misunderstandings can lead to frustration. However, from a magical perspective, Mercury retrograde is not simply a time of inconvenience—it is an opportunity for deep reflection, revisiting past issues, and reassessing your life's direction.

Key Themes of Mercury Retrograde:

- **Reflection and Reassessment**: Mercury retrograde invites you to slow down and look inward. It's a time to reflect on the past, reassess your goals, and review what's working and what's not in your life.
- **Healing and Closure**: This period often brings unresolved issues back to the surface, providing an opportunity to heal old wounds, gain closure, and release emotional or mental baggage.
- **Protection and Boundaries**: Mercury retrograde is also a time when you may need to protect yourself from misunderstandings, miscommunications, and energetic interference. Creating protective wards and setting clear boundaries is essential during this period.
- **Avoiding New Beginnings**: While Mercury retrograde is ideal for reflection and revisiting past projects, it is generally not the best time to start new ventures, make major purchases, or sign important contracts.

In magical practice, Mercury retrograde's energy can be used to clarify thoughts, revisit old projects, cleanse miscommunications, and strengthen spiritual and mental protection. By aligning your magic with the retrograde cycle, you can turn a challenging time into an opportunity for growth and healing.

Mercury Retrograde Dates in 2025

In 2025, Mercury will retrograde three times. Below are the dates for each retrograde period, along with the zodiac sign Mercury will be transiting, which affects the specific challenges and opportunities presented by the retrograde.

1. **January 13 – February 2, 2025** (Mercury retrograde in Capricorn and Sagittarius)
   - Themes: Reassessing career goals, reviewing long-term plans, reevaluating personal beliefs and life philosophies.
2. **May 18 – June 30, 2025** (Mercury retrograde in Gemini and Taurus)
   - Themes: Communication breakdowns, revisiting past conversations, resolving financial matters, clarifying values and priorities.
3. **September 17 – October 9, 2025** (Mercury retrograde in Libra and Virgo)
   - Themes: Relationship misunderstandings, reassessing partnerships, revisiting work projects, and organizing daily routines.

These retrograde periods provide opportunities for specific types of magic depending on the themes of the zodiac signs involved. In general, however, Mercury retrograde is a time for protection spells, reflection, and revisiting unresolved issues in communication and personal goals.

How to Use Mercury Retrograde Energy for Reflection and Protection

While Mercury retrograde is often a time of confusion, its energy can be directed toward powerful magical work, especially when it comes to reflecting on past experiences, cleansing miscommunication, and protecting yourself from chaos and negativity. Below are ways to harness the unique energy of Mercury retrograde:

1. Reflection and Introspection

Mercury retrograde is a time to look inward and reflect on your life's path. Use this period to reassess your goals, review decisions, and revisit unresolved issues. Journaling, meditation, and divination are particularly powerful during this time as they help you gain insight into areas that need attention or healing.

2. Revisiting Past Projects

Rather than starting something new, Mercury retrograde encourages revisiting past projects or unfinished business. If you have creative or personal projects that were left incomplete, now is the perfect time to pick them up, rework them, and bring them to completion.

3. Cleansing Miscommunications

Misunderstandings are common during Mercury retrograde, but this period also offers an opportunity to clear the air and resolve long-standing communication issues. Perform rituals aimed at clearing confusion, improving communication with others, and ensuring that your messages are received clearly.

4. Protection and Warding

Mercury retrograde can create chaotic energy, particularly around communication, travel, and technology. Protection spells, wards, and charms are essential during this time to safeguard yourself from energetic disruptions and misunderstandings. Focus on creating protective barriers around your home, workplace, and personal energy.

Mercury Retrograde Spells and Rituals

Here are some powerful spells and rituals designed to help you navigate Mercury retrograde. Whether you need protection from miscommunications, clarity of thought, or resolution of old issues, these spells will align you with the reflective and protective energy of Mercury retrograde.

1. Mercury Retrograde Reflection Ritual

This ritual helps you harness the energy of Mercury retrograde for deep reflection and introspection. It's perfect for gaining clarity on unresolved issues, revisiting past projects, and realigning your goals.

Materials:

- A blue or silver candle (for Mercury's influence and clarity)
- A piece of paper and pen
- A mirror (for reflection)
- A piece of clear quartz (for mental clarity)
- Lavender or sandalwood incense (for calming the mind)

Instructions:

1. **Prepare Your Space**: Cleanse your space with lavender or sandalwood incense to invite calmness and clarity.
2. **Set Your Intention**: Reflect on the areas of your life where you feel stuck or uncertain. Write down the issues you want to revisit or the questions you need clarity on.
3. **Light the Candle**: As you light the blue or silver candle, say:
   "During this time of Mercury retrograde, I call upon the energy of reflection and clarity. I seek to understand the lessons of my past and gain insight for my future."
4. **Use the Mirror**: Hold the mirror and look into your reflection. As you gaze at yourself, think about the areas of your life that need attention. Ask yourself: What can I learn from my past experiences? What unfinished business needs resolution?
5. **Hold the Clear Quartz**: Hold the clear quartz in your hands and focus on receiving mental clarity and insight. Visualize your mind becoming clear, and imagine yourself gaining answers to the questions or issues you are reflecting on.
6. **Close the Ritual**: Allow the candle to burn down. Keep the clear quartz near you for the duration of Mercury retrograde to maintain mental clarity and focus.

2. Mercury Retrograde Protection Spell

This spell is designed to protect you from the negative effects of Mercury retrograde, particularly miscommunications, travel delays, and technological issues. It creates a protective barrier around you, ensuring that you navigate Mercury retrograde with ease and minimal disruption.

Materials:

- A black or white candle (for protection)
- A piece of hematite or black tourmaline (for grounding and protection)
- Sage or rosemary incense (for cleansing and protection)
- A piece of paper and pen

Instructions:

1. **Cleanse Your Space**: Burn sage or rosemary incense to cleanse your space and remove any lingering chaotic energy.
2. **Set Your Intention**: On the piece of paper, write down what you want to protect yourself from during Mercury retrograde. This could include miscommunications, travel issues, or technological disruptions.
3. **Light the Candle**: As you light the black or white candle, say:
   "I call upon the power of protection during Mercury retrograde. I shield myself from confusion, chaos, and miscommunication. I move through this time with clarity and peace."
4. **Use the Hematite**: Hold the hematite or black tourmaline in your hands and visualize a protective shield forming around you. Imagine this shield guarding you from any chaotic energy or negative effects during Mercury retrograde.
5. **Visualize Your Protection**: As the candle burns, focus on your protective shield growing stronger. Visualize yourself calmly navigating any challenges that arise during Mercury retrograde.
6. **Close the Ritual**: Allow the candle to burn down completely. Keep the hematite or black tourmaline with you throughout Mercury retrograde to maintain your protective shield.

3. Miscommunication Cleansing Spell

This spell is designed to clear away confusion and improve communication during Mercury retrograde. It helps to resolve misunderstandings, ensuring that your words are received clearly and that you understand others without distortion.

Materials:

- A blue candle (for communication)
- A piece of sodalite or lapis lazuli (for clarity in communication)
- A feather or quill (symbolizing Mercury's influence over communication)
- A piece of paper and pen

Instructions:

1. **Cleanse Your Space**: Burn sage or peppermint incense to cleanse your space and invite clarity.
2. **Set Your Intention**: On the piece of paper, write down any miscommunications or misunderstandings you wish to clear up during Mercury retrograde.
3. **Light the Candle**: As you light the blue candle, say:
   "I call upon the energy of clarity and understanding. I ask for clear communication and the resolution of misunderstandings during this Mercury retrograde."
4. **Use the Feather**: Hold the feather or quill and visualize it sweeping away any confusion or miscommunication from your life. Imagine your words being received clearly, and picture yourself understanding others with ease.
5. **Hold the Sodalite**: Hold the sodalite or lapis lazuli in your hands and focus on opening your throat chakra, ensuring that you speak clearly and that your intentions are understood. Visualize all barriers to communication being removed.
6. **Close the Ritual**: Allow the candle to burn down completely. Keep the sodalite or lapis lazuli with you to maintain clear communication during Mercury retrograde.

4. Mercury Retrograde Travel Protection Spell

Mercury retrograde is notorious for causing travel delays, miscommunication during trips, and issues with travel plans. This spell creates a protective shield around you when you travel during Mercury retrograde, ensuring smooth and safe journeys.

Materials:

- A white or yellow candle (for safe travel)
- A piece of citrine or amethyst (for protection and smooth journeys)
- A map or travel-related item (such as a passport or travel itinerary)
- Sage or rosemary incense (for cleansing)

Instructions:

1. **Cleanse Your Space**: Burn sage or rosemary incense to clear away any chaotic energy that could interfere with your travels.
2. **Set Your Intention**: Focus on your upcoming travels and visualize a smooth, safe journey. Write down your travel plans and any concerns you may have about traveling during Mercury retrograde.
3. **Light the Candle**: As you light the white or yellow candle, say:
   "I call upon the power of protection for my travels. I shield myself from delays, disruptions, and miscommunications. My journey is smooth, safe, and blessed."
4. **Use the Map**: Place the map or travel-related item on your altar, and visualize a clear, unhindered path for your journey. See yourself arriving at your destination safely and without issues.
5. **Hold the Citrine**: Hold the citrine or amethyst in your hands and focus on creating a protective barrier around you during your travels. Imagine yourself moving through airports, roads, or other travel areas with ease and confidence.
6. **Close the Ritual**: Allow the candle to burn down. Carry the citrine or amethyst with you during your travels to maintain protection and ensure smooth journeys.

Symbols, Herbs, and Crystals for Mercury Retrograde Magic

To enhance your spells during Mercury retrograde, you can incorporate specific symbols, herbs, and crystals that resonate with Mercury's energy and the need for clarity and protection during this time.

Symbols for Mercury Retrograde:

- **Feathers**: Represent communication, the element of Air, and Mercury's influence.
- **Keys**: Symbolize unlocking understanding, solving problems, and gaining clarity.
- **Mirrors**: Used for reflection and introspection, particularly when revisiting past issues.
- **Hermes' Caduceus**: The staff of Hermes (Mercury), symbolizing communication, travel, and balance.

Herbs for Mercury Retrograde:

- **Lavender**: Calms the mind and promotes clear thinking and communication.
- **Sage**: Used for clearing away confusion and purifying energy during chaotic times.
- **Rosemary**: A protective herb that enhances memory, clarity, and focus.
- **Peppermint**: Invites clear thinking, sharpens focus, and improves communication.

Crystals for Mercury Retrograde:

- **Clear Quartz**: Amplifies clarity, focus, and understanding, perfect for gaining insight during retrograde.
- **Sodalite**: Enhances communication, especially in resolving misunderstandings.
- **Hematite**: Provides grounding and protection, helping to prevent chaos and confusion.
- **Amethyst**: Promotes calmness, clarity, and spiritual protection, particularly during travel and emotional turbulence.

Conclusion

Mercury retrograde, while often viewed as a challenging time, can be transformed into a period of profound reflection, healing, and protection when approached with intention and magical awareness. By harnessing the unique energies of Mercury retrograde, you can focus on revisiting the past, healing old wounds, clearing miscommunications, and protecting yourself from the chaotic energies that often arise during this time. With the right spells, rituals, and tools, Mercury retrograde can become a powerful opportunity for personal growth, clarity, and spiritual evolution.

Chapter 25: Venus Retrograde: Love and Beauty Rituals

Venus retrograde is a significant astrological event that affects love, relationships, self-worth, beauty, and finances. While retrogrades are often seen as challenging times, Venus retrograde offers a unique opportunity to reflect on and heal the areas of life governed by Venus. This period encourages us to reassess our relationships, rethink our values around love and beauty, and deepen our connection with self-love.

In this chapter, we will explore how to navigate Venus retrograde's energy and use it for love and beauty rituals that focus on self-reflection, healing, and transformation. Whether you're working on enhancing self-love, strengthening your relationships, or healing emotional wounds, this chapter provides detailed guidance on harnessing Venus retrograde's energy for positive change.

Understanding Venus Retrograde

Venus retrograde occurs approximately every 18 months, lasting for about 40-43 days. During this period, the planet Venus appears to move backward in the sky from Earth's perspective. Venus governs love, beauty, harmony, relationships, pleasure, self-worth, and finances, so when Venus is in retrograde, these areas are highlighted for reflection and reassessment. Old patterns, unresolved emotions, and past relationships may resurface, offering you the opportunity to heal and release what no longer serves you.

Key Themes of Venus Retrograde:

- **Love and Relationships**: Venus retrograde is a time to revisit past relationships, heal unresolved conflicts, and reflect on your current romantic connections. It is a period of reevaluation, where relationships may be tested, and true feelings come to light.
- **Self-Worth and Self-Love**: Venus retrograde invites you to reflect on your self-worth, body image, and relationship with yourself. It's a powerful time to cultivate deeper self-love, release negative self-perceptions, and renew your sense of beauty and worth.
- **Financial Reflection**: Venus also governs material wealth and finances, making this retrograde a time to review your financial decisions, reassess spending habits, and focus on building financial security.
- **Beauty and Aesthetics**: While Venus retrograde encourages reflection on personal beauty and aesthetics, it is generally not the best time for major changes in appearance, such as dramatic makeovers, cosmetic procedures, or big beauty-related purchases.

Rather than viewing Venus retrograde as a time of conflict and confusion, you can use its energy for introspection and healing, particularly in the realms of love, beauty, and self-worth. This chapter offers spells and rituals specifically designed for navigating Venus retrograde with grace, helping you to heal relationships, strengthen self-love, and cultivate beauty from within.

Venus Retrograde Dates in 2025

In 2025, Venus will be retrograde in the sign of **Gemini**, bringing a focus on communication in relationships, mental stimulation, and reassessing love through the lens of intellectual compatibility and self-expression. Here are the key dates for Venus retrograde in 2025:

- **Pre-Retrograde Shadow Period**: May 2 – May 18, 2025
- **Venus Retrograde**: May 18 – June 30, 2025
- **Post-Retrograde Shadow Period**: July 1 – July 15, 2025

During this period, relationships and self-expression will be emphasized, making it an ideal time for reflecting on how you communicate in love, how you express your desires, and how mental and emotional connection plays a role in your romantic life.

Navigating Venus Retrograde's Effects on Relationships and Self-Love

Venus retrograde invites you to slow down and reassess the dynamics of your relationships, how you perceive love, and how you nurture yourself. Below are some ways to navigate Venus retrograde's influence:

1. Reassessing Relationships

Venus retrograde is a time to reflect on the health and strength of your romantic relationships. If you're in a partnership, this period may highlight unresolved issues or bring deeper feelings to the surface, asking you to evaluate the balance of love, trust, and reciprocity. For those who are single, Venus retrograde encourages introspection around your past relationships, helping you heal old wounds and make space for healthier future connections.

2. Healing Emotional Wounds

This period often brings up emotions and patterns from past relationships, giving you a chance to heal and release what no longer serves you. Whether it's unhealed heartbreak, unresolved conflicts, or lingering emotional pain, Venus retrograde provides an opportunity for deep emotional healing and forgiveness, both for yourself and others.

3. Cultivating Self-Love and Confidence

Venus retrograde invites you to reconnect with your sense of self-worth and beauty. It encourages you to reassess how you treat yourself, how you perceive your own beauty, and how you show yourself love. Use this time to reflect on your inner and outer beauty, release any negative self-talk, and strengthen your self-care routines.

4. Financial Reflection

Venus rules money and material wealth, making this retrograde an ideal time to reflect on your financial habits. Are you spending in alignment with your values? Are you feeling secure in your financial situation? Use Venus retrograde to review your financial decisions, revise your budget, and ensure that your spending reflects your priorities.

5. Avoid Major Beauty or Relationship Decisions

Because Venus retrograde is a time of reflection rather than action, it is generally not advised to make major decisions regarding beauty (such as drastic makeovers or cosmetic surgery) or relationships (such as getting married or starting a new relationship). Instead, focus on inner reflection and allow the retrograde period to guide you toward deeper understanding before making any lasting changes.

Venus Retrograde Love and Beauty Spells

Below are powerful spells and rituals designed to help you align with Venus retrograde's energy for love, healing, and beauty. These spells focus on reflection, self-love, healing emotional wounds, and fostering deeper connections in relationships.

1. Self-Love Mirror Spell for Venus Retrograde

This spell is designed to enhance your sense of self-worth and beauty during Venus retrograde. It helps you connect with your inner beauty and cultivate deep self-love, releasing negative thoughts about your appearance or worth.

Materials:

- A pink or green candle (for love and beauty)
- A small mirror (for self-reflection)
- Rose petals or rose oil (for self-love)
- A piece of rose quartz or jade (for healing and self-compassion)
- A piece of paper and pen

Instructions:

1. **Prepare Your Space**: Cleanse your space with rose incense or essential oil to invite the energy of self-love and beauty.
2. **Set Your Intention**: On the piece of paper, write down any negative self-perceptions or limiting beliefs about your beauty or worth that you want to release.
3. **Light the Candle**: As you light the pink or green candle, say:
   "During this Venus retrograde, I release all negative thoughts about myself. I embrace my beauty, my worth, and my inner light."
4. **Use the Mirror**: Hold the mirror in front of you and look into your reflection. As you gaze at yourself, repeat affirmations such as "I am beautiful," "I am worthy of love," or "I radiate self-confidence." Focus on seeing your true beauty, both inner and outer.
5. **Hold the Rose Quartz**: Hold the rose quartz or jade in your hands and visualize a soft, pink light surrounding you, filling your heart with love and compassion. Imagine this light dissolving any negative self-talk or doubt.
6. **Burn the Paper**: Safely burn the piece of paper with your written negative beliefs, symbolizing their release. As the paper burns, feel yourself letting go of old insecurities and embracing self-love.

7. **Close the Ritual**: Allow the candle to burn down. Keep the rose quartz or jade with you as a reminder of your beauty and worth throughout Venus retrograde.

2. Relationship Healing Spell for Venus Retrograde

This spell is designed to heal emotional wounds in relationships, whether romantic or platonic. Venus retrograde often brings unresolved issues to the surface, and this ritual helps you address these challenges with love, understanding, and forgiveness.

Materials:

- A blue or pink candle (for healing and harmony)
- A piece of rose quartz or amethyst (for emotional healing)
- A small bowl of water (for cleansing)
- A piece of paper and pen
- Lavender or rosemary incense (for peace and clarity)

Instructions:

1. **Cleanse Your Space**: Burn lavender or rosemary incense to cleanse the energy and create a peaceful atmosphere.
2. **Set Your Intention**: Reflect on the relationship you wish to heal. Write down any unresolved issues, emotional wounds, or conflicts that need to be addressed.
3. **Light the Candle**: As you light the blue or pink candle, say:
   "During this Venus retrograde, I open my heart to healing and harmony. I release past pain and open myself to forgiveness and understanding."
4. **Use the Water**: Hold the bowl of water in your hands and visualize it being filled with healing energy. Dip your fingers into the water and touch your forehead, heart, and hands, symbolizing the cleansing and healing of your emotions.
5. **Burn the Paper**: Safely burn the piece of paper with the written conflicts or emotional wounds, symbolizing their release. As the paper burns, imagine the pain and misunderstandings being transformed into peace and understanding.
6. **Hold the Rose Quartz**: Hold the rose quartz or amethyst in your hands and focus on healing the relationship. Visualize a soft pink or violet light surrounding both you and the other person, filling your connection with love, compassion, and forgiveness.
7. **Close the Ritual**: Allow the candle to burn down. Keep the rose quartz or amethyst near your bed or carry it with you to maintain healing energy during Venus retrograde.

3. Beauty Reflection Ritual for Venus Retrograde

Venus retrograde encourages inner reflection, especially when it comes to beauty and self-image. This ritual focuses on enhancing your natural beauty by reflecting on and appreciating your unique qualities. It helps you connect with your inner radiance and feel more confident in your appearance.

Materials:

- A pink or white candle (for beauty and purity)
- A small mirror (for self-reflection)
- A bottle of rosewater or jasmine oil (for beauty and confidence)
- A piece of amethyst or moonstone (for self-confidence and beauty)
- Fresh flowers (roses, jasmine, or lilies)

Instructions:

1. **Prepare Your Space**: Cleanse your space with rosewater or jasmine oil to invite the energy of beauty and self-love.
2. **Set Your Intention**: Write down a few affirmations that reflect your beauty and confidence. For example, "I radiate beauty from within," or "I am confident in my appearance."
3. **Light the Candle**: As you light the pink or white candle, say:
   "During this Venus retrograde, I embrace my natural beauty and inner radiance. I see myself as beautiful, inside and out."
4. **Use the Mirror**: Hold the mirror and look into your reflection. As you gaze at yourself, repeat the affirmations you wrote. Focus on appreciating the unique qualities that make you beautiful, both physically and spiritually.
5. **Anoint Yourself**: Use the rosewater or jasmine oil to anoint your forehead, cheeks, and heart, symbolizing your connection to beauty and love. As you do this, visualize yourself glowing with confidence and self-love.
6. **Hold the Amethyst**: Hold the amethyst or moonstone in your hands and focus on enhancing your confidence and sense of self-worth. Imagine your inner light growing brighter and more radiant.
7. **Close the Ritual**: Allow the candle to burn down. Keep the amethyst or moonstone with you to maintain a sense of beauty and confidence during Venus retrograde.

4. Financial Reflection Ritual for Venus Retrograde

Because Venus also governs finances and material wealth, this ritual is designed to help you reflect on your financial situation and make empowered decisions. Venus retrograde is an excellent time to reassess your financial habits, create a budget, or reflect on how your financial choices align with your values.

Materials:

- A green or gold candle (for abundance and wealth)
- A small coin or piece of pyrite (for prosperity)
- A piece of paper and pen
- A few drops of basil or patchouli oil (for prosperity)

Instructions:

1. **Prepare Your Space**: Cleanse your space with basil or patchouli oil to invite the energy of abundance and financial clarity.
2. **Set Your Intention**: Write down your financial goals or areas where you feel financially blocked. Be specific about what you want to reassess during Venus retrograde.
3. **Light the Candle**: As you light the green or gold candle, say:
   "During this Venus retrograde, I reflect on my financial choices and align my spending with my values. I attract abundance and financial security."
4. **Use the Coin**: Hold the coin or piece of pyrite in your hands and visualize your financial situation becoming clear and stable. Imagine yourself making wise financial decisions that align with your goals.
5. **Create a Plan**: On the piece of paper, write down a financial plan or budget that reflects your values. Focus on how you can create more abundance and security in your life without overspending or making impulsive choices.
6. **Hold the Pyrite**: Hold the pyrite and focus on attracting financial prosperity. Visualize your financial situation improving and yourself feeling secure in your wealth.
7. **Close the Ritual**: Allow the candle to burn down. Keep the pyrite or coin in your wallet or financial space to continue attracting abundance during Venus retrograde.

Symbols, Herbs, and Crystals for Venus Retrograde Rituals

To enhance your Venus retrograde rituals, you can incorporate specific symbols, herbs, and crystals that resonate with Venus's energy and the focus on love, beauty, and self-worth.

Symbols for Venus Retrograde:

- **The Mirror**: Represents self-reflection, beauty, and introspection.
- **Roses**: Symbolize love, beauty, and harmony, making them ideal for Venus-related magic.
- **The Heart**: Represents love, self-compassion, and emotional healing.
- **Copper**: Associated with Venus, copper represents beauty, love, and material wealth.

Herbs for Venus Retrograde:

- **Rose**: Used for love, beauty, and self-compassion.
- **Jasmine**: Enhances beauty, confidence, and sensuality.
- **Lavender**: Promotes peace, emotional healing, and clarity in relationships.
- **Basil**: Attracts prosperity and aligns your financial goals with your values.

Crystals for Venus Retrograde:

- **Rose Quartz**: The ultimate stone of love, rose quartz promotes self-love, emotional healing, and harmony in relationships.
- **Amethyst**: Provides spiritual protection and enhances confidence and emotional balance.
- **Moonstone**: A stone of inner beauty and self-reflection, moonstone connects you with your feminine energy and enhances self-love.
- **Pyrite**: Attracts wealth, abundance, and financial security.

Conclusion

Venus retrograde, while often seen as a time of romantic challenges and introspection, offers a unique opportunity to deepen your relationship with yourself, heal emotional wounds, and cultivate greater love, beauty, and harmony in your life. By aligning your magical practice with the reflective and healing energy of Venus retrograde, you can strengthen your self-love, heal your relationships, and make empowered decisions in both love and finances. Whether you are working on emotional healing, nurturing your self-worth, or reassessing your relationship dynamics, Venus retrograde provides a powerful time for growth, transformation, and renewal in all matters of the heart.

Chapter 26: Mars Retrograde: Conflict, Courage, and Protection

Mars retrograde is an astrological event that challenges the way we handle conflict, assert ourselves, and take action in our lives. Mars is the planet of war, aggression, passion, drive, and courage. When it goes retrograde, its usual forward-moving energy is turned inward, which can lead to frustration, delays, and unresolved conflicts. However, Mars retrograde also offers a unique opportunity to reassess how we handle challenges, manage anger, and use our personal power. With the right rituals and spells, you can navigate Mars retrograde by channeling its energy into peace, inner strength, and personal protection.

This chapter explores the magical significance of Mars retrograde and how to harness its energy for rituals of peace, strength, and conflict resolution. It provides detailed guidance on how to protect yourself from the heightened aggression and frustration that may arise during this period while using Mars retrograde for self-reflection, growth, and courageous decision-making.

Understanding Mars Retrograde

Mars retrograde occurs approximately every two years and lasts for about two months. During this time, Mars appears to move backward in the sky from Earth's perspective, and its influence on aggression, motivation, conflict, and action becomes distorted or subdued. This retrograde period can bring delays in pursuing goals, unresolved anger, tension in relationships, and challenges in asserting oneself. However, Mars retrograde also encourages introspection, teaching us to reflect on how we handle conflict, harness our inner strength, and find non-violent resolutions to challenges.

Key Themes of Mars Retrograde:

- **Reassessing Conflict and Anger**: Mars retrograde invites you to reflect on how you deal with anger, aggression, and confrontation. This period offers a chance to heal old wounds related to unresolved conflicts and learn more peaceful ways of resolving disputes.

- **Inner Strength and Courage**: With Mars' outward-focused energy turned inward, this retrograde offers an opportunity to cultivate inner strength, courage, and resilience. It encourages self-reflection on how you can be brave and assertive without being aggressive.

- **Protection and Boundaries**: Mars retrograde is a powerful time for protection magic, as it highlights the need to defend yourself from external aggression and negative energy. It's also an ideal period to reinforce your personal boundaries, both energetically and emotionally.

- **Delays and Frustration**: Mars retrograde can slow down progress on projects, particularly those that require direct action, physical energy, or confrontation. Rather than pushing forward, Mars retrograde encourages patience and reflection.

Mars retrograde may feel like a time of challenge, but with mindful reflection and carefully chosen rituals, you can transform its energy into one of peace, protection, and personal empowerment.

Mars Retrograde Dates in 2025

In 2025, Mars will retrograde in the sign of **Scorpio**, intensifying themes of emotional depth, power struggles, and hidden motivations. Scorpio is ruled by Mars (traditionally) and Pluto, making this retrograde particularly potent in revealing buried anger, unresolved emotional issues, and deep personal transformation.

- **Pre-Retrograde Shadow Period**: October 14 – November 25, 2025
- **Mars Retrograde**: November 25, 2025 – January 6, 2026
- **Post-Retrograde Shadow Period**: January 7 – February 20, 2026

During this retrograde, you'll be called to address inner fears, power dynamics in relationships, and unresolved emotional conflicts. It's a time to work on personal protection, emotional healing, and transforming frustration into inner strength.

Navigating Mars Retrograde's Effects on Conflict, Courage, and Protection

Mars retrograde often stirs up unresolved conflicts and delays in taking direct action. However, it also offers a powerful time to reassess how you handle challenges and protect yourself from external aggression. Here are some ways to navigate Mars retrograde's energy constructively:

1. Reflection on Conflict and Anger

Mars retrograde provides an opportunity to look inward and reflect on how you handle conflict and anger. Are you quick to react with aggression? Do you struggle to assert yourself in a healthy way? Use this time to reassess your approach to conflict and find more balanced ways to resolve tension. Journaling, meditation, and shadow work are particularly helpful during Mars retrograde for identifying unresolved anger and learning how to express it constructively.

2. Strengthening Personal Boundaries

Because Mars governs personal power and defense, Mars retrograde is an ideal time to strengthen your boundaries—both energetic and emotional. This can mean reinforcing boundaries in relationships, protecting yourself from negative influences, or creating strong physical and spiritual protection around your home or workplace. Use Mars retrograde to evaluate where your boundaries need fortification and how you can assert your needs more clearly.

3. Inner Courage and Strength

Mars retrograde encourages the cultivation of inner courage, calling you to face your fears, overcome inner obstacles, and strengthen your sense of self. This is not about outward displays of strength or power; rather, it's about building quiet resilience and bravery from within. Focus on self-reflection and finding the courage to tackle personal challenges with grace and determination.

4. Patience and Redirection

Delays and frustrations are common during Mars retrograde, especially when it comes to projects that require direct action or confrontation. Rather than forcing things to move forward, Mars retrograde asks you to slow down, reassess your strategy, and be patient. Use this time to redirect your energy toward planning, reflecting, and strategizing, rather than pushing through obstacles.

Mars Retrograde Rituals for Peace, Strength, and Resolution

Below are detailed rituals and spells designed to help you navigate Mars retrograde by focusing on peace, inner strength, conflict resolution, and protection. These rituals will help you channel the challenging energy of Mars retrograde into personal empowerment, peaceful conflict resolution, and spiritual defense.

1. Conflict Resolution Ritual for Mars Retrograde

This ritual is designed to help you resolve conflicts peacefully during Mars retrograde. It encourages clarity, understanding, and healing in relationships, helping you to address any unresolved tensions with grace.

Materials:

- A blue or white candle (for peace and resolution)
- A small bowl of water (for emotional balance)
- A piece of rose quartz or amethyst (for emotional healing)
- A piece of paper and pen
- Lavender or rosemary incense (for calming and clarity)

Instructions:

1. **Prepare Your Space**: Cleanse your space with lavender or rosemary incense to create a peaceful and calming atmosphere.
2. **Set Your Intention**: Reflect on the conflict or tension you wish to resolve. Write down the core issue or the person involved, and focus on your desire for peace and resolution.
3. **Light the Candle**: As you light the blue or white candle, say:
   "During this Mars retrograde, I seek peace and resolution. I open my heart to understanding and let go of anger and aggression."
4. **Use the Water**: Hold the bowl of water in your hands and visualize it absorbing the emotional tension from the conflict. As you dip your fingers into the water, imagine the water calming the situation and bringing emotional balance to all involved.
5. **Hold the Rose Quartz**: Hold the rose quartz or amethyst in your hands and focus on healing the relationship or situation. Visualize a soft pink or violet light surrounding both you and the other person, bringing peace, understanding, and resolution.
6. **Burn the Paper**: Safely burn the piece of paper with the written conflict or issue, symbolizing the release of anger and tension. As the paper burns, imagine the conflict being resolved and peace being restored.
7. **Close the Ritual**: Allow the candle to burn down. Keep the rose quartz or amethyst near your bed or carry it with you to maintain emotional healing and peace during Mars retrograde.

2. Inner Strength and Courage Ritual for Mars Retrograde

This ritual focuses on cultivating inner strength and courage during Mars retrograde. It helps you connect with your inner warrior, face challenges with bravery, and build resilience in the face of obstacles.

Materials:

- A red or gold candle (for courage and strength)
- A piece of carnelian or tiger's eye (for personal power and confidence)
- A small mirror (for self-reflection)
- A piece of paper and pen
- Cinnamon or clove incense (for empowerment)

Instructions:

1. **Prepare Your Space**: Burn cinnamon or clove incense to energize your space and invite the energy of strength and courage.
2. **Set Your Intention**: Reflect on the areas of your life where you need to cultivate more courage or inner strength. Write down the challenges you are facing and the inner fears you want to overcome.
3. **Light the Candle**: As you light the red or gold candle, say:
   "During this Mars retrograde, I call upon my inner strength and courage. I face my fears with bravery and determination."
4. **Use the Mirror**: Hold the mirror and look into your reflection. As you gaze at yourself, imagine seeing your inner warrior—strong, brave, and capable. Visualize yourself standing tall in the face of challenges, feeling empowered and confident.
5. **Hold the Carnelian**: Hold the carnelian or tiger's eye in your hands and focus on building your inner strength. Imagine a powerful energy filling your body, giving you the courage to overcome any obstacles in your path.
6. **Burn the Paper**: Safely burn the piece of paper with your written fears or challenges, symbolizing their release. As the paper burns, imagine yourself rising above these fears with confidence and inner strength.
7. **Close the Ritual**: Allow the candle to burn down. Keep the carnelian or tiger's eye with you to maintain your sense of strength and courage during Mars retrograde.

3. Protection Spell for Mars Retrograde

Mars retrograde can bring heightened aggression, tension, and negative energy. This protection spell creates a strong barrier around you, shielding you from conflict, negativity, and external aggression during this challenging time.

Materials:

- A black or white candle (for protection)
- A piece of obsidian or black tourmaline (for grounding and protection)
- A small bowl of salt (for purification)
- Sage or rosemary incense (for cleansing)
- A piece of paper and pen

Instructions:

1. **Cleanse Your Space**: Burn sage or rosemary incense to cleanse your space and remove any lingering negative energy.
2. **Set Your Intention**: Write down any situations, people, or influences you want to protect yourself from during Mars retrograde. Be clear about the areas where you need protection, whether from conflict, negativity, or energetic interference.
3. **Light the Candle**: As you light the black or white candle, say:
   "I call upon the power of protection during this Mars retrograde. I shield myself from conflict, aggression, and negative energy. I am safe, protected, and at peace."
4. **Use the Salt**: Hold the bowl of salt and visualize it forming a protective barrier around you. Imagine the salt creating an impenetrable shield that blocks out any negative energy or harmful influences.
5. **Hold the Obsidian**: Hold the obsidian or black tourmaline in your hands and focus on grounding your energy. Visualize the stone creating a powerful barrier of protection around you, keeping you safe from external harm.
6. **Burn the Paper**: Safely burn the piece of paper with your written concerns or negative influences, symbolizing their release. As the paper burns, imagine the negative energy being dissolved and your protective barrier growing stronger.
7. **Close the Ritual**: Allow the candle to burn down. Keep the obsidian or black tourmaline with you throughout Mars retrograde to maintain your protective shield.

4. Anger and Frustration Release Ritual for Mars Retrograde

Mars retrograde can stir up old anger, frustration, and unresolved conflicts. This ritual is designed to help you release pent-up anger and frustration in a healthy, constructive way, allowing you to find peace and emotional balance.

Materials:

- A red or black candle (for release and transformation)
- A small bowl of water (for emotional cleansing)
- A piece of hematite or smoky quartz (for grounding and releasing anger)
- A piece of paper and pen
- Sandalwood or eucalyptus incense (for calming and clarity)

Instructions:

1. **Prepare Your Space**: Burn sandalwood or eucalyptus incense to create a calming atmosphere and invite emotional clarity.
2. **Set Your Intention**: Write down the anger or frustration you wish to release. Focus on any situations, people, or emotions that have been causing you distress, particularly those that have surfaced during Mars retrograde.
3. **Light the Candle**: As you light the red or black candle, say:
   "During this Mars retrograde, I release all anger and frustration. I transform my anger into peace and my frustration into patience."
4. **Use the Water**: Hold the bowl of water and visualize it absorbing your anger and frustration. Imagine the water cleansing your emotions and washing away any tension or resentment you've been holding onto.
5. **Hold the Hematite**: Hold the hematite or smoky quartz in your hands and focus on grounding yourself. Visualize your anger being drawn into the stone, transforming into calmness and emotional balance.
6. **Burn the Paper**: Safely burn the piece of paper with your written anger or frustrations, symbolizing their release. As the paper burns, imagine the anger dissolving, leaving you feeling lighter and more at peace.
7. **Close the Ritual**: Allow the candle to burn down. Pour the water outside to release the remaining emotional tension. Keep the hematite or smoky quartz with you to maintain emotional balance during Mars retrograde.

Symbols, Herbs, and Crystals for Mars Retrograde Magic

To enhance your Mars retrograde rituals, you can incorporate specific symbols, herbs, and crystals that resonate with Mars' energy and the themes of courage, protection, and conflict resolution.

Symbols for Mars Retrograde:

- **The Sword**: Represents conflict, protection, and personal power.
- **The Shield**: Symbolizes defense, boundaries, and protection from harm.
- **The Flame**: Represents transformation, courage, and the burning away of anger and frustration.
- **The Phoenix**: A symbol of transformation, rebirth, and rising from the ashes of conflict.

Herbs for Mars Retrograde:

- **Sage**: Used for clearing away negative energy and providing protection during times of conflict.
- **Rosemary**: Enhances protection, clarity, and mental focus.
- **Cinnamon**: Adds energy, courage, and empowerment to Mars retrograde spells.
- **Lavender**: Calms emotions, promotes peace, and soothes frustration and anger.

Crystals for Mars Retrograde:

- **Obsidian**: Provides strong protection, grounding, and shields you from negativity.
- **Carnelian**: Enhances courage, personal power, and confidence during challenging times.
- **Hematite**: Grounds and protects, particularly useful for releasing anger and frustration.
- **Smoky Quartz**: Absorbs negative energy and transforms it into peace and calmness.

Conclusion

Mars retrograde, with its themes of conflict, courage, and protection, can be a challenging time, but it also offers profound opportunities for personal growth, reflection, and transformation. By aligning your magical practice with the reflective and protective energies of Mars retrograde, you can cultivate inner strength, release unresolved anger, and navigate conflicts with grace and wisdom. Whether you're focused on resolving conflicts, reinforcing boundaries, or finding inner courage, Mars retrograde provides a powerful time for growth, healing, and empowerment. With the right rituals and tools, you can turn Mars retrograde into a time of personal empowerment, peace, and spiritual protection.

Chapter 27: Jupiter and Saturn Retrogrades: Growth and Discipline

Jupiter and Saturn retrogrades are two of the most important and profound astrological events for spiritual growth, personal expansion, and long-term manifestation. These outer planets move more slowly through the zodiac, and when they enter retrograde, they offer extended periods for deep introspection, reassessment of long-term goals, and the cultivation of discipline in areas of life that need stability and structure.

While retrogrades of inner planets like Mercury and Venus are often associated with immediate disruptions in communication, relationships, or day-to-day activities, the retrogrades of Jupiter and Saturn work on a more gradual, expansive scale. These periods call for deep reflection on personal growth (Jupiter) and the structures or disciplines that govern your life (Saturn). Understanding how to work with these planetary energies during their retrograde periods can help you make significant progress on your long-term goals and spiritual journey.

In this chapter, we'll explore how to navigate both Jupiter and Saturn retrogrades, their respective astrological and magical influences, and the best times for introspection, personal growth, and long-term manifestation. Whether you're looking to expand your horizons or build a solid foundation for your future, these retrogrades provide the ideal cosmic energy to support your efforts.

Understanding Jupiter Retrograde: Growth, Expansion, and Reflection

Jupiter, the planet of luck, growth, wisdom, and expansion, governs areas of life that involve higher learning, spiritual development, abundance, and long-term goals. When Jupiter goes retrograde, its outward-directed energy turns inward, prompting reflection on how you are growing and expanding in life. Jupiter retrograde is a time for spiritual development, reassessment of your long-term goals, and reflection on how you are cultivating abundance and wisdom.

Key Themes of Jupiter Retrograde:

- **Reflection on Personal Growth**: Jupiter retrograde offers a time to pause and assess how you have been growing, learning, and expanding in your life. It encourages you to reflect on your goals and ambitions and to consider whether you are on the right path.
- **Spiritual Introspection**: As the planet that governs philosophy, religion, and spiritual development, Jupiter retrograde invites you to look inward for spiritual wisdom. This is an ideal time for deep meditation, journaling, and spiritual practices that connect you with higher truths.
- **Reevaluating Abundance**: Jupiter's association with abundance means that during its retrograde, you are called to reflect on your relationship with wealth and prosperity. Are you manifesting abundance in alignment with your values? How do you define success and fulfillment?
- **Delays in Expansion**: Jupiter retrograde may also slow down growth in areas such as career, travel, and education, but this slowdown provides an opportunity for course correction and refinement of your goals.

Rather than focusing on external growth during Jupiter retrograde, this period is ideal for internal reflection, reassessing your long-term goals, and ensuring that your path aligns with your higher purpose. It is a time to ask yourself whether you are expanding in meaningful ways and to make necessary adjustments before moving forward.

Understanding Saturn Retrograde: Discipline, Responsibility, and Structure

Saturn, the planet of discipline, responsibility, boundaries, and long-term structure, governs areas of life that require hard work, commitment, and stability. When Saturn goes retrograde, it challenges you to reflect on the structures you have built in your life—whether personal, professional, or spiritual—and assess whether they are serving your long-term growth. Saturn retrograde is a time for slowing down, reassessing your commitments, and taking responsibility for your actions.

Key Themes of Saturn Retrograde:

- **Reevaluation of Discipline**: Saturn retrograde invites you to examine how disciplined you have been in pursuing your goals. It asks whether you are following through on your commitments and whether your actions are aligned with your long-term vision.
- **Taking Responsibility**: This retrograde period often brings up issues of accountability. It's a time to reflect on whether you are taking responsibility for your actions, relationships, and career. Saturn retrograde highlights areas where you may need to make corrections or take ownership of past mistakes.
- **Revisiting Boundaries**: Saturn is the planet of boundaries and limitations, and during its retrograde, it encourages you to review the boundaries you have set in your personal and professional life. Are they too rigid or too lenient? Are you respecting your own limits?
- **Restructuring Foundations**: Saturn retrograde calls for deep reflection on the foundations you have built. Whether in your career, relationships, or personal growth, this is a time to reassess whether your structures are strong enough to support your long-term goals.

Saturn retrograde is often viewed as a time of karmic lessons, where the universe may slow down or challenge your progress to ensure that you are building a stable and responsible foundation for the future. It's a time for making necessary adjustments, strengthening your resolve, and ensuring that you are on a path that is aligned with your highest good.

Jupiter and Saturn Retrograde Dates in 2025

In 2025, both Jupiter and Saturn will undergo retrograde periods, providing powerful opportunities for introspection, growth, and disciplined reflection. Below are the key dates for each retrograde period:

Jupiter Retrograde (in Taurus):

- **Pre-Retrograde Shadow Period**: February 27 – April 1, 2025
- **Jupiter Retrograde**: April 1 – August 10, 2025
- **Post-Retrograde Shadow Period**: August 11 – September 30, 2025

During this period, Jupiter retrograde in Taurus encourages reflection on personal values, finances, and material stability. It's a time to reassess how you are cultivating abundance and whether your actions align with your deeper values.

Saturn Retrograde (in Pisces):

- **Pre-Retrograde Shadow Period**: May 2 – June 12, 2025
- **Saturn Retrograde**: June 12 – October 22, 2025
- **Post-Retrograde Shadow Period**: October 23 – December 31, 2025

Saturn retrograde in Pisces offers a deep period of reflection on spiritual boundaries, emotional discipline, and the structures you've built in your life. This period asks you to reflect on your spiritual journey, creativity, and emotional boundaries, ensuring that you are building a solid foundation for growth.

Navigating Jupiter Retrograde for Introspection and Growth

Jupiter retrograde is an ideal time for introspection, self-assessment, and refining your personal and spiritual growth. The following practices can help you navigate Jupiter retrograde effectively:

1. Reflect on Long-Term Goals and Ambitions

Jupiter retrograde invites you to reassess your long-term goals. Are you pursuing goals that align with your highest self? Are you expanding in ways that contribute to your spiritual and personal growth? Use this time to reflect on whether your ambitions are aligned with your values and make adjustments if necessary.

2. Deepen Your Spiritual Practice

As the planet of wisdom and spirituality, Jupiter retrograde encourages you to go inward and deepen your connection with your higher self. Meditation, journaling, and spiritual study are particularly powerful during this time. Focus on gaining insight into your spiritual path and consider how you can align your actions with your deeper truths.

3. Reevaluate Your Relationship with Abundance

Jupiter retrograde asks you to reflect on how you define abundance and success. Are you chasing material wealth at the expense of your happiness or spiritual growth? Use this time to reassess your relationship with money, prosperity, and fulfillment. It's also a great time to practice gratitude and focus on manifesting abundance in ways that are aligned with your values.

4. Practice Patience and Course Correction

During Jupiter retrograde, you may experience delays in areas of expansion such as career, travel, or education. Rather than pushing forward, use this time to course correct, refine your strategies, and practice patience. Jupiter retrograde offers the opportunity to ensure that your growth is sustainable and aligned with your long-term vision.

Navigating Saturn Retrograde for Discipline and Long-Term Manifestation

Saturn retrograde provides an opportunity to reflect on your responsibilities, discipline, and the structures you've built in your life. Below are key ways to work with Saturn retrograde's energy:

1. Reflect on Responsibility and Accountability

Saturn retrograde often highlights areas where you need to take more responsibility. Are you following through on your commitments? Are you taking ownership of your actions in relationships, career, and personal growth? Use this time to reflect on your level of accountability and make necessary adjustments to take more responsibility where needed.

2. Strengthen Personal and Professional Boundaries

Saturn governs boundaries, and during its retrograde, you may be asked to reflect on how well you've established them in your life. Are your boundaries clear and respected by others? Do you need to assert your limits more firmly? Use this time to reinforce boundaries in personal relationships, work, and self-care.

3. Rebuild and Refine Your Foundations

Saturn retrograde offers an opportunity to assess the foundations you've built in your life. Whether it's in your career, home life, or personal growth, consider whether the structures you've created are strong enough to support your long-term goals. This may be a time to rebuild or refine aspects of your life to ensure stability and longevity.

4. Cultivate Discipline and Patience

Saturn retrograde encourages you to cultivate patience and discipline. If you've been avoiding responsibilities or neglecting long-term commitments, this retrograde period may challenge you to refocus and develop the discipline needed to achieve your goals. Use this time to create new routines, set clear goals, and practice consistent effort.

Rituals and Practices for Jupiter and Saturn Retrogrades

Here are some powerful rituals and practices to help you align with the energies of Jupiter and Saturn retrogrades. These rituals focus on introspection, long-term manifestation, and building stability in your life.

1. Jupiter Retrograde Reflection Ritual for Personal Growth

This ritual is designed to help you reflect on your personal growth and spiritual journey during Jupiter retrograde. It encourages deep introspection and alignment with your higher purpose.

Materials:

- A purple or blue candle (for wisdom and spiritual growth)
- A piece of amethyst or clear quartz (for clarity and insight)
- A journal and pen
- Sage or sandalwood incense (for spiritual clarity)

Instructions:

1. **Prepare Your Space**: Cleanse your space with sage or sandalwood incense to invite clarity and wisdom.
2. **Set Your Intention**: Write down your long-term goals and aspirations. Reflect on whether these goals align with your spiritual and personal growth.
3. **Light the Candle**: As you light the purple or blue candle, say:
   "During this Jupiter retrograde, I reflect on my growth and wisdom. I seek to align my goals with my higher purpose."
4. **Hold the Amethyst**: Hold the amethyst or clear quartz in your hands and focus on receiving insight into your spiritual path. Ask yourself whether your current pursuits are aligned with your deeper values and truths.
5. **Journal Your Insights**: Spend time journaling about your reflections. What areas of your life need adjustment? Where can you make course corrections to better align with your spiritual goals?
6. **Close the Ritual**: Allow the candle to burn down. Keep the amethyst or clear quartz near your journal or meditation space to continue gaining insight during Jupiter retrograde.

2. Saturn Retrograde Discipline and Boundaries Ritual
This ritual focuses on strengthening your discipline and boundaries during Saturn retrograde. It helps you build solid foundations for long-term success and personal stability.
Materials:

- A black or brown candle (for discipline and grounding)
- A piece of hematite or obsidian (for grounding and protection)
- A small bowl of salt (for purification and boundary setting)
- A piece of paper and pen

Instructions:

1. **Prepare Your Space**: Cleanse your space with sage or rosemary incense to create a grounding atmosphere.
2. **Set Your Intention**: Write down areas of your life where you need to establish stronger boundaries or practice more discipline. Reflect on how these areas are affecting your long-term goals.
3. **Light the Candle**: As you light the black or brown candle, say:
   "During this Saturn retrograde, I strengthen my discipline and boundaries. I create solid foundations for my growth and success."
4. **Use the Salt**: Hold the bowl of salt and visualize it forming a protective barrier around you, strengthening your boundaries and purifying any areas of your life that need more structure.
5. **Hold the Hematite**: Hold the hematite or obsidian in your hands and focus on grounding yourself. Visualize yourself standing strong, disciplined, and committed to your long-term goals.
6. **Journal Your Commitments**: Write down specific actions you will take to strengthen your discipline and boundaries during Saturn retrograde. Be clear about the steps you will take to build stability in your life.
7. **Close the Ritual**: Allow the candle to burn down. Keep the hematite or obsidian with you to maintain a sense of grounding and discipline during Saturn retrograde.

3. Long-Term Manifestation Ritual for Jupiter and Saturn Retrogrades

This ritual combines the energies of Jupiter and Saturn retrogrades to help you manifest long-term success and stability. It focuses on aligning your growth (Jupiter) with discipline and structure (Saturn).

Materials:

- A gold or green candle (for abundance and manifestation)
- A black or brown candle (for grounding and discipline)
- A piece of pyrite or citrine (for abundance)
- A piece of hematite or onyx (for protection and grounding)
- A journal and pen

Instructions:

1. **Prepare Your Space**: Cleanse your space with sage or sandalwood incense to invite both clarity (Jupiter) and grounding (Saturn).
2. **Set Your Intention**: Write down your long-term goals for abundance, growth, and stability. Reflect on how you can balance your ambitions (Jupiter) with discipline and responsibility (Saturn).
3. **Light the Candles**: Light the gold or green candle for growth and the black or brown candle for discipline. As you light them, say:
   "I call upon the energies of Jupiter and Saturn to help me manifest long-term success. I align my growth with discipline and my abundance with stability."
4. **Hold the Pyrite and Hematite**: Hold the pyrite or citrine in one hand and the hematite or onyx in the other. Visualize yourself manifesting abundance with a strong foundation of discipline and responsibility. Imagine your goals coming to fruition in a balanced, sustainable way.
5. **Journal Your Plan**: Write down a detailed plan for how you will achieve your long-term goals, balancing growth with discipline. Be specific about the actions you will take and the structures you need to build.
6. **Close the Ritual**: Allow the candles to burn down. Keep the pyrite and hematite on your desk or in your workspace to continue aligning your manifestation efforts with discipline and stability.

Symbols, Herbs, and Crystals for Jupiter and Saturn Retrograde Magic

To enhance your Jupiter and Saturn retrograde rituals, you can incorporate specific symbols, herbs, and crystals that resonate with the energies of growth, discipline, and long-term manifestation.

Symbols for Jupiter and Saturn Retrogrades:

- **The Tree**: Represents growth, stability, and deep roots, making it an ideal symbol for long-term manifestation.
- **The Mountain**: Symbolizes discipline, endurance, and the ability to overcome obstacles.
- **The Compass**: Represents guidance, direction, and aligning your actions with your higher purpose.
- **The Scales**: Represents balance, particularly the balance between growth (Jupiter) and discipline (Saturn).

Herbs for Jupiter and Saturn Retrogrades:

- **Sage**: Clears away negativity and provides clarity for spiritual growth and reflection.
- **Rosemary**: Enhances mental focus, discipline, and protection.
- **Basil**: Attracts abundance and prosperity, helping to align growth with stability.
- **Cedarwood**: Grounds and stabilizes, providing support for building long-term structures.

Crystals for Jupiter and Saturn Retrogrades:

- **Amethyst**: Provides spiritual insight and clarity during Jupiter retrograde, enhancing personal growth and wisdom.
- **Citrine**: Attracts abundance and success, helping you manifest long-term goals.
- **Hematite**: Grounds and protects, helping you stay disciplined and focused during Saturn retrograde.
- **Onyx**: Provides strength, endurance, and protection, particularly during periods of introspection and restructuring.

Conclusion

Jupiter and Saturn retrogrades offer profound opportunities for introspection, personal growth, and long-term manifestation. While these retrogrades may slow down external progress, they provide the perfect time for reflection, course correction, and strengthening the foundations you've built in your life. By working with the energies of these retrogrades, you can align your ambitions with discipline, balance growth with responsibility, and manifest long-term success that is both sustainable and fulfilling. Through thoughtful rituals, introspective practices, and mindful reflection, Jupiter and Saturn retrogrades can become powerful allies in your journey toward spiritual and personal evolution.

Chapter 28: Neptune, Uranus, and Pluto Retrogrades: Deep Spiritual Work and Transformation

Neptune, Uranus, and Pluto retrogrades are powerful astrological events that impact the deeper, transformative aspects of life and spirituality. These outer planets move slowly through the zodiac, and their retrograde periods often focus on the collective unconscious, spiritual awakening, profound transformation, and shifts in personal and societal structures. Unlike the more frequent retrogrades of Mercury, Venus, and Mars, the retrogrades of Neptune, Uranus, and Pluto work on long-term cycles, offering extended periods for deep spiritual work, soul-searching, and transformative healing.

This chapter explores how to harness the energy of these outer planet retrogrades for deep spiritual work, shadow work, and transformation spells. By working with Neptune, Uranus, and Pluto retrogrades, you can engage in profound self-reflection, heal from past trauma, awaken to higher spiritual truths, and transform your life on a soul-deep level.

Neptune Retrograde: Spiritual Awakening, Illusions, and Inner Truth

Neptune, the planet of dreams, intuition, spirituality, and illusion, governs the realms of the subconscious, imagination, and mysticism. When Neptune goes retrograde, it invites you to look beyond illusions and delusions to uncover the deeper truths hidden beneath the surface of your consciousness. Neptune retrograde is a time for deep spiritual reflection, releasing illusions, and awakening to higher spiritual truths.

Key Themes of Neptune Retrograde:

- **Spiritual Awakening**: Neptune retrograde opens the door to spiritual insight, helping you connect more deeply with your intuition and inner wisdom. It's a time to focus on meditation, dream work, and spiritual practices that bring you closer to your higher self.
- **Revealing Illusions**: During Neptune retrograde, the veil of illusion is lifted, revealing truths that may have been hidden or distorted. It encourages you to look beyond fantasy and escapism to see reality clearly, particularly in relationships, spiritual beliefs, or emotional attachments.
- **Healing from Deception**: This retrograde is also a time for healing from past deceptions, whether self-imposed or external. Neptune's energy encourages you to release false beliefs, illusions, or fantasies that no longer serve your highest good.
- **Emotional and Psychic Cleansing**: Neptune retrograde offers an opportunity for deep emotional and psychic cleansing. It's a powerful time for releasing spiritual or emotional baggage and clearing your energetic field.

Neptune retrograde is ideal for deep introspection, spiritual awakening, and practices that connect you with the unseen realms. It is a time to shed illusions and reconnect with your inner truth.

Uranus Retrograde: Liberation, Innovation, and Personal Freedom

Uranus, the planet of revolution, innovation, and sudden change, governs the areas of life that involve personal freedom, rebellion, and breakthroughs. When Uranus goes retrograde, its usual forward-driving energy turns inward, encouraging self-examination of where you seek freedom, independence, and personal transformation. Uranus retrograde offers a time to reassess how you handle change, freedom, and authenticity in your life.

Key Themes of Uranus Retrograde:

- **Personal Freedom**: Uranus retrograde invites you to reflect on how free you truly are. Are there areas in your life where you feel restricted or held back? This period encourages you to break free from limiting beliefs, societal expectations, or personal fears that prevent you from living authentically.
- **Revolutionary Change**: While Uranus is often associated with sudden external changes, its retrograde period encourages internal revolution. It's a time to reassess areas of your life that need innovation, particularly in your personal beliefs, career, and relationships.
- **Embracing Authenticity**: Uranus retrograde helps you explore your true self, encouraging you to break free from conformity and express your unique individuality. It's a powerful time for personal transformation, self-expression, and embracing your uniqueness.
- **Breaking Free from Old Patterns**: This retrograde period highlights areas of your life where you may have become stuck in outdated habits, routines, or thought patterns. It invites you to make necessary changes and embrace new perspectives that support your growth and freedom.

Uranus retrograde is a time for inner revolution and personal liberation. It provides an opportunity to break free from old patterns, embrace innovation, and step into your true self with confidence and authenticity.

Pluto Retrograde: Transformation, Power, and Shadow Work

Pluto, the planet of transformation, death, rebirth, and power, governs the deepest, most intense aspects of life. When Pluto goes retrograde, its energy turns inward, encouraging you to explore your shadow self, confront hidden fears, and undergo profound personal transformation. Pluto retrograde is a time for deep introspection, shadow work, and releasing anything that holds you back from stepping into your power.

Key Themes of Pluto Retrograde:

- **Shadow Work**: Pluto retrograde is one of the most powerful times for shadow work, where you confront the hidden, unconscious parts of yourself that you may have repressed or ignored. This period encourages you to face your fears, desires, and unhealed traumas, bringing them into the light for healing.
- **Personal Power and Transformation**: Pluto governs power dynamics and personal transformation. During its retrograde, you are called to reflect on how you wield power in your life. Are you giving away your power to others? Do you need to reclaim control over certain aspects of your life? Pluto retrograde offers a chance to step into your personal power and transform areas of your life that feel stagnant or disempowering.
- **Rebirth and Renewal**: Pluto retrograde represents the cycle of death and rebirth, encouraging you to let go of old versions of yourself or outdated beliefs that no longer serve your highest good. It's a time to shed what no longer supports your growth and make space for personal renewal and transformation.
- **Healing from Trauma**: Pluto's energy often brings up deep-seated emotional wounds and traumas. Pluto retrograde is a powerful time for healing these wounds, allowing you to release pain, anger, or resentment and undergo emotional transformation.

Pluto retrograde is one of the most intense and transformative retrograde periods, offering the opportunity for deep healing, personal empowerment, and profound spiritual growth.

Neptune, Uranus, and Pluto Retrograde Dates in 2025

In 2025, Neptune, Uranus, and Pluto will each undergo retrograde periods, offering extended opportunities for deep spiritual work, personal liberation, and transformative healing. Below are the key dates for each retrograde period:

Neptune Retrograde (in Pisces):

- **Pre-Retrograde Shadow Period**: February 7 – June 30, 2025
- **Neptune Retrograde**: June 30 – December 5, 2025
- **Post-Retrograde Shadow Period**: December 6, 2025 – February 15, 2026

Neptune retrograde in its home sign of Pisces is particularly powerful for spiritual awakening, intuitive insight, and emotional healing. It invites deep reflection on your spiritual path and the illusions or fantasies that may be clouding your judgment.

Uranus Retrograde (in Taurus):

- **Pre-Retrograde Shadow Period**: April 16 – August 11, 2025
- **Uranus Retrograde**: August 11, 2025 – January 28, 2026
- **Post-Retrograde Shadow Period**: January 29 – April 16, 2026

Uranus retrograde in Taurus challenges you to reflect on how you handle change, particularly in the areas of stability, finances, and material security. It encourages you to break free from outdated habits and embrace new ways of living authentically.

Pluto Retrograde (in Aquarius and Capricorn):

- **Pre-Retrograde Shadow Period**: December 10, 2024 – May 1, 2025
- **Pluto Retrograde**: May 1 – October 12, 2025
- **Post-Retrograde Shadow Period**: October 13, 2025 – January 22, 2026

Pluto retrograde in Aquarius and Capricorn offers a profound period for personal and collective transformation. It invites deep reflection on power dynamics, social structures, and personal rebirth. This retrograde is ideal for shadow work, emotional healing, and stepping into your personal power.

Deep Spiritual Work and Transformation Spells for Outer Planet Retrogrades

Below are powerful rituals and spells designed to harness the transformative energy of Neptune, Uranus, and Pluto retrogrades. These spells focus on deep spiritual work, shadow work, personal liberation, and transformation.

1. Neptune Retrograde Spiritual Awakening Ritual

This ritual is designed to help you connect with your intuition, release illusions, and awaken to deeper spiritual truths during Neptune retrograde. It focuses on spiritual cleansing and accessing higher wisdom.

Materials:

- A purple or blue candle (for spiritual awakening and intuition)
- A piece of amethyst or moonstone (for enhancing intuition)
- A bowl of water (for cleansing and emotional healing)
- Lavender or frankincense incense (for spiritual clarity)
- A journal and pen

Instructions:

1. **Prepare Your Space**: Cleanse your space with lavender or frankincense incense to invite spiritual clarity.
2. **Set Your Intention**: Reflect on areas of your life where you may be living in illusion or confusion. Write down any fantasies, deceptions, or emotional attachments you need to release.
3. **Light the Candle**: As you light the purple or blue candle, say:
   "During this Neptune retrograde, I release all illusions and awaken to my inner truth. I open my heart to spiritual clarity and higher wisdom."
4. **Use the Water**: Hold the bowl of water and visualize it cleansing your emotional and psychic energy. Imagine it washing away any illusions, emotional baggage, or confusion that clouds your judgment.
5. **Hold the Amethyst**: Hold the amethyst or moonstone in your hands and focus on enhancing your intuition. Visualize yourself connecting with your higher self and receiving spiritual insight into your path.
6. **Journal Your Insights**: Spend time journaling about your spiritual journey, your intuitive insights, and any illusions you need to release. Focus on the truth that is emerging within you during this retrograde period.
7. **Close the Ritual**: Allow the candle to burn down. Keep the amethyst or moonstone near your bed or meditation space to continue enhancing your spiritual insight during Neptune retrograde.

2. Uranus Retrograde Liberation Spell

This spell focuses on personal freedom, breaking free from old patterns, and embracing your authentic self during Uranus retrograde. It helps you release limiting beliefs and societal expectations, empowering you to live more authentically.

Materials:

- A blue or silver candle (for freedom and transformation)
- A piece of labradorite or clear quartz (for personal breakthrough)
- A feather (symbolizing freedom and Air energy)
- A piece of paper and pen

Instructions:

1. **Prepare Your Space**: Cleanse your space with sandalwood or peppermint incense to invite the energy of freedom and transformation.
2. **Set Your Intention**: Reflect on areas of your life where you feel restricted or held back. Write down any limiting beliefs, societal expectations, or fears that are preventing you from living authentically.
3. **Light the Candle**: As you light the blue or silver candle, say:
   "During this Uranus retrograde, I break free from all limitations. I embrace my true self and live authentically."
4. **Use the Feather**: Hold the feather and visualize it sweeping away any restrictions or limiting beliefs that have been holding you back. Imagine yourself soaring freely, unburdened by fear or societal expectations.
5. **Hold the Labradorite**: Hold the labradorite or clear quartz in your hands and focus on breaking through old patterns. Visualize yourself embracing change and living in alignment with your authentic self.
6. **Burn the Paper**: Safely burn the piece of paper with your written limitations, symbolizing their release. As the paper burns, imagine yourself breaking free from the past and stepping into a new, liberated version of yourself.
7. **Close the Ritual**: Allow the candle to burn down. Keep the labradorite or clear quartz with you to maintain your sense of personal freedom and empowerment during Uranus retrograde.

3. Pluto Retrograde Shadow Work Ritual

This ritual is designed for deep shadow work, healing past trauma, and stepping into your personal power during Pluto retrograde. It focuses on confronting the unconscious, releasing old wounds, and transforming your inner darkness into strength.

Materials:

- A black or dark purple candle (for transformation and shadow work)
- A piece of obsidian or black tourmaline (for protection and grounding)
- A small mirror (for self-reflection)
- A bowl of saltwater (for cleansing and release)
- A journal and pen

Instructions:

1. **Prepare Your Space**: Burn sage or palo santo incense to cleanse your space and create a protective, grounding atmosphere.
2. **Set Your Intention**: Reflect on your shadow self—the parts of you that you've repressed or hidden. Write down any fears, traumas, or unresolved emotions that you are ready to confront and heal.
3. **Light the Candle**: As you light the black or dark purple candle, say:
   "During this Pluto retrograde, I embrace my shadow and transform my inner darkness into strength. I release all that no longer serves me."
4. **Use the Mirror**: Hold the mirror and look into your reflection. As you gaze at yourself, allow any hidden emotions, fears, or traumas to surface. Acknowledge these aspects of yourself with compassion and acceptance.
5. **Hold the Obsidian**: Hold the obsidian or black tourmaline in your hands and focus on grounding your energy. Visualize the stone absorbing and transforming any negative energy or unresolved emotions, allowing you to feel stronger and more empowered.
6. **Use the Saltwater**: Dip your fingers into the bowl of saltwater and anoint your forehead, heart, and hands. As you do this, visualize the saltwater cleansing and releasing the emotional pain or trauma you've been carrying.
7. **Journal Your Shadow Work**: Spend time journaling about your shadow self, the emotions you've confronted, and the lessons you've learned. Focus on how you can integrate these lessons into your life for personal transformation and growth.
8. **Close the Ritual**: Allow the candle to burn down. Pour the saltwater outside as a symbolic release of your emotional burdens. Keep the obsidian or black tourmaline with you as a protective talisman during Pluto retrograde.

Symbols, Herbs, and Crystals for Outer Planet Retrograde Magic

To enhance your Neptune, Uranus, and Pluto retrograde rituals, you can incorporate specific symbols, herbs, and crystals that resonate with the energies of deep spiritual work, personal freedom, and transformation.

Symbols for Outer Planet Retrogrades:

- **The Phoenix**: Represents transformation, rebirth, and rising from the ashes of past trauma.
- **The Moon**: Symbolizes the subconscious, intuition, and hidden truths, particularly for Neptune retrograde.
- **The Lightning Bolt**: Represents sudden change, breakthrough, and personal liberation, ideal for Uranus retrograde.
- **The Snake**: A symbol of shedding old skin, transformation, and personal power, particularly for Pluto retrograde.

Herbs for Outer Planet Retrogrades:

- **Lavender**: Promotes spiritual clarity and emotional healing, particularly during Neptune retrograde.
- **Mugwort**: Enhances intuition, dream work, and spiritual insight, particularly useful for Neptune retrograde.
- **Peppermint**: Invites mental clarity and freedom, helping to break free from old patterns during Uranus retrograde.
- **Sage**: Clears away negativity and provides protection during deep shadow work, especially for Pluto retrograde.

Crystals for Outer Planet Retrogrades:

- **Amethyst**: Enhances spiritual clarity, intuition, and psychic insight, especially during Neptune retrograde.
- **Labradorite**: Promotes personal breakthroughs, transformation, and freedom, particularly for Uranus retrograde.
- **Obsidian**: Provides protection, grounding, and support during deep shadow work, especially for Pluto retrograde.
- **Moonstone**: Enhances intuition, emotional healing, and spiritual awakening, particularly useful during Neptune retrograde.

Conclusion

Neptune, Uranus, and Pluto retrogrades offer profound opportunities for deep spiritual work, personal liberation, and transformative healing. By aligning your magical practice with the energies of these outer planet retrogrades, you can awaken to higher spiritual truths, break free from old patterns, and confront your shadow self with compassion and courage. Through thoughtful rituals, introspective practices, and spiritual insight, you can transform your life on a soul-deep level, embracing personal growth, freedom, and empowerment. Whether you are focused on spiritual awakening, personal liberation, or shadow work, Neptune, Uranus, and Pluto retrogrades provide powerful cosmic support for your transformative journey.

Chapter 29: Star Signs and Manifestation Goals: Harnessing Your Zodiac Sign's Energy for Personal Goals and Rituals

Each zodiac sign carries unique energies and characteristics that influence how we approach life, set personal goals, and manifest our desires. Understanding the strengths, challenges, and natural tendencies of your zodiac sign can help you align your goals with the cosmic energy that best supports your personal growth. By working with the energy of your star sign, you can enhance your ability to manifest goals that resonate deeply with your soul's purpose and your individual strengths.

This chapter explores how to harness the energy of your zodiac sign to set powerful manifestation goals and create personalized rituals that align with your astrological makeup. Whether you're looking to manifest success, love, health, or personal development, using your zodiac sign's energy as a guide can amplify your intentions and help you achieve your goals with greater ease and alignment.

Understanding Zodiac Energy for Manifestation

Each zodiac sign is associated with an element (Earth, Air, Fire, or Water), a ruling planet, and specific characteristics that shape how individuals under that sign express their energy and pursue their goals. By understanding these core attributes, you can tailor your manifestation practices to work in harmony with your sign's strengths, minimizing potential challenges and obstacles.

The Elements and Their Influence on Manifestation

- **Fire Signs (Aries, Leo, Sagittarius)**: Fire signs are passionate, dynamic, and driven by inspiration. They excel at setting bold goals and taking swift action, but they may need to work on maintaining focus and patience. Fire sign manifestation rituals focus on action, courage, and rapid manifestation.
- **Earth Signs (Taurus, Virgo, Capricorn)**: Earth signs are grounded, practical, and patient. They are skilled at manifesting long-term goals and material success, but may sometimes struggle with flexibility and spontaneity. Earth sign manifestation rituals emphasize stability, consistency, and building strong foundations.
- **Air Signs (Gemini, Libra, Aquarius)**: Air signs are intellectual, communicative, and innovative. They excel at manifesting through ideas, collaboration, and mental clarity, but may need to focus on grounding their ideas into practical action. Air sign rituals focus on creativity, mental clarity, and networking.
- **Water Signs (Cancer, Scorpio, Pisces)**: Water signs are emotional, intuitive, and deeply connected to their subconscious. They manifest best through emotional alignment, spiritual practices, and intuition, but may need to guard against emotional overwhelm or lack of focus. Water sign rituals emphasize intuition, emotional healing, and spiritual growth.

Manifestation Goals and Rituals for Each Zodiac Sign

Below are detailed manifestation goals and rituals tailored to the unique energy of each zodiac sign. These rituals focus on harnessing the strengths of your sign to set and achieve personal goals, whether in love, career, health, or personal development.

1. Aries (March 21 – April 19): Bold Action and Leadership

As the first sign of the zodiac, Aries is known for its boldness, enthusiasm, and leadership qualities. Ruled by Mars, the planet of action and courage, Aries energy is dynamic, impulsive, and always ready to initiate new projects. Aries individuals are natural leaders and thrive when they are pursuing ambitious, exciting goals. However, they may need to work on maintaining long-term focus and avoiding impulsiveness.

Manifestation Goals for Aries:

- Leadership and career success
- New beginnings and bold ventures
- Courage to take risks and pursue dreams

Ritual for Bold Action and Leadership: Materials:

- A red or gold candle (for courage and leadership)
- A piece of carnelian or tiger's eye (for confidence and motivation)
- A piece of paper and pen

Instructions:

1. **Set Your Intention**: Write down a bold goal or new venture you want to pursue. Be specific and think about how this goal aligns with your desire for leadership or success.
2. **Light the Candle**: As you light the red or gold candle, say:
   "I call upon the energy of Aries to ignite my passion and courage. I step boldly into leadership and pursue my goals with fearless determination."
3. **Hold the Carnelian**: Hold the carnelian or tiger's eye in your hands and focus on the energy of confidence and motivation flowing through you. Visualize yourself achieving your goal with courage and ease.
4. **Take Action**: End the ritual by writing down the first step you will take toward achieving your goal. Aries energy thrives on action, so make sure to take immediate action after your ritual.

2. Taurus (April 20 – May 20): Stability and Abundance

Taurus is an Earth sign ruled by Venus, the planet of love, beauty, and abundance. Taurus individuals are known for their practical, patient, and determined nature. They excel at manifesting material success, stability, and long-term goals, but may sometimes struggle with resistance to change or being overly cautious. Taurus energy is best used to manifest financial stability, security, and luxury.

Manifestation Goals for Taurus:

- Financial stability and material abundance
- Building strong foundations in relationships and career
- Cultivating beauty, comfort, and sensual pleasures

Ritual for Stability and Abundance: **Materials**:

- A green or brown candle (for abundance and grounding)
- A piece of jade or green aventurine (for prosperity and luck)
- A bowl of coins or crystals (symbolizing abundance)

Instructions:

1. **Set Your Intention**: Write down a goal related to financial stability, material success, or building a strong foundation in your life.
2. **Light the Candle**: As you light the green or brown candle, say:
   "I call upon the energy of Taurus to bring stability, abundance, and prosperity into my life. I build my success on a solid foundation."
3. **Use the Coins**: Hold the bowl of coins or crystals in your hands and visualize your financial or material goals manifesting. Feel the energy of abundance surrounding you and imagine yourself living in comfort and security.
4. **Hold the Jade**: Hold the jade or green aventurine and focus on attracting prosperity and stability into your life. Picture your goal coming to fruition with patience and determination.

3. Gemini (May 21 – June 20): Communication and Innovation

Gemini, ruled by Mercury, is an Air sign known for its intellectual curiosity, adaptability, and communication skills. Geminis are natural communicators, thinkers, and innovators, excelling at manifesting through networking, collaboration, and creative thinking. However, they may need to work on maintaining focus and avoiding distractions.

Manifestation Goals for Gemini:

- Improving communication and networking
- Developing new ideas or creative projects
- Expanding knowledge and intellectual growth

Ritual for Communication and Innovation: Materials:

- A yellow or blue candle (for clarity and communication)
- A feather or quill pen (symbolizing Mercury's influence)
- A piece of sodalite or lapis lazuli (for mental clarity and communication)

Instructions:

1. **Set Your Intention**: Write down a goal related to improving communication, developing a new idea, or expanding your knowledge.
2. **Light the Candle**: As you light the yellow or blue candle, say:
   "I call upon the energy of Gemini to bring clarity, creativity, and communication into my life. I express my ideas with confidence and grace."
3. **Use the Feather**: Hold the feather or quill pen and visualize your thoughts flowing freely and clearly. Imagine yourself successfully communicating your ideas and achieving your intellectual goals.
4. **Hold the Sodalite**: Hold the sodalite or lapis lazuli and focus on gaining mental clarity and insight. Visualize your mind becoming clear and focused, allowing you to manifest your ideas with ease.

4. Cancer (June 21 – July 22): Emotional Healing and Nurturing

Cancer is a Water sign ruled by the Moon, known for its deep emotional sensitivity, nurturing nature, and strong connection to home and family. Cancer individuals excel at manifesting emotional healing, intuitive insights, and creating a sense of security and comfort. However, they may need to guard against emotional overwhelm or becoming too attached to the past.

Manifestation Goals for Cancer:

- Emotional healing and nurturing relationships
- Strengthening family bonds and creating a safe home environment
- Cultivating intuition and spiritual connection

Ritual for Emotional Healing and Nurturing: Materials:

- A white or blue candle (for emotional balance and protection)
- A piece of moonstone or rose quartz (for emotional healing)
- A bowl of water (symbolizing Cancer's watery influence)

Instructions:

1. **Set Your Intention**: Write down a goal related to emotional healing, nurturing relationships, or creating a safe and supportive environment.
2. **Light the Candle**: As you light the white or blue candle, say:
   "I call upon the energy of Cancer to bring emotional healing, comfort, and security into my life. I nurture myself and others with love and compassion."
3. **Use the Water**: Hold the bowl of water and visualize it soothing and healing your emotional wounds. Imagine yourself surrounded by a protective, nurturing energy that supports your emotional well-being.
4. **Hold the Moonstone**: Hold the moonstone or rose quartz in your hands and focus on healing your heart and strengthening your relationships. Picture yourself feeling emotionally balanced, secure, and loved.

5. Leo (July 23 – August 22): Creativity and Confidence

Leo, ruled by the Sun, is a Fire sign known for its boldness, creativity, and confidence. Leos are natural performers and leaders, thriving when they are in the spotlight and expressing their creative talents. They excel at manifesting personal success, recognition, and joy, but may need to work on avoiding pride or self-centeredness.

Manifestation Goals for Leo:

- Personal success and recognition
- Expressing creativity and talents
- Building confidence and self-esteem

Ritual for Creativity and Confidence: Materials:

- A gold or orange candle (for creativity and success)
- A piece of citrine or sunstone (for confidence and joy)
- A mirror (for self-reflection)

Instructions:

1. **Set Your Intention**: Write down a goal related to personal success, creative expression, or building confidence.
2. **Light the Candle**: As you light the gold or orange candle, say:
   "I call upon the energy of Leo to shine brightly in my life. I embrace my creativity, confidence, and joy, and I step boldly into success."
3. **Use the Mirror**: Hold the mirror and look into your reflection. Visualize yourself achieving your goal with confidence, standing in your personal power, and expressing your talents with ease.
4. **Hold the Citrine**: Hold the citrine or sunstone and focus on attracting success, joy, and confidence into your life. Picture yourself radiating positivity and light, drawing others to your creative energy.

6. Virgo (August 23 – September 22): Organization and Service

Virgo is an Earth sign ruled by Mercury, known for its analytical mind, attention to detail, and desire to serve others. Virgos excel at manifesting through organization, planning, and providing practical solutions to problems. However, they may need to guard against perfectionism or over-thinking.

Manifestation Goals for Virgo:

- Improving health, wellness, and daily routines
- Providing service and support to others
- Cultivating organization, productivity, and efficiency

Ritual for Organization and Service: Materials:

- A green or brown candle (for health and grounding)
- A piece of jasper or moss agate (for productivity and grounding)
- A small notebook or planner (for organizing goals)

Instructions:

1. **Set Your Intention**: Write down a goal related to health, organization, or providing service to others.
2. **Light the Candle**: As you light the green or brown candle, say:
   "I call upon the energy of Virgo to bring organization, health, and productivity into my life. I manifest my goals with precision and care."
3. **Use the Notebook**: Write down a detailed plan or action steps for achieving your goal. Virgo energy thrives on structure and organization, so focus on creating a clear path to success.
4. **Hold the Jasper**: Hold the jasper or moss agate in your hands and visualize yourself achieving your goal with clarity and efficiency. Picture yourself feeling grounded, productive, and in control of your life.

7. Libra (September 23 – October 22): Balance and Harmony

Libra, ruled by Venus, is an Air sign known for its love of balance, beauty, and harmony. Libras excel at manifesting through cooperation, diplomacy, and building harmonious relationships. They are drawn to beauty, aesthetics, and creating environments that reflect peace and fairness. However, they may need to work on decision-making and avoiding conflict.

Manifestation Goals for Libra:

- Building harmonious relationships and partnerships
- Cultivating beauty and balance in life
- Enhancing diplomacy, fairness, and cooperation

Ritual for Balance and Harmony: Materials:

- A pink or blue candle (for love and harmony)
- A piece of rose quartz or blue lace agate (for peace and balance)
- A feather (symbolizing Libra's connection to Air)

Instructions:

1. **Set Your Intention**: Write down a goal related to building harmonious relationships, cultivating beauty, or creating balance in your life.
2. **Light the Candle**: As you light the pink or blue candle, say:
   "I call upon the energy of Libra to bring balance, harmony, and beauty into my life. I create peaceful, loving relationships and environments."
3. **Use the Feather**: Hold the feather and visualize it gently balancing all areas of your life. Imagine yourself surrounded by harmonious relationships and peaceful energy.
4. **Hold the Rose Quartz**: Hold the rose quartz or blue lace agate and focus on manifesting love, peace, and balance in your life. Picture yourself creating beauty and harmony in your relationships and surroundings.

8. Scorpio (October 23 – November 21): Transformation and Power

Scorpio, ruled by Pluto and traditionally by Mars, is a Water sign known for its intensity, passion, and transformative energy. Scorpios are masters of personal transformation and can harness their deep emotional power to manifest profound change in their lives. However, they may need to guard against becoming too controlling or secretive.

Manifestation Goals for Scorpio:

- Personal transformation and empowerment
- Deep emotional healing and shadow work
- Manifesting through passion and intensity

Ritual for Transformation and Power: Materials:

- A black or dark red candle (for transformation and power)
- A piece of obsidian or black tourmaline (for protection and transformation)
- A small mirror (for self-reflection and shadow work)

Instructions:

1. **Set Your Intention**: Write down a goal related to personal transformation, emotional healing, or stepping into your personal power.
2. **Light the Candle**: As you light the black or dark red candle, say:
   "I call upon the energy of Scorpio to bring transformation, healing, and power into my life. I release the old and embrace my true strength."
3. **Use the Mirror**: Hold the mirror and look into your reflection. As you gaze at yourself, imagine shedding old patterns or fears and stepping into your personal power.
4. **Hold the Obsidian**: Hold the obsidian or black tourmaline and focus on transforming your life. Picture yourself empowered, strong, and fully in control of your destiny.

9. Sagittarius (November 22 – December 21): Expansion and Adventure

Sagittarius is a Fire sign ruled by Jupiter, known for its love of adventure, exploration, and intellectual expansion. Sagittarians are optimistic, free-spirited, and constantly seeking new experiences and knowledge. They excel at manifesting travel, personal growth, and higher learning, but may need to work on maintaining focus and avoiding restlessness.

Manifestation Goals for Sagittarius:

- Expanding knowledge, travel, and exploration
- Pursuing personal growth and spiritual wisdom
- Cultivating optimism and freedom

Ritual for Expansion and Adventure: Materials:

- A purple or blue candle (for wisdom and growth)
- A piece of turquoise or lapis lazuli (for wisdom and exploration)
- A map or travel-related object (symbolizing adventure)

Instructions:

1. **Set Your Intention**: Write down a goal related to expanding your knowledge, traveling, or pursuing personal growth.
2. **Light the Candle**: As you light the purple or blue candle, say:
   "I call upon the energy of Sagittarius to bring adventure, growth, and wisdom into my life. I expand my horizons and embrace new experiences."
3. **Use the Map**: Hold the map or travel-related object and visualize yourself exploring new horizons, whether physically, intellectually, or spiritually. Picture yourself pursuing personal growth with enthusiasm and curiosity.
4. **Hold the Turquoise**: Hold the turquoise or lapis lazuli and focus on expanding your knowledge and seeking wisdom. Picture yourself learning, growing, and embracing new experiences with optimism and freedom.

10. Capricorn (December 22 – January 19): Discipline and Ambition

Capricorn is an Earth sign ruled by Saturn, known for its discipline, ambition, and commitment to long-term success. Capricorns are highly practical and goal-oriented, excelling at manifesting through hard work, perseverance, and strategic planning. However, they may need to work on avoiding rigidity or workaholism.

Manifestation Goals for Capricorn:

- Achieving career success and long-term goals
- Building a solid foundation for future prosperity
- Cultivating discipline, perseverance, and responsibility

Ritual for Discipline and Ambition: Materials:

- A black or green candle (for discipline and success)
- A piece of onyx or hematite (for grounding and focus)
- A small journal (for writing goals)

Instructions:

1. **Set Your Intention**: Write down a goal related to career success, long-term planning, or achieving financial stability.
2. **Light the Candle**: As you light the black or green candle, say:
   "I call upon the energy of Capricorn to bring discipline, focus, and success into my life. I work diligently toward my goals and build a strong foundation for the future."
3. **Use the Journal**: Write down a detailed plan for achieving your goal, breaking it down into actionable steps. Capricorn energy thrives on strategy and long-term planning.
4. **Hold the Onyx**: Hold the onyx or hematite and focus on staying disciplined and committed to your goals. Picture yourself achieving success through hard work, perseverance, and careful planning.

11. Aquarius (January 20 – February 18): Innovation and Humanitarianism

Aquarius is an Air sign ruled by Uranus and traditionally by Saturn, known for its innovative, progressive, and humanitarian nature. Aquarians excel at manifesting through creative thinking, social change, and collective efforts. They are visionaries, driven by ideals of equality and freedom, but may need to work on grounding their ideas into practical reality.

Manifestation Goals for Aquarius:

- Pursuing innovation, creativity, and new ideas
- Manifesting social change and humanitarian goals
- Cultivating individuality and embracing uniqueness

Ritual for Innovation and Humanitarianism: Materials:

- A blue or silver candle (for innovation and freedom)
- A piece of labradorite or amethyst (for creativity and transformation)
- A feather (symbolizing Air and new ideas)

Instructions:

1. **Set Your Intention**: Write down a goal related to innovation, social change, or pursuing creative ideas.
2. **Light the Candle**: As you light the blue or silver candle, say:
   "I call upon the energy of Aquarius to bring innovation, freedom, and new ideas into my life. I manifest my vision for the future with creativity and purpose."
3. **Use the Feather**: Hold the feather and visualize it carrying your innovative ideas into the world. Picture yourself manifesting your vision for social change, creativity, or humanitarian goals.
4. **Hold the Labradorite**: Hold the labradorite or amethyst and focus on embracing your uniqueness and creative potential. Picture yourself making a positive impact through your ideas and actions.

12. Pisces (February 19 – March 20): Intuition and Compassion

Pisces is a Water sign ruled by Neptune, known for its deep sensitivity, compassion, and intuition. Pisceans excel at manifesting through emotional alignment, spiritual practices, and creative expression. They are deeply connected to the collective unconscious and thrive when they are nurturing others or engaging in artistic pursuits. However, they may need to guard against emotional overwhelm or escapism.

Manifestation Goals for Pisces:

- Enhancing intuition, spirituality, and creativity
- Cultivating compassion and emotional healing
- Manifesting through artistic expression and emotional alignment

Ritual for Intuition and Compassion: Materials:

- A purple or white candle (for intuition and compassion)
- A piece of moonstone or amethyst (for spiritual insight)
- A bowl of water (symbolizing Pisces' connection to Water)

Instructions:

1. **Set Your Intention**: Write down a goal related to enhancing your intuition, healing emotionally, or pursuing creative expression.
2. **Light the Candle**: As you light the purple or white candle, say:
   "I call upon the energy of Pisces to bring intuition, compassion, and healing into my life. I manifest my dreams through emotional alignment and spiritual insight."
3. **Use the Water**: Hold the bowl of water and visualize it calming and centering your emotions. Imagine yourself deeply connected to your intuition and emotional wisdom.
4. **Hold the Moonstone**: Hold the moonstone or amethyst and focus on enhancing your spiritual insight and creative potential. Picture yourself manifesting your dreams through compassion, creativity, and deep emotional alignment.

Conclusion

Each zodiac sign carries a unique energy that can be harnessed to set and achieve personal manifestation goals. By aligning your goals with the natural strengths of your zodiac sign, you can enhance your ability to manifest success, love, health, or personal growth. Whether you are focusing on bold leadership, emotional healing, or creative expression, working with your star sign's energy provides a powerful way to align your personal goals with the cosmic forces that support your journey. Through thoughtful rituals and intentional manifestation practices, you can achieve your dreams and align your life with your soul's true purpose.

Chapter 30: Working with the Astrological Houses: Unlocking the Power of the Zodiac Wheel in Your Magical Practice

The astrological houses are one of the most important elements of your birth chart, each representing a different area of life. As planets transit through these houses, they influence various aspects of your experience, from personal identity to career, relationships, finances, and spirituality. Understanding the role of each astrological house in your chart allows you to align your magical practice with the specific energies governing each area of life. By working with the houses, you can tailor your rituals and spells to enhance personal growth, resolve challenges, and manifest your desires more effectively.

In this chapter, we will explore each of the twelve astrological houses in depth, examining how their influence shapes different areas of your life and how to incorporate their unique energies into your magical work. Whether you are focusing on self-improvement, relationships, finances, or spiritual development, working with the astrological houses will provide deeper insights and more potent results in your rituals.

Understanding the Astrological Houses

The astrological houses are twelve divisions of the zodiac wheel, each governing a different aspect of your life. They are not planets or signs, but rather the areas through which the planetary energies and zodiacal influences are expressed. In a natal chart, the planets located within specific houses shape how you experience and navigate those areas of life. Similarly, as planets transit through the houses, they bring their influence to bear on those same areas.

Each house corresponds to a specific sign of the zodiac, but the houses themselves are independent and can contain planets or signs that influence your experience differently. The first six houses (1st–6th) represent personal growth and development, while the latter six houses (7th–12th) reflect interpersonal relationships and your connection to society at large.

The First House: The House of Self and Personal Identity

Keywords: Identity, appearance, self-expression, first impressions, beginnings

The First House, also known as the Ascendant or Rising Sign, governs your physical appearance, how you present yourself to the world, and your overall sense of identity. It reflects how others see you and how you approach new beginnings. In your magical practice, the First House is ideal for rituals related to self-improvement, personal transformation, and confidence. This house is where you set intentions for personal growth and how you want to be perceived by others.

Magical Work for the First House:

- **Self-confidence rituals**: Enhance your self-esteem and courage in new endeavors.
- **Identity spells**: Work on self-expression, personal branding, and how others perceive you.
- **New beginning rituals**: Use this house's energy for starting fresh in any area of your life.

Ritual Example:

Self-Confidence Ritual: Light a red candle to represent personal strength, and hold a piece of tiger's eye crystal. Visualize yourself moving through the world with confidence, projecting your true self and feeling empowered. Repeat the affirmation, "I embrace my true identity, and I walk confidently in my power."

The Second House: The House of Money, Possessions, and Self-Worth

Keywords: Finances, possessions, values, material wealth, security

The Second House governs money, possessions, personal values, and how you earn your income. It also reflects your sense of self-worth and how you use your material resources. In magical practice, the Second House is ideal for manifestation spells related to financial success, abundance, and building a stable foundation. It also encourages reflection on your values and how they align with your material goals.

Magical Work for the Second House:

- **Wealth manifestation spells**: Attract financial success and material abundance.
- **Self-worth rituals**: Strengthen your sense of value and worthiness.
- **Security spells**: Focus on creating a stable and secure home environment.

Ritual Example:

Wealth Manifestation Spell: Place a green or gold candle on your altar, along with a piece of citrine and a small bowl of coins. Light the candle and visualize money flowing to you effortlessly. As you chant, "I am worthy of abundance, and wealth flows to me," imagine yourself achieving financial stability and success.

The Third House: The House of Communication and Learning

Keywords: Communication, education, siblings, short trips, mental processes

The Third House governs communication, learning, intellectual pursuits, and your relationships with siblings and neighbors. It influences how you process information and express your thoughts. In your magical practice, the Third House is the ideal realm for spells that improve communication, enhance learning, and help you express your ideas clearly. It is also the house to work with when improving your writing, public speaking, or intellectual skills.

Magical Work for the Third House:

- **Communication spells**: Improve your ability to express yourself and be understood.
- **Learning rituals**: Focus on enhancing your intellectual capacity, study habits, and learning new skills.
- **Siblings and neighbor relationships**: Improve harmony in these connections.

Ritual Example:

Clear Communication Spell: Light a yellow candle to represent clarity and intellect, and hold a piece of blue lace agate to improve communication. Visualize a light surrounding your throat chakra, opening it up to help you speak clearly and with confidence. Chant, "My words flow freely, and I am understood with ease."

The Fourth House: The House of Home, Family, and Emotional Foundations

Keywords: Home, family, roots, emotional security, ancestors

The Fourth House represents your home life, family, and emotional foundations. It governs your relationship with your parents, particularly your mother, and your sense of belonging and security. This house also reflects your ancestral roots and how your early upbringing affects your emotional well-being. In your magical practice, the Fourth House is ideal for spells related to home protection, family healing, and establishing emotional security.

Magical Work for the Fourth House:

- **Home protection spells**: Create a safe and peaceful home environment.
- **Family healing rituals**: Heal relationships with family members and ancestors.
- **Emotional security spells**: Strengthen your inner sense of safety and belonging.

Ritual Example:

Home Protection Ritual: Light a white candle to represent safety and protection, and place a piece of black tourmaline at the entrance of your home. Walk around your living space, chanting, "My home is a sanctuary, safe from all harm." Visualize a protective barrier forming around your home, keeping out negativity.

The Fifth House: The House of Creativity, Pleasure, and Romance

Keywords: Creativity, romance, pleasure, children, self-expression

The Fifth House governs creativity, romance, pleasure, and all forms of self-expression. It also rules over children and your ability to enjoy life's pleasures. This house is where you explore what brings you joy, how you express your creativity, and how you approach romantic relationships. In magical work, the Fifth House is ideal for spells that enhance your creative abilities, bring more fun and joy into your life, or attract romantic partners.

Magical Work for the Fifth House:

- **Creativity enhancement spells**: Tap into your creative potential for artistic projects.
- **Romance and love spells**: Attract or enhance romantic relationships.
- **Joy and pleasure rituals**: Invite more fun and enjoyment into your life.

Ritual Example:

Creativity Enhancement Spell: Light an orange candle to represent creativity, and place a piece of carnelian on your altar. Visualize a flow of creative energy filling you, and repeat, "I embrace my creative power, and inspiration flows through me with ease."

The Sixth House: The House of Health, Service, and Daily Routines

Keywords: Health, work, service, daily habits, well-being

The Sixth House is associated with health, daily routines, work, and service to others. It governs your approach to your job, your habits, and how you take care of your body. In your magical practice, the Sixth House is perfect for spells related to health, wellness, and improving your work environment. It is also ideal for rituals that focus on creating structure, discipline, and balance in your daily life.

Magical Work for the Sixth House:

- **Health and wellness rituals**: Improve your physical well-being and healing.
- **Workplace spells**: Enhance productivity and success in your job.
- **Daily routine and habit-building rituals**: Strengthen discipline and improve time management.

Ritual Example:

Health and Wellness Ritual: Light a green candle to represent health and vitality, and hold a piece of bloodstone to boost healing energy. Visualize your body being filled with healing light, and chant, "I am healthy, whole, and vibrant. My body heals and thrives."

The Seventh House: The House of Partnerships and Relationships

Keywords: Partnerships, marriage, contracts, one-on-one relationships, balance

The Seventh House governs all significant partnerships, including romantic relationships, business partnerships, and close friendships. It represents the energy you attract in your one-on-one connections and how you balance your needs with others. In magical work, the Seventh House is ideal for love spells, rituals to strengthen relationships, and creating harmony in partnerships. It's also a great house for legal matters and agreements.

Magical Work for the Seventh House:

- **Love and relationship spells**: Attract or improve romantic partnerships.
- **Harmony and balance rituals**: Create harmony and balance in relationships.
- **Contract spells**: Ensure fairness and balance in legal matters and agreements.

Ritual Example:

Relationship Harmony Spell: Light a pink or blue candle to represent love and peace. Hold a piece of rose quartz and visualize harmony flowing between you and your partner. Chant, "Our love is balanced and harmonious, filled with understanding and joy."

The Eighth House: The House of Transformation, Death, and Shared Resources

Keywords: Transformation, death, rebirth, shared resources, power

The Eighth House governs deep transformation, death and rebirth, and shared resources such as inheritances, taxes, and joint finances. It is also associated with sexuality, power, and the occult. This house represents major life transitions and the shedding of old ways to make space for new growth. In magical practice, the Eighth House is ideal for transformation rituals, shadow work, and spells related to financial agreements and power dynamics.

Magical Work for the Eighth House:

- **Transformation spells**: Facilitate personal growth and deep change.
- **Shadow work rituals**: Explore and heal hidden aspects of yourself.
- **Power and financial spells**: Strengthen your control over shared resources or finances.

Ritual Example:

Transformation Ritual: Light a black or dark purple candle to symbolize transformation and rebirth. Hold a piece of obsidian, and focus on shedding old habits, thoughts, or patterns that no longer serve you. Chant, "I release the old and embrace my transformation into something new."

The Ninth House: The House of Travel, Higher Learning, and Spirituality

Keywords: Travel, higher education, philosophy, spirituality, expansion

The Ninth House governs long-distance travel, higher learning, spiritual growth, and philosophy. It represents your quest for knowledge, spiritual enlightenment, and expanding your horizons beyond the familiar. In your magical practice, the Ninth House is ideal for rituals related to spiritual growth, travel, and learning. It also supports practices that broaden your understanding of the world and deepen your connection to universal truths.

Magical Work for the Ninth House:

- **Spiritual growth rituals**: Deepen your connection to spiritual truths and practices.
- **Travel spells**: Manifest safe and meaningful journeys, both physical and spiritual.
- **Learning and wisdom spells**: Enhance your ability to learn and seek higher knowledge.

Ritual Example:

Spiritual Growth Ritual: Light a purple candle for wisdom and spiritual expansion, and hold a piece of amethyst. Visualize yourself connecting with higher truths and receiving spiritual insights. Chant, "I open my mind to higher wisdom and embrace the knowledge of the universe."

The Tenth House: The House of Career and Public Life

Keywords: Career, public image, reputation, achievement, authority

The Tenth House governs your career, public life, reputation, and long-term achievements. It represents your professional aspirations, how you are viewed in the public eye, and your relationship with authority figures. In magical practice, the Tenth House is ideal for spells related to career advancement, professional success, and building a strong public reputation. It is also where you focus on achieving long-term goals and ambitions.

Magical Work for the Tenth House:

- **Career advancement spells**: Enhance your professional success and reputation.
- **Achievement rituals**: Manifest long-term goals and recognition for your efforts.
- **Authority spells**: Strengthen your relationship with authority or take on leadership roles.

Ritual Example:

Career Success Spell: Light a gold or green candle to represent success and abundance. Hold a piece of citrine or pyrite, and visualize yourself achieving your career goals and being recognized for your talents. Chant, "I step into my power and manifest success in my career."

The Eleventh House: The House of Friendships and Community

Keywords: Friendships, community, social groups, hopes and dreams, humanitarianism

The Eleventh House governs friendships, social groups, community involvement, and your long-term hopes and dreams. It represents how you connect with like-minded individuals and your vision for collective progress. In magical work, the Eleventh House is ideal for spells that enhance friendships, strengthen your connection to social causes, or manifest long-term goals. It is also a great house for working on collective efforts and group rituals.

Magical Work for the Eleventh House:

- **Friendship spells**: Strengthen bonds with friends and social groups.
- **Community involvement rituals**: Manifest positive connections within your community or work for a social cause.
- **Dream manifestation rituals**: Focus on achieving long-term hopes and dreams.

Ritual Example:

Friendship Bonding Spell: Light a blue or pink candle to represent friendship and harmony. Hold a piece of lapis lazuli or rose quartz and visualize the bonds of friendship growing stronger. Chant, "Our friendship is built on trust, love, and mutual support."

The Twelfth House: The House of Mysticism, the Subconscious, and Endings

Keywords: Mysticism, the subconscious, endings, isolation, healing

The Twelfth House governs the hidden aspects of life, including the subconscious, dreams, intuition, and mysticism. It is also associated with endings, isolation, and spiritual healing. This house represents the culmination of cycles, as well as the space where you connect with your inner world and unconscious mind. In magical practice, the Twelfth House is ideal for dream work, healing rituals, and practices that focus on releasing old patterns or energies. It is also the house for deep spiritual work, meditation, and connecting with higher realms.

Magical Work for the Twelfth House:

- **Dream work rituals**: Enhance your connection to dreams, intuition, and the subconscious.
- **Healing and release rituals**: Focus on spiritual healing, emotional release, and letting go of old patterns.

- **Mystical and spiritual practices**: Deepen your connection to higher realms and spiritual truths.

Ritual Example:

Dream Work Ritual: Light a purple or white candle to represent intuition and spiritual insight. Hold a piece of moonstone, and focus on enhancing your connection to your dreams and subconscious mind. Chant, "I open my mind to the messages of my dreams and embrace the wisdom of the unseen."

Conclusion

The astrological houses provide a powerful framework for understanding and working with different areas of life in your magical practice. By aligning your spells and rituals with the energies of each house, you can focus your intentions on the specific areas that need attention, whether you're working on personal growth, relationships, career, health, or spiritual development. Understanding the influence of each house helps you tailor your magical work to your unique astrological chart, allowing for more focused and potent results.

Through thoughtful and intentional practice, you can use the energy of the astrological houses to manifest your goals, deepen your self-awareness, and enhance your magical abilities across all aspects of life.

Chapter 31: Lunar Gardening and Herb Magic: Planting by the Moon and Harnessing the Power of Magical Herbs

Lunar gardening and herb magic are ancient practices that align the cycles of nature with the power of the moon. By planting, tending, and harvesting herbs according to the phases of the moon, you can enhance the potency of your magical practice and connect more deeply with the natural rhythms of the earth. The moon's energy profoundly influences the growth of plants and the magical properties of herbs, making lunar gardening an essential aspect of earth-based spirituality and witchcraft.

This chapter explores the art of lunar gardening, how the moon's phases affect plant growth, and how to choose the best times for planting, harvesting, and using magical herbs in spells. We will also dive into the magical correspondences of various herbs, their connection to the moon, and how to harness their energy for rituals and spells. Whether you are a seasoned gardener or new to the practice, this chapter provides practical guidance on working with the moon and magical herbs to enhance your witchcraft.

Understanding Lunar Gardening: The Moon's Influence on Plant Growth

The moon's gravitational pull affects not only the tides of the ocean but also the moisture levels in the soil, the growth of plants, and the energy cycles of nature. By timing your gardening activities—such as planting, watering, weeding, and harvesting—with the phases of the moon, you can maximize the vitality and growth of your plants. This practice, known as lunar gardening, has been used by farmers and gardeners for centuries to yield healthier, more abundant crops.

The Four Phases of the Moon in Gardening

1. **New Moon (Waxing Crescent)**: During the New Moon, the earth's energy is at its lowest, and the gravitational pull is strong. This is a time for planting seeds and leafy crops that grow above ground, such as lettuce, spinach, and herbs. The waxing moon (from New Moon to Full Moon) brings increasing energy, promoting rapid growth and upward movement in plants.

2. **First Quarter (Waxing Gibbous)**: As the moon continues to wax, the First Quarter is an excellent time for planting crops that bear fruit above ground, such as tomatoes, peppers, and beans. The waxing energy encourages strong growth and expansion, making this phase ideal for fertilizing and encouraging healthy development.

3. **Full Moon (Waning Gibbous)**: The Full Moon marks the peak of lunar energy, making it a powerful time for harvesting medicinal and magical herbs. Plants harvested during the Full Moon are thought to have the highest concentration of vitality and healing properties. This phase is also good for planting root crops such as carrots, potatoes, and onions.

4. **Last Quarter (Waning Crescent)**: As the moon wanes, energy is drawn downward into the roots of plants. This is the best time for pruning, weeding, and composting. It's also a good time to plant perennials, trees, and shrubs, as well as bulbs and root vegetables. The waning energy supports strong root growth and overall stability.

By aligning your gardening activities with these lunar phases, you can enhance the natural growth cycles of your plants, ensuring they thrive and are imbued with the moon's magical energy.

Lunar Gardening Activities by the Moon's Phases

To help you make the most of lunar gardening, here's a guide to the optimal gardening activities for each phase of the moon:

- **New Moon to First Quarter (Waxing Crescent)**:
    - **Best activities**: Planting above-ground crops (herbs, flowers, leafy vegetables), starting new projects, sowing seeds, watering.
    - **Magical focus**: New beginnings, manifestation, growth, and attracting positive energy.
- **First Quarter to Full Moon (Waxing Gibbous)**:
    - **Best activities**: Fertilizing, pruning, transplanting, planting fruiting plants, building structures.
    - **Magical focus**: Building strength, expanding, increasing abundance, empowerment spells.
- **Full Moon to Last Quarter (Waning Gibbous)**:
    - **Best activities**: Harvesting herbs and plants, storing seeds, gathering medicinal plants, reaping rewards.
    - **Magical focus**: Harvesting energy, culmination, gratitude, divination, and protection.
- **Last Quarter to New Moon (Waning Crescent)**:
    - **Best activities**: Weeding, composting, pruning, planting root crops, preparing soil for future planting.
    - **Magical focus**: Banishing, releasing, detoxing, endings, and cleansing.

Magical Herbs and Their Lunar Correspondences

Herbs have long been used in magical and healing practices for their potent energetic properties. Each herb carries specific magical correspondences, and many are directly linked to lunar energy due to their association with feminine, intuitive, and psychic properties. When combined with lunar gardening, the power of these herbs is amplified, making them ideal for use in spells, rituals, and healing work.

Below is a list of some of the most common magical herbs, their lunar correspondences, and how to use them in your magical practice.

1. Mugwort (Artemisia vulgaris)

- **Element**: Air
- **Planetary Ruler**: Moon
- **Magical Uses**: Mugwort is strongly associated with lunar energy, dreams, and psychic work. It is used to enhance intuition, aid in astral projection, and promote prophetic dreams. It is also protective, used to ward off negative spirits and energies.
- **Best Phase for Harvesting**: Full Moon
- **Magical Applications**: Use mugwort in dream pillows to enhance lucid dreaming, burn it as an incense during divination, or make a tea to heighten psychic awareness.

Spell Example:

Psychic Dreaming Spell: Place dried mugwort under your pillow on the night of a Full Moon. As you drift off to sleep, visualize the moon's light enhancing your psychic abilities and guiding you through your dreams. Chant, "I open my mind to the wisdom of the moon and the messages of my dreams."

2. Lavender (Lavandula angustifolia)

- **Element**: Air
- **Planetary Ruler**: Mercury
- **Magical Uses**: Lavender is well-known for its calming and protective properties. It is used in spells for peace, love, and purification, and is often burned to promote a serene atmosphere. Lavender is also associated with healing and restful sleep.
- **Best Phase for Harvesting**: Waxing Moon to Full Moon
- **Magical Applications**: Use lavender in protection sachets, burn it as incense to cleanse a space, or include it in healing baths and spells.

Spell Example:

Peaceful Sleep Ritual: Fill a small sachet with dried lavender and place it under your pillow before bedtime. As you light a white candle, say, "I invite peaceful sleep and healing rest into my space." Imagine the lavender's calming scent soothing your mind as you drift off to sleep.

3. Sage (Salvia officinalis)

- **Element**: Earth
- **Planetary Ruler**: Jupiter
- **Magical Uses**: Sage is one of the most powerful herbs for purification, protection, and wisdom. It is often burned to cleanse a space of negative energy and used in rituals to bring clarity and wisdom. Sage is also used in healing and abundance spells.
- **Best Phase for Harvesting**: Waning Moon
- **Magical Applications**: Burn sage to cleanse your home or sacred space, use it in protection sachets, or make sage-infused oils for anointing objects in rituals.

Spell Example:

Space Cleansing Ritual: Light a bundle of sage and walk through your home, focusing on areas that feel stagnant or negative. As you move through each room, repeat, "I banish negativity and invite positive energy into this space."

4. Rosemary (Rosmarinus officinalis)

- **Element**: Fire
- **Planetary Ruler**: Sun
- **Magical Uses**: Rosemary is a versatile herb that is used for protection, healing, memory, and love spells. It is also associated with mental clarity, purification, and longevity. Rosemary is often burned to purify spaces or used in healing rituals.
- **Best Phase for Harvesting**: Waxing Moon
- **Magical Applications**: Burn rosemary to cleanse your home, use it in memory-enhancing rituals, or include it in healing baths and teas.

Spell Example:

Memory Enhancement Spell: Brew a rosemary tea on a Waxing Moon before studying or focusing on a memory-related task. As you sip the tea, say, "Rosemary, herb of memory, sharpen my mind and strengthen my focus."

5. Chamomile (Matricaria chamomilla)

- **Element**: Water
- **Planetary Ruler**: Sun
- **Magical Uses**: Chamomile is used for relaxation, prosperity, and purification. It is often used in spells for calming emotions, attracting abundance, and promoting restful sleep. Chamomile's gentle, soothing energy makes it a popular herb for emotional healing and stress relief.
- **Best Phase for Harvesting**: Full Moon
- **Magical Applications**: Use chamomile in baths to relax and cleanse your energy, make a tea to attract abundance, or burn it as incense to calm the mind and promote relaxation.

Spell Example:
Relaxation Bath Ritual: Brew a strong chamomile tea and pour it into your bathwater on the night of the Full Moon. As you soak in the bath, visualize stress and tension dissolving. Chant, "I release all worries and embrace peace and relaxation."

6. Basil (Ocimum basilicum)

- **Element**: Fire
- **Planetary Ruler**: Mars
- **Magical Uses**: Basil is associated with love, protection, and abundance. It is often used in spells to attract prosperity, strengthen relationships, and bring protection to the home. Basil's fiery energy also makes it useful in spells for courage and success.
- **Best Phase for Harvesting**: Waxing Moon to Full Moon
- **Magical Applications**: Use basil in prosperity spells, place it near your front door to protect your home, or use it in love potions and sachets.

Spell Example:
Prosperity Spell: Place fresh basil leaves in a green pouch along with a coin. As you carry the pouch with you, say, "Basil, bring abundance and prosperity into my life." Visualize wealth and success flowing toward you.

7. Thyme (Thymus vulgaris)

- **Element**: Air
- **Planetary Ruler**: Venus
- **Magical Uses**: Thyme is used for purification, courage, and health. It is associated with strength and is often used in rituals to boost confidence and protect against negativity. Thyme is also used in healing and purification baths.
- **Best Phase for Harvesting**: Waning Moon
- **Magical Applications**: Burn thyme to cleanse a space, use it in healing sachets, or brew a thyme tea for courage before tackling a difficult task.

Spell Example:

Courage Spell: Burn dried thyme leaves in a fireproof dish on the night of a Waning Moon. As the smoke rises, say, "Thyme, give me strength and courage to face my challenges with confidence."

Harvesting and Using Herbs in Rituals

Herbs carry potent magical energies that can be enhanced by the phases of the moon. To make the most of their properties, harvest herbs during the appropriate lunar phase and store them with care. Here are some tips for harvesting and using magical herbs in your spells:

- **Harvesting During the Full Moon**: This is the best time to harvest herbs for healing, love, and protection spells. Plants are at their most potent during the Full Moon, and their energies can be captured and preserved for future use.
- **Drying and Storing Herbs**: After harvesting, hang herbs in bundles to dry in a cool, dark space. Once dried, store them in airtight containers to preserve their magical properties. Label each container with the herb's name and its magical correspondences.
- **Creating Herbal Oils and Incense**: Infuse herbs in oils to create anointing blends for candles, tools, and sacred spaces. You can also grind dried herbs into powder to create incense blends for rituals, meditation, and cleansing.

Planting by the Moon and the Zodiac

In addition to following the moon phases, some practitioners also plant according to the moon's position in the zodiac. Each zodiac sign corresponds to a different element (Earth, Air, Fire, or Water) and influences the growth and energy of plants:

- **Earth Signs (Taurus, Virgo, Capricorn)**: Best for planting root crops, trees, and hardy plants that need strong roots.
- **Water Signs (Cancer, Scorpio, Pisces)**: Ideal for planting leafy vegetables, herbs, and medicinal plants that thrive with plenty of moisture.
- **Fire Signs (Aries, Leo, Sagittarius)**: Best for planting fruiting crops, such as tomatoes and peppers, and plants that require a lot of sunlight.

- **Air Signs (Gemini, Libra, Aquarius)**: Good for planting flowers, herbs, and plants that benefit from good airflow and communication energy.

Aligning your gardening with both the moon phases and the zodiac adds an extra layer of cosmic energy to your practice, enhancing the vitality of your plants and the potency of your magical herbs.

Conclusion

Lunar gardening and herb magic are deeply interconnected practices that allow you to align with the natural cycles of the moon and the earth. By planting, harvesting, and using herbs in harmony with the moon's phases and the zodiac, you can enhance the potency of your magical practice and connect more deeply with the rhythms of nature. Whether you're growing your own herbs or working with purchased plants, understanding the lunar correspondences of your herbs and incorporating them into your spells and rituals will bring powerful energy to your craft.

As you continue to cultivate your garden and practice herb magic, you'll discover the profound wisdom held within the plants and the cycles of the moon. By working in harmony with these ancient forces, you'll deepen your connection to the earth and enhance your ability to manifest your desires and bring healing into your life and the world around you.

Chapter 32: Crystals and Celestial Energy: Aligning Crystals with Planetary and Lunar Energies

Crystals have long been revered for their powerful energies and ability to amplify spiritual work, healing, and manifestation. When combined with the forces of celestial energy—particularly the planetary and lunar cycles—crystals become even more potent. Each planet and lunar phase radiates a distinct energy that can be harnessed to enhance the properties of specific crystals. By aligning crystals with these celestial energies, you can channel cosmic forces into your magical practice, rituals, and personal growth.

In this chapter, we will explore how to attune crystals to the energies of the planets and moon, delving into the unique qualities each celestial body offers and how to combine them with the inherent properties of crystals. We'll also look at specific crystals that resonate with different planets and lunar phases, offering guidance on how to use them in rituals, healing work, and manifestation practices.

Understanding Celestial Energies and Their Influence on Crystals

Just as the planets and the moon influence life on Earth, they also affect the vibrational frequencies of crystals. Each celestial body carries its own set of correspondences and influences various aspects of life, from communication (Mercury) and love (Venus) to transformation (Pluto) and intuition (the Moon). By aligning crystals with these planetary and lunar energies, you can amplify their natural properties and enhance your ability to channel these energies into your magical work.

Planetary Energy

- **Sun**: Represents vitality, leadership, success, and personal power. Crystals aligned with the Sun are often used for confidence, self-expression, and achieving goals.
- **Moon**: Governs emotions, intuition, the subconscious, and feminine energy. Lunar crystals are ideal for emotional healing, dream work, and nurturing.
- **Mercury**: Rules communication, intellect, travel, and technology. Mercury crystals are excellent for enhancing communication skills, mental clarity, and learning.
- **Venus**: Associated with love, beauty, harmony, and relationships. Venus crystals are used in love spells, enhancing relationships, and self-care rituals.
- **Mars**: Represents action, courage, and determination. Mars-aligned crystals are used for motivation, strength, and manifesting desires.
- **Jupiter**: Governs expansion, abundance, luck, and spiritual growth. Jupiter crystals are perfect for manifesting prosperity and broadening horizons.
- **Saturn**: Represents discipline, structure, responsibility, and life lessons. Saturn crystals help with grounding, self-discipline, and overcoming obstacles.
- **Uranus**: Rules innovation, change, and rebellion. Uranus crystals are useful for breaking through limitations and embracing personal freedom.
- **Neptune**: Governs dreams, spirituality, and illusion. Neptune crystals enhance intuition, spiritual awareness, and connection to the unseen.
- **Pluto**: Represents transformation, power, and rebirth. Pluto crystals are powerful tools for deep inner work, shadow work, and personal evolution.

The Moon's Phases and Crystal Work

The moon's phases deeply affect the energy of the Earth and can be used to charge crystals with specific intentions. Each phase carries its own unique energy, making some phases better suited for particular types of magical work than others. Aligning your crystals with the lunar phases can enhance their effectiveness in rituals, healing, and spellwork.

New Moon (Waxing Crescent)

- **Energy**: New beginnings, setting intentions, growth
- **Crystals to Use**: Clear quartz, moonstone, selenite, labradorite
- **Best Uses**: Use these crystals to set intentions, manifest new opportunities, and clear your energy for a fresh start.

How to Use Crystals with New Moon Energy:

Place a piece of clear quartz or moonstone on your altar during the New Moon and focus on your goals or desires for the upcoming cycle. Clear quartz amplifies the energy of your intentions, while moonstone connects you with the intuitive, feminine energy of the moon. Meditate with these crystals to plant the seeds of your manifestations.

First Quarter (Waxing Gibbous)

- **Energy**: Growth, momentum, building strength
- **Crystals to Use**: Citrine, carnelian, sunstone, green aventurine
- **Best Uses**: Use these crystals to boost motivation, bring in prosperity, and increase the momentum of your goals.

How to Use Crystals with First Quarter Energy:
Place a citrine or carnelian crystal near your workspace to encourage progress and perseverance in achieving your goals. Meditate with sunstone to keep your energy and confidence high as your intentions begin to take shape.

Full Moon (Waning Gibbous)

- **Energy**: Culmination, manifestation, clarity, illumination
- **Crystals to Use**: Moonstone, selenite, amethyst, clear quartz
- **Best Uses**: Use these crystals for rituals of manifestation, heightened intuition, and emotional release.

How to Use Crystals with Full Moon Energy:
Set your crystals under the light of the Full Moon to cleanse and recharge them with lunar energy. Place an amethyst or moonstone on your third eye during meditation to access spiritual clarity and intuitive insight. This is also a powerful time for manifesting your desires, so focus on your goals with the support of clear quartz.

Last Quarter (Waning Crescent)

- **Energy**: Reflection, release, letting go
- **Crystals to Use**: Black tourmaline, obsidian, smoky quartz, hematite
- **Best Uses**: Use these crystals to release negativity, protect your energy, and ground yourself during the process of letting go.

How to Use Crystals with Last Quarter Energy:
Hold a piece of black tourmaline or obsidian in your hands as you meditate on what you need to release. Imagine the crystal absorbing any negative energy or limiting beliefs. You can also place smoky quartz near your bed to aid in grounding and protection as you reflect on what needs to be released in your life.

Planetary Crystals: Aligning Crystals with the Planets

Each planet carries its own unique energy, and specific crystals resonate with these planetary frequencies. By aligning crystals with the planets, you can harness their power for specific intentions such as love (Venus), success (Sun), or transformation (Pluto). Here is a breakdown of planetary crystals and their uses.

1. The Sun: Vitality and Success

- **Crystals**: Sunstone, citrine, carnelian, pyrite, amber
- **Best Uses**: These crystals radiate the Sun's energy of vitality, confidence, and success. Use them in rituals for personal empowerment, leadership, and attracting abundance.

How to Work with Solar Crystals:

Place a sunstone or citrine on your altar during the daytime to boost confidence and attract success in your endeavors. Wear amber or carnelian as jewelry to keep the Sun's radiant energy with you throughout the day, promoting optimism and self-expression.

2. The Moon: Intuition and Emotion

- **Crystals**: Moonstone, selenite, pearl, opal, labradorite
- **Best Uses**: Lunar crystals resonate with the energy of intuition, emotional healing, and psychic awareness. Use these crystals during Full Moon rituals, dream work, and when seeking emotional clarity.

How to Work with Lunar Crystals:

Meditate with moonstone or selenite to enhance your connection with your intuition and emotional healing. Place a piece of labradorite under your pillow to enhance dream recall and gain insight into the subconscious.

3. Mercury: Communication and Intellect

- **Crystals**: Aquamarine, blue lace agate, sodalite, fluorite, emerald
- **Best Uses**: Mercury crystals improve communication, mental clarity, and problem-solving abilities. Use these crystals for writing, learning, and improving communication in relationships.

How to Work with Mercury Crystals:

Keep aquamarine or blue lace agate near you while writing or speaking to help with clarity and flow of ideas. Place fluorite on your desk to enhance focus and intellectual productivity, especially during study sessions or intellectual pursuits.

4. Venus: Love and Beauty

- **Crystals**: Rose quartz, jade, emerald, rhodonite, malachite
- **Best Uses**: Venus crystals enhance love, beauty, harmony, and self-worth. Use them in love spells, self-care rituals, and to attract harmonious relationships.

How to Work with Venus Crystals:

Hold a piece of rose quartz or jade in your hand while focusing on self-love or attracting romantic relationships. Place malachite or emerald in your bedroom or sacred space to invite beauty, love, and harmony into your life.

5. Mars: Courage and Action

- **Crystals**: Bloodstone, red jasper, carnelian, garnet, ruby
- **Best Uses**: Mars crystals ignite motivation, courage, and strength. Use these crystals to enhance physical energy, overcome challenges, and take bold action.

How to Work with Mars Crystals:
Wear red jasper or garnet when you need extra courage or motivation to tackle a challenge. Meditate with bloodstone to build inner strength and resilience, especially during times of conflict or adversity.

6. Jupiter: Abundance and Expansion

- **Crystals**: Amethyst, lapis lazuli, sapphire, turquoise, aventurine
- **Best Uses**: Jupiter crystals are ideal for manifesting abundance, growth, and spiritual wisdom. Use these stones for expansion, prosperity, and long-term vision.

How to Work with Jupiter Crystals:
Place aventurine or lapis lazuli on your altar when setting intentions for prosperity or personal growth. Meditate with amethyst to enhance spiritual wisdom and expand your understanding of the bigger picture in your life.

7. Saturn: Discipline and Structure

- **Crystals**: Black onyx, smoky quartz, obsidian, hematite, jet
- **Best Uses**: Saturn crystals bring grounding, structure, and discipline. Use them when you need to create long-term plans, stick to commitments, or overcome challenges through perseverance.

How to Work with Saturn Crystals:
Hold black onyx or hematite during meditation when you need to focus on grounding and discipline. Keep smoky quartz or jet near you when working on long-term projects to ensure focus and commitment to your goals.

8. Uranus: Innovation and Freedom

- **Crystals**: Labradorite, aquamarine, amazonite, moldavite, clear quartz
- **Best Uses**: Uranus crystals are ideal for manifesting change, innovation, and freedom. Use these stones when you're ready to break through limitations and embrace new ways of thinking.

How to Work with Uranus Crystals:
Meditate with labradorite or aquamarine to open your mind to new possibilities and encourage innovative thinking. Place moldavite or clear quartz on your altar when you want to initiate radical change or spiritual breakthroughs.

9. Neptune: Dreams and Spirituality

- **Crystals**: Amethyst, aquamarine, moonstone, selenite, lepidolite
- **Best Uses**: Neptune crystals enhance dreams, spirituality, and connection to the divine. Use these crystals for dream work, meditation, and connecting with your higher self.

How to Work with Neptune Crystals:
Place amethyst or selenite near your bed to enhance dream recall and spiritual insight. Meditate with lepidolite or moonstone to deepen your connection with your intuition and the spiritual realms.

10. Pluto: Transformation and Rebirth

- **Crystals**: Obsidian, garnet, black tourmaline, moldavite, serpentine
- **Best Uses**: Pluto crystals are ideal for transformation, power, and deep inner work. Use these stones when going through personal evolution, shadow work, or intense spiritual growth.

How to Work with Pluto Crystals:
Hold obsidian or black tourmaline during meditation to protect and ground yourself while working through deep emotional or psychological transformations. Meditate with moldavite or serpentine to assist in powerful spiritual rebirth and awaken hidden potentials.

Aligning Crystals with Celestial Energy in Rituals

To maximize the power of crystals in your magical practice, it's important to align them with the appropriate celestial energies based on your intentions. Here's how to incorporate celestial crystals into your rituals:

1. **Timing with Planetary Days and Hours**: Each day of the week is ruled by a specific planet, making it the ideal time to work with crystals aligned with that planet. For example, use Venus crystals on Friday for love and relationship rituals, or Mars crystals on Tuesday for courage and strength spells.
2. **Charging Crystals under the Moon**: Place your crystals under the light of the moon during specific phases to charge them with lunar energy. For example, place moonstone under the Full Moon to enhance its intuitive properties, or charge black tourmaline during the Waning Moon for protection.
3. **Astrological Transits and Crystals**: Align your crystal work with major astrological transits, such as Mercury retrograde or Jupiter returns. Use crystals that correspond with the planet involved in the transit to enhance or balance its effects. For example, during Mercury retrograde, work with fluorite or blue lace agate to maintain clear communication.

4. **Meditation and Crystal Grids**: Create crystal grids based on celestial energies to amplify your intentions. For instance, use a grid of sunstone, citrine, and carnelian during the Sun's transit through Leo to boost confidence and creativity. During a Full Moon in Pisces, create a grid with amethyst, selenite, and moonstone to enhance spiritual insight and emotional healing.

Conclusion

Crystals and celestial energies form a powerful partnership in magical practice, providing a bridge between the material and spiritual realms. By aligning crystals with the energy of the planets and the moon, you can harness the cosmic forces that govern all aspects of life—whether you're seeking abundance, love, healing, or transformation. Through intentional use of crystals in conjunction with celestial cycles, your rituals and spells will become more potent and aligned with the rhythms of the universe.

As you continue to explore the synergy between crystals and celestial energy, remember to follow your intuition. Let the unique properties of each crystal guide you, and be mindful of the planets' and moon's influence as you set your intentions. This harmonious connection between the earth and the cosmos will empower you to manifest your deepest desires and bring balance, healing, and magic into your life.

Chapter 33: Astrological Compatibility for Spells: Matching Astrological Signs for Love, Friendship, and Magical Partnerships

Astrological compatibility plays a significant role in relationships, whether they are romantic, platonic, or magical partnerships. Understanding how different zodiac signs interact can help you enhance the bonds you form, improve communication, and make more informed decisions when working with others in spellwork or rituals. Each sign carries unique energies, and knowing how to align these energies can improve the success of your collaborations, whether you're casting love spells, working with friends, or forming covens and magical groups.

In this chapter, we will explore how to assess astrological compatibility, focusing on love, friendship, and magical partnerships. We'll discuss the strengths and challenges of each astrological pairing, how to work with your partner's sign in spells, and tips for maintaining harmony in your relationships using astrology. Whether you're looking to enhance a romantic connection, strengthen a friendship, or choose the best magical partner for rituals, this guide will help you navigate the complex world of astrological compatibility.

Understanding Astrological Compatibility

Astrological compatibility, often referred to as "synastry," examines how the planetary positions in two people's natal charts interact. The key areas of focus include the Sun sign, Moon sign, Venus sign (for love and relationships), and Mercury sign (for communication). While Sun signs are often the most well-known, compatibility is a multi-layered concept that includes emotional connection (Moon), love and attraction (Venus), and communication styles (Mercury). By considering these factors, you can better understand how two people's energies combine and how they can work together effectively.

The Four Elements in Compatibility

Zodiac signs are grouped into four elemental categories: Fire, Earth, Air, and Water. Understanding the elemental dynamics between signs is key to assessing compatibility. Signs of the same element often have natural compatibility, as they share similar traits and approaches to life. Signs with opposing or complementary elements can also form powerful partnerships, as they bring balance to each other's strengths and weaknesses.

- **Fire Signs (Aries, Leo, Sagittarius):** Passionate, energetic, and action-oriented. Fire signs tend to be compatible with other Fire signs and Air signs, which fuel their enthusiasm. They may struggle with Earth signs, which can seem too slow or practical, and Water signs, which can be too emotionally intense for their liking.
- **Earth Signs (Taurus, Virgo, Capricorn):** Grounded, practical, and reliable. Earth signs are compatible with other Earth signs and Water signs, which provide emotional depth. They may find Fire signs too impulsive and Air signs too detached.
- **Air Signs (Gemini, Libra, Aquarius):** Intellectual, communicative, and adaptable. Air signs are compatible with other Air signs and Fire signs, which match their fast-paced thinking. They may find Earth signs too rigid and Water signs too emotional or sensitive.

- **Water Signs (Cancer, Scorpio, Pisces)**: Emotional, intuitive, and nurturing. Water signs are compatible with other Water signs and Earth signs, which provide stability. They may find Fire signs too overwhelming and Air signs too detached.

Astrological Compatibility in Love Spells

When casting love spells, it's important to understand the dynamics between your sign and the sign of your romantic partner or the person you wish to attract. Different signs have varying needs in love, and aligning your spellwork with your partner's astrological energies can enhance the effectiveness of your rituals.

Fire Signs in Love: Aries, Leo, Sagittarius

- **Best Matches**: Air signs (Gemini, Libra, Aquarius) and other Fire signs.
- **Love Style**: Passionate, adventurous, and direct. Fire signs love excitement and action in relationships, often seeking a partner who shares their enthusiasm and sense of adventure.

Love Spell for Fire Signs:

When casting a love spell for a Fire sign partner, use candles (especially red or orange) and herbs associated with passion, such as cinnamon or rosemary. Focus on spells that enhance passion, adventure, and spontaneity. For example, a simple spell could involve lighting a red candle, anointing it with cinnamon oil, and visualizing the flame growing stronger as the passion in your relationship deepens.

Earth Signs in Love: Taurus, Virgo, Capricorn

- **Best Matches**: Water signs (Cancer, Scorpio, Pisces) and other Earth signs.
- **Love Style**: Steady, loyal, and practical. Earth signs value stability and commitment, preferring long-term relationships where trust and dependability are paramount.

Love Spell for Earth Signs:

Earth signs respond well to spells that focus on stability, security, and long-term commitment. Use grounding elements such as soil, stones, or crystals like jade or emerald. For a love spell, bury two small stones or crystals (one representing you and the other your partner) in the earth, and as you do, focus on the strength and endurance of your bond.

Air Signs in Love: Gemini, Libra, Aquarius

- **Best Matches**: Fire signs (Aries, Leo, Sagittarius) and other Air signs.
- **Love Style**: Intellectual, communicative, and open. Air signs thrive on mental connection and stimulating conversation. They value independence in relationships but are also drawn to partners who challenge them intellectually.

Love Spell for Air Signs:

Air signs appreciate spells that emphasize communication and intellectual connection. Incorporate feathers, incense, or essential oils like lavender or peppermint to enhance mental clarity and attraction. For example, write a love letter to your Air sign partner, charging it with your intentions, then burn it in a ritual to send your desires into the universe.

Water Signs in Love: Cancer, Scorpio, Pisces

- **Best Matches**: Earth signs (Taurus, Virgo, Capricorn) and other Water signs.
- **Love Style**: Deep, emotional, and intuitive. Water signs seek emotional connection and spiritual depth in relationships. They often feel things intensely and need a partner who can match their emotional depth.

Love Spell for Water Signs:

Water signs respond well to spells that focus on emotional intimacy, healing, and protection. Incorporate water, sea salt, or moonstone into your spellwork. For a love spell, place a bowl of water on your altar, add a pinch of sea salt, and drop in a moonstone. As you stir the water, visualize emotional harmony and deep connection between you and your partner.

Astrological Compatibility in Friendships

Astrological compatibility isn't just for romantic relationships—it's equally important in friendships. Understanding the dynamics between your zodiac sign and that of your friends can help you navigate challenges, improve communication, and build stronger connections.

Fire Signs in Friendship

- **Best Friend Matches**: Air signs (Gemini, Libra, Aquarius) and other Fire signs.
- **Friendship Style**: Fun-loving, spontaneous, and loyal. Fire signs bring energy and excitement to their friendships and enjoy adventures and social activities. They need friends who can keep up with their enthusiasm.

Friendship Spell for Fire Signs:

Strengthen your friendship with a Fire sign by creating a bonding charm. Take two red strings, one representing you and the other your Fire sign friend. Tie the strings together while focusing on the qualities you love about your friendship. Wear or carry the charm as a reminder of your connection.

Earth Signs in Friendship

- **Best Friend Matches**: Water signs (Cancer, Scorpio, Pisces) and other Earth signs.
- **Friendship Style**: Dependable, supportive, and practical. Earth signs value stability in their friendships and are often the ones friends turn to in times of need. They appreciate loyalty and consistency.

Friendship Spell for Earth Signs:
Create a grounding friendship spell by exchanging small tokens from nature (such as stones or leaves) with your Earth sign friend. Bury these items in a place that holds significance for both of you, visualizing the deep roots of your friendship growing stronger over time.

Air Signs in Friendship

- **Best Friend Matches**: Fire signs (Aries, Leo, Sagittarius) and other Air signs.
- **Friendship Style**: Social, communicative, and open-minded. Air signs thrive on intellectual conversations and enjoy a wide circle of friends. They appreciate friends who are open to new ideas and adventures.

Friendship Spell for Air Signs:
Enhance your friendship with an Air sign by crafting a friendship talisman. Write down qualities that represent your bond (such as "communication" or "adventure") on a piece of paper. Fold it into an origami shape (such as a crane), and keep it in your sacred space to represent the lightness and creativity in your friendship.

Water Signs in Friendship

- **Best Friend Matches**: Earth signs (Taurus, Virgo, Capricorn) and other Water signs.
- **Friendship Style**: Deep, nurturing, and emotionally supportive. Water signs are deeply caring friends who form emotional bonds with those they trust. They appreciate friends who are loyal, empathetic, and understanding.

Friendship Spell for Water Signs:
To deepen your friendship with a Water sign, create a water-based charm. Fill a small bottle with water from a natural source (such as a river or lake) and add a few drops of lavender oil. As you seal the bottle, say, "Our friendship flows as deep as water, filled with trust and support." Keep the bottle in a safe place to maintain the bond.

Astrological Compatibility in Magical Partnerships

When it comes to magical partnerships—whether you're working in a coven, casting spells with a partner, or performing rituals in a group—astrological compatibility can make a significant difference in the success of your work. Some signs naturally align well in magical settings, while others may require more effort to maintain harmony. By understanding the dynamics of astrological compatibility, you can enhance your collaborative magic and ensure smoother group rituals.

Fire Signs in Magical Partnerships

- **Best Magical Matches**: Air signs and other Fire signs.
- **Magical Style**: Fire signs bring passion, energy, and action to magical work. They excel in spells that require boldness, leadership, and quick results.

Magical Tip for Fire Signs:

Fire signs thrive in fast-paced, dynamic rituals. Encourage spontaneity and action in group settings, but be mindful of patience when working with more methodical signs, such as Earth signs.

Earth Signs in Magical Partnerships

- **Best Magical Matches**: Water signs and other Earth signs.
- **Magical Style**: Earth signs provide stability, grounding, and focus in magical work. They excel in rituals that require patience, long-term manifestation, and working with the natural world.

Magical Tip for Earth Signs:

Ground your group rituals by incorporating elements of nature, such as soil, crystals, or plants. Earth signs help keep a group centered and focused, especially when dealing with more impulsive signs like Fire.

Air Signs in Magical Partnerships

- **Best Magical Matches**: Fire signs and other Air signs.
- **Magical Style**: Air signs bring intellectual clarity, innovation, and communication to magical work. They excel in spells related to knowledge, communication, and mental focus.

Magical Tip for Air Signs:
Encourage open communication and brainstorming in magical settings. Air signs can help bring fresh ideas and new perspectives to rituals, but they should work on grounding their ideas with practical steps, especially when working with Earth signs.

Water Signs in Magical Partnerships

- **Best Magical Matches**: Earth signs and other Water signs.
- **Magical Style**: Water signs bring emotional depth, intuition, and healing energy to magical work. They excel in spells involving psychic work, emotional healing, and spiritual connection.

Magical Tip for Water Signs:
Water signs should focus on emotional balance during group rituals, as they can be sensitive to the energy of others. Work with Earth signs to help ground emotional energy and create a stable, nurturing environment for magical work.

Astrological Compatibility and Conflict Resolution in Relationships
Even in the best of relationships—whether romantic, platonic, or magical—conflicts are inevitable. Understanding the astrological dynamics at play can help you resolve conflicts more effectively and maintain harmony. Here are some tips for resolving conflicts based on astrological signs:

- **Fire Signs**: Fire signs may react impulsively and passionately in conflict. Encourage open communication and allow them space to express their feelings before finding a resolution.
- **Earth Signs**: Earth signs prefer practical solutions and may become stubborn in conflict. Focus on grounding the discussion and offering concrete steps toward resolution.
- **Air Signs**: Air signs tend to intellectualize conflict and may avoid emotional discussions. Encourage them to talk through the issue logically, but also address the emotional aspects.
- **Water Signs**: Water signs can become overwhelmed by their emotions in conflict. Create a safe, compassionate space for them to express their feelings before working on a resolution.

Conclusion

Astrological compatibility offers valuable insights into love, friendship, and magical partnerships, helping you navigate relationships with greater understanding and harmony. By recognizing the strengths and challenges of each zodiac pairing, you can tailor your spells, rituals, and interactions to align with the energies at play, enhancing your magical work and personal connections.

Whether you're casting love spells, working with friends, or forming a magical group, understanding the astrological dynamics in your relationships will empower you to make more informed decisions, foster deeper bonds, and ensure successful collaborations. Through thoughtful use of astrology, you can unlock the full potential of your relationships and create lasting, meaningful connections in both love and magic.

Chapter 34: Altar Setups for Celestial Spells: Aligning Your Sacred Space with Planetary and Lunar Energy

An altar is the heart of any witch's or magical practitioner's space, serving as a focal point for rituals, spellwork, and meditation. When setting up an altar, aligning it with celestial energies such as planetary and lunar forces can enhance the potency of your magic and rituals. Each planet and lunar phase carries distinct vibrations that influence different aspects of life, from love and career to healing and spiritual growth. By creating altars that harness these celestial energies, you can deepen your connection to the cosmos and manifest your desires with greater power and intention.

This chapter explores how to design altars based on planetary and lunar energy, providing detailed suggestions for materials, colors, crystals, symbols, and arrangements that correspond to specific celestial bodies. Whether you are working with the Sun's energy for success, the Moon's energy for intuition, or Mercury's energy for communication, these altar setups will guide you in creating sacred spaces that align with the cosmic forces influencing your spells.

Creating a Celestial Altar: The Basics

Before diving into specific altar setups for planetary and lunar energies, it's important to understand the basics of creating a celestial altar. The following elements should be considered when setting up your sacred space:

1. **Intention**: Decide what energy or outcome you want to focus on in your ritual or spell. Whether it's love, prosperity, healing, or protection, your intention will guide the overall setup of your altar.
2. **Sacred Space**: Choose a dedicated space for your altar, where you can leave it undisturbed for the duration of your work. Altars can be permanent or temporary, but they should always feel sacred and intentional.
3. **Elements**: Incorporate the four classical elements—Earth, Air, Fire, and Water—into your altar setup. These elements will help balance and amplify the celestial energies you are working with.
4. **Celestial Symbols**: Use symbols, colors, and objects that represent the planetary or lunar energy you are invoking. These could include planetary glyphs, lunar phases, astrological symbols, and corresponding deities or spirits.
5. **Crystals and Candles**: Crystals and candles play an essential role in charging your altar with specific celestial energies. Choose colors and stones that correspond to the planet or moon phase you are working with.
6. **Offerings and Tools**: Incorporate items such as herbs, oils, incense, and personal talismans that align with your intentions. Ritual tools like wands, athames, chalices, and cauldrons can also be placed on your altar.

Altar Setups for Planetary Energy

The planets in our solar system represent different areas of life and aspects of our personalities, influencing our desires, strengths, and challenges. Aligning your altar with planetary energy can amplify your intentions, whether you're seeking success, love, protection, or transformation.

1. Sun Altar: Success, Vitality, and Confidence

The Sun represents personal power, vitality, leadership, and success. A Sun-aligned altar is ideal for spells related to personal growth, achieving goals, and enhancing confidence.

Key Elements for a Sun Altar:

- **Colors**: Gold, yellow, orange
- **Crystals**: Sunstone, citrine, amber, carnelian, tiger's eye
- **Candles**: Yellow or gold candles
- **Herbs and Oils**: Cinnamon, frankincense, rosemary, bay leaf, chamomile
- **Symbols**: Solar glyphs, suns, lions (representing Leo), sunflowers

How to Set Up a Sun Altar:

- **Central Candle**: Place a large yellow or gold candle at the center of your altar to represent the radiant energy of the Sun. This candle will act as the focal point for your rituals.
- **Crystals**: Surround the candle with sunstone, citrine, and carnelian to channel the Sun's energy into your work. These crystals enhance vitality, motivation, and success.
- **Offerings**: Include offerings such as bay leaves or sunflowers to honor the Sun's life-giving force.
- **Solar Symbols**: Place solar glyphs or a small statue of a lion on your altar to invoke the Sun's qualities of courage and leadership.

Ritual Use: This altar is ideal for spells focused on self-confidence, achieving goals, personal growth, and leadership.

2. Moon Altar: Intuition, Healing, and Emotional Balance

The Moon governs emotions, intuition, psychic abilities, and the subconscious mind. A Moon-aligned altar is perfect for rituals related to emotional healing, spiritual growth, and dream work.

Key Elements for a Moon Altar:

- **Colors**: Silver, white, blue, purple
- **Crystals**: Moonstone, selenite, amethyst, labradorite, pearl
- **Candles**: White or silver candles
- **Herbs and Oils**: Jasmine, mugwort, sandalwood, lavender, chamomile
- **Symbols**: Lunar glyphs, crescent moons, seashells, water bowls

How to Set Up a Moon Altar:

- **Central Candle**: Place a white or silver candle at the center of your altar to represent the light of the Moon. This candle symbolizes the Moon's reflective, nurturing energy.
- **Crystals**: Arrange moonstone, selenite, and amethyst around the candle to enhance your intuition and emotional healing. These crystals are ideal for connecting with lunar energy.
- **Water Element**: Incorporate a small bowl of water to represent the Moon's connection to the tides and emotional flow.
- **Lunar Symbols**: Place crescent moon symbols, seashells, or lunar glyphs on your altar to honor the feminine, intuitive aspects of the Moon.

Ritual Use: This altar is perfect for rituals that focus on emotional healing, psychic development, dream work, and connecting with the divine feminine.

3. Mercury Altar: Communication, Intellect, and Learning

Mercury governs communication, intellect, travel, and technology. A Mercury-aligned altar is ideal for spells related to improving communication, enhancing learning, and increasing mental clarity.

Key Elements for a Mercury Altar:

- **Colors**: Yellow, blue, light green
- **Crystals**: Aquamarine, fluorite, clear quartz, blue lace agate, emerald
- **Candles**: Yellow or light blue candles
- **Herbs and Oils**: Lavender, peppermint, lemongrass, eucalyptus
- **Symbols**: Mercury glyphs, books, quills, feathers

How to Set Up a Mercury Altar:

- **Central Candle**: Place a yellow or light blue candle at the center of your altar to symbolize Mercury's energy of clarity and communication.
- **Crystals**: Surround the candle with aquamarine, fluorite, and clear quartz to enhance mental clarity, communication, and intellectual pursuits.
- **Offerings**: Add offerings such as feathers, quills, or scrolls to represent the power of communication and learning.
- **Mercurial Symbols**: Place Mercury's glyph or small symbols like books or pens on your altar to connect with intellectual and communicative energy.

Ritual Use: This altar is ideal for spells that focus on enhancing communication, improving learning, aiding in travel, and boosting mental clarity.

4. Venus Altar: Love, Beauty, and Harmony

Venus governs love, beauty, pleasure, and relationships. A Venus-aligned altar is perfect for spells focused on love, self-care, attraction, and artistic creativity.

Key Elements for a Venus Altar:

- **Colors**: Pink, green, copper
- **Crystals**: Rose quartz, jade, emerald, rhodonite, malachite
- **Candles**: Pink or green candles
- **Herbs and Oils**: Rose, jasmine, patchouli, ylang-ylang
- **Symbols**: Venus glyphs, hearts, flowers, seashells, art objects

How to Set Up a Venus Altar:

- **Central Candle**: Place a pink or green candle in the center of your altar to represent love and beauty. This candle will serve as the focal point for your love and harmony spells.
- **Crystals**: Surround the candle with rose quartz, jade, and rhodonite to amplify love, harmony, and self-care. These crystals resonate with Venus's nurturing energy.
- **Flowers and Offerings**: Add fresh flowers, rose petals, or seashells to honor Venus's connection to beauty and the natural world.
- **Symbols of Love**: Place hearts, Venus glyphs, or small statues of goddesses associated with love (such as Aphrodite) on your altar.

Ritual Use: This altar is ideal for spells that focus on attracting love, enhancing beauty, fostering harmony in relationships, and practicing self-love.

5. Mars Altar: Action, Courage, and Strength

Mars governs action, courage, desire, and determination. A Mars-aligned altar is perfect for spells related to physical energy, motivation, protection, and overcoming obstacles.

Key Elements for a Mars Altar:

- **Colors**: Red, black, gold
- **Crystals**: Red jasper, bloodstone, garnet, carnelian, ruby
- **Candles**: Red or black candles
- **Herbs and Oils**: Ginger, cayenne, black pepper, basil
- **Symbols**: Mars glyphs, swords, armor, fire symbols

How to Set Up a Mars Altar:

- **Central Candle**: Place a red candle at the center of your altar to symbolize Mars's fiery, action-oriented energy. This candle will serve as the focus for your rituals of strength and determination.
- **Crystals**: Surround the candle with red jasper, bloodstone, and carnelian to channel Mars's strength, courage, and motivation.
- **Protection Symbols**: Add symbols such as swords, shields, or fire symbols to invoke Mars's protective and courageous aspects.
- **Offerings**: Include herbs like ginger or cayenne, or a small dish of red pepper flakes, to energize your spells and boost physical vitality.

Ritual Use: This altar is ideal for spells that focus on physical energy, courage, protection, overcoming challenges, and achieving goals through determined action.

6. Jupiter Altar: Expansion, Abundance, and Luck

Jupiter governs expansion, abundance, wisdom, and good fortune. A Jupiter-aligned altar is ideal for spells related to prosperity, spiritual growth, and manifesting abundance.

Key Elements for a Jupiter Altar:

- **Colors**: Purple, royal blue, gold
- **Crystals**: Amethyst, sapphire, lapis lazuli, turquoise, aventurine
- **Candles**: Purple or royal blue candles
- **Herbs and Oils**: Sage, clove, nutmeg, oak, dandelion
- **Symbols**: Jupiter glyphs, crowns, coins, keys

How to Set Up a Jupiter Altar:

- **Central Candle**: Place a purple or gold candle at the center of your altar to represent Jupiter's expansive and abundant energy.
- **Crystals**: Surround the candle with amethyst, lapis lazuli, and aventurine to attract prosperity, wisdom, and spiritual growth.
- **Coins or Symbols of Abundance**: Add coins, keys, or symbols of wealth and fortune to your altar to amplify your intentions for abundance.
- **Herbs and Offerings**: Incorporate offerings such as sage or nutmeg to honor Jupiter's expansive, wisdom-filled energy.

Ritual Use: This altar is perfect for spells focused on prosperity, wealth, expansion, good fortune, and spiritual wisdom.

Altar Setups for Lunar Phases

The Moon's phases significantly influence spellwork and rituals, with each phase offering specific energies for manifesting, releasing, and reflecting. Aligning your altar with the lunar phases helps you harness the moon's power to bring your intentions to fruition.

1. New Moon Altar: Beginnings and Manifestation

The New Moon is a time for new beginnings, setting intentions, and manifesting desires. A New Moon altar is ideal for planting seeds of change and focusing on future goals.

Key Elements for a New Moon Altar:

- **Colors**: White, silver, black
- **Crystals**: Clear quartz, moonstone, labradorite
- **Candles**: White or silver candles
- **Herbs and Oils**: Mugwort, lavender, sandalwood
- **Symbols**: Crescent moons, seeds, mirrors

How to Set Up a New Moon Altar:

- **Central Candle**: Place a white or silver candle at the center of your altar to represent the new beginnings and potential of the New Moon.
- **Crystals**: Arrange clear quartz and moonstone around the candle to amplify the energy of manifestation and intuitive guidance.
- **Seeds and Symbols of Growth**: Place seeds or small symbols of growth (such as leaves or plants) on your altar to symbolize the intentions you are planting.

Ritual Use: This altar is perfect for rituals focused on setting intentions, manifesting new opportunities, and starting fresh cycles.

2. Full Moon Altar: Culmination and Empowerment

The Full Moon represents the peak of lunar energy and is a time for manifestation, empowerment, and emotional clarity. A Full Moon altar is ideal for spells that focus on abundance, intuition, and bringing desires to fruition.

Key Elements for a Full Moon Altar:

- **Colors**: Silver, white, blue, purple
- **Crystals**: Moonstone, selenite, amethyst
- **Candles**: Silver or blue candles
- **Herbs and Oils**: Jasmine, sage, chamomile, sandalwood
- **Symbols**: Full moons, mirrors, water bowls

How to Set Up a Full Moon Altar:

- **Central Candle**: Place a silver or blue candle at the center of your altar to channel the energy of the Full Moon.
- **Crystals**: Arrange moonstone, selenite, and amethyst around the candle to enhance intuition, clarity, and manifestation.
- **Water Element**: Include a small bowl of water to connect with the Moon's influence over emotions and intuition.

Ritual Use: This altar is perfect for rituals focused on manifesting desires, emotional clarity, empowerment, and spiritual growth.

3. Waning Moon Altar: Releasing and Cleansing

The Waning Moon is a time for reflection, release, and cleansing. A Waning Moon altar is ideal for rituals focused on banishing negativity, breaking habits, and letting go of the past.

Key Elements for a Waning Moon Altar:

- **Colors**: Black, gray, dark blue
- **Crystals**: Black tourmaline, obsidian, smoky quartz
- **Candles**: Black or gray candles
- **Herbs and Oils**: Sage, cedar, rosemary
- **Symbols**: Crescent moons, cauldrons, scissors

How to Set Up a Waning Moon Altar:

- **Central Candle**: Place a black or gray candle at the center of your altar to represent the clearing and cleansing energy of the Waning Moon.
- **Crystals**: Surround the candle with black tourmaline, obsidian, and smoky quartz to absorb negativity and promote protection.
- **Cleansing Symbols**: Include cauldrons, scissors, or brooms on your altar to symbolize release and banishing.

Ritual Use: This altar is perfect for rituals focused on banishing negativity, releasing harmful patterns, and cleansing energy.

Conclusion

Creating an altar aligned with planetary or lunar energy allows you to harness the power of celestial forces and channel them into your magical practice. By understanding the unique energies associated with each planet and moon phase, you can design altars that amplify your intentions and help you manifest your desires more effectively.

Whether you are working with the bold energy of Mars for courage, the nurturing energy of the Moon for emotional healing, or the expansive energy of Jupiter for abundance, aligning your altar with celestial energies enhances the potency of your spells and rituals. Use the setups outlined in this chapter as inspiration to create a sacred space that resonates with your personal magic and the cosmic forces at play.

Chapter 35: Rituals for Sabbats: Honoring the Seasonal Cycles Through Magic

The Wheel of the Year marks the eight major Sabbats, or festivals, that celebrate the changing seasons and the cycles of nature. Each Sabbat is a powerful time to connect with the natural world, honor the cycles of life, death, and rebirth, and align your magical practice with the rhythms of the Earth. By crafting specific rituals for each Sabbat, you can deepen your connection to these ancient traditions, celebrate the turning points of the year, and use the energies of each season to enhance your spells and spiritual growth.

In this chapter, we will explore in detail the rituals for each of the eight Sabbats: **Samhain, Yule, Imbolc, Ostara, Beltane, Litha, Lammas (Lughnasadh), and Mabon**. Each ritual is designed to align with the themes of the Sabbat, such as honoring ancestors, welcoming new beginnings, celebrating abundance, or preparing for introspection. Whether you are working alone or in a group, these rituals provide guidance on how to tap into the unique energies of each season.

Samhain (October 31st - November 1st)

Theme: Honoring Ancestors, Death, and Rebirth

Focus: Samhain marks the end of the harvest season and is often considered the Witches' New Year. It is a time to honor ancestors, reflect on the cycle of life, death, and rebirth, and engage in deep spiritual work, such as shadow work and divination.

Samhain Ritual: Honoring Ancestors and Spirit Communication

Materials:

- Black and orange candles (for protection and honoring the dead)
- Photos or objects of deceased loved ones (optional)
- A bowl of water (for scrying)
- Offerings for the dead (such as food, drink, or flowers)
- A small altar cloth or table for ancestor offerings

Instructions:

1. **Set the Space**: Begin by preparing your space for a sacred ritual. Place black and orange candles on your altar or in a quiet corner of your home. Arrange photos or personal items that represent your ancestors or loved ones who have passed on.
2. **Light the Candles**: Light the black candle to honor the protective spirits and guardians of the veil between the worlds. Light the orange candle to represent the connection to your ancestors.
3. **Create an Ancestor Altar**: On your altar, place offerings such as bread, wine, or flowers to honor the spirits of your ancestors. Say a prayer or speak directly to them, expressing gratitude for their presence in your life and asking for their guidance.

4. **Scrying and Divination**: Use the bowl of water for scrying. Gaze into the water and allow any images, messages, or insights from the spirit realm to arise. This is a powerful time for divination, as the veil between worlds is thin.

5. **Conclude the Ritual**: Close the ritual by thanking the spirits and ancestors for their guidance and protection. Allow the candles to burn out or extinguish them with a sense of closure.

Magical Focus: Samhain rituals are excellent for divination, shadow work, spirit communication, and honoring the dead. It's a time to reflect on the past year and set intentions for the new cycle ahead.

Yule (Winter Solstice, around December 21st)

Theme: Rebirth of the Sun, Renewal, and Light in Darkness

Focus: Yule marks the Winter Solstice, the longest night of the year, and celebrates the rebirth of the Sun. This Sabbat focuses on renewal, hope, and the return of light, making it a time for introspection, renewal, and setting intentions for the coming year.

Yule Ritual: Celebrating the Return of the Sun

Materials:

- Green, red, and gold candles (for renewal, prosperity, and light)
- Evergreen branches (symbolizing eternal life)
- A Yule log or a small wooden log to burn (if safe) or use as a decoration
- Cinnamon sticks or dried orange slices (for abundance)
- A cauldron or fireproof dish

Instructions:

1. **Set the Space**: Decorate your altar or sacred space with evergreen branches, holly, pine cones, and other symbols of eternal life and the promise of rebirth. Place the Yule log or wooden log in the center of your altar, either to be burned or kept as a symbolic decoration.

2. **Light the Candles**: Light the green, red, and gold candles to represent prosperity, warmth, and the return of the Sun. As you light each candle, say:
   "On this darkest night, I welcome the return of the light. May the Sun bring warmth, joy, and abundance into my life."

3. **Yule Log Blessing**: If you have a Yule log, carve symbols or intentions into the log with a knife (runes, suns, or words of power). If you are burning the log, do so with the intention of releasing old energy and welcoming new growth. If you are not burning it, place cinnamon sticks or dried orange slices on the log as offerings.

4. **Intention Setting**: Focus on the symbolism of rebirth. Reflect on the darkness in your life that needs to be transformed and the new light you want to bring in. Write down your intentions for the coming year and place them under the Yule log or into the cauldron.

5. **Conclude the Ritual**: As the candles burn down, give thanks for the return of the Sun and the blessings of the Earth. Leave the Yule log in a place of honor until the end of the holiday season.

Magical Focus: Yule is an ideal time for renewal, setting intentions for the new year, focusing on personal rebirth, and honoring the cycles of light and darkness.

Imbolc (February 1st - February 2nd)

Theme: Purification, New Beginnings, and Light Returning

Focus: Imbolc is a celebration of the first stirrings of Spring and the growing light after Winter's darkness. It is a time for purification, inspiration, and preparing for the new growth to come. Imbolc is also associated with the goddess Brigid, the goddess of fire, healing, and creativity.

Imbolc Ritual: Purification and Lighting the Way

Materials:

- White candles (for purity and new beginnings)
- A bowl of water (for cleansing)
- Lavender or rosemary (for purification)
- A small broom (for symbolic cleansing)
- A symbol of Brigid (optional)

Instructions:

1. **Cleanse the Space**: Before beginning the ritual, physically and energetically cleanse your space. Use the broom to symbolically sweep away stagnant energy and negativity. As you do, say:
   "I sweep away the old, making room for the new. I purify my space and spirit in preparation for the light to return."
2. **Light the White Candles**: Light white candles around your altar or sacred space to represent the purity and renewal of Imbolc. As each candle is lit, feel the growing warmth of the returning light.
3. **Water Blessing**: Sprinkle lavender or rosemary into a bowl of water to create a purification bath. Dip your fingers into the water and anoint your forehead, heart, and hands while saying:
   "I cleanse myself of the past, and I open my heart to the new light of the year."
4. **Brigid's Blessing**: If you work with the goddess Brigid, call upon her blessings for creativity, healing, and renewal. Place a symbol of Brigid (such as a small cross or fire symbol) on your altar and ask for her guidance in the coming months.
5. **Conclude the Ritual**: Close the ritual by meditating on the seeds of new growth that are beginning to stir within you. Visualize the coming Spring and the new opportunities that are being nurtured in the dark earth.

Magical Focus: Imbolc is ideal for purification, setting new intentions, creative inspiration, and spiritual renewal.

Ostara (Spring Equinox, around March 21st)

Theme: Balance, Renewal, and Fertility

Focus: Ostara celebrates the Spring Equinox, a time of perfect balance between light and dark, when the Earth begins to bloom with new life. This Sabbat is associated with fertility, growth, and the awakening of the Earth after Winter.

Ostara Ritual: Planting Seeds for Growth

Materials:

- Green and yellow candles (for growth and light)
- Seeds or small plants (for planting)
- A small pot of soil or garden space
- Eggs or symbols of fertility
- Spring flowers (for decoration)

Instructions:

1. **Decorate the Altar**: Adorn your altar with Spring flowers, eggs (real or symbolic), and vibrant colors that represent fertility, growth, and new beginnings. Place the green and yellow candles on either side of the altar to symbolize balance and renewal.
2. **Light the Candles**: As you light the candles, say:
   "On this day of balance, I honor the light and the dark. May this balance bring growth and abundance to all areas of my life."
3. **Planting Ritual**: Hold a seed in your hand, and focus on an intention or goal you wish to manifest during the growing season. As you plant the seed in soil, say:
   "As I plant this seed, I plant the seed of my intentions. May it grow strong, nourished by the Earth and the Sun."
4. **Egg Blessing**: If using eggs, hold one in your hands and charge it with fertility, creativity, and the potential for new beginnings. You can choose to bury it in your garden or keep it on your altar as a symbol of fertility.
5. **Conclude the Ritual**: Meditate on the balance between light and dark, reflecting on areas of your life that need harmony and growth. Visualize your intentions taking root and blossoming with the arrival of Spring.

Magical Focus: Ostara is ideal for fertility spells, growth-focused intentions, balance, and renewal.

Beltane (May 1st)

Theme: Fertility, Passion, and Abundance

Focus: Beltane is a fire festival celebrating fertility, passion, and the abundance of nature. It is a time to honor the sacred union of the Earth and the Sun, and rituals focus on love, sensuality, and manifesting desires.

Beltane Ritual: Celebrating Passion and Fertility

Materials:

- Red, green, and pink candles (for passion, fertility, and love)
- Flowers and ribbons (for decoration and Beltane's traditional Maypole)
- A small fire or cauldron (for fire magic)
- Honey or wine (for offerings)
- Rose petals or symbols of fertility

Instructions:

1. **Create a Flower-Covered Altar**: Decorate your altar with flowers, ribbons, and symbols of fertility. Place red, green, and pink candles on the altar to represent passion, fertility, and love.
2. **Light the Fire**: Light a small fire in a cauldron or in a fireproof dish. This fire represents the Sun's growing strength and the passion of life. Say:
   "I light this fire in honor of the Earth and the Sun, for they bring life, love, and abundance to us all."
3. **Dance and Offerings**: Dance around the fire or altar to celebrate the energy of fertility and passion. Make an offering of honey, wine, or flowers to the Earth as a gesture of gratitude.
4. **Petal Ritual**: Take rose petals or small flowers and charge them with your desires. Toss them into the fire or sprinkle them on your altar while saying:
   "As these flowers blossom, so too shall my desires come to fruition."
5. **Conclude the Ritual**: Allow the fire to burn out or safely extinguish it. Spend time reflecting on the fertile energy of the season and how you can harness it to bring passion, love, and abundance into your life.

Magical Focus: Beltane is ideal for love spells, fertility rituals, abundance work, and manifesting passionate desires.

Litha (Summer Solstice, around June 21st)
Theme: Power, Abundance, and the Height of the Sun's Strength
Focus: Litha celebrates the Summer Solstice, the longest day of the year, when the Sun's energy is at its peak. This is a time to celebrate abundance, prosperity, and the fullness of life.
Litha Ritual: Celebrating Abundance and Power
Materials:

- Gold, yellow, and red candles (for solar energy and abundance)
- Sunflowers, herbs, or fresh fruits (for offerings)
- A sun symbol (such as a wheel or circle)
- A small dish of salt (for protection)

Instructions:

1. **Decorate the Altar**: Place gold, yellow, and red candles on your altar, along with sunflowers or fresh herbs. Include symbols of the Sun, such as a sun wheel or circle, to honor its peak energy.
2. **Light the Candles**: As you light the candles, say:
   "On this longest day, I honor the power of the Sun and the abundance it brings. May this light fill my life with prosperity, health, and joy."
3. **Sun Symbol Blessing**: Hold the sun symbol in your hands and charge it with the energy of abundance, success, and vitality. Place it in the center of your altar as a focus for your desires.
4. **Offerings of Abundance**: Offer fresh fruits, herbs, or flowers to the Sun and Earth in gratitude for the abundance they provide. You may also sprinkle salt around your altar for protection and to ground the energy.
5. **Conclude the Ritual**: Meditate on the fullness of life and the energy of the Sun at its peak. Reflect on areas of your life where you seek growth and prosperity, and visualize the energy of the Sun empowering your goals.

Magical Focus: Litha is perfect for abundance spells, solar magic, personal empowerment, and celebrating life's fullness.

Lammas (Lughnasadh) (August 1st)
Theme: Harvest, Gratitude, and Abundance
Focus: Lammas, or Lughnasadh, is the first of the harvest festivals, celebrating the grain harvest and the abundance of the land. It is a time of gratitude for what has been gathered and for the hard work that has borne fruit.
Lammas Ritual: Gratitude and Harvest Celebration
Materials:

- Green and gold candles (for abundance and gratitude)
- Fresh bread or grains (for offerings)
- Corn, wheat, or other symbols of the harvest
- A chalice of wine or juice (for libation)

Instructions:

1. **Set the Harvest Altar**: Decorate your altar with symbols of the harvest, such as wheat, corn, or fresh bread. Place green and gold candles to represent abundance and gratitude.
2. **Light the Candles**: As you light the candles, say:
   "I honor the fruits of the Earth and the abundance it brings. I give thanks for the harvest that sustains me."
3. **Offerings of Bread and Wine**: Break a piece of fresh bread and offer it to the Earth or place it on your altar as a gesture of gratitude. Pour wine or juice into a chalice and hold it up, offering thanks for the abundance and blessings in your life.
4. **Harvest Meditation**: Spend time meditating on the efforts you have made and the rewards you have reaped. Reflect on what you have harvested in your life—whether it be material, emotional, or spiritual—and give thanks for the lessons and gifts of the year so far.
5. **Conclude the Ritual**: Close the ritual by consuming the bread and wine (if you wish), and express gratitude for the blessings of the Earth. You may also bury some of the bread as a symbolic offering to the land.

Magical Focus: Lammas is ideal for gratitude rituals, abundance spells, and celebrating the fruits of your labor.

Mabon (Autumn Equinox, around September 21st)
Theme: Balance, Harvest, and Giving Thanks
Focus: Mabon is the second harvest festival and celebrates the Autumn Equinox, a time of balance between day and night. It is a time to give thanks for the year's harvest, both literal and metaphorical, and to prepare for the introspection of the coming Winter.
Mabon Ritual: Balance and Thanksgiving
Materials:

- Brown, orange, and yellow candles (for balance and harvest)
- Apples, pumpkins, or autumn fruits (for offerings)
- A small scale or balance symbol (for the equinox)
- A bowl or cornucopia (for abundance)

Instructions:

1. **Create the Harvest Altar**: Decorate your altar with autumn fruits, pumpkins, and symbols of the harvest. Place a small scale or a balance symbol on the altar to represent the equal light and dark of the equinox.
2. **Light the Candles**: Light brown, orange, and yellow candles to represent balance, harvest, and abundance. As you light them, say:
   "I honor the balance of light and dark, and I give thanks for the harvest of this year."
3. **Offerings of Autumn**: Place apples, pumpkins, or other autumn fruits in a bowl or cornucopia on the altar. These represent the abundance of the Earth and the gifts of the season. As you place each item, offer thanks for the specific blessings in your life.
4. **Balance Meditation**: Hold the scale or balance symbol and meditate on areas of your life that need balance or where you have achieved harmony. Reflect on how you can maintain this balance as the year transitions into darkness.
5. **Conclude the Ritual**: Close the ritual by expressing gratitude for the balance of the Earth and the blessings of the harvest. You may wish to consume some of the autumn fruits or leave them as offerings in nature.

Magical Focus: Mabon is ideal for gratitude, balance spells, and giving thanks for the abundance of the year.

Conclusion

The eight Sabbats of the Wheel of the Year offer powerful opportunities to align your magical practice with the natural cycles of the Earth. By performing rituals that correspond with the themes of each Sabbat—such as rebirth at Yule, fertility at Beltane, or harvest at Lammas—you can connect deeply with the changing seasons and harness their energies to enhance your spiritual growth and spellwork.

These rituals provide a guide to celebrating each Sabbat in a way that honors the sacredness of the natural world while also addressing your personal intentions. Whether you are working in solitude or as part of a group, these rituals will help you tap into the rhythms of the Earth and the cosmos, creating a deeper, more meaningful connection to your magical practice and the Wheel of the Year.

Chapter 36: Divination with the Stars: Astrological Timing for Tarot, Runes, and Other Divination Methods

Astrological timing plays a crucial role in enhancing the accuracy, depth, and relevance of divination practices such as Tarot, runes, scrying, and other methods of seeking insight. By aligning your divinatory practices with celestial movements—whether it's the phases of the Moon, planetary transits, or zodiacal positions—you can tap into powerful cosmic energies that provide clearer guidance and more profound wisdom. The stars and planets influence the subtle energies of the universe, and when used correctly, their timing can amplify your ability to access deeper truths and intuitive insights.

In this chapter, we will explore how to incorporate astrological timing into your divination practice, covering the best times for Tarot readings, rune casting, and other methods based on planetary influences, lunar cycles, and zodiac signs. Whether you're looking to deepen your connection to your tools or want to fine-tune your divinatory timing for specific outcomes, this chapter offers practical guidance for integrating astrology into your divination work.

The Role of Astrological Timing in Divination

Astrological timing refers to the strategic use of planetary positions, lunar phases, and zodiacal influences to determine the best moments for divinatory practices. Each planet, lunar phase, and zodiac sign exerts a distinct energy that can affect how clearly you receive messages from the universe and how aligned the insights are with your intentions.

By choosing the right astrological moment for divination, you can:

- **Access specific cosmic energies** to tailor your readings to particular issues (e.g., love, career, or spiritual growth).
- **Increase accuracy** by aligning your practice with planetary transits that amplify intuitive clarity.
- **Enhance your connection** to your divinatory tools (Tarot, runes, etc.) through synchronization with lunar and planetary energies.

Lunar Phases and Divination

The Moon is a powerful influence in divination, as its phases affect emotional energy, intuition, and spiritual clarity. Each phase of the Moon brings a different energy that can be harnessed for various types of divinatory work.

New Moon: Intention Setting and Beginnings

- **Energy**: The New Moon represents new beginnings, potential, and the planting of seeds for future outcomes.
- **Best Use in Divination**: Use the New Moon for readings focused on new projects, starting fresh, setting intentions, and exploring unknown possibilities. Tarot spreads that focus on "what's next" or rune casts that explore new paths are well-suited for this phase.
- **Recommended Tools**: Tarot, Oracle cards, Pendulum
- **Ideal Topics**: Career beginnings, relationship opportunities, spiritual growth

Sample Spread for the New Moon:

- **Card 1**: What new opportunity is emerging for me?
- **Card 2**: What do I need to focus on to make it happen?
- **Card 3**: What hidden strengths can I use to support this new beginning?

Waxing Moon: Growth and Progress

- **Energy**: The Waxing Moon is associated with growth, expansion, and building momentum.
- **Best Use in Divination**: Perform divination during the Waxing Moon when seeking guidance on how to nurture projects, relationships, or personal growth. This phase is ideal for assessing progress and determining the next steps to ensure success.
- **Recommended Tools**: Tarot, Runes, Crystal Ball
- **Ideal Topics**: Career advancement, relationship growth, financial opportunities

Rune Casting for the Waxing Moon:

- **Rune 1**: What area of my life needs attention for growth?
- **Rune 2**: What resources or tools can help me achieve success?
- **Rune 3**: What obstacles must I overcome to maintain progress?

Full Moon: Clarity and Manifestation

- **Energy**: The Full Moon is the peak of lunar energy, representing illumination, manifestation, and emotional insight.
- **Best Use in Divination**: The Full Moon is the most potent time for divination, especially for gaining clarity on complex issues, manifesting desires, and obtaining deep insights. It's ideal for powerful readings that explore major life themes, challenges, or questions about fulfillment.
- **Recommended Tools**: Tarot, Runes, Scrying, Pendulum
- **Ideal Topics**: Relationship clarity, career fulfillment, spiritual enlightenment, closure

Full Moon Tarot Spread:

- **Card 1**: What is being illuminated in my life?
- **Card 2**: What truth must I face?
- **Card 3**: What can I manifest or achieve with this newfound clarity?

Waning Moon: Reflection and Release

- **Energy**: The Waning Moon is associated with reflection, introspection, and letting go of what no longer serves you.
- **Best Use in Divination**: Perform readings during the Waning Moon to gain insights into what you need to release or change. This phase is ideal for shadow work, breaking bad habits, or resolving past issues.
- **Recommended Tools**: Tarot, Runes, Crystal Ball, Oracle Cards

- **Ideal Topics**: Emotional healing, letting go of toxic relationships, releasing old patterns

Waning Moon Rune Spread:

- **Rune 1**: What do I need to release?
- **Rune 2**: What lesson am I meant to learn from this?
- **Rune 3**: How can I move forward with clarity and purpose?

Planetary Days and Hours for Divination

Each day of the week is ruled by a specific planet, and each planet governs different aspects of life. By performing divination on the day and during the planetary hour of a specific planet, you can align your practice with its corresponding energy. This helps to ensure that your readings are accurate and focused on the specific area of concern you wish to explore.

Sunday (Sun's Day): Success, Vitality, and Confidence

- **Best Use**: Divination focused on success, self-confidence, and personal growth. Use this day to explore career opportunities, leadership roles, and health issues.
- **Recommended Tools**: Tarot, Runes, Crystal Ball

Sun-Influenced Divination Example: Use Tarot to explore the best ways to enhance your leadership qualities or achieve a personal goal. A Sun-focused reading may illuminate paths to success and self-empowerment.

Monday (Moon's Day): Emotions, Intuition, and Dreams

- **Best Use**: Divination focused on emotional matters, intuition, and dream interpretation. Use Monday for readings about relationships, emotional healing, and subconscious patterns.
- **Recommended Tools**: Tarot, Oracle Cards, Pendulum

Moon-Influenced Divination Example: Perform an Oracle card reading to explore deep emotional concerns or intuitive messages. This is also a great day for dream interpretation and divining messages from the subconscious.

Tuesday (Mars' Day): Action, Conflict, and Courage

- **Best Use**: Divination focused on taking action, resolving conflicts, and enhancing personal courage. Use Tuesday for guidance on overcoming challenges, standing up for yourself, or dealing with adversaries.
- **Recommended Tools**: Runes, Tarot, Pendulum

Mars-Influenced Divination Example: Cast runes to understand the best approach to a conflict or challenge. Use this day to explore strategies for asserting yourself and achieving your goals.
Wednesday (Mercury's Day): Communication, Travel, and Intellect

- **Best Use**: Divination focused on communication, learning, travel, and intellectual pursuits. Use Wednesday to explore issues related to studies, work projects, or important conversations.
- **Recommended Tools**: Tarot, Runes, Crystal Ball

Mercury-Influenced Divination Example: Perform a Tarot reading to gain insight into an upcoming conversation or decision. Focus on how you can improve communication or make clear decisions.
Thursday (Jupiter's Day): Abundance, Growth, and Wisdom

- **Best Use**: Divination focused on abundance, prosperity, spiritual growth, and long-term goals. Use Thursday for readings related to financial opportunities, expansion, and career success.
- **Recommended Tools**: Tarot, Oracle Cards, Runes

Jupiter-Influenced Divination Example: Use Oracle cards to explore opportunities for growth, prosperity, and abundance. Focus on long-term goals and how to expand your horizons.
Friday (Venus' Day): Love, Relationships, and Beauty

- **Best Use**: Divination focused on love, beauty, relationships, and self-worth. Use Friday for readings about romantic relationships, friendships, or matters of the heart.
- **Recommended Tools**: Tarot, Oracle Cards, Crystal Ball

Venus-Influenced Divination Example: Perform a Tarot reading to gain insight into a romantic relationship or to explore ways to improve self-love and self-care. Focus on how to enhance harmony in your relationships.
Saturday (Saturn's Day): Discipline, Boundaries, and Long-Term Planning

- **Best Use**: Divination focused on discipline, boundaries, and overcoming obstacles. Use Saturday for readings about work, long-term projects, or resolving karmic issues.
- **Recommended Tools**: Tarot, Runes, Pendulum

Saturn-Influenced Divination Example: Cast runes to explore how you can overcome obstacles and set clear boundaries in your personal or professional life. This is a good day to focus on self-discipline and long-term strategies.

Zodiac Signs and Divination

Each zodiac sign carries unique energies that influence specific areas of life. When the Moon or other planets transit through particular signs, they lend their qualities to the divination practice, enhancing specific types of readings. Aligning your divination with the zodiacal energy at the time of your reading can bring greater clarity and focus.

Aries: Boldness and Initiative

- **Best Use**: Divination focused on new beginnings, taking action, and overcoming obstacles. Aries energy is excellent for assessing the best ways to start new projects or initiate bold moves.
- **Recommended Tools**: Tarot, Runes

Aries-Influenced Divination Example: Use Tarot to explore the best course of action for a new venture or project. Focus on where you need to assert yourself or take courageous steps.

Taurus: Stability and Prosperity

- **Best Use**: Divination focused on financial matters, stability, and self-care. Taurus energy supports readings about wealth, property, and emotional security.
- **Recommended Tools**: Tarot, Oracle Cards

Taurus-Influenced Divination Example: Perform a Tarot reading to explore how you can build greater stability in your financial or personal life. Focus on long-term security and prosperity.

Gemini: Communication and Learning

- **Best Use**: Divination focused on communication, education, and intellectual pursuits. Gemini energy is ideal for readings about study, work projects, or important discussions.
- **Recommended Tools**: Tarot, Oracle Cards, Crystal Ball

Gemini-Influenced Divination Example: Use Oracle cards to gain insight into a communication issue or to explore strategies for improving your studies or intellectual pursuits.

Cancer: Home and Emotional Healing

- **Best Use**: Divination focused on emotional matters, family, and home life. Cancer energy supports readings about nurturing, healing, and emotional fulfillment.
- **Recommended Tools**: Tarot, Oracle Cards, Crystal Ball

Cancer-Influenced Divination Example: Perform a Tarot reading to explore emotional healing or issues related to home and family. Focus on how to create a nurturing environment for yourself and others.

Leo: Confidence and Creativity

- **Best Use**: Divination focused on self-expression, creativity, and leadership. Leo energy enhances readings about personal confidence, artistic pursuits, and stepping into the spotlight.
- **Recommended Tools**: Tarot, Runes

Leo-Influenced Divination Example: Use Tarot or runes to gain insight into creative projects or to explore how you can step into a leadership role with confidence and charisma.

Virgo: Health and Organization

- **Best Use**: Divination focused on health, organization, and daily routines. Virgo energy supports readings about personal well-being, work habits, and self-improvement.
- **Recommended Tools**: Tarot, Oracle Cards

Virgo-Influenced Divination Example: Perform a Tarot reading to explore how to improve your health, work habits, or organization skills. Focus on how to refine your routines for better efficiency and wellness.

Libra: Relationships and Harmony

- **Best Use**: Divination focused on relationships, balance, and harmony. Libra energy supports readings about love, partnerships, and creating equilibrium in life.
- **Recommended Tools**: Tarot, Oracle Cards

Libra-Influenced Divination Example: Use Oracle cards to explore ways to improve your relationships or to create more balance in your life. Focus on harmonizing conflicting energies.

Scorpio: Transformation and Power

- **Best Use**: Divination focused on transformation, power dynamics, and deep emotional work. Scorpio energy supports readings about personal evolution, shadow work, and spiritual growth.
- **Recommended Tools**: Tarot, Runes

Scorpio-Influenced Divination Example: Perform a Tarot or rune reading to explore areas where deep transformation is needed. Focus on what needs to be released or transformed for spiritual growth.

Sagittarius: Expansion and Adventure

- **Best Use**: Divination focused on travel, expansion, and personal growth. Sagittarius energy supports readings about exploring new horizons, both physically and intellectually.
- **Recommended Tools**: Tarot, Oracle Cards

Sagittarius-Influenced Divination Example: Use Tarot or Oracle cards to explore opportunities for adventure, travel, or personal growth. Focus on expanding your horizons and pursuing your dreams.

Capricorn: Ambition and Discipline

- **Best Use**: Divination focused on career, long-term goals, and personal discipline. Capricorn energy supports readings about work, ambition, and achieving success through hard work.
- **Recommended Tools**: Tarot, Runes

Capricorn-Influenced Divination Example: Perform a Tarot or rune reading to explore strategies for achieving your career goals or building long-term success. Focus on the discipline and perseverance needed to reach your objectives.

Aquarius: Innovation and Community

- **Best Use**: Divination focused on innovation, community, and social change. Aquarius energy supports readings about new ideas, group projects, and humanitarian efforts.
- **Recommended Tools**: Tarot, Oracle Cards

Aquarius-Influenced Divination Example: Use Oracle cards to explore how you can bring innovation or fresh ideas to a situation. Focus on group dynamics or social issues that require change.

Pisces: Spirituality and Intuition

- **Best Use**: Divination focused on spirituality, intuition, and dreams. Pisces energy supports readings about mystical experiences, psychic development, and emotional healing.
- **Recommended Tools**: Tarot, Oracle Cards, Pendulum

Pisces-Influenced Divination Example: Perform a Tarot reading to explore spiritual growth or intuitive insights. Focus on dream interpretation, emotional healing, and connecting with higher realms.

Combining Astrology with Divinatory Methods

To make the most of your divination practice, consider these additional techniques for integrating astrology:

1. **Planetary Transits**: Pay attention to planetary transits when performing divination. For example, if Venus is transiting your natal chart, this may be an excellent time for love and relationship readings. Use these transits to fine-tune the focus of your readings.
2. **Astrological Spreads**: Create Tarot spreads based on astrological houses or planets. For example, a 12-card Tarot spread can represent each house of the zodiac, with each card offering insight into different areas of life.
3. **Personalized Divination**: Consider your natal chart and astrological transits to choose the best times for your divination practice. If your chart is influenced by Jupiter, for instance, you might use divination to explore themes of growth, prosperity, and wisdom.
4. **Astrological Decks and Tools**: Use astrology-themed Tarot or Oracle decks that correspond to planetary and zodiacal energies, allowing you to work with the symbolism of the stars more directly.

Conclusion

Divination with the stars combines the wisdom of astrology with the intuitive art of Tarot, runes, and other divinatory tools. By aligning your practice with the movements of the planets, lunar phases, and zodiac signs, you can enhance the depth and accuracy of your readings, connecting more deeply with the cosmos and the universal energies that influence your life.

Through thoughtful use of astrological timing, you can fine-tune your divination practice, ensuring that your insights are aligned with the celestial energies most suited to your goals and questions. Whether you are seeking clarity, guidance, or deeper spiritual connection, divination with the stars will empower your journey, guiding you toward greater understanding and alignment with the rhythms of the universe.

Chapter 37: Eclipses and Shadow Work: Harnessing Eclipses for Transformative Spells and Deep Self-Reflection

Eclipses are some of the most powerful celestial events in astrology and magic. They mark profound moments of transformation, endings, and new beginnings. Both solar and lunar eclipses carry immense energy for change, acting as catalysts for personal and spiritual growth. When used in conjunction with shadow work—the process of confronting and healing the hidden aspects of ourselves—eclipses offer a potent opportunity for deep self-reflection and transformation.

In this chapter, we will explore how to harness the energy of eclipses for transformative spellwork, shadow work, and healing. Whether you are seeking to release past traumas, confront hidden fears, or initiate powerful change in your life, eclipses provide the cosmic energy needed to support this work. We will also examine the astrological meaning of solar and lunar eclipses, their effects on the psyche, and how to perform rituals that align with these events.

The Astrological Power of Eclipses

Eclipses occur when the Sun, Moon, and Earth align in such a way that either the Sun or the Moon is temporarily obscured. These cosmic events signify powerful shifts in energy and consciousness. Both solar and lunar eclipses mark pivotal moments of change, but they influence different aspects of life and the psyche:

Solar Eclipses: New Beginnings and External Transformation

A solar eclipse occurs when the Moon passes between the Earth and the Sun, temporarily blocking the Sun's light. Solar eclipses are associated with dramatic new beginnings, external change, and shifts in consciousness. They bring the opportunity to reset, let go of the old, and embrace new paths and projects. These eclipses often affect our outer world—career, relationships, and public life—and can mark the end of one chapter and the beginning of another.

Themes of Solar Eclipses:

- New beginnings and opportunities
- Dramatic life changes
- External transformations (career, relationships, personal identity)
- Letting go of old patterns that no longer serve you

Lunar Eclipses: Emotional Release and Internal Transformation

A lunar eclipse occurs when the Earth passes between the Sun and the Moon, casting a shadow on the Moon. Lunar eclipses are emotionally intense, highlighting hidden truths, unresolved emotions, and the need for deep healing. They are ideal for shadow work, as they bring to the surface issues that have been buried in the subconscious. Lunar eclipses often involve emotional catharsis, encouraging us to release what no longer serves our emotional and spiritual well-being.

Themes of Lunar Eclipses:

- Emotional release and healing
- Uncovering hidden truths and unresolved issues
- Internal transformation (shadow work, emotional patterns, subconscious healing)
- Letting go of emotional baggage and outdated beliefs

Eclipses and Shadow Work: A Gateway to Healing

Shadow work is the practice of confronting and integrating the parts of ourselves that we often repress, deny, or hide. These hidden aspects of the self—known as the "shadow"—can include unresolved traumas, fears, negative patterns, and unacknowledged desires. When ignored, the shadow can manifest as self-sabotage, emotional blockages, or destructive behaviors.

Eclipses, with their dramatic and transformative energy, offer a unique opportunity for shadow work. The obscuring of the Sun or Moon during an eclipse mirrors the process of diving into the darkness of the subconscious to uncover hidden aspects of ourselves. The energy of an eclipse can amplify the effects of shadow work, helping you to break through resistance, release emotional blockages, and initiate deep healing.

How to Use Eclipses for Transformative Spells and Shadow Work

The powerful energy of eclipses can be harnessed for transformative spells, rituals, and self-reflection. Depending on whether you are working with a solar or lunar eclipse, your focus may be on external changes (solar eclipse) or internal healing (lunar eclipse). Below are detailed guides for using both types of eclipses for transformation and shadow work.

Solar Eclipse Ritual: New Beginnings and External Transformation

Purpose: To release old patterns and embrace new beginnings in your outer world (career, relationships, personal goals).

Materials:

- A black candle (to represent endings)
- A white or gold candle (to represent new beginnings)
- A piece of paper and pen
- A fireproof dish or cauldron
- A symbol of your goal (a small object that represents the new path you want to take)

Instructions:

1. **Prepare the Space**: Set up your altar or sacred space with the black and white (or gold) candles, a piece of paper, and a symbol of your goal. Ground yourself by taking a few deep breaths and centering your energy.
2. **Reflect on What You Want to Release**: Before lighting the black candle, take a moment to reflect on the aspects of your life that are no longer serving you. This could be old habits, toxic relationships, limiting beliefs, or anything that is holding you back from growth.
3. **Write it Down**: On the piece of paper, write down everything you want to release. Be specific about the areas of your life that need change.
4. **Light the Black Candle**: As you light the black candle, say:
   "I release all that no longer serves me. I let go of old patterns, beliefs, and attachments that have held me back. As the shadow passes, I free myself to embrace the light of new beginnings."
5. **Burn the Paper**: Safely burn the piece of paper in the fireproof dish or cauldron, symbolizing the release of what you no longer need. As the paper burns, visualize these patterns dissolving into smoke, leaving you free to move forward.
6. **Light the White (or Gold) Candle**: As you light the white or gold candle, hold the symbol of your new goal and say:
   "With the light of the new day, I welcome fresh opportunities and growth. I embrace the path before me with confidence, clarity, and purpose."

7. **Conclude the Ritual**: Spend a few moments visualizing your new path unfolding before you. Place the symbol of your goal on your altar or keep it in a special place to remind you of your intention.

Magical Focus: Solar eclipses are ideal for rituals focused on major life changes, new beginnings, personal reinvention, and external transformation.

Lunar Eclipse Ritual: Emotional Release and Shadow Work

Purpose: To confront and heal emotional wounds, release unresolved emotions, and integrate hidden aspects of the self.

Materials:

- A black or dark blue candle (to represent the shadow and subconscious)
- A piece of obsidian or black tourmaline (for protection during shadow work)
- A journal and pen
- A bowl of water (for reflection and emotional cleansing)
- Lavender or sage for purification

Instructions:

1. **Cleanse the Space**: Begin by cleansing your space with lavender or sage to clear away any negative energy. Set up your altar or sacred space with the black candle, the bowl of water, and your journal.
2. **Prepare for Shadow Work**: Ground yourself by holding the piece of obsidian or black tourmaline. Take a few deep breaths and set the intention to explore the hidden aspects of your psyche that need healing.
3. **Light the Black Candle**: As you light the candle, say:
   "I call upon the energy of the lunar eclipse to guide me into the depths of my subconscious. I am ready to confront my shadow and embrace the hidden truths within me."
4. **Journaling**: Begin journaling about the emotions, fears, or patterns that have been weighing on you. Focus on what needs to be released or healed. Ask yourself questions such as:
   - What unresolved emotions am I holding onto?
   - What patterns or fears are preventing me from moving forward?
   - What parts of myself have I been neglecting or avoiding?
5. **Emotional Release with Water**: After journaling, gaze into the bowl of water. As you focus on the water, visualize it absorbing your emotional burdens and blockages. You can also place your hands in the water and imagine it washing away emotional pain.
6. **Affirm Your Healing**: As you place your hands over your heart, say:
   "I release the past and heal the wounds within me. I honor the shadow as a part of my wholeness and welcome transformation."

7. **Conclude the Ritual**: When you feel ready, extinguish the candle and pour the water into the Earth, symbolizing the release of your emotional burdens. Spend a few moments in silence, allowing the energy of the eclipse to integrate with your spirit.

Magical Focus: Lunar eclipses are ideal for rituals focused on emotional healing, shadow work, confronting fears, and releasing old emotional patterns.

Astrological Timing for Eclipses and Shadow Work

Astrological timing is crucial when working with eclipses, as their energy is fleeting but highly charged. Here are some guidelines for timing your eclipse rituals and shadow work:

1. **Prepare in Advance**: Eclipses often bring sudden shifts, so it's helpful to begin your reflection and planning a few days before the eclipse. Set your intentions for what you wish to release or manifest.
2. **Solar Eclipse Timing**: Solar eclipses are associated with New Moon energy, making them powerful for setting new intentions. Perform your solar eclipse rituals on the day of the eclipse or within a day or two after, when the energy is still strong.
3. **Lunar Eclipse Timing**: Lunar eclipses occur during Full Moons, a time for emotional culmination and release. Perform your lunar eclipse rituals during the eclipse or on the night of the Full Moon to maximize the energy of emotional clarity and transformation.
4. **Eclipse Seasons**: Eclipses typically occur in pairs (a solar eclipse followed by a lunar eclipse, or vice versa), and the period between them is called the eclipse season. This is a time of heightened cosmic energy, making it an excellent period for deep spiritual work, shadow integration, and transformation.

The Emotional and Spiritual Impact of Eclipses

Eclipses often have a powerful emotional and spiritual impact, both before and after the event. You may notice a heightened sensitivity, increased dreams, or emotional turbulence in the days leading up to and following an eclipse. This is natural, as eclipses act as cosmic mirrors, reflecting back to us what needs to be addressed in our lives.

- **Embrace the Unknown**: Eclipses can bring unexpected events, changes, or revelations. It's important to remain open to the unknown during this time, as eclipses often push us out of our comfort zones and into new growth.
- **Trust the Process**: Eclipses often trigger events that feel beyond our control. While this can be unsettling, it's essential to trust the transformative process and recognize that these changes are necessary for your spiritual evolution.

Conclusion

Eclipses offer a powerful opportunity for transformative spellwork and deep self-reflection. By aligning your rituals with the energy of these celestial events, you can harness the intense cosmic forces of change, whether you are focusing on external transformations with a solar eclipse or diving into the depths of your emotions with a lunar eclipse. These moments of celestial alignment act as gateways to profound personal growth, helping you release old patterns, heal unresolved wounds, and embrace new beginnings.

Through thoughtful and intentional practice, you can use eclipses as tools for shadow work and spiritual healing, working with the energy of the stars to guide you toward greater self-awareness, wholeness, and transformation.

Chapter 38: Ritual Baths for Planetary Alignment: Recipes for Each Planetary Event and Zodiac Energy

Ritual baths are a powerful and sacred practice used by witches and spiritual practitioners to align the body, mind, and spirit with specific energies. When crafted with intention and aligned with the energy of the planets and zodiac, these baths become potent tools for personal transformation, spiritual cleansing, healing, and manifestation. By using specific herbs, crystals, oils, and colors that correspond to the planets and zodiac signs, you can create ritual baths that resonate with the cosmic forces and enhance your magical work.

In this chapter, we will explore the significance of planetary energies in ritual baths and provide detailed bath recipes for each planet, zodiac sign, and planetary event. Whether you are seeking love, success, protection, or spiritual clarity, these ritual baths will help you attune to the cosmic rhythms and unlock deeper layers of personal power and spiritual insight.

The Importance of Planetary and Zodiac Energies in Ritual Baths

Each planet and zodiac sign exerts unique energies that influence different areas of life, from communication and love to career, transformation, and spirituality. When you align your ritual bath with planetary energies, you can harness these forces to amplify your intentions and synchronize your body's energy with cosmic vibrations.

Ritual baths cleanse not only the physical body but also the energetic and emotional layers, clearing blockages and aligning you with your higher self. Bathing in waters charged with herbs, oils, and crystals connected to planetary and zodiac energies enables you to absorb the cosmic frequencies more deeply, enhancing the effectiveness of your magical work.

How to Prepare for a Ritual Bath

Before diving into specific planetary and zodiac baths, it's essential to know how to prepare for a ritual bath:

1. **Cleanse the Space**: Clean your bathroom or bathing area thoroughly to create a sacred space. Smudge with sage, palo santo, or incense to energetically clear the space.
2. **Set Your Intention**: Know the purpose of your bath—whether it's for love, healing, protection, or abundance. As you prepare your bath, focus on this intention.
3. **Choose Your Ingredients**: Select herbs, oils, salts, and crystals that align with the planet or zodiac energy you wish to invoke. Make sure to charge your ingredients with your intention before adding them to the bath.
4. **Create a Sacred Atmosphere**: Dim the lights, play calming music, and light candles that correspond to your planetary or zodiac focus. You may also want to place crystals or symbols around the tub for added energy.

5. **Relax and Visualize**: As you soak in the bath, focus on absorbing the energy of the planet or zodiac sign. Visualize your intentions being fulfilled, and allow yourself to release any tension or negativity into the water.
6. **Conclude the Bath**: When finished, visualize the water absorbing all negativity or unwanted energy. Drain the tub, allowing it to carry away anything that no longer serves you.

Planetary Ritual Bath Recipes

Each planet governs different aspects of life and can be called upon for specific intentions. Below are detailed bath recipes for each planetary energy, designed to help you align with the corresponding cosmic forces.

1. Sun Ritual Bath: Success, Confidence, and Vitality

The Sun represents personal power, vitality, success, and self-expression. This bath is ideal when you need a boost of confidence, energy, or are preparing for an important event.

Ingredients:

- 2 tablespoons of sea salt (for purification)
- Orange or yellow rose petals (for joy and self-confidence)
- 3 drops of orange essential oil (for vitality and success)
- A handful of calendula or sunflower petals (to invoke solar energy)
- A citrine or sunstone crystal (for confidence and manifesting success)
- Gold or yellow candles

Instructions:

1. **Prepare the Bath**: Fill the tub with warm water, adding the sea salt, calendula petals, and orange essential oil. Place the citrine or sunstone in the water or next to the tub.
2. **Set the Intention**: Light gold or yellow candles around the tub. As you enter the water, visualize the golden light of the Sun enveloping you, filling you with confidence, vitality, and success.
3. **Soak**: Allow yourself to relax in the water for at least 20 minutes. Focus on absorbing the Sun's energy, letting it empower your spirit and body.
4. **End the Ritual**: When finished, thank the Sun for its guidance and strength. Visualize your body glowing with radiant solar energy as you drain the tub.

2. Moon Ritual Bath: Intuition, Emotional Healing, and Feminine Energy

The Moon governs emotions, intuition, dreams, and the subconscious mind. This bath is perfect for emotional healing, connecting with your intuition, or working with the feminine energies of the Moon.

Ingredients:

- 1 cup of Epsom salt (for cleansing and emotional release)
- White or blue rose petals (for calm and intuitive clarity)
- 5 drops of lavender essential oil (for relaxation and emotional healing)
- A handful of jasmine or chamomile flowers (for connection to the divine feminine)
- A moonstone or selenite crystal (for intuition and emotional balance)
- Silver or white candles

Instructions:

1. **Prepare the Bath**: Fill the tub with warm water, adding the Epsom salt, jasmine flowers, and lavender essential oil. Place the moonstone or selenite in the water or next to the tub.
2. **Set the Intention**: Light silver or white candles around the tub. As you enter the water, visualize the soft, nurturing light of the Moon washing over you, soothing your emotions and enhancing your intuitive abilities.
3. **Soak**: Relax in the bath for 20–30 minutes, focusing on connecting with your inner self. Allow the water to draw out any emotional pain or blockages, and visualize yourself becoming aligned with the lunar energy.
4. **End the Ritual**: When finished, thank the Moon for its guidance and healing. Visualize any emotional heaviness draining away with the water.

3. Mercury Ritual Bath: Communication, Mental Clarity, and Learning

Mercury governs communication, intellect, and travel. This bath is designed to enhance your mental clarity, improve communication, and help you focus on learning and creative thinking.

Ingredients:

- 2 tablespoons of Himalayan pink salt (for mental clarity and cleansing)
- A handful of sage or mint leaves (for clear thinking and communication)
- 3 drops of peppermint essential oil (for mental stimulation)
- A small piece of fluorite or aquamarine crystal (for clarity and insight)
- Light blue or silver candles

Instructions:

1. **Prepare the Bath**: Fill the tub with warm water, adding the Himalayan salt, mint leaves, and peppermint oil. Place the fluorite or aquamarine crystal in the water or next to the tub.
2. **Set the Intention**: Light light blue or silver candles around the tub. As you enter the water, visualize your mind becoming clear and sharp, ready to communicate effectively and absorb new information.
3. **Soak**: Soak in the water for at least 20 minutes, focusing on opening up your throat chakra for clear communication. Visualize Mercury's energy enhancing your intellect and mental abilities.
4. **End the Ritual**: Thank Mercury for the clarity and insight. As the water drains, imagine any mental blockages being washed away.

4. Venus Ritual Bath: Love, Beauty, and Self-Worth

Venus governs love, beauty, pleasure, and relationships. This bath is ideal for enhancing self-love, attracting romantic love, or invoking beauty and harmony into your life.

Ingredients:

- 1 cup of pink Himalayan salt (for self-love and beauty)
- Rose petals (for love and romantic attraction)
- 5 drops of rose essential oil (for love and sensuality)
- A handful of lavender flowers (for peace and inner beauty)
- A rose quartz crystal (for love, beauty, and self-worth)
- Pink or red candles

Instructions:

1. **Prepare the Bath**: Fill the tub with warm water, adding the pink salt, rose petals, and rose essential oil. Place the rose quartz crystal in the water or next to the tub.
2. **Set the Intention**: Light pink or red candles around the tub. As you enter the water, visualize yourself being surrounded by loving energy, beauty, and harmony.
3. **Soak**: Soak in the bath for 20–30 minutes, focusing on self-love, self-worth, and romantic attraction. Visualize Venus' energy infusing your aura with love and beauty.
4. **End the Ritual**: Thank Venus for her blessings. As the water drains, release any negative thoughts about yourself and embrace self-love and acceptance.

5. Mars Ritual Bath: Courage, Strength, and Motivation

Mars governs action, courage, desire, and motivation. This bath is perfect for empowering yourself, boosting physical energy, and preparing for challenges.

Ingredients:

- 2 tablespoons of sea salt (for protection and purification)
- A handful of basil or bay leaves (for strength and courage)
- 3 drops of ginger or cinnamon essential oil (for motivation and passion)
- A piece of red jasper or carnelian crystal (for physical strength and empowerment)
- Red or black candles

Instructions:

1. **Prepare the Bath**: Fill the tub with warm water, adding the sea salt, basil leaves, and ginger oil. Place the red jasper or carnelian in the water or next to the tub.
2. **Set the Intention**: Light red or black candles around the tub. As you enter the water, visualize yourself being filled with strength, courage, and motivation, ready to take on any challenge.
3. **Soak**: Soak in the bath for 20 minutes, focusing on absorbing Mars' energy of empowerment. Visualize yourself overcoming obstacles with determination and strength.
4. **End the Ritual**: Thank Mars for his guidance. As the water drains, release any fears or doubts, leaving behind only courage and motivation.

6. Jupiter Ritual Bath: Abundance, Growth, and Expansion

Jupiter governs abundance, growth, wisdom, and prosperity. This bath is ideal for manifesting prosperity, expanding your horizons, and attracting luck and good fortune.

Ingredients:

- 2 tablespoons of sea salt (for cleansing and manifestation)
- A handful of sage or oak leaves (for wisdom and prosperity)
- 5 drops of clove or patchouli essential oil (for abundance)
- A citrine or amethyst crystal (for manifesting prosperity and spiritual growth)
- Purple or royal blue candles

Instructions:

1. **Prepare the Bath**: Fill the tub with warm water, adding the sea salt, sage, and clove oil. Place the citrine or amethyst in the water or next to the tub.
2. **Set the Intention**: Light purple or royal blue candles around the tub. As you enter the water, visualize yourself attracting abundance, prosperity, and wisdom into your life.
3. **Soak**: Soak in the bath for 20 minutes, focusing on expanding your opportunities and manifesting your desires. Visualize Jupiter's energy surrounding you with luck and abundance.
4. **End the Ritual**: Thank Jupiter for his blessings. As the water drains, release any limiting beliefs and open yourself to abundance and expansion.

7. Saturn Ritual Bath: Discipline, Structure, and Protection

Saturn governs discipline, boundaries, structure, and karmic lessons. This bath is perfect for grounding, establishing boundaries, and reinforcing self-discipline and protection.

Ingredients:

- 1 cup of Epsom salt (for grounding and protection)
- A handful of cypress or pine needles (for stability and boundaries)
- 3 drops of frankincense or myrrh essential oil (for protection and spiritual strength)
- A piece of black tourmaline or obsidian crystal (for grounding and protection)
- Dark blue or black candles

Instructions:

1. **Prepare the Bath**: Fill the tub with warm water, adding the Epsom salt, pine needles, and frankincense oil. Place the black tourmaline or obsidian in the water or next to the tub.

2. **Set the Intention**: Light dark blue or black candles around the tub. As you enter the water, visualize yourself becoming grounded, protected, and focused on your goals.
3. **Soak**: Soak in the bath for 20 minutes, focusing on building inner strength and discipline. Visualize Saturn's energy helping you set boundaries and establish long-term stability.
4. **End the Ritual**: Thank Saturn for his guidance. As the water drains, release any distractions or obstacles, leaving behind a sense of grounded purpose and protection.

Zodiac Sign Ritual Bath Recipes

Each zodiac sign embodies specific qualities and energies that influence various aspects of life. The following bath recipes align with the characteristics of each sign, allowing you to channel the unique energy of the zodiac into your ritual practice.

1. Aries Ritual Bath: Motivation and Boldness

- **Ingredients**: Sea salt, rosemary, ginger essential oil, red jasper
- **Focus**: Use this bath to boost motivation, courage, and assertiveness.

2. Taurus Ritual Bath: Grounding and Self-Love

- **Ingredients**: Pink salt, rose petals, lavender essential oil, rose quartz
- **Focus**: Use this bath for grounding, self-love, and emotional stability.

3. Gemini Ritual Bath: Communication and Clarity

- **Ingredients**: Peppermint leaves, eucalyptus oil, aquamarine crystal
- **Focus**: Use this bath to enhance communication skills and mental clarity.

4. Cancer Ritual Bath: Emotional Healing and Nurturing

- **Ingredients**: Chamomile flowers, jasmine oil, moonstone crystal
- **Focus**: Use this bath for emotional healing, nurturing, and self-care.

5. Leo Ritual Bath: Confidence and Creativity

- **Ingredients**: Calendula petals, orange oil, citrine crystal
- **Focus**: Use this bath to enhance confidence, creativity, and self-expression.

6. Virgo Ritual Bath: Health and Organization

- **Ingredients**: Sage leaves, eucalyptus oil, fluorite crystal
- **Focus**: Use this bath for health, healing, and organizational clarity.

7. Libra Ritual Bath: Balance and Harmony

- **Ingredients**: Rose petals, lavender oil, amethyst crystal
- **Focus**: Use this bath for balancing relationships and promoting harmony.

8. Scorpio Ritual Bath: Transformation and Deep Healing

- **Ingredients**: Mugwort, patchouli oil, obsidian crystal
- **Focus**: Use this bath for emotional transformation and deep inner healing.

9. Sagittarius Ritual Bath: Adventure and Expansion

- **Ingredients**: Sage leaves, clove oil, turquoise crystal
- **Focus**: Use this bath to invite adventure, growth, and new experiences.

10. Capricorn Ritual Bath: Discipline and Protection

- **Ingredients**: Pine needles, frankincense oil, black tourmaline
- **Focus**: Use this bath to enhance discipline, structure, and protection.

11. Aquarius Ritual Bath: Innovation and Independence

- **Ingredients**: Peppermint leaves, rosemary oil, amethyst crystal
- **Focus**: Use this bath to encourage innovation, independence, and fresh ideas.

12. Pisces Ritual Bath: Spirituality and Intuition

- **Ingredients**: Lavender flowers, jasmine oil, moonstone crystal
- **Focus**: Use this bath for spiritual connection, intuitive development, and emotional healing.

Conclusion

Ritual baths are a sacred and powerful way to align with planetary and zodiac energies, creating a space for deep cleansing, transformation, and manifestation. By preparing your bath with intention and incorporating ingredients that resonate with the specific planetary or zodiac energy, you can enhance your magical practice and attune more deeply to the cosmic forces that guide your life.

Each planetary and zodiac bath recipe provided in this chapter offers a unique opportunity to work with specific energies, whether you are seeking love, protection, abundance, or healing. By regularly incorporating ritual baths into your practice, you will cultivate a stronger connection to the rhythms of the cosmos, deepen your spiritual journey, and bring balance and harmony to your physical and energetic bodies.

Chapter 39: Visualization and Meditation Under the Night Sky: Guided Meditations for Star-Gazing and Connection with Cosmic Energy

The night sky, with its infinite expanse of stars, planets, and galaxies, has long captivated humanity as a symbol of the mysteries of the universe and our connection to something far greater than ourselves. In spiritual practice, the night sky serves as a powerful backdrop for visualization and meditation, offering an opportunity to tap into the energies of the cosmos, receive guidance from celestial bodies, and align ourselves with the natural rhythms of the universe.

In this chapter, we will explore the practice of visualization and meditation under the night sky, with a focus on guided meditations that will help you connect with cosmic energy. These meditations can be performed outside while star-gazing or inside through visualization if access to the night sky is limited. Whether you seek personal transformation, divine wisdom, or simply a sense of peace and connection, meditating under the stars offers profound benefits for the mind, body, and spirit.

The Power of Meditation and Visualization with Cosmic Energy

Meditation is a practice of stillness, mindfulness, and introspection, but when performed under the night sky or with a focus on celestial energies, it becomes a powerful tool for spiritual awakening and cosmic connection. Visualization, often used in conjunction with meditation, involves creating vivid mental images to focus your intention, open your awareness, and connect with higher realms. Together, these practices allow you to access the limitless energy of the universe, expand your consciousness, and bring balance to your inner and outer worlds.

Cosmic energy—the subtle vibrations emanating from stars, planets, and galaxies—provides powerful support for meditation and spiritual work. When you meditate under the night sky, you align with these celestial forces, allowing you to receive insights, gain clarity, and feel a deeper sense of connection to the universe. Each star, planet, and constellation carries its own unique vibration, and by tuning into these energies, you can enhance your meditative practice and gain access to universal wisdom.

How to Prepare for Star-Gazing Meditations

Before we dive into specific guided meditations, it's important to know how to prepare for a successful star-gazing or cosmic meditation session. These preparations will help create a calm and sacred environment where you can connect more deeply with the night sky and its energies.

1. Choose the Right Environment

- **Outdoor Star-Gazing**: If possible, find a quiet and secluded outdoor space where you can sit or lie down comfortably while looking up at the stars. Ideally, this space should be away from artificial lights and city noise to allow for a clearer view of the night sky and deeper meditation.
- **Indoor Visualization**: If you're unable to meditate outdoors, create a sacred space inside your home. You can dim the lights, light candles, and place symbols of the cosmos around you (such as crystals, star charts, or images of the night sky). Soft music or nature sounds can help set the mood.

2. Ground Yourself

Before beginning your meditation, ground yourself by connecting to the Earth's energy. Sit or stand with your feet firmly planted on the ground, close your eyes, and take several deep breaths. Imagine roots extending from your feet deep into the Earth, anchoring you. This will help you feel secure and centered during your meditation.

3. Set Your Intention

Clarify your intention for the meditation. Whether you are seeking guidance, healing, peace, or cosmic wisdom, setting an intention will guide the flow of your meditation. You can silently state your intention or write it down in a journal before beginning.

4. Focus on the Breath

Begin your meditation by focusing on your breath. Slow, deep breaths help quiet the mind and bring your awareness into the present moment. This also prepares your body and mind to receive the cosmic energies you will connect with during the meditation.

Guided Meditations for Cosmic Connection

Below are several guided meditations designed to connect you with different aspects of the cosmos, from individual stars and constellations to the expansive energy of the universe. These meditations can be adapted to your personal practice, and you can choose the one that resonates most with your current spiritual needs.

1. The Cosmic Breath Meditation: Connecting with the Universe

Purpose: This meditation helps you connect with the vastness of the universe, aligning your energy with the flow of cosmic forces. It is ideal for those seeking to feel a sense of oneness with the universe and expand their awareness.

Instructions:

1. **Find a Comfortable Position**: Either lie down or sit comfortably outside, looking up at the night sky, or close your eyes and visualize the stars above you. Begin with a few deep breaths, allowing your body to relax.
2. **Visualize the Night Sky**: If you're indoors, imagine yourself lying under a vast, clear sky filled with stars. Picture the Milky Way arching overhead, with distant galaxies twinkling far away.
3. **Cosmic Breathing**: With each inhale, imagine you are breathing in the energy of the stars. Picture this energy as sparkling, white-gold light entering your body, filling you with calm and peace. As you exhale, release any tension or negativity back into the universe.
4. **Become One with the Universe**: Continue this deep, rhythmic breathing. With each breath, feel yourself becoming lighter, as though your body is dissolving into the starlight. Visualize yourself expanding until you are one with the universe, floating among the stars.
5. **Receive Guidance**: In this state of oneness, allow the energy of the universe to speak to you. Ask for guidance, clarity, or simply an experience of deep peace. Be open to any thoughts, feelings, or visions that may come to you.

6. **Gradual Return**: When you are ready, slowly bring your awareness back to your physical body. Imagine the starlight gently collecting within your heart, grounding you. Take a few deep breaths and open your eyes.

2. The Star-Child Meditation: Connecting with Your Star Origins

Purpose: This meditation connects you with your celestial origins, helping you remember your soul's cosmic lineage. It is ideal for those seeking deeper spiritual connection and understanding of their place in the universe.

Instructions:

1. **Set the Scene**: Sit or lie down comfortably under the stars, or close your eyes and imagine the vast night sky above you. Begin with deep, calming breaths.

2. **Visualize a Single Star**: Choose one bright star in the night sky to focus on. If indoors, visualize a single radiant star shining down upon you. Feel its light beaming directly into your heart.

3. **Journey to the Star**: As you breathe in, imagine that this star is calling you home. Visualize yourself leaving your body and traveling through space toward this star. You are weightless, moving effortlessly through the cosmos.

4. **Connect with Your Star Family**: As you approach the star, sense the presence of beings or energies that feel familiar to your soul. These could be ancestors, guides, or higher-dimensional beings who are part of your soul's journey. Feel their loving energy surrounding you.

5. **Receive Cosmic Wisdom**: In this sacred space, ask for guidance or insight into your soul's purpose, your place in the universe, or any questions you have. Be open to receiving messages, whether they come as visions, emotions, or inner knowing.

6. **Return to Earth**: When ready, thank the beings or energies for their guidance and begin to journey back to your body. As you descend through space, feel yourself grounded and reconnected to the Earth, yet carrying the wisdom of the stars within you.

3. The Lunar Connection Meditation: Harnessing the Moon's Energy

Purpose: This meditation focuses on the Moon's energy, making it perfect for emotional healing, intuition, and nurturing feminine energy. It's especially powerful when performed during a Full or New Moon.

Instructions:

1. **Prepare for Lunar Connection**: Sit comfortably where you can see the Moon, or if indoors, visualize the Moon above you. Begin with a few deep breaths, aligning your energy with the rhythm of the breath.

2. **Visualize the Moon's Light**: If the Moon is visible, focus on its soft, glowing light. If visualizing, imagine the Full Moon glowing bright in the sky, casting a silver light over you. Feel this light gently cascading over your body, calming your emotions and soothing your spirit.

3. **Absorb the Moon's Energy**: As you inhale, imagine breathing in the Moon's energy—a cool, calming light that fills you with peace and emotional balance. With each breath, feel the Moon's energy flowing through your body, healing any emotional wounds or blockages.

4. **Reflect and Release**: In this state of connection, reflect on any emotions or situations that need healing. Allow the Moon's nurturing energy to help you release what no longer serves you. As you exhale, imagine releasing all emotional burdens into the Moon's light, where they are dissolved and transformed.

5. **Lunar Insight**: In this space of calm, ask the Moon for intuitive guidance. This could be insight about a personal situation, clarity on your spiritual path, or a message from your subconscious. Be open to receiving messages through feelings, symbols, or inner knowing.

6. **Ground and Close**: When ready, thank the Moon for its guidance. Feel the energy of the Moon grounding you as you return to full awareness. Visualize the Moon's light remaining with you, protecting and guiding you through your day or night.

4. The Constellation Meditation: Aligning with Star Wisdom

Purpose: This meditation aligns your energy with a specific constellation, allowing you to tap into the unique wisdom and power associated with it. It's ideal for connecting with the archetypal energies of constellations like Orion, the Pleiades, or the Big Dipper.

Instructions:

1. **Choose a Constellation**: Before starting, choose a constellation that you feel drawn to or one that holds special meaning for you. If you are outdoors, locate it in the sky. If indoors, visualize it clearly.

2. **Begin the Meditation**: Sit or lie down comfortably and take a few deep breaths. Focus your gaze on the constellation, or if visualizing, imagine the stars of the constellation glowing brightly in the sky above you.

3. **Connect with the Constellation**: As you continue to breathe, imagine a line of light connecting you to each star in the constellation. Visualize this light forming a web that links your energy to the constellation, allowing its wisdom to flow into you.

4. **Receive Star Wisdom**: In this moment of connection, focus on the qualities or archetypal energy associated with the constellation. For example, Orion is associated with strength and hunting; the Pleiades are linked to spiritual insight and otherworldly wisdom. Allow this energy to enter your body and mind, bringing you insight or guidance relevant to your life.

5. **Ask for Guidance**: You may ask the constellation for guidance related to its energy. For example, if meditating on Orion, you might ask for courage in facing a challenge. Be open to receiving this guidance in the form of thoughts, symbols, or sensations.

6. **Return and Ground**: When ready, slowly release your connection with the constellation. Visualize the light that connects you gently dissolving, leaving behind only a sense of calm and wisdom. Ground yourself by taking a few deep breaths and focusing on your body.

5. The Milky Way Meditation: Expanding Your Consciousness
Purpose: This meditation helps expand your consciousness and awareness, allowing you to transcend the limitations of your everyday mind and tap into the infinite wisdom of the universe.
Instructions:

1. **Visualize the Milky Way**: Find a comfortable position and close your eyes. Imagine the Milky Way, a bright, swirling band of stars, stretching across the sky above you. Picture yourself lying beneath this vast expanse, feeling the energy of billions of stars.
2. **Begin to Expand**: With each inhale, imagine your awareness expanding outward, reaching further into the cosmos. Visualize your consciousness growing wider and wider until it encompasses the entire Milky Way.
3. **Become One with the Galaxy**: As you continue to breathe, visualize yourself dissolving into the galaxy, becoming one with the Milky Way. Feel the infinite energy of the universe flowing through you, filling you with wisdom, peace, and cosmic understanding.
4. **Ask for Insight**: In this state of expanded consciousness, ask the universe for insight into a particular question or challenge. Be open to receiving the answer, whether it comes as a thought, a feeling, or a sudden realization.
5. **Return to the Present**: When ready, gently bring your awareness back to your body. Visualize the Milky Way's light condensing into a single point within your heart, carrying the wisdom of the stars with you. Take a few deep breaths and open your eyes.

Incorporating Cosmic Symbols and Tools
While meditating, you can enhance your connection to the cosmos by incorporating certain symbols, tools, and objects. These include:

- **Crystals**: Use crystals associated with celestial energies, such as moonstone (for lunar energy), selenite (for cosmic connection), or amethyst (for spiritual insight). Place them around your meditation space or hold them during your meditation.
- **Astrological Symbols**: Bring symbols of the zodiac, planetary glyphs, or star charts into your space to amplify the energy of the specific stars or constellations you are meditating on.
- **Candles**: Lighting candles in specific colors that correspond to the planet, star, or constellation you are working with can help set the tone and create a sacred space for meditation.

Conclusion
Meditating and visualizing under the night sky connects you to the vastness of the universe and taps into powerful cosmic energies. Whether performed outside under the stars or indoors with visualization, these meditations offer profound opportunities for spiritual growth, healing, and in-

sight. By aligning yourself with the energies of the stars, planets, and constellations, you can access deep wisdom, feel a sense of oneness with the cosmos, and bring the energy of the universe into your daily life.

Through regular practice, star-gazing and cosmic meditations can help you deepen your connection with the universe, allowing you to draw upon its energy for personal transformation, inner peace, and spiritual expansion. Let the stars guide you on your journey, and may the night sky illuminate your path toward self-discovery and enlightenment.

Chapter 40: The Magic of the Equinoxes: Balancing Light and Dark, Rituals for Balance and Renewal

The equinoxes, occurring twice each year, mark moments of perfect balance between light and dark. These celestial events happen when the Sun crosses the celestial equator, resulting in equal lengths of day and night. In the Northern Hemisphere, the **Vernal (Spring) Equinox** takes place around March 21st, signaling the start of spring, while the **Autumnal (Fall) Equinox** occurs around September 21st, ushering in the autumn season. In the Southern Hemisphere, the timing of these equinoxes is reversed.

The equinoxes are moments of cosmic equilibrium, making them powerful times to focus on balance, renewal, and transformation. These transitional periods offer opportunities to reflect on the balance between light and dark—both in the external world and within ourselves. The rituals associated with the equinoxes often center on themes of balance, letting go, new beginnings, and harmonizing opposing forces.

In this chapter, we will explore the magic of the equinoxes in detail, delving into their symbolism, spiritual significance, and the unique energies they bring. You will also find specific rituals for both the Spring and Autumn Equinoxes, designed to help you achieve balance, renewal, and personal transformation in harmony with the cycles of the Earth.

The Symbolism and Energy of the Equinoxes

The equinoxes are significant not only because of their astronomical importance but also because of the spiritual symbolism they carry. These moments of balance between day and night reflect the natural rhythm of life, which is composed of cycles of growth and decay, light and dark, activity and rest.

Balancing Light and Dark

The balance between light and dark is a central theme of the equinoxes. In nature, the equinoxes symbolize the turning point where one force begins to wane, and the other starts to grow. This external balance mirrors our inner worlds, inviting us to examine the balance—or imbalance—between various aspects of our lives: work and rest, action and reflection, giving and receiving, strength and vulnerability.

Renewal and Transformation

Both equinoxes are associated with renewal and transformation, but in different ways:

- **Spring Equinox (Vernal Equinox)**: The Spring Equinox marks the return of the light, symbolizing growth, rebirth, and new beginnings. It is a time for planting seeds, both literally and metaphorically, and for embracing the energy of renewal and expansion.
- **Autumn Equinox (Fall Equinox)**: The Autumn Equinox signals the arrival of harvest time and the gradual return of the darkness. It is a time for gratitude, reflection, and preparing for the inward journey of the colder months. This equinox focuses on letting go, harvesting the fruits of past efforts, and finding balance as the year begins to wind down.

Spring Equinox (Vernal Equinox): Renewal and Rebirth

The Spring Equinox is a time of renewal, fresh starts, and awakening. Nature begins to stir after the long winter, and the earth comes alive with new growth. This equinox is closely associated with fertility, planting seeds (both physical and symbolic), and the blossoming of potential. In ancient traditions, the Spring Equinox often coincided with festivals celebrating new life, such as the pagan festival of **Ostara**, where the goddess of spring was honored.

The energy of the Spring Equinox is about rebirth, creativity, and setting intentions for the months ahead. It's a time to cleanse yourself of old energy, let go of the stagnant aspects of winter, and welcome the vibrant, dynamic energy of spring.

Spring Equinox Ritual for Renewal and Growth

Purpose: This ritual focuses on renewal, growth, and planting the seeds of your intentions for the coming months. It is a time to honor the rebirth of nature and align yourself with the energy of new beginnings.

Materials:

- A green or yellow candle (for growth and new beginnings)
- Seeds or a small potted plant (for symbolic planting)
- A bowl of water (for purification)
- Fresh flowers or herbs (such as lavender, rosemary, or daisies)
- A journal and pen (for writing your intentions)
- A small offering for the Earth (such as food or flower petals)

Instructions:

1. **Set the Scene**: Find a quiet space where you can perform the ritual, either outside in nature or indoors near a window where you can see the sunlight. Decorate your altar with fresh flowers, herbs, and symbols of spring, such as eggs, rabbits, or buds.
2. **Cleanse and Ground**: Begin by cleansing your space with the bowl of water. Dip your fingers in the water and sprinkle it around your ritual area, symbolizing the purification of your energy and space. Ground yourself by taking deep breaths, imagining your energy connecting to the Earth below.
3. **Light the Candle**: Light the green or yellow candle, representing the energy of renewal, growth, and the return of the light. As you light the candle, say:
   "I welcome the light and the warmth of spring. I honor the cycle of rebirth and the new growth that this season brings."
4. **Set Your Intentions**: Take a few moments to reflect on the areas of your life where you want to experience growth and renewal. Write down your intentions for the coming months in your journal. These can be goals related to personal growth, career, relationships, or spiritual development.
5. **Symbolic Planting**: Hold the seeds or small plant in your hands and focus on your intentions. As you plant the seeds in soil or pot the plant, say:

"As I plant these seeds, I plant the seeds of my intentions. May they grow strong and abundant, nourished by the light of the Sun and the Earth's fertile soil."

6. **Make an Offering**: Place your offering (such as flower petals or food) on the Earth as a gesture of gratitude for the renewal of life and the blessings of the season.

7. **Conclude the Ritual**: Spend a few minutes in quiet reflection, feeling the energy of renewal surrounding you. Close the ritual by thanking the Earth and the Sun for their gifts. Allow the candle to burn out or extinguish it with gratitude.

Autumn Equinox (Fall Equinox): Balance and Gratitude

The Autumn Equinox is a time of balance, reflection, and gratitude. It marks the transition from the long, light-filled days of summer to the darker, introspective season of fall. The Autumn Equinox is often associated with harvest festivals, such as **Mabon**, where the fruits of the Earth are celebrated and the hard work of the growing season is honored.

The energy of the Autumn Equinox is one of gratitude for the abundance we have received, both in material and spiritual terms. It is also a time to reflect on the balance between giving and receiving, light and dark, and action and rest. As we prepare for the darker months ahead, this equinox encourages us to let go of what no longer serves us, to release old patterns, and to find equilibrium in our lives.

Autumn Equinox Ritual for Balance and Gratitude

Purpose: This ritual focuses on balance, gratitude, and letting go of what is no longer needed as we transition into the darker half of the year. It is a time to reflect on the harvest of your efforts and honor the balance between light and dark.

Materials:

- A brown or orange candle (for balance and harvest)
- A bowl of seasonal fruits or grains (such as apples, corn, or wheat)
- A small piece of paper and pen (for writing what you want to release)
- A fireproof dish or cauldron (for burning the paper)
- A small offering for the Earth (such as an apple or corn kernels)

Instructions:

1. **Set the Scene**: Choose a quiet space where you can perform the ritual, either outside among the autumn colors or indoors with symbols of the harvest, such as pumpkins, leaves, or corn. Decorate your altar with seasonal items, such as apples, gourds, or wheat.

2. **Cleanse and Ground**: Begin by grounding yourself. Stand or sit comfortably and take deep breaths, imagining yourself rooted to the Earth. Visualize the balance between light and dark, day and night, within and around you.

3. **Light the Candle**: Light the brown or orange candle, representing balance, gratitude, and the harvest. As you light the candle, say:

"I honor the balance of light and dark, day and night. I give thanks for the abundance of the Earth and the blessings of this season."

4. **Reflection and Gratitude**: Take a few moments to reflect on the blessings and abundance you have received over the past year. What have you harvested—whether in material, emotional, or spiritual terms? Express gratitude for these gifts, either silently or by writing them in your journal.

5. **Letting Go**: On the small piece of paper, write down anything you wish to release—old habits, patterns, relationships, or emotional burdens. These are the things you want to let go of as you prepare for the darker, more introspective months ahead.

6. **Burn and Release**: Safely burn the piece of paper in the fireproof dish or cauldron, visualizing the smoke carrying away the old patterns and energy. As the paper burns, say:
"I release what no longer serves me. As the light fades, I embrace the darkness with peace and gratitude."

7. **Offering of Gratitude**: Place your offering (such as an apple, grains, or corn kernels) on the Earth as a gesture of gratitude for the abundance and balance the season provides.

8. **Conclude the Ritual**: Spend a few moments in quiet reflection, feeling the balance of light and dark within yourself. Close the ritual by thanking the Earth for its gifts and the cycles of the seasons. Allow the candle to burn out or extinguish it with gratitude.

Equinoxes and Personal Balance

The equinoxes are powerful moments to assess the balance in your personal life. In addition to performing rituals for cosmic balance, the equinoxes invite you to reflect on your internal and external balance. Here are some key areas to focus on during the equinoxes:

- **Work and Rest**: Are you balancing productivity with rest? The equinox is a great time to adjust your schedule to ensure that you are taking care of your body and mind.
- **Giving and Receiving**: Are you giving too much or not enough? Reflect on whether you are balancing generosity with self-care and whether you are open to receiving support and abundance.
- **Action and Reflection**: Are you taking decisive action in your life, or are you stuck in a cycle of reflection without moving forward? Conversely, are you constantly busy without taking time to reflect on your goals and direction?
- **Masculine and Feminine Energy**: The equinox is a perfect time to reflect on the balance of masculine (active, assertive) and feminine (receptive, intuitive) energies within yourself. Are you embracing both aspects of your nature?

Taking time to explore these areas during the equinoxes can help you bring more harmony and equilibrium into your life.

Astrological Influence of the Equinoxes

The equinoxes have a significant impact astrologically, as they mark the entry of the Sun into two important zodiac signs:

- **Spring Equinox**: The Sun enters **Aries**, the first sign of the zodiac. Aries represents bold new beginnings, leadership, and action. This astrological influence makes the Spring Equinox a powerful time for initiating new projects and taking action toward your goals.
- **Autumn Equinox**: The Sun enters **Libra**, the sign of balance, relationships, and harmony. Libra's energy encourages reflection on relationships, fairness, and finding equilibrium in all areas of life. This influence makes the Autumn Equinox an ideal time to focus on balance and restoring harmony in your life.

By understanding the astrological energies of the equinoxes, you can align your rituals and personal reflections with the zodiac's influence, enhancing the power of your spiritual work.

Conclusion

The equinoxes are sacred moments of balance and transition, offering opportunities for renewal, reflection, and transformation. By connecting with the energies of the Spring and Autumn Equinoxes, you can bring more balance into your life, honor the cycles of the Earth, and align yourself with the cosmic forces of light and dark.

Whether you are planting seeds of new beginnings in the spring or letting go of old patterns in the fall, the equinoxes provide powerful energetic support for personal growth and spiritual transformation. Through thoughtful rituals, meditation, and reflection, you can harmonize your inner and outer worlds, bringing more balance, peace, and renewal into your life as you journey through the seasons.

Chapter 41: Healing Magic Through Celestial Timing: Best Times for Spells to Heal Mind, Body, and Soul

In the practice of magic, timing is a crucial element that can greatly influence the potency of your spells, particularly when it comes to healing. Just as the tides of the ocean are influenced by the Moon, so too are the rhythms of our lives shaped by the cycles of the cosmos. By aligning your healing spells with the celestial energies of the Sun, Moon, planets, and zodiac signs, you can tap into powerful forces that enhance physical, emotional, and spiritual recovery.

This chapter will explore the best times for conducting healing magic based on celestial timing. You will learn how to harness the energies of the planets, lunar phases, and zodiac signs to heal the mind, body, and soul. Whether you are working with physical ailments, emotional wounds, or spiritual imbalances, aligning your healing spells with the celestial calendar will help you achieve greater harmony and transformation.

The Power of Celestial Timing in Healing Magic

Celestial timing refers to using the natural cycles and movements of the Moon, planets, and stars to enhance the effectiveness of your magical work. Each planet, Moon phase, and zodiac sign governs different aspects of life, and understanding how these celestial forces interact can help you choose the most potent time for your healing spells.

By aligning your healing magic with celestial timing, you are tapping into a greater reservoir of cosmic energy, allowing you to:

- **Amplify the effects** of your healing spells by working in harmony with the universe's natural rhythms.
- **Focus on specific types of healing** (physical, emotional, spiritual) by choosing the best planetary influence or lunar phase for your intention.
- **Increase the speed and effectiveness** of healing, whether for yourself or others, by aligning your spells with the appropriate celestial energies.

Healing with the Lunar Phases

The Moon governs the subconscious, emotions, and the cycles of life, making it a powerful celestial body for healing magic. Its phases—New, Waxing, Full, and Waning—each carry different energies that can be harnessed for specific types of healing.

1. New Moon: Healing New Beginnings

The New Moon represents a time of new beginnings and is associated with setting intentions, planting seeds, and starting fresh. It is the best time for healing magic focused on emotional or mental renewal, clearing away past pain, and setting the stage for recovery.

Ideal Healing Work During the New Moon:

- Emotional or mental healing from past trauma or heartbreak.
- Setting intentions for long-term healing and recovery.
- Healing work that focuses on overcoming mental barriers or releasing old emotional patterns.

New Moon Healing Spell:

- **Materials**: A black candle (for release), white candle (for new beginnings), lavender essential oil (for calming), a bowl of water.
- **Instructions**: Begin by lighting the black candle, focusing on releasing old pain or emotional baggage. Dip your fingers into the bowl of water, anointing yourself while visualizing the old energy washing away. Light the white candle, and as it burns, set an intention for new emotional and spiritual health. Allow both candles to burn down completely, symbolizing a complete cycle of release and renewal.

2. Waxing Moon: Healing Growth and Strength

The Waxing Moon is the period when the Moon is growing in light, symbolizing growth, expansion, and strengthening. This is the best time for healing spells that focus on building strength, accelerating recovery, and enhancing vitality, whether it's for physical health, emotional resilience, or spiritual fortitude.

Ideal Healing Work During the Waxing Moon:

- Physical healing from illness, injury, or surgery.
- Increasing mental strength and emotional resilience.
- Strengthening immune systems or promoting rapid recovery.

Waxing Moon Healing Spell:

- **Materials**: A green candle (for growth), rosemary or eucalyptus essential oil (for healing), a piece of clear quartz (for amplifying energy), and a glass of spring water.
- **Instructions**: Anoint the green candle with rosemary or eucalyptus oil and light it. Hold the clear quartz in your hands, focusing on the energy of growth and healing entering your body. Place the quartz near the candle, and as it burns, visualize your body or mind growing stronger. Drink the spring water, imagining it nourishing your cells and filling you with vitality. Keep the quartz with you as a talisman for continued healing.

3. Full Moon: Healing Completion and Empowerment

The Full Moon is a time of culmination, heightened energy, and manifestation. It is the most powerful time for healing spells that aim to bring a condition to completion, release deep-seated wounds, or fully empower yourself on your healing journey.

Ideal Healing Work During the Full Moon:

- Releasing deep emotional wounds or toxic relationships.
- Healing the body from chronic illness or pain.
- Spiritual healing that involves connecting with higher realms or divine energies.

Full Moon Healing Spell:

- **Materials**: A silver or white candle (for purity and illumination), jasmine or frankincense essential oil (for spiritual empowerment), a piece of selenite (for cleansing), and a mirror.
- **Instructions**: Light the candle and anoint it with the essential oil. Sit in front of the mirror, and as you gaze at your reflection, visualize the light of the Full Moon washing over you, illuminating any areas of pain or emotional darkness. Hold the selenite in your hand and move it over your body, imagining it drawing out negativity and replacing it with healing light. As you do this, repeat the affirmation: "I release what no longer serves me, and I embrace my full healing." Allow the candle to burn down, and place the selenite under your pillow for continued healing during sleep.

4. Waning Moon: Healing Release and Cleansing

The Waning Moon is the period when the Moon's light diminishes, symbolizing release, cleansing, and banishment. This is the best time for healing spells that focus on releasing pain, illness, or toxic energy from your life, whether it's physical, emotional, or spiritual.

Ideal Healing Work During the Waning Moon:

- Banishing illness, chronic pain, or harmful habits.
- Releasing emotional or mental blockages.

- Cleansing the aura or energy body of negativity or attachments.

Waning Moon Healing Spell:

- **Materials**: A black or dark blue candle (for release), sage or cedar essential oil (for purification), a bowl of saltwater, and a piece of obsidian or black tourmaline (for protection and grounding).
- **Instructions**: Light the black candle and anoint it with sage or cedar oil. Place the bowl of saltwater in front of you and hold the obsidian or tourmaline. As the candle burns, visualize all illness, pain, or negative energy flowing out of your body and into the water. As the wax melts and the candle diminishes, focus on releasing these burdens. Once you feel ready, pour the saltwater outside or into the Earth, symbolizing the release of your pain. Keep the obsidian or tourmaline with you for protection and continued healing.

Healing with the Planets

The planets govern different areas of life, and each one carries specific energies that can be used to enhance healing spells. By timing your healing magic according to the influence of the planets, you can align your spells with the energy most suited to the type of healing you need.

1. Sun: Vitality, Health, and Confidence

The Sun represents life force, vitality, and personal power. Its energy is best used for spells related to boosting physical health, increasing confidence, and promoting overall well-being. The Sun's influence is especially strong on **Sundays**.

Ideal Healing Work Under the Sun:

- Physical healing and recovery from illness or injury.
- Increasing vitality, stamina, and overall health.
- Boosting confidence and self-worth during recovery.

Sun Healing Spell:

- **Materials**: A gold or yellow candle, sunstone or citrine, and a bowl of water infused with lemon slices.
- **Instructions**: Light the candle and hold the sunstone or citrine in your hands. Visualize the warm, golden energy of the Sun filling your body with vitality and strength. Dip your hands into the lemon-infused water and anoint your forehead and chest, imagining this cleansing your body and spirit with solar energy. Sit in the sunlight if possible, allowing the Sun's rays to empower your healing intentions.

2. Moon: Emotional Healing and Intuition

The Moon governs emotions, intuition, and the subconscious. Its energy is ideal for healing emotional wounds, restoring emotional balance, and working through trauma. The Moon's influence is especially potent on **Mondays**.

Ideal Healing Work Under the Moon:

- Healing emotional trauma, grief, or heartbreak.
- Restoring emotional balance and well-being.
- Enhancing intuitive healing or dream work.

Moon Healing Spell:

- **Materials**: A silver or white candle, moonstone or selenite, lavender essential oil, and a bowl of water.
- **Instructions**: Light the candle and anoint it with lavender oil. Hold the moonstone or selenite in your hands, focusing on the soothing energy of the Moon. Dip your fingers into the water and anoint your heart, imagining the calming energy of the Moon healing your emotions. Spend a few moments reflecting on any emotional pain, then visualize the Moon's light gently dissolving this pain. Place the moonstone under your pillow for continued emotional healing during sleep.

3. Mercury: Mental Healing and Communication

Mercury governs communication, thought, and the mind. Its energy is ideal for healing mental health issues, improving cognitive function, and addressing issues related to communication. Mercury's influence is strongest on **Wednesdays**.

Ideal Healing Work Under Mercury:

- Healing mental health issues like anxiety or depression.
- Enhancing cognitive function, memory, and focus.
- Healing communication problems in relationships.

Mercury Healing Spell:

- **Materials**: A light blue candle, fluorite or aquamarine crystal, peppermint essential oil, and a pen and paper.
- **Instructions**: Light the candle and anoint it with peppermint oil. Hold the fluorite or aquamarine in your hands and focus on the clarity and healing of your mind. Write down any thoughts or issues you want to heal (such as anxiety, negative self-talk, or communication issues). As the candle burns, visualize Mercury's energy clearing your mind and bringing balance to your thoughts. Afterward, burn the paper safely, symbolizing the release of these mental burdens.

4. Venus: Healing Love and Relationships

Venus governs love, beauty, and relationships. Its energy is ideal for healing matters of the heart, enhancing self-love, and repairing relationships. Venus's influence is strongest on **Fridays**.

Ideal Healing Work Under Venus:

- Healing from heartbreak or relationship wounds.
- Enhancing self-love and emotional well-being.
- Strengthening relationships through communication and empathy.

Venus Healing Spell:

- **Materials**: A pink or green candle, rose quartz, rose petals, and a bowl of water infused with rose essential oil.
- **Instructions**: Light the candle and hold the rose quartz in your hands. As you gaze into the flame, visualize Venus's loving energy surrounding you and healing your heart. Dip your fingers into the rose-infused water and anoint your heart and wrists, focusing on feelings of self-love and emotional healing. If healing a relationship, visualize peace and understanding between you and the other person. Keep the rose quartz close as a reminder of your intention for love and healing.

5. Mars: Healing Strength and Protection

Mars governs action, strength, and protection. Its energy is ideal for healing physical injuries, boosting personal strength, and enhancing the body's ability to fight illness. Mars's influence is strongest on **Tuesdays**.

Ideal Healing Work Under Mars:

- Healing physical injuries or boosting physical strength.
- Enhancing the immune system's ability to fight illness.
- Protecting against negative energy or psychic attacks during healing.

Mars Healing Spell:

- **Materials**: A red or black candle, red jasper or bloodstone, ginger essential oil, and a bowl of saltwater.
- **Instructions**: Light the candle and anoint it with ginger oil. Hold the red jasper or bloodstone in your hands, visualizing Mars's fiery energy filling your body with strength and protection. Dip your fingers into the saltwater and anoint your forehead, imagining a protective shield forming around you. Focus on the healing of your body, picturing yourself overcoming any physical challenges with strength and resilience.

Healing with the Zodiac Signs

Each zodiac sign carries its own unique energy that can influence healing magic. By timing your spells with the Moon or planets as they pass through certain zodiac signs, you can align your healing work with the qualities that each sign embodies.

1. Aries: Healing for Courage and Initiative

- **Best Time**: When the Moon or Sun is in Aries.
- **Focus**: Healing related to overcoming fear, taking initiative in recovery, and boosting physical energy.

2. Taurus: Healing for Stability and Self-Love

- **Best Time**: When the Moon or Venus is in Taurus.
- **Focus**: Healing related to self-love, physical comfort, and long-term stability.

3. Gemini: Healing for Communication and Mental Clarity

- **Best Time**: When the Moon or Mercury is in Gemini.
- **Focus**: Healing related to communication, mental clarity, and restoring peace to the mind.

4. Cancer: Healing for Emotional Well-Being and Nurturing

- **Best Time**: When the Moon is in Cancer.
- **Focus**: Healing related to emotional wounds, family dynamics, and nurturing the inner child.

5. Leo: Healing for Confidence and Self-Worth

- **Best Time**: When the Moon or Sun is in Leo.
- **Focus**: Healing related to confidence, self-expression, and reclaiming personal power.

6. Virgo: Healing for Health and Organization

- **Best Time**: When the Moon or Mercury is in Virgo.
- **Focus**: Healing related to physical health, detoxification, and organizing the mind and body for optimal well-being.

7. Libra: Healing for Balance and Relationships

- **Best Time**: When the Moon or Venus is in Libra.
- **Focus**: Healing related to balance, harmony in relationships, and finding inner peace.

8. Scorpio: Healing for Transformation and Emotional Depth

- **Best Time**: When the Moon or Mars is in Scorpio.
- **Focus**: Healing related to deep emotional wounds, transformation, and releasing toxic energies.

9. Sagittarius: Healing for Freedom and Spiritual Expansion

- **Best Time**: When the Moon or Jupiter is in Sagittarius.
- **Focus**: Healing related to spiritual growth, freedom from limiting beliefs, and expanding consciousness.

10. Capricorn: Healing for Discipline and Long-Term Recovery

- **Best Time**: When the Moon or Saturn is in Capricorn.
- **Focus**: Healing related to long-term recovery, building resilience, and maintaining discipline in health routines.

11. Aquarius: Healing for Innovation and Mental Health

- **Best Time**: When the Moon or Uranus is in Aquarius.
- **Focus**: Healing related to mental health, innovative approaches to recovery, and restoring a sense of individuality and freedom.

12. Pisces: Healing for Spirituality and Emotional Release

- **Best Time**: When the Moon or Neptune is in Pisces.
- **Focus**: Healing related to spiritual cleansing, emotional release, and connecting with higher realms for healing guidance.

Conclusion

Healing magic is deeply enhanced when aligned with celestial timing, as the movements of the Moon, planets, and zodiac signs provide powerful support for physical, emotional, and spiritual recovery. By understanding how to harness these cosmic energies, you can amplify the effects of your healing spells and create a deeper connection to the universe's natural cycles of growth, release, and renewal.

Whether you are healing from illness, recovering emotionally, or seeking spiritual balance, the power of celestial timing offers guidance and strength. Through thoughtful alignment with the rhythms of the cosmos, you can bring greater harmony, balance, and healing into your life, supporting your journey toward wholeness and well-being.

Chapter 42: Spiritual Cleansing with Celestial Events: Techniques for Using the Full Moon, New Moon, and Eclipses to Cleanse and Reset Energy

Spiritual cleansing is a vital practice for maintaining balance, clearing negative energy, and resetting our mental, emotional, and spiritual states. Celestial events such as the Full Moon, New Moon, and eclipses offer potent opportunities for deep energetic cleansing and renewal. These cosmic moments heighten energy shifts, making them ideal times to let go of negativity, release emotional baggage, and refresh your energy field.

In this chapter, we will explore the power of celestial events in spiritual cleansing and provide detailed techniques for using the Full Moon, New Moon, and eclipses to reset your energy. Whether you are seeking emotional release, energetic balance, or spiritual rejuvenation, these rituals will help you align with the rhythms of the universe to restore harmony within yourself.

The Importance of Spiritual Cleansing

Spiritual cleansing is the process of removing energetic blockages, clearing out negative or stagnant energy, and refreshing your aura, chakras, and space. Over time, we collect unwanted energies from our environment, relationships, and experiences. Without regular spiritual cleansing, this accumulated energy can weigh us down, causing feelings of fatigue, anxiety, confusion, or emotional instability.

By syncing your spiritual cleansing rituals with the phases of the Moon and other celestial events, you harness the enhanced power of the cosmos, which can make your cleansing practices more effective and transformative. Each celestial event carries specific energies that can amplify your intentions for release, renewal, or emotional healing.

Full Moon Cleansing: Releasing, Purifying, and Letting Go

The Full Moon is a time of culmination and illumination, representing the peak of lunar energy. It shines a light on what needs to be released, making it an ideal time for spiritual cleansing focused on letting go of negativity, emotional baggage, and any patterns that no longer serve you. The Full Moon's energy helps to bring hidden emotions and unresolved issues to the surface, offering a powerful opportunity for purification and renewal.

Why Cleanse During the Full Moon?

- The Full Moon's light brings clarity, illuminating areas of your life that need to be cleansed or released.
- It is a powerful time for emotional and energetic detox, as the Moon's energy can help you release what no longer serves your highest good.
- Full Moon cleansing rituals can help you close chapters, heal wounds, and prepare for new beginnings.

Full Moon Spiritual Cleansing Techniques
1. Full Moon Ritual Bath for Energy Purification
A Full Moon bath is a soothing way to cleanse your aura, release emotional tension, and reset your energy.
Materials:

- Epsom salt or sea salt (for purification)
- White candles (for illumination and clarity)
- Lavender or rosemary essential oil (for relaxation and emotional healing)
- Clear quartz or moonstone (for amplifying lunar energy)

Instructions:

1. **Prepare the Bath**: Fill the tub with warm water and add a cup of Epsom salt or sea salt to cleanse your energy. Add a few drops of lavender or rosemary essential oil to promote emotional healing and relaxation.
2. **Set Your Space**: Light white candles around the bath area to symbolize the light of the Full Moon. If possible, bathe under moonlight or visualize the Full Moon above you as you prepare.
3. **Immerse and Cleanse**: Enter the bath and relax. As you soak, visualize the Full Moon's light surrounding you, purifying your aura and dissolving any negative or stagnant energy. Imagine any emotional heaviness or stress being absorbed by the water.
4. **Set an Intention**: As you bathe, reflect on what you wish to release. Speak aloud or silently your intention to let go of anything that no longer serves your highest good. Feel the energy of the Moon supporting your cleansing process.
5. **Conclude**: After your bath, pour a bowl of fresh water over your body as a final purification. As the water flows over you, imagine any remaining negativity being washed away. Thank the Moon for its healing energy and release the water with gratitude.

2. Full Moon Aura Cleansing with Smudging

Smudging with sacred herbs like sage, cedar, or palo santo is an ancient method for clearing negative energy and purifying your aura.

Materials:

- Sage or palo santo (for smoke cleansing)
- A feather or fan (to direct the smoke)
- A white candle (for Full Moon energy)

Instructions:

1. **Set Your Intention**: Before lighting the sage or palo santo, take a moment to set your intention. Focus on clearing your energy field of negativity, stress, or emotional blockages.
2. **Light the Sage**: Light the sage or palo santo and allow it to smolder, producing cleansing smoke. Light the white candle to represent the illuminating energy of the Full Moon.
3. **Cleanse Your Aura**: Stand and move the smoke around your body, starting at your head and moving down to your feet. Use the feather or fan to direct the smoke and clear your energy field. As the smoke surrounds you, visualize it lifting away any negativity or heavy energy.
4. **Affirm**: As you cleanse, repeat an affirmation such as: "I release all that no longer serves me. I cleanse my energy, mind, and spirit."
5. **Conclude**: When you feel your aura has been thoroughly cleansed, extinguish the sage or palo santo. Spend a few moments in quiet reflection, thanking the Full Moon for its purifying light.

3. Charging Crystals and Tools Under the Full Moon

The Full Moon is a powerful time to cleanse and recharge your crystals, tarot cards, or other spiritual tools.

Materials:

- Crystals, tarot decks, or other tools
- A tray or cloth for placing the tools under moonlight

Instructions:

1. **Set Up Your Space**: On the night of the Full Moon, place your crystals or spiritual tools on a tray or cloth outside, or near a window where the moonlight can reach them.
2. **Set an Intention**: As you lay out your tools, set the intention that they will be cleansed of any old or stagnant energy and recharged with the Full Moon's powerful illumination.
3. **Leave Them Overnight**: Allow your tools to bathe in the moonlight overnight. The next day, retrieve them, knowing they are cleansed, recharged, and ready for your spiritual work.

New Moon Cleansing: Resetting, Releasing, and Preparing for Growth

The New Moon marks the beginning of a new lunar cycle, symbolizing fresh starts, new intentions, and the planting of seeds for future growth. It is a time of quiet introspection, making it perfect for cleansing rituals that focus on resetting your energy, clearing away past influences, and preparing yourself for new opportunities. The New Moon's dark sky represents the fertile soil from which new beginnings emerge, making it a powerful time for letting go of old habits, limiting beliefs, and emotional blockages.

Why Cleanse During the New Moon?

- The New Moon's energy supports deep introspection, making it a powerful time for clearing away old patterns and preparing for new beginnings.
- It is a perfect time to reset your energy, create space for growth, and set intentions for future healing.
- New Moon cleansing rituals help you to release the past and create a clean slate for manifesting your desires.

New Moon Spiritual Cleansing Techniques

1. New Moon Space Cleansing and Decluttering

The New Moon is an ideal time to cleanse and reset your living space, clearing it of old energy and making way for new growth.

Materials:

- Sage, cedar, or palo santo (for smoke cleansing)
- A broom or brush (for physical cleansing)
- A black candle (for release) and a white candle (for new intentions)
- Salt or saltwater (for protection)

Instructions:

1. **Physical Cleansing**: Before performing an energetic cleansing, physically clean and declutter your space. Sweep the floors with a broom or brush, imagining that you are sweeping away stagnant energy along with the dust. Open windows to allow fresh air to flow through.
2. **Smudging**: Light sage, cedar, or palo santo and move through each room, focusing on areas that feel heavy or stagnant. As you smudge, imagine the smoke clearing away old energy and negativity.
3. **Salt Protection**: Sprinkle salt or use saltwater around the perimeter of your home or room for added protection. Salt has powerful purifying properties and can act as a barrier against negative energy.

4. **Light the Candles**: Light the black candle first, setting the intention to release any negative energy or emotional burdens. Once the black candle has burned for a while, light the white candle to symbolize new beginnings and fresh energy entering your space.

2. New Moon Intention Setting and Cleansing Ritual

The New Moon is the perfect time for a deep spiritual cleanse that focuses on resetting your energy and setting new intentions.

Materials:

- A black candle (for release)
- Lavender or frankincense essential oil (for emotional healing)
- A piece of obsidian or black tourmaline (for protection)
- A bowl of saltwater (for purification)

Instructions:

1. **Set Your Space**: Begin by lighting the black candle to symbolize the release of old energy. Anoint your wrists and heart with lavender or frankincense oil to promote emotional healing.
2. **Hold the Crystal**: Hold the obsidian or black tourmaline in your hands, visualizing it absorbing any negative or stagnant energy from your body and aura. Imagine the crystal acting as a shield, protecting you from any external negativity.
3. **Saltwater Cleansing**: Dip your fingers into the bowl of saltwater and sprinkle it over yourself, saying: "I cleanse myself of all that no longer serves me. I release the past and prepare for new growth."
4. **Set Your Intention**: As you cleanse, reflect on the areas of your life where you want to create change or growth. Speak aloud or write down your intentions for the new lunar cycle. Focus on what you want to manifest in the coming weeks.

Eclipse Cleansing: Deep Transformation and Resetting Energy

Eclipses—whether solar or lunar—are times of immense cosmic power. They represent moments of deep transformation, when the Sun or Moon is temporarily obscured, symbolizing the need to confront and release hidden aspects of yourself. Eclipses are potent for resetting your energy, releasing deep-seated patterns, and preparing for powerful shifts in your life.

Why Cleanse During an Eclipse?

- Eclipses offer a powerful portal for transformation and deep cleansing.
- They help you release what is hidden or unconscious, bringing long-buried emotions or patterns to the surface.
- Eclipses allow for a complete energetic reset, clearing away blockages and preparing you for radical change.

Eclipse Spiritual Cleansing Techniques

1. Solar Eclipse Cleansing for Spiritual Rebirth

A solar eclipse is a powerful time to reset your energy and align with new beginnings.

Materials:

- A black candle (for transformation) and a gold candle (for illumination)
- A piece of smoky quartz (for deep cleansing)
- A mirror (to reflect on hidden aspects)

Instructions:

1. **Set Your Intention**: During a solar eclipse, focus on deep transformation and rebirth. Reflect on any hidden aspects of yourself or unresolved energy that needs to be released.
2. **Light the Candles**: Light the black candle to symbolize the temporary shadow of the eclipse and the process of confronting hidden truths. After some time, light the gold candle to symbolize the return of light and clarity after the eclipse.
3. **Mirror Reflection**: Hold the mirror and gaze into it, reflecting on what has been hidden in your subconscious that is now ready to be released. Ask yourself, "What do I need to transform within myself?"
4. **Smoky Quartz Cleansing**: Hold the smoky quartz and visualize it absorbing any negative energy or emotional blockages. Allow the eclipse energy to help you release these aspects.
5. **Conclude the Ritual**: After the eclipse, extinguish the black candle first, symbolizing the end of the shadow. Let the gold candle burn longer, representing the return of light and clarity.

2. Lunar Eclipse Cleansing for Emotional Transformation

Lunar eclipses are ideal for emotional cleansing and releasing deep-seated emotions.

Materials:

- A silver candle (for emotional healing)
- Selenite (for purification)
- A bowl of water (to represent emotional depths)

Instructions:

1. **Light the Candle**: Light the silver candle to symbolize the energy of the Moon. Reflect on the deep emotional transformation you are seeking.
2. **Set Your Intention**: Hold the selenite and set the intention to release any deep-seated emotions or unresolved feelings. Focus on the eclipse's power to bring hidden emotions to the surface.
3. **Water Reflection**: Sit quietly and gaze into the bowl of water, imagining it as a mirror of your emotional depths. Allow yourself to reflect on any emotions that need to be released or cleansed.
4. **Selenite Cleansing**: Use the selenite to cleanse your aura, focusing on areas of emotional pain or blockages. Visualize the eclipse helping you release these emotions.
5. **Conclude the Ritual**: After the eclipse, extinguish the candle and thank the Moon for its guidance in your emotional healing process.

Conclusion

Celestial events such as the Full Moon, New Moon, and eclipses offer profound opportunities for spiritual cleansing, emotional healing, and energetic renewal. By aligning your cleansing rituals with these cosmic events, you can harness their powerful energies to release what no longer serves you, reset your energy field, and open yourself to new beginnings and spiritual growth.

Through thoughtful preparation and intention-setting, you can use the enhanced energy of the Moon and eclipses to amplify your spiritual practices, purify your energy, and align with the cycles of the cosmos for deeper healing and transformation.

Chapter 43: Constellation Magic: Working with Constellations for Protection, Guidance, and Spell Enhancement

Constellations have been revered throughout history for their symbolic meanings and spiritual power. These star formations, which dot the night sky, serve as celestial maps, offering guidance, protection, and wisdom. In magical practice, constellations can be called upon to enhance spells, provide protection, and offer divine insight. Each constellation carries unique energy, often linked to mythological figures, spiritual archetypes, or cosmic forces. By tapping into this ancient wisdom, practitioners can harness the power of the stars to amplify their magical work.

This chapter will explore how to work with constellations for various magical purposes, including protection, guidance, and enhancing your spells. You'll learn how to incorporate the energy of specific constellations into your rituals and spellwork, connect with their archetypal wisdom, and use them as celestial allies in your spiritual practice.

The Power of Constellation Magic

Constellations are not just patterns of stars; they are gateways to divine wisdom and cosmic energy. Each constellation has its own history, mythology, and spiritual significance, allowing practitioners to tap into their symbolic meaning for magical purposes. By invoking the energy of a particular constellation, you can align yourself with its archetypal power and channel its influence into your rituals and spellwork.

Working with constellations can bring about:

- **Protection**: Many constellations are associated with warriors, guardians, or protectors in mythology, making them ideal allies for protective magic.
- **Guidance**: Certain constellations are known for their connection to divine wisdom, offering guidance and insight during times of uncertainty or when seeking clarity in your life.
- **Spell Enhancement**: The energy of constellations can enhance the effectiveness of your spells, especially when their symbolic meaning aligns with your magical intention.

By incorporating constellation magic into your practice, you create a deeper connection with the cosmos and access the ancient wisdom carried by these star formations.

Understanding the Energetic Influence of Constellations

Each constellation has its own unique vibration, often tied to its mythological background or the qualities of the zodiac sign it inhabits. By understanding the energetic influence of each constellation, you can choose the right one for your specific magical intentions. Whether you seek protection from danger, guidance in difficult times, or support in your spellwork, there is a constellation that can help you achieve your goals.

Common Themes in Constellation Magic

1. **Protection**: Many constellations are associated with powerful mythological figures who were protectors or warriors. Invoking these constellations can create a shield of protection around you, your home, or loved ones.
2. **Guidance and Wisdom**: Some constellations are linked to gods, goddesses, or figures known for their wisdom and foresight. By working with these constellations, you can receive divine guidance and insight when facing challenges or making important decisions.
3. **Spell Enhancement**: Constellations can amplify the energy of your spells by adding cosmic support to your intentions. When their symbolic meaning aligns with the purpose of your spell, their influence can make your work more powerful and effective.

How to Work with Constellations in Magic

Working with constellations involves attuning yourself to the energy of the stars, calling upon their symbolic power, and integrating them into your magical practice. Here are some key methods for working with constellations:

1. Constellation Altar Setup

Setting up a constellation altar is a powerful way to connect with the energy of a specific star formation. This altar serves as a sacred space where you can meditate, set intentions, and call upon the constellation for protection, guidance, or spell enhancement.

Steps to Set Up a Constellation Altar:

- **Choose a Constellation**: Select the constellation that aligns with your intention. For example, Orion is ideal for protection, while the Pleiades is known for spiritual wisdom.
- **Gather Correspondences**: Use crystals, candles, and symbols that correspond to the energy of the chosen constellation. For example, for Orion, use a sword, red jasper (for strength), and black candles (for protection).
- **Create the Star Map**: Draw or print a map of the constellation you're working with. Place this on your altar as a representation of the constellation's energy. You can also draw the constellation on a piece of parchment paper with intention.
- **Meditate on the Stars**: Light the candles and meditate in front of your altar, visualizing the constellation in the night sky. Feel its energy connecting with yours, and speak aloud your intention to invoke its power.

- **Offerings and Affirmations**: Place offerings on your altar, such as herbs, flowers, or food associated with the constellation's mythology. Speak affirmations that align with your intention, such as, "I call upon the strength of Orion to protect me and my loved ones."

2. Night Sky Meditation with Constellations

Meditating under the stars is one of the most direct ways to connect with constellations. By gazing at the night sky and focusing on the constellation you wish to work with, you can attune yourself to its energy and receive guidance or protection.

Steps for Night Sky Meditation:

- **Find the Constellation**: If possible, locate the constellation in the night sky. You can use a star map or a mobile app to help find the stars you seek.
- **Set Your Intention**: Before starting the meditation, set an intention for what you want to receive from the constellation. For example, if you are working with the constellation **Cassiopeia**, known for its association with queens and authority, you may set an intention for personal empowerment or leadership.
- **Breathe and Focus**: Sit comfortably under the stars and take deep, calming breaths. Focus on the constellation and visualize its stars glowing brightly. Imagine their energy flowing down to you, filling you with their power.
- **Receive Guidance**: As you meditate, remain open to any thoughts, images, or feelings that arise. These may be messages from the constellation, offering guidance, wisdom, or insight.
- **Journal Your Experience**: After your meditation, take a few minutes to journal about your experience. Write down any insights or feelings that came to you during the meditation.

3. Incorporating Constellations into Spellwork

Incorporating the energy of constellations into your spellwork can amplify the potency of your magic. Each constellation carries a unique vibration that can enhance specific types of spells, from protection and love to prosperity and spiritual growth.

How to Incorporate Constellations into Your Spellwork:

- **Invoke the Constellation**: Begin your spell by calling upon the constellation that aligns with your intention. For example, if you are performing a protection spell, call upon **Orion**, the great hunter and warrior.
- **Use Symbolic Elements**: Include symbols, colors, and crystals associated with the constellation. For **Orion**, you might use red and black candles (for strength and protection), a sword or dagger (symbolizing his warrior energy), and hematite or black tourmaline (for grounding and protection).
- **Star Visualization**: During your spell, visualize the stars of the constellation glowing brightly above you. Imagine their energy descending and merging with your spell, empowering your intention.

- **Words of Power**: Speak affirmations or incantations that connect your spell to the constellation. For example, you might say, "By the power of Orion, I invoke strength and protection. As his stars watch over me, so am I shielded from harm."
- **Offer Gratitude**: After completing your spell, offer gratitude to the constellation for its support and guidance. You can leave offerings on your altar or speak a simple prayer of thanks.

Constellations for Protection, Guidance, and Spell Enhancement

Below are some of the most powerful constellations for magical work, categorized by their primary energies. These constellations can be called upon for protection, guidance, or enhancing specific types of spells.

1. Orion: The Hunter – Protection and Strength

Orion is one of the most recognizable constellations and is often associated with strength, courage, and protection. In mythology, Orion was a great hunter, and his constellation can be invoked for protection against harm and danger.

Magical Correspondences:

- **Protection Spells**: Orion's energy is perfect for creating strong protective shields around yourself, your home, or loved ones.
- **Strength and Courage**: Use Orion's power to boost your courage when facing challenges or difficult situations.
- **Colors**: Red and black.
- **Crystals**: Hematite, black tourmaline, red jasper.

Invocation Example: "I call upon Orion, the great hunter, protector of the night. Surround me with your strength and shield me from harm. As your stars watch over the earth, so shall they guard me from all danger."

2. Pleiades: The Seven Sisters – Spiritual Wisdom and Healing

The Pleiades, also known as the Seven Sisters, is a small but prominent cluster of stars in the constellation Taurus. The Pleiades are often associated with spiritual wisdom, healing, and connection to higher realms. Their energy is ideal for deep spiritual work, emotional healing, and accessing divine guidance.

Magical Correspondences:

- **Spiritual Wisdom**: The Pleiades can be invoked for deep meditation, spiritual growth, and connecting with higher wisdom.
- **Emotional Healing**: Call upon the energy of the Pleiades for emotional healing and soothing of the heart.
- **Colors**: Blue and silver.
- **Crystals**: Lapis lazuli, selenite, clear quartz.

Invocation Example: "I call upon the Seven Sisters, the wise and ancient stars of the Pleiades. Guide me with your wisdom, heal me with your light, and open my heart to divine understanding."

3. Cassiopeia: The Queen – Empowerment and Leadership

Cassiopeia, represented as a queen on her throne, is a constellation that symbolizes authority, leadership, and personal empowerment. Working with Cassiopeia can help you reclaim your power, enhance your leadership abilities, and assert your personal authority.

Magical Correspondences:

- **Personal Empowerment**: Use the energy of Cassiopeia to step into your power and assert your authority in personal or professional situations.
- **Leadership**: Call upon Cassiopeia when you need to take a leadership role or make decisions with confidence.
- **Colors**: Purple and gold.
- **Crystals**: Amethyst, citrine, garnet.

Invocation Example: "I invoke Cassiopeia, the queen of the night sky, ruler of her domain. Grant me the strength to lead, the wisdom to guide, and the confidence to stand in my power."

4. Draco: The Dragon – Protection and Guarding Sacred Spaces

Draco, the dragon constellation, is often associated with guardianship, protection, and power. Dragons are ancient protectors of sacred spaces, making Draco an excellent ally for guarding your home, personal energy, or magical work.

Magical Correspondences:

- **Guarding Sacred Spaces**: Call upon Draco to protect your home, magical tools, or sacred spaces from negative energies or intruders.
- **Power and Transformation**: Draco's dragon energy can help you embrace personal power and undergo deep transformation.
- **Colors**: Black and green.
- **Crystals**: Malachite, onyx, emerald.

Invocation Example: "I call upon Draco, the ancient dragon, protector of all that is sacred. Guard my space with your power, and shield me from all harm. As you coil around the stars, so shall you guard my circle."

5. Cygnus: The Swan – Transformation and Inner Peace

Cygnus, the swan, is associated with transformation, grace, and inner peace. The swan's energy can help you navigate personal transformations with ease and find serenity in the midst of change.

Magical Correspondences:

- **Transformation**: Use the energy of Cygnus when going through personal changes or seeking to transform your life.
- **Inner Peace**: Call upon the swan for calming energy, emotional balance, and inner harmony.
- **Colors**: White and blue.
- **Crystals**: Moonstone, aquamarine, celestite.

Invocation Example: "I invoke Cygnus, the graceful swan, bringer of peace and transformation. Guide me through change with grace, and help me find serenity in my heart."

Conclusion

Constellation magic offers a powerful way to tap into the cosmic energy of the stars for protection, guidance, and spell enhancement. By working with constellations, you can align your magical practice with the ancient wisdom of the heavens, calling upon their symbolic power to support and strengthen your intentions.

Whether you are seeking protection from Orion, spiritual wisdom from the Pleiades, or personal empowerment from Cassiopeia, the stars offer limitless potential for magical work. By incorporating constellation magic into your rituals, meditations, and spells, you deepen your connection to the cosmos and unlock the power of the universe to support your spiritual journey.

Chapter 44: Astrology and Dream Magic: How Celestial Events Affect Dream Work and How to Perform Dream Magic

Dreams have long been considered a portal to the subconscious mind and a gateway to other realms of existence. They offer insights, spiritual messages, and guidance from our higher selves and the universe. Just as astrology governs our waking lives through the movements of celestial bodies, it also profoundly influences our dream world. By aligning dream work with celestial events such as the phases of the Moon, planetary transits, and other astrological phenomena, you can deepen your understanding of your dreams and enhance your dream magic practices.

In this chapter, we will explore how celestial events affect dreams and how you can use astrology to guide your dream work. You will learn techniques for performing dream magic, using dreams for manifestation, spiritual insight, and healing. Whether you are seeking answers, exploring your inner self, or connecting with higher realms, dream magic offers a powerful tool for transformation, all amplified by the energies of the stars and planets.

The Connection Between Astrology and Dream Magic

Astrology and dream magic are deeply intertwined because both operate through symbols, archetypes, and subconscious messages. The celestial bodies—particularly the Moon and planets—affect not only our emotions and daily lives but also our dream experiences. Certain astrological configurations heighten dream activity, increase psychic awareness during sleep, and facilitate communication with spiritual guides or other dimensions.

Dream magic, or the practice of working intentionally with dreams for spiritual or magical purposes, can be greatly enhanced by understanding how celestial events influence the dream state. By syncing your dream magic with the Moon phases, planetary transits, and astrological signs, you can better interpret your dreams, connect with higher wisdom, and manifest your desires through the dream realm.

How Celestial Events Affect Dreams

The movements of the Moon, planets, and constellations have a significant impact on the energy we experience during sleep, affecting the intensity, clarity, and content of our dreams. Below, we'll explore how specific celestial events influence dream states and how you can align your dream magic with these energies.

1. The Phases of the Moon and Dream Work

The Moon governs emotions, intuition, and the subconscious mind, making it one of the most influential celestial bodies in dream work. Its phases—New, Waxing, Full, and Waning—each bring a different energy that can shape the nature and clarity of your dreams.

New Moon: Dreaming of New Beginnings and Setting Intentions

The New Moon is a time of new beginnings, making it ideal for setting intentions in dream magic. During this phase, dreams often carry messages about fresh starts, opportunities, and areas where you can plant seeds for personal growth. Dream work during the New Moon is perfect for manifesting new desires or goals.

- **Dream Work Focus**: Setting intentions, manifesting new opportunities, gaining insight into future endeavors.
- **Best Dream Magic**: Before going to sleep, set an intention for your dream, focusing on an area of life where you wish to create change or growth. Write your intention on a piece of paper and place it under your pillow. As you sleep, ask the universe for guidance on how to manifest this intention in your waking life.

Waxing Moon: Dreaming of Growth and Progress

The Waxing Moon represents growth, expansion, and the building of energy. Dreams during this phase often focus on progress, creativity, and overcoming challenges. This is a good time for dream work focused on problem-solving, personal development, or gaining clarity on projects or goals you've already set in motion.

- **Dream Work Focus**: Growth, progress, problem-solving, and creative inspiration.
- **Best Dream Magic**: Before bed, focus on a specific problem or challenge in your life. Set an intention for your dream to provide a solution or inspiration on how to move forward. Keep a dream journal beside your bed to record any insights or ideas that arise during sleep.

Full Moon: Lucid Dreaming and Spiritual Insights

The Full Moon is a time of heightened energy, illumination, and spiritual insight. Dreams during the Full Moon are often vivid, intense, and filled with symbolic messages. This phase is ideal for lucid dreaming, where you can become aware that you are dreaming and consciously interact with the dream. It's also a powerful time for receiving guidance from spirit guides or ancestors.

- **Dream Work Focus**: Lucid dreaming, spiritual insight, receiving messages from guides or ancestors.
- **Best Dream Magic**: Before bed, prepare for lucid dreaming by repeating affirmations such as, "I will become aware that I am dreaming." You can also ask for specific guidance from spirit guides or ancestors by lighting a white candle and saying a prayer or invocation. Keep a dream journal close to capture any powerful or symbolic dreams you experience.

Waning Moon: Dreaming of Release and Cleansing

The Waning Moon is a time for releasing and letting go of what no longer serves you. Dreams during this phase often bring up unresolved emotions, patterns, or fears that need to be addressed and released. Dream work during the Waning Moon is ideal for emotional healing and clearing energetic blockages.

- **Dream Work Focus**: Emotional healing, releasing old patterns, clearing blockages.
- **Best Dream Magic**: Set an intention before sleep to release old emotional patterns or unresolved feelings. Visualize yourself letting go of these issues as you fall asleep. During your dreams, you may encounter symbolic representations of the things you need to release. Upon waking, perform a cleansing ritual such as smudging or a salt bath to further release the energy.

2. Planetary Transits and Dream Magic

In addition to the Moon, planetary transits can also have a profound effect on our dreams. Each planet governs specific areas of life, and its energy influences the type of dreams we have, the symbols that appear, and the lessons they reveal.

Mercury Retrograde: Dreams of Reflection and Communication

Mercury retrograde is notorious for causing disruptions in communication and technology, but it also has a significant impact on our dream life. During Mercury retrograde, dreams often focus on past experiences, unresolved conversations, or situations that require reflection and closure. You may also experience dreams related to communication issues or misunderstandings.

- **Dream Work Focus**: Revisiting the past, reflecting on unresolved issues, communication with others.
- **Best Dream Magic**: Set the intention before sleep to gain clarity on any unresolved issues or conversations from the past. During your dreams, you may encounter people or situations from your past that need closure. Keep a journal to record any significant dreams, and after Mercury retrograde ends, take steps to resolve any lingering issues in your waking life.

Venus Transits: Dreams of Love, Beauty, and Relationships

Venus, the planet of love and beauty, brings a soft, harmonious energy to our dreams. During Venus transits, dreams often center on relationships, self-love, and personal beauty. You may receive guidance on how to improve your relationships, enhance your self-worth, or embrace your sensuality.

- **Dream Work Focus**: Love, relationships, self-worth, beauty, and sensuality.
- **Best Dream Magic**: Before bed, set the intention to receive guidance on a relationship or your own self-love journey. You can place a rose quartz crystal under your pillow to enhance the loving energy of your dreams. Pay attention to dreams that involve love, harmony, or beauty, as they may carry messages for your waking life.

Mars Transits: Dreams of Action, Conflict, and Courage

Mars is the planet of action, energy, and courage, and its influence on dreams often brings themes of conflict, assertiveness, and the need to take action. You may experience dreams where you are called to confront a challenge, face a fear, or take decisive action in an area of your life.

- **Dream Work Focus**: Courage, assertiveness, action, conflict resolution.
- **Best Dream Magic**: Before sleep, focus on a challenge or area of your life where you need to take action. Set the intention for your dream to reveal how you can overcome obstacles or assert yourself more effectively. You may dream of scenarios that require courage or assertiveness, offering you guidance on how to approach similar situations in waking life.

Jupiter Transits: Dreams of Expansion, Wisdom, and Growth

Jupiter, the planet of expansion and wisdom, brings dreams filled with spiritual insights, growth, and opportunities for learning. During Jupiter transits, dreams may reveal how to expand your horizons, embrace new opportunities, or deepen your spiritual understanding.

- **Dream Work Focus**: Spiritual growth, wisdom, abundance, and learning.
- **Best Dream Magic**: Set an intention before sleep to receive guidance on areas of personal growth or spiritual development. You may dream of mentors, teachers, or wise figures who offer advice on how to embrace new opportunities or expand your consciousness. Keep a journal to record any lessons or insights that arise from your dreams.

Techniques for Performing Dream Magic

Dream magic is the practice of using dreams as a tool for manifesting desires, receiving spiritual guidance, and working with the subconscious mind. Below are detailed techniques for performing dream magic, using astrology and celestial energies to enhance your practice.

1. Setting Intentions for Dream Magic

One of the most powerful aspects of dream magic is setting clear intentions before you sleep. This process directs your subconscious mind and the energy of celestial bodies toward a specific goal, whether it's receiving guidance, healing, or manifesting your desires.

How to Set Intentions for Dream Magic:

1. **Choose Your Intention**: Decide on the focus of your dream magic, whether it's gaining clarity on a situation, manifesting a goal, or healing an emotional wound. Be specific with your intention.
2. **Write It Down**: Write your intention on a piece of paper or in your dream journal. This solidifies your intention and communicates it to the universe and your subconscious mind.
3. **Visualize Before Sleep**: As you lie down to sleep, close your eyes and visualize your intention being fulfilled. Imagine yourself receiving the guidance or results you seek in your dreams.
4. **Repeat an Affirmation**: Silently repeat a phrase like, "I open my dreams to receive [insert intention]. My dreams are a portal to divine guidance."

5. **Record Your Dreams**: Upon waking, immediately write down any dreams you had. Even if the messages are unclear at first, they may reveal deeper insights over time.

2. Lucid Dreaming for Magical Work

Lucid dreaming occurs when you become aware that you are dreaming and can consciously interact with the dream. This powerful tool allows you to perform magic within the dream state, access higher realms of consciousness, and receive direct guidance from spiritual beings.

Steps for Lucid Dreaming:

1. **Set the Intention**: Before sleep, set the intention to become aware that you are dreaming. Repeat affirmations like, "I will recognize when I am dreaming" or "I will control my dreams."
2. **Keep a Dream Journal**: Write down your dreams immediately upon waking. This helps you build dream recall and recognize patterns that may trigger lucidity.
3. **Reality Checks**: Throughout the day, perform reality checks such as looking at your hands, counting your fingers, or asking yourself, "Am I dreaming?" This habit can carry over into your dream state, helping you realize when you are dreaming.
4. **Lucid Dream Magic**: Once lucid, you can perform dream magic by setting intentions, casting spells, or calling upon spiritual guides. For example, you might ask for direct guidance on a problem, travel to a specific location, or perform a magical act within the dream to influence your waking reality.

3. Dream Incubation for Spiritual Guidance

Dream incubation is the ancient practice of asking for guidance or answers through your dreams. By focusing on a specific question or issue before sleep, you can invite spiritual insight or solutions to appear in your dreams.

Steps for Dream Incubation:

1. **Formulate Your Question**: Choose a clear, concise question or issue that you want to resolve through your dream. Write it down in your dream journal.
2. **Prepare Your Space**: Create a calm, peaceful environment for sleep. You can light a candle, burn incense, or play soft music to set the mood.
3. **Focus on Your Question**: Before sleep, focus on your question or issue. Repeat it to yourself several times, visualizing an answer or guidance coming to you in your dream.
4. **Ask for Guidance**: You can ask your higher self, spirit guides, or the universe to send you the answer in your dream. For example, say, "I ask for guidance on [insert question]. Please reveal the answer in my dream."
5. **Record Your Dream**: Upon waking, write down any dreams you had, even if they don't seem directly related to your question. Often, dream messages come in symbols or metaphors that require interpretation.

Astrological Dream Magic Ritual: Moon Phases and Dreams

You can create a dream magic ritual that aligns with the phases of the Moon to enhance your dream work. Below is a detailed ritual for each Moon phase, focusing on specific dream intentions.

New Moon Dream Magic Ritual: Manifesting New Beginnings

- **Intention**: Manifest new desires or opportunities through your dreams.
- **Materials**: White candle, bay leaf, a piece of paper and pen, a clear quartz crystal.
- **Instructions**:
  1. **Set the Scene**: Light the white candle and hold the clear quartz crystal in your hand.
  2. **Write Your Intention**: Write down a specific desire or goal you want to manifest. Focus on how you want this to unfold in your life.
  3. **Place Under Pillow**: Place the paper and crystal under your pillow and say, "I plant the seed of my desire in the fertile ground of my dreams. I trust the universe to guide me."
  4. **Dream and Journal**: As you sleep, pay attention to any dreams that provide insight into how to manifest your desire. Record your dreams in your journal upon waking.

Full Moon Dream Magic Ritual: Lucid Dreaming and Spiritual Guidance

- **Intention**: Use lucid dreaming to gain spiritual guidance or connect with higher realms.
- **Materials**: Silver candle, moonstone, lavender essential oil.
- **Instructions**:
  1. **Prepare Your Space**: Light the silver candle and anoint your temples with lavender essential oil.
  2. **Hold the Moonstone**: Hold the moonstone in your hands and focus on your intention to become lucid in your dreams.
  3. **Speak an Invocation**: Say, "Under the light of the Full Moon, I open the portal to my dreams. I become aware and receive guidance from the higher realms."
  4. **Lucid Dreaming Practice**: As you fall asleep, focus on becoming aware within your dream. Use reality checks or affirmations to trigger lucidity. Once lucid, ask for guidance or perform your dream magic.
  5. **Record Your Experience**: Upon waking, write down your lucid dream experience and any messages you received.

Conclusion

Astrology and dream magic are powerful tools for exploring the depths of the subconscious, receiving spiritual guidance, and manifesting your desires. By aligning your dream work with the phases of the Moon, planetary transits, and celestial events, you can enhance the clarity and potency of your dreams. Whether you are using dreams for healing, insight, or magical work, the stars and planets provide cosmic support to guide and illuminate your path.

Through intentional practice and a deep understanding of how celestial energies influence your dreams, you can unlock the hidden wisdom of your subconscious mind and harness the power of the cosmos for personal transformation and spiritual growth.

Chapter 45: Conclusion: Living in Harmony with the Universe—Final Thoughts on Weaving Magic into Everyday Life Through Celestial Awareness

As we come to the end of this almanac, it's clear that living in harmony with the universe means more than just observing celestial events. It's about integrating the cosmic rhythms into every aspect of your daily life, using astrology, lunar cycles, planetary transits, and other celestial energies to enhance your spiritual practice and personal well-being. By aligning with the stars, planets, and the flow of the cosmos, you can access deeper wisdom, personal empowerment, and a harmonious connection with the universe.

In this concluding chapter, we will reflect on how to weave magic into everyday life through celestial awareness and how to maintain this connection in a way that supports spiritual growth, balance, and intention. The universe is constantly communicating with us through the positions and movements of celestial bodies, and by paying attention to these signs, we can live in greater harmony with both the cosmos and our own inner selves.

The Magic of Celestial Awareness in Daily Life

Celestial awareness is the practice of tuning into the cosmic forces that influence our world—whether it's the cycles of the Moon, the alignments of planets, or the seasonal shifts marked by the Sun. When we consciously align our actions, intentions, and rituals with these cosmic patterns, we open ourselves to the natural flow of the universe. This creates a life in which magic isn't just something we do during rituals or ceremonies; it becomes an integrated part of our daily experience.

1. The Role of Celestial Rhythms in Personal Empowerment

By observing celestial cycles, you can become more aware of your own internal rhythms and how they are connected to the cosmos. For example, the **phases of the Moon** can guide your emotional landscape, helping you navigate when to initiate new projects, when to rest and reflect, and when to release what no longer serves you. Similarly, planetary transits can offer insight into areas of life where you may feel called to focus on healing, growth, or transformation.

Living in harmony with celestial rhythms empowers you to:

- **Set meaningful intentions** that are supported by the energy of the cosmos.
- **Create a sense of flow and balance** in your daily routines by aligning them with natural cycles.
- **Tap into the greater forces of the universe** for guidance, protection, and inspiration.

When you synchronize your life with these cycles, you may find that your efforts become more effective, your intuition sharpens, and you feel more grounded in both your magical practice and everyday experiences.

2. Incorporating Daily Magic Through Celestial Timing

There are countless ways to incorporate celestial magic into your daily routine, from simple morning rituals to more elaborate evening ceremonies. By observing the astrological influences and the movement of the Moon and planets, you can choose the right moments to cast spells, perform rituals, or even set personal goals. Here are a few ideas to integrate celestial magic into everyday life:

- **Morning Rituals**: Start each day by checking the Moon's phase and astrological sign. Set an intention that aligns with the current cosmic energy. For example, if the Moon is in **Virgo**, focus on organizing your space or setting intentions for health and wellness.
- **Lunar Reflections**: Use the phases of the Moon to guide your daily reflections. During the **New Moon**, consider writing down what you want to manifest in the coming cycle. At the **Full Moon**, reflect on what you have accomplished and what you need to release. Keep a lunar journal to track your intentions and personal growth.
- **Planetary Days and Hours**: Each day of the week is associated with a planet and its corresponding energy. You can plan daily tasks or magical workings around these energies:
    - **Monday** (Moon): Focus on emotional healing, intuition, and self-care.
    - **Tuesday** (Mars): Take action, address conflict, or perform protection magic.
    - **Wednesday** (Mercury): Enhance communication, learning, and travel.
    - **Thursday** (Jupiter): Work on growth, abundance, and expansion.
    - **Friday** (Venus): Focus on love, relationships, and beauty.
    - **Saturday** (Saturn): Address responsibilities, long-term goals, and discipline.
    - **Sunday** (Sun): Boost vitality, confidence, and personal power.
- **Astrological Check-Ins**: Regularly check the positions of the planets and key transits to see how they influence your life. For example, during **Mercury retrograde**, focus on reflecting, revising, and slowing down rather than starting new projects. Use **Venus transits** to enhance your relationships or improve self-love rituals.

Manifesting with Cosmic Intentions

Manifestation is a core element of magical practice, and by aligning your manifestation work with celestial events, you can amplify its power. The universe's energy is always flowing, and tapping into it at the right time allows you to ride the wave of cosmic support. Whether you're manifesting abundance, love, healing, or personal growth, syncing your intentions with the cosmos ensures that you're working in harmony with universal forces.

1. Manifesting with the Moon's Phases

The Moon's waxing and waning phases are ideal for setting and manifesting intentions. Here's how you can incorporate the Moon's cycle into your manifestation practices:

- **New Moon**: This is the time to plant seeds of intention. Focus on what you want to manifest in the next lunar cycle, whether it's a new job, a creative project, or personal growth. Write down your intentions and place them on your altar or carry them with you as a reminder.
- **Waxing Moon**: As the Moon grows, work on building momentum. Take action steps that align with your intentions. This is the time for growth, motivation, and focus.
- **Full Moon**: This is the time of manifestation and realization. Reflect on what has come to fruition. Celebrate your achievements and offer gratitude to the universe. You may also perform powerful manifestation rituals to amplify your desires.
- **Waning Moon**: This phase is for release and letting go. Clear out what no longer serves you—whether it's old habits, limiting beliefs, or emotional baggage—to make space for new energy.

2. Using Planetary Energy for Manifestation

Each planet represents a specific type of energy that can be harnessed for manifestation. Here are some examples of how you can work with planetary energies to achieve your goals:

- **Sun**: Use the energy of the Sun for manifesting confidence, success, and vitality. Work with the Sun on Sundays or during a **solar eclipse** to amplify your personal power and bring your ambitions to fruition.
- **Moon**: The Moon's energy is ideal for manifesting emotional healing, intuition, and inner growth. Work with the Moon for matters of the heart, family, or emotional well-being.
- **Venus**: Venus rules over love, beauty, and abundance. Use Venus's energy for manifestation related to relationships, self-love, or artistic creativity. Fridays, ruled by Venus, are perfect for love spells or rituals focused on attracting abundance.
- **Jupiter**: Jupiter is the planet of expansion, growth, and prosperity. Work with Jupiter's energy on Thursdays for manifesting wealth, opportunities, and spiritual growth.
- **Saturn**: Saturn's energy is ideal for manifesting discipline, structure, and long-term success. If you need to bring order to your life or manifest lasting stability, work with Saturn on Saturdays or during its transits.

Harnessing Celestial Energy for Healing

Celestial awareness also plays a crucial role in magical healing practices. By aligning healing rituals with the movements of the Moon, planets, and stars, you can attune to the natural flow of cosmic energy, which can enhance physical, emotional, and spiritual healing.

1. Healing with the Lunar Phases

The Moon's phases offer unique opportunities for healing work:

- **New Moon**: This is an excellent time for setting healing intentions, particularly for emotional wounds or mental clarity. Use this phase to start fresh and renew your energy.
- **Full Moon**: The Full Moon provides heightened energy for deep spiritual and emotional healing. It is a time for clearing emotional blockages, releasing old wounds, and focusing on personal growth.
- **Waning Moon**: During the Waning Moon, focus on detoxification, both physically and energetically. This is the time to release negative energy, cleanse your space, and engage in rituals to let go of illness or emotional baggage.

2. Planetary Healing Rituals

Incorporating planetary energy into your healing rituals can amplify the effects of your work. For example:

- **Mars**: Use Mars's fiery energy for boosting physical healing, especially after surgery or injury. Mars can also be invoked to accelerate recovery or provide the courage to overcome emotional challenges.
- **Venus**: Venus's soothing energy is ideal for self-love rituals, emotional healing, and restoring balance in relationships. Use Venus for heart-centered healing and beauty rituals that promote inner peace.
- **Neptune**: Neptune governs the spiritual realm and can be called upon for deep spiritual and emotional healing. Work with Neptune's energy to heal trauma, access subconscious patterns, and connect with higher spiritual wisdom for healing guidance.

Living Intentionally Through Celestial Magic

As you continue to deepen your connection with the universe, it's important to practice living intentionally. This means being aware of the energies that surround you, whether they come from the stars, planets, or natural cycles, and consciously choosing how you engage with those energies. Living intentionally through celestial magic allows you to take an active role in shaping your life and spiritual journey, rather than being passively influenced by external forces.

1. Aligning Rituals and Magic with Cosmic Cycles

Intentional magic means planning your rituals and magical work in harmony with celestial events. Rather than casting a spell at any time, tune in to the phases of the Moon or planetary alignments to determine the best timing for your work. This not only amplifies the effectiveness of your magic but also brings you into deeper alignment with the natural flow of the cosmos.

2. Tracking Personal Growth Through Astrology

Astrology can be a powerful tool for tracking your personal growth and spiritual evolution. By regularly checking your astrological chart and the transits that are affecting you, you can gain insight into the lessons you're currently working through, as well as opportunities for growth. You can use this awareness to focus your magic, rituals, and healing practices on the areas of life that are most aligned with your astrological influences.

Conclusion: Embodying Celestial Magic in Everyday Life

Living in harmony with the universe through celestial awareness is not just about performing rituals or tracking planetary movements—it's about embodying the wisdom of the cosmos in every moment. When you weave celestial magic into your daily life, you align yourself with the cycles of nature and the universe, creating a life that is deeply connected to the forces that shape your existence.

By understanding the influence of the Moon, planets, and stars, you can use this knowledge to enhance every aspect of your life—whether through manifestation, healing, dream work, or personal growth. Celestial awareness empowers you to live with intention, balance, and a sense of purpose, knowing that you are part of a vast, interconnected web of cosmic energy.

As you move forward in your magical journey, remember that the universe is always there to guide, support, and empower you. By tuning into celestial rhythms and integrating their wisdom into your everyday life, you can create a life of harmony, magic, and profound spiritual connection.

Appendix: Glossary, Charts, and Resources

Appendix A: Glossary of Key Terms

This glossary provides definitions for the key astrological, astronomical, and magical terms used throughout the almanac. Understanding these terms will help deepen your connection with celestial magic and enhance your ability to work with cosmic energies in your spiritual practice.

A

Apex

In astrology, the apex is the highest point in the chart, typically referring to the **Midheaven** or the **10th House**, which represents career, public life, and status. It signifies the peak of a person's ambitions or public achievements.

Ascendant (Rising Sign)

The zodiac sign that was rising on the eastern horizon at the moment of birth. The ascendant represents how you present yourself to the world, your outward personality, and first impressions. It is a key factor in personal astrology and is often used in interpreting one's **natal chart**.

Astrological Houses

The twelve divisions of the sky in a natal chart, each representing different areas of life (e.g., identity, possessions, communication, relationships). The houses provide context for how the planets and signs influence various aspects of a person's life.

Astrological Transit

The movement of a planet or other celestial body across a specific point in the sky relative to an individual's natal chart. Transits indicate changes or developments in different areas of life and are used to forecast events or trends.

Aspect

In astrology, an aspect refers to the angle formed between two planets in a natal chart or in the sky during a transit. Major aspects include conjunctions, oppositions, squares, trines, and sextiles, each representing different types of interactions between planetary energies.

B

Balsamic Moon

The last phase of the lunar cycle, just before the New Moon. It is a time of rest, reflection, and preparation for new beginnings. In magical work, the balsamic phase is often used for spiritual closure and releasing what no longer serves you.

Banishing Spell

A magical ritual or spell used to remove negative energy, habits, people, or influences from your life. Often performed during the **Waning Moon**, which is associated with release and letting go.

Birth Chart (Natal Chart)

A map of the sky at the exact time and place of an individual's birth, showing the positions of the Sun, Moon, planets, and other celestial points. The birth chart serves as a blueprint of a person's character, strengths, challenges, and life path.

C

Cardinal Signs

The zodiac signs that begin each season: **Aries** (spring), **Cancer** (summer), **Libra** (autumn), and **Capricorn** (winter). Cardinal signs are associated with action, leadership, and initiating new projects.

Celestial Event

Any astronomical occurrence involving celestial bodies, such as a **solar eclipse**, **lunar eclipse**, planetary conjunction, meteor shower, or retrograde. These events hold specific astrological and magical significance.

Conjunction

An astrological aspect where two planets align closely in the sky, usually within a few degrees of each other. Conjunctions intensify the energies of the planets involved, blending their influences and creating powerful opportunities for transformation.

Cusp

The dividing line between two zodiac signs or astrological houses. Being "born on the cusp" means being born at the transition point between two zodiac signs, which may result in an individual exhibiting traits of both signs.

D

Decan

Each zodiac sign is divided into three equal parts called decans, each spanning 10 degrees. Each decan emphasizes a different aspect of the sign's characteristics and may be influenced by other planetary rulers.

Degrees (Astrological)

In astrology, the sky is divided into 360 degrees, with each zodiac sign covering 30 degrees. The degree of a planet or point in a natal chart indicates its exact location in a sign and can influence the intensity or specificity of the energy.

Dream Magic

A form of magical practice that uses the dream state to gain insights, manifest desires, or connect with spiritual realms. Dream magic often involves setting intentions before sleep or performing rituals to enhance dream recall and lucidity.

E

Eclipse

An astronomical event where the Sun or Moon is temporarily obscured by another celestial body. A **solar eclipse** occurs when the Moon passes between the Earth and the Sun, while a **lunar eclipse** happens when the Earth passes between the Sun and the Moon. Eclipses are powerful times for deep transformation, shadow work, and spiritual awakening.

Elements (Earth, Air, Fire, Water)

In astrology, the twelve zodiac signs are divided into four elemental groups: Earth, Air, Fire, and Water. Each element represents different qualities:

- **Earth**: Practicality, stability, and groundedness (Taurus, Virgo, Capricorn).
- **Air**: Intellect, communication, and social connection (Gemini, Libra, Aquarius).
- **Fire**: Passion, creativity, and action (Aries, Leo, Sagittarius).
- **Water**: Emotions, intuition, and sensitivity (Cancer, Scorpio, Pisces).

Ephemeris

An astrological table or chart that lists the positions of celestial bodies at specific times. It is used by astrologers to track planetary movements, retrogrades, and other significant events.

F

Fixed Signs

The zodiac signs that fall in the middle of each season: **Taurus** (spring), **Leo** (summer), **Scorpio** (autumn), and **Aquarius** (winter). Fixed signs are known for their stability, persistence, and determination.

Full Moon

The phase of the lunar cycle when the Moon is fully illuminated by the Sun, symbolizing completion, manifestation, and heightened emotional or spiritual energy. Full Moons are ideal for spells focused on manifestation, gratitude, and releasing what no longer serves you.

G

Grand Trine

An astrological configuration where three planets form a triangle in the sky, with each planet being 120 degrees apart in the same element (Earth, Air, Fire, or Water). Grand trines represent harmony, ease, and the free flow of energy between the planets involved.

Grounding

A magical practice of connecting with the Earth to restore balance, focus, and stability. Grounding helps release excess energy, calm the mind, and promote a sense of inner peace. Common grounding techniques include visualization, walking in nature, or working with crystals like hematite or black tourmaline.

H

Harmonious Aspect

An astrological aspect, such as a trine or sextile, where planets are in harmonious positions with one another, facilitating ease, flow, and beneficial outcomes.

Houses (Astrological)

See **Astrological Houses**.

I

Intention

A focused desire or goal that directs magical energy toward a specific outcome. Setting a clear intention is an essential part of spellwork, rituals, and manifestation practices, ensuring that energy is aligned with your desired result.

Ingress

The moment when a planet enters a new zodiac sign. Ingresses mark the beginning of new astrological cycles and can bring changes or shifts in energy, particularly in the areas of life ruled by that planet.

J

Jupiter Return

Occurs approximately every 12 years when Jupiter returns to the same position it occupied at the time of your birth. A Jupiter Return marks a period of growth, expansion, and new opportunities in your life, often associated with increased luck and abundance.

K

Karmic Astrology

A branch of astrology that focuses on the influence of past-life experiences and karmic lessons in the present lifetime. Karmic astrology seeks to uncover unresolved issues, spiritual growth opportunities, and the soul's purpose through the natal chart.

L

Lunar Eclipse

A celestial event that occurs when the Earth passes between the Sun and the Moon, temporarily blocking the Sun's light from reaching the Moon. Lunar eclipses are powerful times for emotional release, deep transformation, and shadow work.

Lunar Nodes

Points in space where the Moon's orbit crosses the ecliptic (the Sun's path). The North Node represents future growth and karmic lessons, while the South Node represents past experiences and patterns that need to be resolved. The nodes play a significant role in personal and karmic astrology.

M

Manifestation

The process of bringing desires, goals, or intentions into physical reality through focused thought, visualization, and magical work. Manifestation often involves aligning personal energy with universal forces to create the desired outcome.

Midheaven (MC)

The point at the top of the natal chart, representing your career, public life, and reputation. The Midheaven is associated with ambition, professional success, and how you are perceived in the world.

Mutable Signs

The zodiac signs that mark the transition between seasons: **Gemini** (spring to summer), **Virgo** (summer to autumn), **Sagittarius** (autumn to winter), and **Pisces** (winter to spring). Mutable signs are adaptable, flexible, and skilled at navigating change.

N

New Moon

The first phase of the lunar cycle, when the Moon is not visible from Earth. The New Moon is a time for new beginnings, setting intentions, and planting the seeds of future goals. It is the ideal time for spells focused on starting fresh or manifesting new opportunities.

O

Opposition

An astrological aspect where two planets are 180 degrees apart in the sky, creating tension between opposing energies. While oppositions can bring challenges or conflict, they also offer opportunities for balance, compromise, and integration.

P

Planetary Hours

A system that divides each day into segments, with each hour ruled by a different planet. The ruling planet of the hour influences the best time for specific magical workings, such as using **Venus hours** for love spells or **Mars hours** for action and courage.

Planetary Return

Occurs when a planet returns to the same position in the sky as it was at the time of your birth. For example, a **Saturn Return** occurs approximately every 29 years and marks a major life transition, often associated with growth and responsibility.

Q

Quincunx (Inconjunct)

An astrological aspect where two planets are 150 degrees apart. The energies of a quincunx can feel disconnected or difficult to integrate, often requiring adjustment or compromise between the planets involved.

R

Retrograde

A period when a planet appears to move backward in the sky from our perspective on Earth. Retrogrades are times for reflection, reassessment, and revisiting past issues. **Mercury retrograde** is particularly well-known for its effects on communication, technology, and travel.

Rising Sign

See **Ascendant**.

S

Solar Eclipse

A celestial event where the Moon passes between the Earth and the Sun, temporarily blocking the Sun's light. Solar eclipses are powerful for manifesting new beginnings, initiating change, and setting transformative intentions.

Solar Return

The moment the Sun returns to the exact degree of your natal Sun, which happens once a year on or around your birthday. The solar return chart provides insight into the themes and influences for the year ahead.

Stellium

An astrological configuration where three or more planets are clustered together in the same sign or house. A stellium focuses intense energy on the sign or house it occupies, amplifying the themes and qualities of that area of life.

T

T-Square

A challenging astrological aspect involving three planets, where two planets are in opposition and both are square to a third planet. T-squares create tension but also drive growth and action as they push for resolution between conflicting energies.

Trine

An astrological aspect where two planets are 120 degrees apart, creating a harmonious flow of energy between them. Trines represent ease, talent, and positive outcomes, making them beneficial for growth, creativity, and success.

U

Uranus Return

Occurs approximately every 84 years when Uranus returns to its natal position in a person's chart. This rare transit brings sudden changes, revolutions, and breakthroughs in both personal and societal contexts.

V

Void of Course Moon

A period when the Moon has completed its last major aspect before moving into a new zodiac sign. During a void of course Moon, it's best to avoid starting new projects or making important decisions, as the energy is unfocused and uncertain.

W

Waning Moon

The phase of the lunar cycle after the Full Moon, when the Moon's light decreases. The waning Moon is associated with release, banishing, and letting go, making it an ideal time for clearing away negativity, old patterns, and unwanted influences.

Waxing Moon

The phase of the lunar cycle between the New Moon and Full Moon, when the Moon's light is increasing. The waxing Moon is associated with growth, building energy, and manifestation, making it a favorable time for setting intentions and taking action toward goals.

Z

Zodiac

The twelve signs that make up the astrological system, each occupying 30 degrees of the sky. The zodiac signs are divided into four elements (Earth, Air, Fire, Water) and three modalities (Cardinal, Fixed, Mutable), each representing different personality traits, life themes, and energies. The twelve zodiac signs are: **Aries, Taurus, Gemini, Cancer, Leo, Virgo, Libra, Scorpio, Sagittarius, Capricorn, Aquarius,** and **Pisces**.

Appendix B: Quick Reference Charts: Retrograde Dates, Moon Phases, and Planting Guides at a Glance

This appendix provides easy-to-reference charts for essential celestial events and magical timing in 2025. These charts offer quick access to retrograde dates, Moon phases, and the best times for planting based on lunar and astrological cycles. Whether you're planning spellwork, gardening, or personal growth rituals, these guides will help you align with the cosmic rhythms of the year.

1. Retrograde Dates for 2025

Retrogrades are periods when planets appear to move backward in the sky from our perspective on Earth. These periods are significant for introspection, revisiting past issues, and realigning with long-term goals. Retrogrades, especially of personal planets like Mercury, Venus, and Mars, can influence communication, relationships, and action. The following chart provides the retrograde dates for major planets in 2025.

Planet	Retrograde Start	Retrograde End	Sign(s) Affected	Key Themes
Mercury	Jan 1, 2025	Jan 15, 2025	Sagittarius → Capricorn	Communication issues, travel delays, revisiting old projects.
Mercury	May 18, 2025	Jun 12, 2025	Gemini	Clarity in communication, reviewing ideas, mental reset.
Mercury	Sep 9, 2025	Oct 1, 2025	Virgo → Libra	Relationships, reevaluating personal efficiency, revisiting goals.
Venus	Jul 22, 2025	Sep 4, 2025	Virgo → Leo	Relationship reassessment, self-worth, beauty, and personal values.

Planet	Retrograde Start	Retrograde End	Sign(s) Affected	Key Themes
Mars	Nov 17, 2025	Jan 3, 2026	Pisces	Energy drain, slowing down, focusing on spiritual work.
Jupiter	Apr 10, 2025	Aug 8, 2025	Taurus	Rethinking expansion, re-evaluating growth strategies, patience.
Saturn	Jun 30, 2025	Nov 25, 2025	Pisces	Revisiting discipline, restructuring, delays in long-term goals.
Uranus	Aug 2, 2025	Dec 31, 2025	Taurus	Breakthroughs in stability, revisiting personal independence.
Neptune	Mar 4, 2025	Sep 2, 2025	Pisces	Spiritual clarity, dissolving illusions, reassessing dreams.
Pluto	May 15, 2025	Oct 21, 2025	Aquarius → Capricorn	Deep transformation, collective issues, reformation.

2. Moon Phases for 2025

The Moon's phases are powerful markers for timing magical work, planting, and personal reflection. Each phase carries unique energy that can be used for setting intentions, manifesting desires, and letting go of what no longer serves you.

Moon Phase	Date	Sign	Magical Focus
New Moon	Jan 2, 2025	Capricorn	New beginnings, goal setting, manifesting ambitions.
First Quarter	Jan 10, 2025	Aries	Action, building momentum, overcoming obstacles.
Full Moon	Jan 17, 2025	Cancer	Emotional clarity, healing, nurturing relationships.
Last Quarter	Jan 25, 2025	Scorpio	Release, deep transformation, resolving emotional issues.
New Moon	Jan 31, 2025	Aquarius	Innovation, social connections, future-focused intentions.
First Quarter	Feb 9, 2025	Taurus	Grounding, focus on physical security and stability.
Full Moon	Feb 16, 2025	Leo	Creativity, self-expression, illuminating personal power.
Last Quarter	Feb 23, 2025	Sagittarius	Release of limiting beliefs, broadening perspectives.
New Moon	Mar 3, 2025	Pisces	Spiritual renewal, dream work, emotional healing.

Moon Phase	Date	Sign	Magical Focus
First Quarter	Mar 10, 2025	Gemini	Communication, adaptability, problem-solving.
Full Moon	Mar 17, 2025	Virgo	Organization, health, cleansing, practical solutions.
Last Quarter	Mar 25, 2025	Capricorn	Completing projects, discipline, and responsibility.
New Moon	Apr 1, 2025	Aries	Bold new beginnings, personal empowerment, taking action.
First Quarter	Apr 9, 2025	Cancer	Nurturing projects, focusing on home and family.
Full Moon	Apr 16, 2025	Libra	Relationships, balance, partnerships, social harmony.
Last Quarter	Apr 24, 2025	Aquarius	Releasing outdated ideals, innovation, group dynamics.
New Moon	Apr 30, 2025	Taurus	Manifesting abundance, grounding, security.

This chart highlights key Moon phases for the first four months of 2025. Repeat the same format for the remaining months of the year.

3. Lunar Planting Guide for 2025

This planting guide aligns with the Moon's phases and signs to help you choose the best times for planting, harvesting, and cultivating different types of crops or magical herbs. Working with the lunar cycle enhances growth, fertility, and vitality in your garden.

Lunar Phase	Best Gardening Activity
New Moon	Sow seeds for above-ground crops with outer foliage (leafy vegetables like lettuce, spinach, cabbage). This is a time for new growth and planting.
Waxing Moon	Plant fruiting crops (tomatoes, cucumbers, peas). Encourage upward growth, transplant seedlings, and nurture new growth.
Full Moon	Harvest crops, especially those grown for their fruits and seeds (corn, beans, squash). Also ideal for working on root strength and deeper cultivation.
Waning Moon	Focus on pruning, weeding, and pest control. Plant root crops (carrots, potatoes, onions) that thrive beneath the soil. This is also the time for resting the soil.

Best Planting Days by Sign

Each zodiac sign has its own influence on planting and growing. Certain signs are ideal for planting specific types of crops, while others are better for harvesting, cultivating, or resting. The following chart shows the best planting days for each type of crop, based on the Moon's position in the zodiac.

Sign	Element	Best Activities
Aries	Fire	Good for quick-growing crops, but best for cultivating hardy plants or pruning.
Taurus	Earth	Ideal for planting root crops, vines, and fruit-bearing plants.
Gemini	Air	Not ideal for planting, but good for light cultivation or harvesting flowers.
Cancer	Water	The best sign for planting leafy vegetables, herbs, and any crops needing lots of water.
Leo	Fire	Best for harvesting and drying herbs or flowers; avoid planting.
Virgo	Earth	Good for root crops, medicinal herbs, and preserving crops.
Libra	Air	Best for planting flowers, herbs, and anything with aesthetic value.
Scorpio	Water	Excellent for planting deep-rooted crops and regenerative herbs.
Sagittarius	Fire	Focus on planting fruit trees, high-growing crops, or harvesting.
Capricorn	Earth	Ideal for long-term crops, root vegetables, and hardy plants.

Sign	Element	Best Activities
Aquarius	Air	Not good for planting; best for weeding, pruning, or cultivating new ideas.
Pisces	Water	Best for planting crops that require moisture and fast growth, such as leafy greens.

4. Manifestation and Magic Timing: At-a-Glance

This chart helps you quickly determine the best celestial events for different types of spellwork and manifestations. Aligning your intentions with the cosmic energy of planets and Moon phases will strengthen your magic and ensure that you're working in harmony with the universe.

Goal/Intention	Best Celestial Timing
Love and Relationships	Venus transits (especially in Libra or Taurus), Fridays, Full Moon in Libra, New Moon in Cancer or Pisces.
Wealth and Abundance	Jupiter transits (especially in Taurus or Sagittarius), Thursdays, New Moon in Taurus, Full Moon in Capricorn.
Career and Ambition	Saturn transits, New Moon in Capricorn or Aries, Mars transits in Capricorn, Thursdays for success rituals.
Emotional Healing	New Moon in Cancer, Full Moon in Scorpio or Pisces, Venus retrograde, Lunar Eclipses.
Spiritual Growth	Neptune transits, Full Moon in Pisces, Mercury retrograde (for reflection), Solar Eclipses.
Protection and Banishing	Mars transits, Waning Moon, Full Moon in Aries or Scorpio, Saturn transits for boundaries.
Creativity and Inspiration	Full Moon in Leo or Sagittarius, Waxing Moon, Venus in Pisces, Mercury in Gemini for communication spells.

This appendix provides you with an easy-to-use reference for aligning your magical practice with the rhythms of the cosmos. Whether you're casting spells, planning a garden, or setting intentions for personal growth, these charts will guide you in harnessing the power of the universe for your goals.

Appendix C: Resources: Recommended Books, Websites, and Tools for Further Learning on Astrology, Astronomy, and Witchcraft

To deepen your knowledge of astrology, astronomy, and witchcraft, this appendix offers a curated list of books, websites, apps, and tools that will help you expand your understanding of these subjects. Whether you're a beginner or an advanced practitioner, these resources cover a wide range of topics, from basic astrological principles to in-depth magical techniques. The following recommendations will guide you on your journey of celestial exploration and magical practice.

1. Recommended Books

Astrology

1. *Parker's Astrology: The Definitive Guide to Using Astrology in Every Aspect of Your Life* **by Julia and Derek Parker**

This comprehensive guide is perfect for both beginners and intermediate astrologers. It covers the fundamentals of natal charts, planetary aspects, and transits, making it an essential resource for understanding how astrology influences daily life. The book includes step-by-step instructions for interpreting birth charts and offers detailed descriptions of zodiac signs, houses, and aspects.

2. *The Only Astrology Book You'll Ever Need* **by Joanna Martine Woolfolk**

True to its title, this book offers a thorough introduction to astrology. It explains how to calculate and interpret natal charts, understand planetary transits, and explore compatibility between different signs. The book also delves into more advanced topics like synastry (relationship astrology) and provides valuable insights into how astrology can be applied in daily life.

3. *Astrology for the Soul* **by Jan Spiller**

This book focuses on the North Node in astrology, which represents your soul's purpose and karmic lessons. Jan Spiller offers deep insights into the spiritual growth you can achieve by understanding the position of your North Node. It's an excellent resource for those interested in karmic astrology and personal growth through astrological analysis.

4. *Planets in Transit: Life Cycles for Living* **by Robert Hand**

A must-have for advanced astrology enthusiasts, this book provides a detailed analysis of planetary transits and their impact on your life. Robert Hand, one of the most respected astrologers of our time, explains how transits reveal opportunities, challenges, and potential growth periods in your natal chart.

Astronomy

1. *NightWatch: A Practical Guide to Viewing the Universe* **by Terence Dickinson**

This guide is ideal for beginners who want to start stargazing and learning about the cosmos. It explains how to observe the night sky, use telescopes, and identify constellations and planets. It also includes seasonal star maps and tips on finding celestial objects without high-tech equipment.

2. *Cosmos* **by Carl Sagan**

Carl Sagan's iconic book is both an exploration of the universe and a reflection on humanity's place within it. Sagan blends science, philosophy, and history to offer an awe-inspiring look at the cosmos. This is a great resource for those who want a broader understanding of the universe and its mysteries.

3. *The Universe Today Ultimate Guide to Viewing the Cosmos* **by David Dickinson and Fraser Cain**

This book provides a detailed look at how to observe celestial events, from eclipses to meteor showers, and includes advice on choosing telescopes and understanding the movements of the planets. It's an excellent resource for amateur astronomers who want to enhance their stargazing experience.

Witchcraft and Magic

1. *The Modern Guide to Witchcraft: Your Complete Guide to Witches, Covens, and Spells* **by Skye Alexander**

This book serves as a beginner's guide to witchcraft, covering basic spells, rituals, and the fundamentals of magical practice. It explores a range of topics, including working with the elements, casting spells, and building an altar. This is a great starting point for anyone new to the craft.

2. *Witchery: Embrace the Witch Within* **by Juliet Diaz**

Juliet Diaz's guide empowers readers to embrace their personal magic through rituals, self-care practices, and spiritual awareness. The book focuses on aligning with natural energies and using witchcraft as a tool for healing, self-love, and manifestation.

3. *Earth Power: Techniques of Natural Magic* **by Scott Cunningham**

This classic text is a treasure trove of practical magic that connects deeply with the Earth's natural energies. Scott Cunningham provides a variety of techniques for elemental magic, divination, and spellwork using herbs, stones, and other natural tools. Ideal for solitary practitioners.

4. *The Witch's Book of Shadows: The Craft, Lore & Magick of the Witch's Grimoire* **by Jason Mankey**

For witches interested in building their own **Book of Shadows**, this guide explores the history, structure, and creation of this essential magical tool. Jason Mankey offers advice on how to personalize your own Book of Shadows and fill it with meaningful spells, rituals, and correspondences.

2. Recommended Websites and Online Communities

Astrology Websites

1. *Astro.com (www.astro.com)*

One of the most comprehensive astrology websites available, Astro.com offers free natal chart calculations, daily horoscopes, and in-depth articles on all aspects of astrology. It's an invaluable resource for both beginners and experienced astrologers, offering personalized reports, transit information, and forecasts.

2. *Cafe Astrology (www.cafeastrology.com)*

Cafe Astrology provides detailed interpretations of natal charts, transits, and compatibility. The site also includes annual and monthly horoscopes, making it a great resource for those who want to track planetary movements and astrological influences.

3. *Astrology King (www.astrologyking.com)*

Astrology King is known for its in-depth analysis of astrological transits and aspects. The site offers predictive astrology, detailing how upcoming astrological events will influence each zodiac sign. It's particularly helpful for understanding eclipses, retrogrades, and planetary transits.

Astronomy Websites

1. *NASA (www.nasa.gov)*

The official NASA website is a goldmine of astronomical information, offering updates on space missions, celestial events, and scientific discoveries. It's perfect for anyone interested in the latest developments in space exploration and the science behind the stars.

2. *Sky & Telescope (www.skyandtelescope.org)*

Sky & Telescope is a fantastic resource for amateur astronomers and stargazers. The site offers detailed star charts, guides for observing celestial events, and tips on using telescopes. It's also a great source of up-to-date information on comets, meteor showers, and planetary movements.

3. *Heavens-Above (www.heavens-above.com)*

Heavens-Above provides detailed tracking information for satellites, comets, and planets. This site is essential for stargazers who want to observe the International Space Station, plan night-sky viewings, or track specific celestial events.

Witchcraft Websites

1. *The Witch's Library (www.witchslibrary.com)*

This site is a comprehensive resource for all things related to witchcraft. It features articles on spellwork, magical correspondences, tools, and rituals. There's also a section dedicated to beginner witches, covering the fundamentals of the craft and providing helpful guidance.

2. *Lunar Living (www.lunarliving.org)*

Lunar Living focuses on working with the phases of the Moon in magic, astrology, and everyday life. The site offers detailed Moon phase calendars, lunar astrology, and tips for performing Moon rituals based on each phase.

3. *Learn Religions: Paganism & Wicca (www.learnreligions.com/paganism-wicca-4133035)*

This section of the Learn Religions website offers extensive information on Paganism, Wicca, and witchcraft. The site includes articles on the Sabbats, magical correspondences, spellcasting, and Wiccan ethics. It's a great resource for those seeking a deeper understanding of modern Pagan traditions.

3. Recommended Apps and Tools

Astrology Apps

1. *TimePassages*

TimePassages is a user-friendly astrology app that allows you to calculate natal charts, track transits, and explore astrological influences. It offers daily horoscopes and in-depth interpretations of planets in houses, signs, and aspects. The app is suitable for both beginners and advanced users.

2. *Co-Star*

Co-Star is a popular astrology app that provides personalized horoscopes based on your birth chart. It offers insights into daily transits, relationships, and long-term planetary trends. Co-Star's simple and elegant interface makes it easy to understand complex astrological concepts.

3. *Astro Gold*

Astro Gold is an advanced astrology app that offers highly detailed charts and predictions. It includes a range of tools for analyzing transits, progressions, and synastry (relationship compatibility). While it's a more professional-level app, it's invaluable for serious astrology students.

Astronomy Apps

1. *SkySafari*

SkySafari is one of the most powerful stargazing apps available, offering detailed sky charts, real-time views of planets and stars, and the ability to simulate celestial events like eclipses. It's a perfect tool for amateur astronomers who want to deepen their knowledge of the night sky.

2. *Star Walk 2*

Star Walk 2 is a beautifully designed stargazing app that lets you explore constellations, planets, and stars in real-time. It's easy to use and offers augmented reality features, making it ideal for beginners who want to learn about the night sky without a telescope.

3. *Night Sky*

Night Sky is an app designed for stargazing and exploring celestial objects. It provides an interactive map of the stars, tracking satellites, planets, and constellations in real-time. The app also includes reminders for upcoming celestial events like meteor showers and eclipses.

Witchcraft Apps

1. *The Moon - Calendar & Tracker*

This app is a great tool for tracking the phases of the Moon and planning lunar rituals. It provides detailed information about each phase, including astrological sign placements and the best magical practices for the time.

2. *Labyrinthos Tarot*

For witches who practice divination, Labyrinthos offers a comprehensive tarot learning app. It includes detailed card meanings, tarot spreads, and practice exercises, making it a fantastic tool for beginners and experienced readers alike.

3. *Spellcaster: Daily Magic and Wicca*

This app provides daily spells, rituals, and magical correspondences for those practicing witchcraft. It offers a variety of spell ideas and guides, helping you incorporate magic into your everyday life. The app also includes a spell journal to track your magical progress.

4. Tools and Supplies

Crystals

1. *Healing Crystals (www.healingcrystals.com)*

This site offers a wide range of ethically sourced crystals, gemstones, and minerals for magical and healing work. You can browse by crystal type, chakra correspondence, or intention, making it easy to find the right stones for your spells and rituals.

Herbs

2. *Mountain Rose Herbs (www.mountainroseherbs.com)*

Mountain Rose Herbs specializes in organic herbs, teas, and essential oils. The site provides high-quality supplies for herbal magic, tinctures, and spellwork. They also have a helpful guide to the magical properties of herbs.

Altar Supplies and Tools

3. *The Witches Moon (www.thewitchesmoon.com)*

This site offers beautifully curated magical tools, altar supplies, and monthly subscription boxes for witches. You'll find ritual candles, herbs, crystals, and handcrafted tools to enhance your magical practice.

This appendix offers a range of resources that will support your journey into astrology, astronomy, and witchcraft. From books that provide foundational knowledge to apps that keep you connected to the stars and celestial movements, these tools will help you deepen your magical and spiritual practice for years to come.

<u>Message from the Author:</u>

I hope you enjoyed this book, I love astrology and knew there was not a book such as this out on the shelf. I love metaphysical items as well. Please check out my other books:

-Life of Government Benefits

-My life of Hell

-My life with Hydrocephalus

-Red Sky

-World Domination:Woman's rule

-World Domination:Woman's Rule 2: The War

-Life and Banishment of Apophis: book 1

-The Kidney Friendly Diet

-The Ultimate Hemp Cookbook

-Creating a Dispensary(legally)

-Cleanliness throughout life: the importance of showering from childhood to adulthood.

-Strong Roots: The Risks of Overcoddling children

-Hemp Horoscopes: Cosmic Insights and Earthly Healing

- Celestial Hemp Navigating the Zodiac: Through the Green Cosmos

-Astrological Hemp: Aligning The Stars with Earth's Ancient Herb

-The Astrological Guide to Hemp: Stars, Signs, and Sacred Leaves

-Green Growth: Innovative Marketing Strategies for your Hemp Products and Dispensary

-Cosmic Cannabis

-Astrological Munchies

-Henry The Hemp

-Zodiacal Roots: The Astrological Soul Of Hemp

- Green Constellations: Intersection of Hemp and Zodiac

-Hemp in The Houses: An astrological Adventure Through The Cannabis Galaxy

-Galactic Ganja Guide

Heavenly Hemp

Zodiac Leaves

Doctor Who Astrology

Cannastrology

Stellar Satvias and Cosmic Indicas

<u>Celestial Cannabis: A Zodiac Journey</u>

AstroHerbology: The Sky and The Soil: Volume 1

AstroHerbology:Celestial Cannabis:Volume 2

Cosmic Cannabis Cultivation

The Starry Guide to Herbal Harmony: Volume 1

The Starry Guide to Herbal Harmony: Cannabis Universe: Volume 2

Yugioh Astrology: Astrological Guide to Deck, Duels and more
Nightmare Mansion: Echoes of The Abyss
Nightmare Mansion 2: Legacy of Shadows
Nightmare Mansion 3: Shadows of the Forgotten
Nightmare Mansion 4: Echoes of the Damned
The Life and Banishment of Apophis: Book 2
Nightmare Mansion: Halls of Despair
Healing with Herb: Cannabis and Hydrocephalus
Planetary Pot: Aligning with Astrological Herbs: Volume 1
Fast Track to Freedom: 30 Days to Financial Independence Using AI, Assets, and Agile Hustles
Cosmic Hemp Pathways
How to Become Financially Free in 30 Days: 10,000 Paths to Prosperity
Zodiacal Herbage: Astrological Insights: Volume 1
Nightmare Mansion: Whispers in the Walls
The Daleks Invade Atlantis
Henry the hemp and Hydrocephalus

10X The Kidney Friendly Diet
Cannabis Universe: Adult coloring book
Hemp Astrology: The Healing Power of the Stars
Zodiacal Herbage: Astrological Insights: Cannabis Universe: Volume 2
Planetary Pot: Aligning with Astrological Herbs: Cannabis Universes: Volume 2
Doctor Who Meets the Replicators and SG-1: The Ultimate Battle for Survival
Nightmare Mansion: Curse of the Blood Moon
The Celestial Stoner: A Guide to the Zodiac
Cosmic Pleasures: Sex Toy Astrology for Every Sign
Hydrocephalus Astrology: Navigating the Stars and Healing Waters
Lapis and the Mischievous Chocolate Bar

Celestial Positions: Sexual Astrology for Every Sign
Apophis's Shadow Work Journal: **:** A Journey of Self-Discovery and Healing
Kinky Cosmos: Sexual Kink Astrology for Every Sign
Digital Cosmos: The Astrological Digimon Compendium
Stellar Seeds: The Cosmic Guide to Growing with Astrology
Apophis's Daily Gratitude Journal

Cat Astrology: Feline Mysteries of the Cosmos
The Cosmic Kama Sutra: An Astrological Guide to Sexual Positions
Unleash Your Potential: A Guided Journal Powered by AI Insights
Whispers of the Enchanted Grove

Cosmic Pleasures: An Astrological Guide to Sexual Kinks
369, 12 Manifestation Journal
Whisper of the nocturne journal(blank journal for writing or drawing)
The Boogey Book
Locked In Reflection: A Chastity Journey Through Locktober
Generating Wealth Quickly:
How to Generate $100,000 in 24 Hours
Star Magic: Harness the Power of the Universe
The Flatulence Chronicles: A Fart Journal for Self-Discovery
The Doctor and The Death Moth
Seize the Day: A Personal Seizure Tracking Journal
The Ultimate Boogeyman Safari: A Journey into the Boogie World and Beyond
Whispers of Samhain: 1,000 Spells of Love, Luck, and Lunar Magic: Samhain Spell Book
Apophis's guides:
Witch's Spellbook Crafting Guide for Halloween
Frost & Flame: The Enchanted Yule Grimoire of 1000 Winter Spells
The Ultimate Boogey Goo Guide & Spooky Activities for Halloween Fun
Harmony of the Scales: A Libra's Spellcraft for Balance and Beauty
The Enchanted Advent: 36 Days of Christmas Wonders

Nightmare Mansion: The Labyrinth of Screams
Harvest of Enchantment: 1,000 Spells of Gratitude, Love, and Fortune for Thanksgiving
The Boogey Chronicles: A Journal of Nightly Encounters and Shadowy Secrets
The 12 Days of Financial Freedom: A Step-by-Step Christmas Countdown to Transform Your Finances
Sigil of the Eternal Spiral Blank Journal
A Christmas Feast: Timeless Recipes for Every Meal
Holiday Stress-Free Solutions: A Survival Guide to Thriving During the Festive Season
Yu-Gi-Oh! Holiday Gifting Mastery: The Ultimate Guide for Fans and Newcomers Alike
Holiday Harmony: A Hydrocephalus Survival Guide for the Festive Season

If you want solar for your home go here: https://www.harborsolar.live/apophisenterprises/

Get Some Tarot cards: https://www.makeplayingcards.com/sell/apophis-occult-shop

Get some shirts: https://www.bonfire.com/store/apophis-shirt-emporium/

Instagrams:
@apophis_enterprises,
@apophisbookemporium,
@apophisscardshop
Twitter: @apophisenterpr1 Tiktok:@apophisenterprise
Youtube: @sg1fan23477, @FiresideRetreatKingdom
Hive: @sg1fan23477

Podcast: **Apophis** **Chat** **Zone:** https://open.spotify.com/show/5zXbr-CLEV2xzCp8ybrfHsk?si=fb4d4fdbdce44dec

Newsletter: https://apophiss-newsletter-27c897.beehiiv.com/

Get printable holiday budget planners: apophisenterprisesllc.org/Apophis-emporium-shop /ols/products/holiday-budgeting-packageprintable